MULTI-AGENCY WORK IN CRIMINAL JUST

C000269430

Theory, policy and practice

Second Edition

Edited by Aaron Pycroft and Dennis Gough

P

First published in Great Britain in 2019 by

Policy Press
University of Bristol
1-9 Old Park Hill
Bristol
BS2 8BB
UK
t: +44 (0)117 954 5940
pp-info@bristol.ac.uk
www.policypress.co.uk

North America office:
Policy Press
c/o The University of Chicago Press
1427 East 60th Street
Chicago, IL 60637, USA
t: +1 773 702 7700
f: +1 773-702-9756
sales@press.uchicago.edu
www.press.uchicago.edu

British Library Cataloguing in Publication Data
A catalogue record for this book is available from the British Library

Library of Congress Cataloging-in-Publication Data
A catalog record for this book has been requested

ISBN 978-1-4473-4024-9 paperback
ISBN 978-1-4473-4025-6 ePub
ISBN 978-1-4473-4026-3 Mobi
ISBN 978-1-4473-4027-0 ePdf

Cover design by Hayes Design
Front cover image: iStock
Printed and bound in Great Britain by CMP, Poole
Policy Press uses environmentally responsible print partners

Contents

List of tables and figures

Tables

Figures

Notes on contributors

Claudia Cox is a Senior Teaching Fellow at the Institute of Criminal Justice Studies, University of Portsmouth, UK. She is currently studying for her PhD exploring the interpretation, implementation and impact of policy in relation to the policing of ethnic minority communities. Her research interests include the diversity of the police workforce, police culture, and trust and confidence in policing. Previous research has included an exploration into the lack of diversity in specialist policing units, particularly armed policing, with findings contributing to the reform of recruitment processes for Authorised Firearms Officers in several UK police forces.

Dr John Fox is a Senior Lecturer in Police Studies within the Institute of Criminal Justice Studies at the University of Portsmouth. He was awarded his MSc (with distinction) in Criminology and Criminal Justice by the University of Surrey, and his PhD in the discipline of Sociology also by University of Surrey with research concerning police investigative techniques and guidance, and homicide investigation in the UK and US. He is a former senior police officer and Head of Public Protection in a large police force. He is currently a member of the National Policing Childhood Death Working Group and has represented the Police Service on various government working parties and committees concerning child abuse and related issues. He was Lord Laming's police advisor and assessor on the Victoria Climbié Inquiry. He has conducted many multi-agency serious case reviews as Independent Lead Reviewer and has sat on four Local Safeguarding Children Boards. He is an Associate Trainer for the College of Policing in respect of child death investigation. His publications/research interests include: serious case reviews, multi-agency child death investigation, discretion in police investigation, police training and guidance.

Dr Dennis Gough is course leader for the Professional Doctorate in Criminal Justice (DCrimJ) at the University of Portsmouth. Prior to this appointment, he was Director of Community Justice leading the University of Portsmouth's work to provide the academic underpinning to probation officer training in London, the South of England and Wales. His Doctoral research was concerned with volunteer peer mentors in the penal voluntary sector.

Dr Anita Green D.Nursing, MA, BA (Hons), RCNT, RGN, RMN is Associate Director of Nurse Education for Sussex Partnership NHS Foundation Trust and Visiting Professor at the School of Health Sciences, University of Surrey.

Her research interests include; dual diagnosis – the service user experience; pre-registration care profession education; motivational interviewing; women's experience of substance misuse and mental health services.

John Grieve CBE, QPM, BA (Hons), MPhil, Hon DL is Professor Emeritus at London Metropolitan University. He is a former senior Scotland Yard detective and former head of CT Investigations and Senior National CT Coordinator. He has taught all over the world and written extensively on policing and criminal justice issues including leadership, intelligence, diversity, hate crime, crisis management and other counter terrorism issues.

Dr Nathan Hall is Associate Head (Academic) at the Institute of Criminal Justice Studies at the University of Portsmouth. He has been researching and publishing in the field of hate crime for almost 20 years, and is a member of a number of national and local criminal justice hate crime independent advisory groups. He is currently working on the third edition of his monograph *Hate Crime*.

Zoë Jackson has, since its inception in 2011 and as a founder member, been the Operations Manager at Aurora New Dawn, a charity based in the south-east of England, providing support to individuals who have experienced domestic abuse, sexual violence and/or stalking. Zoë has worked in the domestic abuse, sexual violence and stalking arena for over 15 years, including several years of frontline work with both high risk victims of domestic abuse, and with victims of sexual violence. Zoë holds a Law degree (LLB) from the University of Bristol and a master's degree (MSc) in Criminology and Criminal Psychology from the University of Portsmouth. An experienced trainer and facilitator, with particular expertise in the effective assessment and management of risk in domestic abuse cases, Zoë has trained a variety of professional groups. Her work is focused on the needs, experiences and safety of victims, both within the criminal justice system and beyond.

Lesley Laver is a Legal Psychologist, a teacher of Forensic Psychology, and a Registered Intermediary with the Ministry of Justice. She holds an MSc in Forensic Psychology, a Graduate Diploma in Psychology and a Bachelor of Laws. She has worked with children, young people and vulnerable adults in a variety of contexts (including education, policing, courts and community settings) and her research seeks to improve equality and justice for vulnerable people in conflict with the law.

Dr Sarah Lewis is a Prison Reformer and Director of Penal Reform Solutions. She currently works within prisons facilitating the Growth Project, which embraces a research-informed participatory approach. Further to this, she works for the Council of Europe, developing rehabilitation programmes in the Balkans. Dr Sarah Lewis has worked as a Probation Practitioner and Senior Academic at the Institute for Criminal Justice Studies. Her interests are Nordic prisons, participatory research, creative methodologies, prison reform, rehabilitation and rehabilitative climates and culture.

Barry Loveday BA Hons, MPhil has been a Reader in Criminal Justice: Administration at the University of Portsmouth since 2001. He has written widely on police management and accountability and has also worked for two London Think Tanks: IPPR and Policy Exchange. He has also served as a member of the Community Safety Advisers Board at the Local Government Association. In 2005 he was invited to present an independent evaluation to the Prime Minister's Strategy Unit of the government's planned amalgamation of police forces in England and Wales.

Dr Michael Nash is Emeritus Professor of Criminology, at the Institute of Criminal Justice Studies, University of Portsmouth. He is a former senior probation officer with experience of working in maximum security prisons. Research and publications have focused on public protection policy with emphasis on those assessed as high risk of harm and potentially dangerous. He has researched multi-agency collaboration in this field since the earliest days of its existence with particular emphasis on the way in which public protection collaboration has impacted on the culture of police and probation services. More recently research has focused on the issue of serious further offending and the assessment of those released from custody concerning their potential to perpetrate further serious harm. A future project is planned around the 'learning of lessons' in cases where serious harm has followed the release of offenders into the community.

Graham Noyce BSc, BA, MA, RNLD, FHEA, Approved MH Practitioner, is a senior lecturer in social work at the University of Portsmouth. He is a practising approved mental health professional and also works for the Health and Care Professions Council. He advises the Care Quality Commission on their inspection reviews of mental health services. His areas of research include forensic mental practice, mental health care and practice, the law and best outcomes for service users travelling through the mental health system.

Dr Nicholas Pamment is a Principal Lecturer and Associate Head (Students) at the Institute of Criminal Justice Studies, University of Portsmouth, having previously worked in various roles for a Youth Offending Team (YOT). Following a BSc (Hons) and MSc, he completed his doctorate within the area of community reparation and restorative justice for young offenders. He has published studies within the fields of policing; multi-agency working; research methodology; community sentences and wildlife crime.

Dr Aaron Pycroft is Reader in Criminal Justice and Social Complexity in the Institute of Criminal Justice Studies at the University of Portsmouth. He has had extensive practice and management experience working with complex needs. His main research interests are in the development of phenomenological approaches to complexity theory and its application to empowering the practices and ethics of criminal justice.

Sue Roberts is a senior lecturer in Politics and Public Administration at the University of Portsmouth. Her background is in local and national government having had 15 years as a manager in public service. Sue's research interests are in community safety, policing, public sector multi-agency partnerships and collaborative working. She managed an EU project in Romania and Bulgaria, in partnership with the University of Macerata in Italy to bring partnership working training to the emerging democracies in Europe. She retains strong links with local multi-agency partnerships and groups across Sussex, Surrey, Hampshire and the north of England. She is currently researching violent crime among young people in London and is working towards the completion of her PhD.

Dr Jacki Tapley is a Principal Lecturer in Victimology and Criminology at the Institute of Criminal Justice Studies, University of Portsmouth. Prior to joining ICJS in 2000, Jacki worked as a probation officer in Dorset. Her teaching and research focus on victims of crime and her specialist areas include victims of sexual violence, domestic abuse and fraud, the role of victims in the criminal justice system, the implementation of policies and legislation, and professional cultures. She works closely with the police and the Crown Prosecution Service, and is the Independent Facilitator for the Wessex CPS VAWG Scrutiny Panel and a member of the Hampshire Victim and Witness Working Group. She is a member of the Victim Commissioner's Advisory Board, and a trustee for Aurora New Dawn, a domestic abuse, sexual violence and stalking charity. Her research contributes to national policy and was used to inform the government's Victims Strategy (2018) in England and Wales.

Dr Marie-Edith Tiquet has over 14 years' experience in the health and social care sector and an extensive background in criminal justice and substance misuse service design and delivery, holding practitioner and operational management positions. She recently completed her Professional Doctorate in Criminal Justice, looking at the impact of coercion on service users' engagement in community drug and alcohol treatment. She has a keen interest in substance misuse, the concept of coercion and partnership working.

Jemma Tyson is a Senior Lecturer in Criminology at the University of Portsmouth, England. Her research interests focus on disablist hate crime and criminal justice responses. Jemma's PhD examines police service provision for victims of learning disablist hate crime and builds on the findings of her master's thesis on a related topic; the latter was conducted in partnership with the UK Cross Government Hate Crime Programme. She has published in this field and is an Independent Advisory Group member for the Hate Crime Programme and Hampshire Constabulary. In addition, she sits on the CPS Wessex Hate Crime Scrutiny Panel and has also represented the UK government at international hate crime events.

Dr Andy Williams is a Principal Lecturer and Associate Head of Research at the Institute of Criminal Justice Studies, University of Portsmouth. Having completed his doctorate in 2003, which consisted of an ethnography of the Paulsgrove demonstrations in 2000, he has developed academic courses and practitioner training in understanding risk and dangerousness for violent and sexual offenders. He is co-author (with Mike Nash) of *The anatomy of serious further offending* (2008, Oxford University Press) and *The handbook of public protection* (2010, Routledge). His recent books are *The myth of moral panics* (with Bill Thompson, 2014, Routledge) and *Forensic criminology* (2015, Routledge). He has undertaken numerous evaluations of public protection systems including an evaluation of the Integrated Management IRiS model for Avon and Somerset Police and Probation services (2014), Hampshire's Violent Offender Intervention Programme (2016, for Hampshire's Police and Crime Commissioner) and Aurora New Dawn's DVA Cars™ initiative (2018). His current research primarily focuses on an online ethnography of online grooming and anti-child sex offender ('Paedophile' Hunter) activist groups.

Dr Jane Winstone has qualifications in sociology, psychology and counselling as well as a diploma in social work and a PhD in criminology, focusing on youth crime and the impact of multi-agency intervention pre and post release from youth custody. Before moving to the University of Portsmouth in 1999 to launch the probation training qualification, Jane worked as a probation officer where she developed her interests in mental health, ethical research and professional practice. She continued to pursue these as specialist areas throughout her university career. Following her recent retirement, Jane works as a trustee for a charity with a role to lead in her areas of expertise. She is also a member of the NHS Research Ethics Committee for London-Surrey.

Introduction

Aaron Pycroft and Dennis Gough

Synopsis and aims

The book will develop the concept of multi-agency working in criminal justice by bringing together probation, policing, prison, social work, criminological and organisational studies perspectives. Since the publication of the first edition of this book in 2010, there has not been another book that focuses specifically on multi-agency working in criminal justice from the range of perspectives that we are offering and across the range of offender groups. The chapters will bring together up-to-date theory, policy and practice in an accessible way that is entirely relevant to practitioners and students in the criminal justice system. Multi-agency working continues to be a core focus in criminal justice and allied work, with government continuing to invest significantly in training criminal justice professionals. This book is entirely relevant to students who are studying and training to become probation officers, police officers, social workers or other professions related to criminal justice.

The second edition of this book has a deliberately broader focus than the first. The first edition focused almost exclusively on the changing landscape of probation in England and Wales and how many aspects of probation strategy and actions were founded upon multi-agency relations. From work to reduce recidivism and successfully reform offenders to strategies designed to manage, constrain and protect, multi-agency arrangements were analysed as the de facto approach to a vast array of what was termed 'probation practice'. Indeed, one of the themes of the earlier book was that such work to reform and protect could increasingly be considered as the criminal justice practices of local government, charities, private enterprise and citizens. However, what was omitted in the first book takes a central place in this second edition, namely the governmental logics and strategies to reduce crime across the broad spectrum of criminal justice. This includes policing, prisons and other custodial settings and a range of statutory and non-statutory organisations, all examined through the lens of multi-agency working.

The need to appreciate and comprehend the porous and fluid nature of traditional statutory, private and voluntary sector boundaries in contemporary criminal justice policy was best exemplified by the Conservative government's announcement that the competition to run HMP Wrexham (now HMP Berwyn) had been successfully *won* by the statutory sector via HM Prison Service. However, on closer inspection, despite the prison being won and operated by the statutory sector, HMP Wrexham would also see almost a third of the prison outsourced to private and voluntary providers ostensibly to provide the best rehabilitative environment by combining endeavours from inside and outside of the state. The then Prisons Minister, Andrew Selous, stated,

> The construction of the new prison in North Wales is already underway as part of the Prison New Capacity and Unit Cost Programmes. I can confirm that the new prison will be operated by Her Majesty's Prison Service (HMPS) but with 34% of service provision outsourced, including the running of the large industrial workshop complex. This new model will bring the public, voluntary and private sectors together, working to provide the best rehabilitative environment and to tackle re-offending rates. (Ministry of Justice, press release, 24 February 2015)[1]

Many of the chapters in this book talk about or reference the realities of austerity funding and the ways in which government seeks to save money in the face of economic problems. The above example is one of many that practitioners and service users will be familiar with, as well as its concomitant operating issues. In addressing those issues this book seeks to reflect on theoretical analysis of political economy with particular reference to neoliberal policies in the first two chapters. The first chapter by Dennis Gough sets the context for understanding the predicaments that policy makers have faced in addressing crime with particular reference to Foucault's governmentality thesis. In the second chapter Aaron Pycroft then takes the theme of neoliberalism and applies it to practice in the criminal justice system with a call to try and resist the implications of these policies for already marginal people. These two chapters are an invitation to engage with the taken for granted concepts of multi-agency working and to use the approaches discussed as a tool of analysis with the other chapters.

The second part of the book examines the main multi-agency frameworks for criminal justice. Barry Loveday and Sue Roberts discuss the important development of having directly elected Police and Crime Commissioners, and the politicisation of responses to crime and how this impacts on the delivery of justice; in his chapter Andy Williams provides a case example of integrated offender management and how this works in practice with respect to colocation and information sharing; Mike Nash analyses the role of Multi-Agency Public Protection Arrangements (MAPPAs) and the problems of 'othering' sex offenders along with questioning a simplistic risk based classification system for allocating resources; Jacki Tapley and Zoë Jackson highlight the ways in which victims of domestic abuse are called on to take greater responsibility themselves for tackling that abuse rather than government tackling root causes. All of these chapters highlight good practice but demonstrate the necessity of an ongoing evolution whereby a collection of agencies may just be 'joined-up worrying' in practice.

The third part of the book then moves onto policing. Claudia Cox focuses on community policing in diverse communities, and the ways in which they have become more accountable to more individuals and organisations and the implications for practice. John Fox addresses the ways in which the police investigate child protection cases and the ways in which austerity and other priorities have impacted on capacity to do this well; Jemma Tyson and Nathan Hall examine the definitions and impact of hate crime and the necessity of multi-agency working in addressing it, as well as the importance of doing straightforward things well. The issue of terrorism is then addressed by John Grieve who finds problems in the current approaches but argues that much can be learnt from the bottom up approaches of the hate crime strategy.

The fourth part of the book then considers custodial settings. One of the themes that emerges from these chapters is the importance of listening to the voices of those involved. Lesley Laver takes a practice based approach to interviewing children who are suspects and the different roles and agencies involved and tries to see the process and experience from the child's perspective. This is followed by Sarah Lewis' practice based example of engaging prisoners to reform the prison environment and how this affects all of the key stakeholders in building a positive environment. The following chapter by Graham Noyce examines the problematic marketplace for out of area placements for service users with mental health problems and how this needs to be addressed within case management approaches. The problem of complex needs and dual diagnosis within the forensic population and the importance of motivational working is discussed by Anita Green and Aaron Pycroft.

The final part focuses on community interventions, with Jane Winstone discussing ways in which the good lives model can be implemented for people with mental health problems in the criminal justice system. Marie-Edith Tiquet then examines the use of treatment orders for substance misuse and alcohol, and the vexed problems of outcome measurement and the use of coercion. Finally, Nick Pamment addresses youth justice and developments in treating young offenders from a child protection perspective rather than as criminals per se.

In many ways the book covers far more ground than the first edition, which of course reflects developments in policy and practice. There are omissions, and we have not covered everything that we would have liked to, such as gangs and more on women offenders. In part this has been due to problems with the attitude that neoliberal universities take towards certain kinds of outputs and the ways in which these are valued and judged by the standards of the Research Excellence Framework (REF). Chapters in edited books are not rated highly with respect to impact. Our argument is that impact should be precisely about shaping practice in the criminal justice system and that the knowledge and experience contained in this book is essential for students and practitioners, and that the academic life and impact is far more than the REF. However the practicalities of publishing an edited book on time has meant that we have lost some contributions, but nonetheless we hope that you find what we have published interesting, thought-provoking and useful.

Note

[1]   www.gov.uk/government/news/new-prison-to-be-run-by-her-majestys-prison-service-hmps accessed 19/2/19

1

Multi-agency working and the governance of crime control

Dennis Gough

> **Aims of the chapter**
> - To provide a theoretical context for the book.
> - To analyse the political economy of developments in the governance of crime.
> - To utilise Foucault's governmentality thesis to examine the ways in which government seeks to shape and control organisations.

This chapter seeks to uncover and make sense of the theoretical underpinnings of multi-agency arrangements by analysing approaches to criminal justice policy which move beyond the state or what Rhodes has called the 'governance' of societal problems. Rhodes (1995: 1) states that 'governance signifies a change in the meaning of government, referring to a new process of governing; or a changed condition of ordered rule; or the new method by which society is governed'. As such, the governance of crime control includes discourses relating to a wide ranging participation in partnership, contestability, marketisation and privatisation arrangements. As Pierre and Peters (2000) note, these new strategies will increasingly centre on the government's efforts to steer the crime control endeavours of others. The chapter attempts to move beyond a mere tracing and description of the different institutional arrangements that serve to identify how, for example policing has changed. Rather, the chapter connects the development of complex multi-agency arrangements, found in antisocial behaviour and preventative work, the policing of public and private space and the punishment and rehabilitation of offenders with political and societal developments particularly in relation to the nature of contemporary government and the fluid relationships between the state and law and order (Crawford, 1999).

In order to achieve this, the chapter will utilise theoretical insights and perspectives which centre on the multiplicity of ways by which governments seek to control and shape organisations and citizens' conduct afforded through the lens of Foucault's notion of governmentality. This chapter firstly details the backdrop to recent societal, economic and political changes which challenge established and rational modernist criminological thought. Secondly, the chapter discusses emergent theoretical perspectives in criminology, centring around governmentality, which attempts to shed light on the contemporary mainstreaming of traditionally non-penal and non-state actors in the criminal justice system. The chapter concludes by highlighting how successive governments' mainstreaming of non-state actors in criminal justice policy and practice requires a broader criminological imagination than has been afforded thus far in mainstream criminology. A broader imagination would incorporate and reflect a variety of governmental ways of thinking about policing, punishment and rehabilitation.

Late modernity and challenges to big government and crime control

Any analysis of the relationship between government strategies to reduce crime and the new mainstreaming of the private, voluntary and community sector groups needs to be situated against the political, economic and social changes which have challenged and reshaped the boundaries of criminology in the period described as late modernity. Only by outlining and analysing the sheer variety of political, social and economic challenges since the late 1970s can the involvement of voluntary organisations and volunteers in the field of community justice and rehabilitation be fully understood and articulated.

Contemporary criminology is emerging out of the new political, economic and social world of the 1970s and presents a set of significant challenges to the discipline. The rapid and profound changes to our society have been of significant interest to a number of sociologists and criminologists (Garland and Sparks, 2000; Stenson, 2001; Taylor, 1999). Indeed, Taylor (1999: 10) notes how

> the analysis of crime itself (the object of analysis of any serious 'criminological' project) must be located in relation to the fundamental transformation of social formation that is currently in progress (resulting from a deep crisis in the pre-existing configurations of social and economic organization).

Criminology has witnessed a profound set of cultural, political and social undertaken changes in Western capitalist democracies brought about by the changing nature of capitalist production, such as mass consumerism, globalisation, the restructuring of the labour market and the growth of unemployment. The cumulative impact of such profound transformations is something which Lea and Hallsworth (2013: 19) have termed 'rewriting the scripts governing social structure, class relations and politics in the advanced capitalist countries of the industrial North'. Similarly, Garland (2001) notes the economic and ideological force of capitalist production to be the most basic transformative force in the modern times. For Garland (2001) many of the profound economic and social changes during the latter part of the 20th century can be ascribed to the process of capital accumulation, the unerring search for new markets for capitalist growth including previously sacralised public sector work. In short, during the post war period government was conceptualised to be 'big' in that it assumed both an active and central role in managing economic and social life, guaranteeing opportunities to create markets and profit while ensuring that the population were guaranteed health, wellbeing and prosperity (Garland, 2001: 81). Since 1945 in Western Europe and USA, the interventionist welfare state was central to the delivery of what had previously been deemed as private actions and behaviour. Whether one considers the fields of policing, punishment, education or health, the post war interventionist state can be conceptualised as incorporating a variety of national, regulatory agencies assuming a degree of expertise and control of formally unregulated activity. Thus this Keynesian interventionist state is best exemplified by the creation of a welfare state, an expanded 'public sector' and the rapid development of a largely state sponsored professionalised middle class in society.

However, this post war settlement of remarkable growth in both capital accumulation and living standards in Western capitalist economies was abruptly ended in the early 1970s. This crisis in economic growth arose as a result of the cumulative effects of the rise in the price of oil, economic recession and negative growth and finally the competition from newly competitive economies of developing countries in a globalised economy. As Hobsbawm (1994: 15) noted, global capitalism undermined national institutions and interests and 'for many purposes, notably in economic affairs, the globe is now the primary operational unit and older units, such as the national economies defined by the politics of territorial states, are reduced to complications of transnational activities'.[1] Whole industries which had been the mainstay of the industrialised economy had all but disappeared. Importantly during the fiscal crisis in the 1970s, public expenditure outran income from taxation and led to a radical and accelerated restructuring of the labour market with the shedding of millions of predominantly male, heavy manufacturing jobs and created a labour market that was characterised not by stable, high paid careers with significant employment protections but by precarious, low paid and part time positions (Taylor, 1999: 14).

Since the 1970s crisis in capitalism, Western nations have borne witness to great transformations in class relations. Increasingly, the skilled working class have shifted their interests away from a sense of collectivism in favour of 'asocial individualism' (Hobsbawm, 1994: 15) and free market economics. As such, we are used to the favouring of individualistic rather than collective tendencies in how we live our lives or solve societal problems (Garland, 2001). Indeed, while such freeing up of old collectivism could be seen by many as liberating and offering opportunities to progress and consume, it also brought with it new problems linked to these new individual freedoms.

In addition, and interwoven with the political and economic changes outlined above, we have born witness to social changes to the family, epitomised by increasing numbers of women wanting or needing to enter the workforce, increased rates of divorce and family structures, a decrease in family size and a rise in different family formations, and the creation of the teenager as a separate and largely unsupervised member of society. Moreover, a society characterised by profound changes in the stretching of time, space and communication brought about by mass ownership of cars, technological developments and affordable travel. Transformations in communities and families have at their core the entry of women into the labour market to fill the burgeoning jobs in the service sectors.[2] The rise in work for women impacted on family structure. Garland (2001) highlights a noticeable decline in birth rate during this period with women beginning a family later in life, having fewer children and returning to work after childbirth. Possibly the most startling social transformation relating to the family structure during this period is the rate at which marriages ended in divorce. In England the rate of divorce and separation increased sharply as did the number of children being raised in single parent households.[3] As Garland (2001: 83) notes, the scale of the transformation in family life was so significant that

> in the space of only 40 years the traditional image of the nuclear family – a married couple living together with children – had come to bear little relation to the real domestic lives of most of the population in America and Britain.

New economic and social realities and the relationship to crime

The period of late modernity has then witnessed the coexistence of rising consumption, general affluence and a concomitant rise in the overall crime rate in every Western industrialised nation, something Garland (2001) has termed an 'epistemological crisis'. Indeed as Taylor (1999: 16) notes, it is a sociological and cultural shock to find the uncritical acceptance of a constantly developing and improving society to be a fallacy. The rise in recorded crime during a period of a general rise in general living standards and prosperity is significant. In England and Wales the police recorded crime rate doubled between 1955 and 1964 from 500,000 to 1 million crimes (Reiner, 2007: 62–63). By 1965 the crime rate had doubled again and then doubled again by 1990 as a result of the increase in absolute and relative deprivation rates (Taylor, 1999: 16). Late modern economic and social transformation had clearly made society a more criminogenic milieu with increased opportunities for crime and reduced levels of social control afforded by the family and church. In addition, an ever increasing number of individuals were losing out in the changes to the labour market and welfare restructuring, and were 'at risk' of crime. This included an increasingly large number of teenage males enjoying time outside of the home and hence outside of family and work controls. As Currie said, as a result of the interconnectedness of the economic, the social or community and the familial when discussing violent crime,

> we are likely to see great structural inequalities and community fragmentation and weakened ability of parents to monitor and supervise their children – and a great many other things all going on at once, all entwined with each other, and all affecting the crime rate (Currie, 1997, cited in Reiner, 2007: 80)

Neoliberal and conservative mentalities as an antidote to the late modern problem of crime

Dean (2010) and Reiner (2007) have outlined the increasing turn to a duality of conservative and neoliberal rationalities of government since the 1970s as a way to solve political, social and economic challenges in Western states. As Crawford (1999: 25) notes, the challenge to the post war interventionist state has been found in a rejection of the expectation that the state was expected to hand down answers to ameliorate society's problems and meet human need. Rather, since the 1970s, political thought has centred on how all sectors, communities and citizens have become implicated and mobilised in the task of resolving them.

While the neoliberal term or concept has been used in a multiplicity of ways which often incorporate communitarianism or neo-conservative political ideology, here the term is used to refer to a sea change in the government of liberal democracies since the 1960s and 1970s. After the Second World War, government was largely understood as an activity undertaken by a national welfare state acting on behalf on a singular 'domain' understood as society (Dean, 2010: 176). Indeed, the Keynesian attempts to govern and intervene in the health of the economy and society is encapsulated in the attempts to secure full employment and care for people from the cradle to the grave. As such, the state took on a wide range of social and economic obligations principally by the use of state investment in sectors such as transportation, public utilities, housing and manufacturing that were vital to mass production and consumption. Harvey (1989, in Smart, 2003: 122) notes that 'governments also moved to provide a strong underpinning to the social wage through expenditure covering social security, health care, education, housing and the like'.

However, by the late 1970s this post war settlement of centralised state planning, high levels of economic development and the provision of social care from the cradle to the grave was coming under increasing challenge by academics and political leaders who began to envisage the state as too large, too expensive and restricting the freedoms of entrepreneurial individuals. Indeed, any conceptualisation of a crisis of the state really alludes to a fundamental lack of confidence with the Keynesian welfare state's ability to manage and encourage economic prosperity.

A key aspect of Garland's (1996, 2000, 2001) central thesis on the government of crime control stems from the view that, since the late 1970s, governments' constructions of, and approaches to reduce, crime and disorder have been reconfigured as a result of a collective experience of crime and insecurity in society. For Garland (2001: 110) government has a central predicament around contemporary crime control. First, governments of all persuasions see the need to withdraw their universal claim to be the most effective provider of security in the face of entrenched high crime rates; and second and concomitantly, politicians are concerned about the disastrous political implications of doing so in the face of the politicisation of crime and punishment. As a consequence, in the last 30 years of the 20th century, governments of all persuasions had to develop new approaches and adaptations to the predicament of rising crime rates, particularly in relation to violent and property crime and the increased politicisation of crime. The presence of crime in society has been understood as a normal social fact and the state has had to adapt its strategies in accordance with this new mentality. This central predicament or weakness of the state around crime and punishment is played out in a multiplicity of ways and in policy decisions that can sometimes appear fragmented, contradictory or volatile. Rather than identifying a grand narrative such as discipline or reform, rehabilitation or correction, Rose (2000a) identifies a range of competing and complementary ways of thinking and acting on the crime problem. As a result, the field of crime control and punishment includes both inclusionary and exclusionary thoughts and practices, particularly when one considers responses to the politicised and racialised problem of crime and punishment. The older ways of governments addressing crime by invoking 'social' notions of treatment, welfare and rehabilitation now coexist and compete with radically different urges to manage and exclude with strategies to empower and accept personal responsibility. As Rose (2000a: 183) highlights,

> Demands for exemplary sanctions against offenders are accompanied by schemes for naming and shaming and blaming focused on the relations between offender and victim. The prisoner is to be incapacitated or the prisoner is to be taught life skills and entrepreneurship, or the prisoner is to be stigmatized and made to accept moral culpability or the prisoner is to be helped to reintegrate into society. The spread of community types of correction such as fines, probation orders, community service and so forth go hand in hand with an inexorable increase in the prison population and the constant expansion of the prison building programme.

Conservative, law and order government agendas

Responding to crime has emerged as an issue at the core of government activity as a result of substantial transformations in economic and social life (Stenson, 2001). In the last 30 years of the 20th century, the discipline of criminology has had to respond to fundamental changes in government thinking in relation to how it should conceptualise the crime problem and best respond to it. In particular, while the Keynesian welfare state helped to create a society where most if not all benefited from economic prosperity and a rise in living standards until the 1970s economic crisis, the welfare state began to be attacked, in light of rising crime rates, not as merely a poor and ineffective government strategy to reduce criminality but rather as a problem that can lead to or underpin higher rates of criminal behaviour in society.

The social and economic transformations detailed earlier have led to a generalised sense of insecurity in late modern society. It is this feeling of insecurity that has affected nearly all Western capitalist nations, fuelling a demand for protection from crime and lawlessness by citizens and a general punitive response to lawbreaking. Feelings of insecurity run high and amount to demands for safety and security from government which become hard to meet. Conservative 'tough on crime' responses to crime and criminals which posit that offenders are rational actors who can be deterred or incapacitated from criminal behaviour have increasingly found favour in comparison to those that afford reintegrative and welfarist solutions (Bell, 2011: 2). Sections of the public, with significant feelings of insecurity and dislocation, respond with a much greater sense of condemnation to crime. They are much less willing to countenance sympathy for the offender who has abused his or her freedoms in society. In penal policy criminal behaviour has come to be conceptualised much more in terms of the offender's danger or risk to a community of law abiding citizens marked by fear, insecurities about crime and victimisation and condemnation of the law breaker. Less time is given to the notion that offenders can be changed or afforded second chances and rather more is given to their neutralisation or 'management' through harsh criminal sentencing and regulatory controls. In policing zero tolerance approaches and the metaphor of war have been used to highlight an increasingly harsh and robust approach to policing.

Furthermore, a common experience of victimisation, or the fear of becoming victimised, has led to what Garland (2001) has called a 'crime complex' whereby general fears and concerns are shaped through the lens of crime and victimisation. Allied to this sense of insecurity and the political foregrounding of crime and punishment came the perception that crime will continue to rise, even when the crime rates stagnated or fell, and that crime was a problem of ineffective control, with the statutory pillars of the penal and criminal justice system deemed ineffective and broken rather than enjoying any sense of legitimacy and public support.

Garland (1996) notes how a range of expressive government assertions may take the form of a criminology of the 'other' where governments deny the central predicament of the state's new limitations to afford security by a politicised neo-conservative reaction involving tougher legislation and increased incarceration which moves away from rational decision making based on proportionality. Similarly, expressive modes of punishment such as shaming the offender or militaristic bootcamps are as a result of a governmental discourse around crime and punishment which is expressive, deliberately emotional, harsh and unforgiving. As Garland (1996: 461) notes,

> It is a criminology of the alien other which represents criminals as dangerous members of a distinct racial and social groups which bear little resemblance to 'us'. It is moreover a criminology which trades in images, archetypes and anxieties, rather than careful analysis and research findings, more a politicised discourse of the unconscious than a detailed form of knowledge for power.

The turn to neoliberal governmental rationalities

However, such conservative punitive strategies created while denying the realities of high crime rates and subsequently 'acting out' over crime by demonstrations of sovereign power are only one aspect of an array of solutions to the governmental predicament regarding crime control (Garland, 2001). What has received rather less academic attention is my central concern in relation to governmental strategies that incorporate multi-agency working. These changes in approaches to criminal justice have been much 'quieter' (Loader and Sparks, 2007: 80) and less prominent in the academic literature. Nevertheless, the fluidity in governmental, institutional and administrative arrangements regarding how the field of criminal justice has been reconfigured to cope with rising crime rates and concurrent demands for economic efficiencies and effectiveness remain important considerations to understand.

The neoliberal rationalities of government have been most significantly found in the work of F.A. Hayek's work (1994) *The road to serfdom* and the political ideas of Keith Joseph and Margaret Thatcher. All agree that the only solution to economic decline is the belief in the power of free markets and in taking individual responsibility to address societal problems. It is worthwhile recounting what Thatcher stated in 1987 as evidence of an emerging neoliberal rationality which decentred state welfarism and emphasised personal responsibility.

> I think we've been through a period where too many people have been given to understand that if they have a problem, it's the government's job to cope with it. 'I have a problem I'll get a grant.' 'I'm homeless, the government must house me.' They're casting their problems on society. And, you know there is no such thing as society. There are individual men and women and there are families. And no government can do anything except through people, and people must look to themselves first. It is our duty to look after ourselves, and then to look after our neighbour. (Thatcher, quoted in Dean 2010: 177)

Thatcher outlines above three strands of neoliberal political rationality which outline the core of neoliberal thinking around the excesses of government and the freedoms of individualism that underpin the reform of penal policy and the emerging marketisation of fields such as community justice and rehabilitation. This new emerging thinking about the relationship of the individual to the state can be built around the three tenets of individual responsibility rather than state dependency, the foregrounding of freedom and autonomy via participation and reliance on market principles and relations, and finally a multiplicity of governance arrangements unsettling the previous reliance upon the public sector and state. While neoliberalism has been often invoked but ill defined, this work uses the analytical framework of Mudge (2008), who conceptualises neoliberalism firstly as an *intellectual idea or 'face'* in that it is a concept distinguished by its Anglo-American transnationalism and the unadulterated emphasis of the free market as the source and providers of human freedom. Secondly, Mudge (2008: 704) notes neoliberalism's *bureaucratic face* in the expression of neoliberal ideologies in state policy and action. She highlights how neoliberal ideas are expressed in state liberalisation, the deregulation of previously 'sacralised' public services and government activities to privatisation and the loosening of left versus right divisions in politics. Finally, Mudge (2008: 705) highlights a third *political face* of neoliberalism which attempts to move beyond parochial party politics to encompass political elites, interest groups, grassroots organisations and private groups to lobby for a common sense approach to and unquestioned foregrounding of the market. While definitions of neoliberalism abound, Bourdieu's notion of an 'ideological system that holds the market sacred, born within the human or social sciences and refined in a network of Anglo-American–centric knowledge producers, expressed in different ways within the institutions of the post war nation state and their political fields' encapsulates the three faces of neoliberalism outlined here (Mudge, 2008: 706).

The neoliberal governmental rationality has developed where the remedies to social problems such as crime and disorder lay less with the state and government but increasingly more so in the private and civil spheres of endeavour. The construction by government of quasi or artificial markets such as those in adult social care or probation and rehabilitation were envisaged as an alternative to government characterised by excessive state expenditure, increased bureaucracy, economic stagnation and dependency were increasingly articulated by neoliberal thinkers and policy makers. The centrality and 'truths' of markets in neoliberal thinking is best summarised by Keith Joseph: 'Markets are a state of nature which has spontaneously evolved and to disregard their rules is as pointless as attempting to ignore the laws of gravity' (Joseph in Turner, 2011: 123).

The neoliberal notion of the state is one which should actively create markets in public sector utilities and duties such as community justice, in what are reconsidered and reconceptualised in the language of market pluralism as single state *monopolies* (Bell, 2011). However, the emphasis here on the enduring yet reconfigured role of the state does rather contradict assertions that the state has become 'hollowed out' or rolled back. Rather, neoliberal politics involve the shifting of state intervention from service delivery to new forms of governance underpinned by logic of competition, marketisation, deregulation and activation policies in order to achieve renewed capitalist growth.

In order to capture the increasing presence of market based developments and a plurality of actors in crime control, Garland (2001: 124) constructs a governmental approach he terms a 'responsibilisation strategy' to mobilise non-state actors in an attempt to extend the reach of the state's interests. He states that creative linkages between state organisations are encouraged and non-statutory bodies in both the private and not for profit sector are joined and activated to carry out crime control work. Similarly, the notion of responsibilisation can also be extended to the citizens themselves, who are encouraged to take control and manage their own of sense of insecurity by purchasing security services and adapting their own behaviour so as to minimise the possibility of victimhood. This governmental strategy of 'responsibilisation' is therefore

> an enhanced network of more or less directed, more or less informal crime control, complementing and extending the formal controls of the criminal justice state? Instead of imagining they can monopolize crime control, or exercising their sovereign powers … state agencies now adopt a strategic relation to other forces of social control. They seek to build broader alliances, enlisting the 'governmental' powers of private actors and shaping them to the ends of crime control. (Garland, 2001: 124)

Despite the emergence of new strategies that attempt to share the responsibility of crime control via new practices such as partnership working or marketisation approaches (Crawford, 1999), this new conceptualisation of crime control 'beyond the state' has had a limited impact on the world of criminal justice. Appreciating the plurality in punishment and rehabilitation has arrived late in comparison to other areas of the criminal justice system such as policing and the crime prevention field. Academic attention to private policing and security is well established with the work of Button (2007) and Von Hirsch et al (2002) and the development of the field of crime prevention work involving voluntary sector and private sector involvement has been expertly charted by the work of Crawford (1999). Indeed, the identification and analysis of responsibilisation strategies in Garland's (2001) work has largely been conceptualised as relevant and indicative of changes to governmental strategies in crime preventative strategies such as situational crime prevention. Indeed he states that a 'new rationality of crime control – a new way of thinking and acting that differs quite radically from previous modes of crime control… involving a whole new infrastructure of arrangements whereby state and non-state agencies coordinate their practices to enhance community safety' relates to preventative work where the private and penal voluntary sectors will flourish in a dispersed, disorganised field of preventative endeavour (Garland, 2000: 349).

As such, it is the realm of policing and crime prevention that criminology has documented a move to localised, community based crime prevention initiatives which have activated business, community organisations, local authorities and police services. Rather than the state handing down authoritative answers to complex, localised crime problems, the community or locale itself is implicated in the task of resolving the problems they are experiencing through the creation of local partnerships or complex webs of preventative work (Crawford, 1999).

Analysing plurality in criminal justice: Foucault's governmentality thesis

Within criminology, the influence of Michel Foucault's work is enormous. Foucault's later work around governmentality has been described as his 'second wave' to emphasise its growing influence of academic criminological thinking. In essence, his work around governmentality developed from his earlier perspectives in *Discipline and punish* (1977), which located a diffused power in society designed to create individuals as 'docile bodies' brought to conformity by social control and the disciplinary power of government. Foucault's latter work on governmentality paid more attention to a multiplicity of ways in which populations and individuals are governed including the governance of individuals as active subjects whose attitudes and choices of behaviour come to be conjoined with the aims of governing authorities (Dean, 2010; Burchell et al, 1991).

Indeed, Foucault's work on neoliberal governmentality offers both a new perspective which emphasises the multiplicity of actors involved the shaping of free citizens' behaviour and a powerful new analytic to how crime and criminality is problematised, the way crime and offenders are thought about and acted upon in a practical sense. At its core, the governmentality analytic refers to the range of governmental rationalities and practices, associated with liberal rule, by which populations are rendered thinkable and measurable for the purposes of government (Foucault, 1980). As an array of technologies of government, governmentality is understood as the analysis of strategies, techniques and procedures through which different authorities seek to enact programmes of government which can be a 'complex assemblage of diverse forces, techniques, devices that promise to regulate decisions and actions of individuals, groups and organisations in relation to authoritative criteria' (Rose and Miller, 1992; Burchell, 1996: 42). State power is effectively *translated* into the work of other actors and relations of authority. In terms of an analysis of contemporary neoliberal political ideology, Rose and Miller (1992) have developed Foucault's analysis to discussion of power beyond the state. Power, they argue, should be viewed as a matter of networks and alliances rather than the direct imposition of state or sovereign will. Rose and Miller's (1992) analysis presupposes that within the networks of governance are chains of actors, all with their own subjectivity, who translate centre objectives down the chain. Here, they see the importance of 'governing at a distance', involving multiple actors who blur the demarcation of state and civil, public and private.

Such an approach is particularly applicable to neoliberal political ideology which encourages private entrepreneurship in social matters and dealing with social problems such as crime. As such,

> political power is exercised today though a profusion of shifting alliances between diverse authorities in projects to govern a multitude of facets of economic activity, social life and individual conduct. Power is not so much a matter of imposing constraints upon citizens as of 'making up' citizens capable of bearing a kind of regulated freedom. (Rose and Miller, 1992: 174)

While the art of government has been described by Foucault (Burchell et al, 1991) as essentially a problem solving exercise, Dean (2010) reminds us that it intrinsically links to questions of morality. The attempt to shape conduct implies the idea of a prescribed standard against which conduct should be measured rather than the freedom to act as one might wish. This sense of directing conduct is important in late modern society where responsibility for one's behaviour is increasingly seen as the responsibility of the individual themselves. Government therefore asserts how individuals ought to conduct themselves whether that is to be crime free, healthy and fit, employable and self-improving and to correct oneself when the individual does not meet the standard (Dean, 2010:19). Foucault's 'governmentality' thesis has been developed further by Rose and Miller who have traced an analysis of neoliberal power 'beyond the state' or 'at a distance'. Their work to, first, trace the analytical thinking around neoliberal government and, second, the governmental technologies of neoliberalism have emphasised the decentring of the state and the incorporation of a multiplicity of actors and the shaping of the behaviour of autonomous subjects. This is documented by Pratt (1997: 133) when he states that neoliberalism as programme of government 'shifts the general burden of risk management away from the state and its agencies and onto the self, in partnership with non-state forms of expertise and governance'.

Conclusion: shadow states and plural policing and punishment

The disciplines of criminology and criminal justice are therefore situated against significant political and social change in society. Garland and Sparks (2000: 1) go so far as to say that criminology's subject matter is 'centrally implicated in the major transformations of our time'. As a result of such tumultuous political, social and economic transformations detailed above, criminal justice scholars need to shift their traditional focus and frameworks of analysis to have contemporary relevance. As such, criminology and criminal justice 'must be a subject that constantly reconstitutes itself if it is to come to terms with the social and legal worlds that is aspires to comprehend and which it intends to intervene' (Garland and Sparks, 2000: 3).

This work is an edited collection that extends beyond modernist criminological thinking, which has traditionally been focused upon a narrow conceptualisation of the sovereign state and its criminal justice system, with a focus on law making professionals employed by the institutional pillars of state, the police service and prison and probation services.

However, this collection is a small part of a more fluid and liquid criminology that has been developing whereby criminologists have begun to appreciate and chart the ways in which regulatory powers or governance arrangements impact significantly and deeply upon individual citizens' lives and the way in which the provision of security or prevention of crime have become the focus of a wider range of authorities. These extend the reach of the criminal justice system and introduce new knowledge, expertise and methods. Indeed, the focus on multi-agency working in criminal justice involving the private, voluntary sectors and local government echoes Rose's (2000b: 324) argument for a decentring of analysis away from the 'criminal justice system encapsulated in "codes, courts and constables"'.

In charting the contemporary landscape of crime, order and control, Loader and Sparks (2007) argue that one of criminology's contemporary habits is an unerring focus on the sovereign state which needs to be reconsidered in order to appreciate new governmental strategies in criminal justice. The criminal justice system is continually fragmenting and becoming pluralised involving non-state bodies from the private, voluntary and community sectors and involving new professionals who traditionally have not had a crime control remit. Garland and Sparks (2000:4) note how

> The continuing erosion of clear cut distinctions between the public and the private realms of crime control, together with the displacement of the criminal justice state from centre stage in the production of security and crime control, have had a major impact.

As a result the political discourse constructed by opposing sides such as the public versus private, or state versus civil society and government versus the market does not adequately characterise the diversity of ways in which government rule is shaped through all these organisations and fields of practice. As such, we need to be aware of governmental *inventiveness* and the nuanced changing ways of governing populations and individuals.

A criminology which ignores the increasing plurality of voices, expertise and authority on crime matters continues to focus on the outdated notion that the criminal justice state is the sole solution to crime problems and is also responsible for the delivery of those solutions. In discussing how late modern crime control is volatile, uneven and contradictory, criminologists such as O'Malley (1999) and Garland (2001) encourage us to see how the power of the state has been sustained even though the statutory actors of police and prisons have been challenged by a market logic and partially replaced by private interests and actors. As such, in contemporary times we witness with respect to crime control the 'flexing of the muscles of the displaced state' (Bauman, 1999, in Loader and Sparks, 2007: 81) in a response to increased demands for safety and security from citizens. As such, this enables us to conceptualise a change in the nature of the state power from 'an imagined state as being a centralized body within any nation, a collective actor with a monopoly of the legitimate use of force in a demarcated territory' (Rose, 1999: 1) to one which is fragmented, has new flows and alliances with private and other interests on a localised and globalised scale.

This edited collection refigures the criminological mirror not only to be fixed upon the reconfigurations apparent in the 'state system', but also to encapsulate newer and broader governmental strategies around the relationships between state, civil society and citizens.

As Beckett and Murakawa (2012) highlight by limiting any analysis of punishment to the harsh, expressive actions of the state, criminology fails to open and illuminate the broader 'shadow carceral state' emerging beyond the confines of the more visible criminal law and justice institutions. They usefully remind us that 'the penal system has become not only larger, but also more legally hybrid and institutionally variegated than is sometimes recognised' particularly when government strategies demand that penal control grow without the requisite costs (Beckett and Murakawa, 2012: 223). Furthermore, Miller (2014) details how faith based charities and voluntary organisations involved in re-entry in the USA enable the state to extend its reach into the communities and lives of the poor and hardest to reach during a period of fiscal retrenchment. Similarly, Kaufman et al (2016: 2) note how 'the penal state reaches beyond carceral confinement and the well documented iterations of this confinement through civil laws and regulations, bureaucratic operations, and for profit and non-profit nongovernmental organizations'. As such, these scholars have begun to conceptualise resettlement and re-entry activities as a hybridised field that activates human actors in voluntary, private and state agencies to intervene in offenders' lives in particular ways.

However, by conceptualising new and important regulatory forms of control as being merely 'other to state' or 'beyond the state' rather than an analysis of exactly what they are' (Armstrong and McAra, 2006: 8) criminology is only just broadening its understanding of fragmented policing and penal fields. A rather thicker analytical frame is essential in detailing the rich complexity of the power to punish in late modernity where the state presents itself as *simultaneously* sovereign and decentred. Contemporary criminology and penology therefore need to continue to respond to punitive arrangements which involves new actors and practices, stretching the penal gaze beyond courts, prisons and probation officers to new networks and multiple 'architectures of punishment' across penal and civil spheres. Neoliberal political rationality locates civil society and civil institutions as key to the neoliberal project. The activities of charities and non-governmental organisations are not considered as part of the state but rather as art of governance arrangements actively reforming and transforming what has traditionally been state activity as its remoulds itself into a range of governance functions of a huge range of providers of criminal justice.

This chapter has charted the recent blend of neoliberal and neo-conservative governmental mentalities in crime control. It has highlighted how harsh coercion, restraint and domination are to the fore particularly when moralistic and paternalistic neo-conservative mentalities are powerful. In an increasingly fluid and complex society, studies around governmentality offer criminologists a move away from totalising and centrist theorisations of coercive sovereign power. Governmentality opens up understandings of the governance of others and of open ended ways of thinking about government (Rose and Miller, 1992). Armstrong and McAra (2006) speak of the need for an analysis which recognises the porous nature of punishment's borders and the need to move beyond the simplistic notion that punishment is the state's response to law breaking. This edited collection is a deliberate broadening out of our analytical lens away from codes, courts and constables to perhaps charities, companies and citizens in analysing contemporary arrangements in the policing and punishment of law breakers.

Summary of key learning points

Multi-agency working arrangements are considered central to the government of social and criminal problems in contemporary times.

Whilst often multi-agency arrangements are analysed by their effectiveness, this chapter has attempted to link such arrangements to social theory. In doing so it charts how crime problems, and those responsible for addressing them, are conceptualised increasingly beyond the state involving community groups and business.

Notes

[1] For example, the decline in manufacturing industry in the USA as a percentage of the total economy fell from 25.9% in 1970 to 17.5% in 1990 – it fell from 38.7% to 22.5% in the UK over the same period (Taylor, 1999)

[2] The rate of married women entering the world of work rose from 14% of the total population in 1951 to over 50% in 1980 in the US. Similar rises were experienced in the UK, where women formed 29% of the active workforce in 1951 rising to 43% by 1991 (Garland, 2001).

[3] In 1938 only 1 in 38 marriages in England ended in divorce compared to 1 in 2.2 by the mid-1980s (Garland, 2001: 83). In the USA in the 1990s the number of children born to a single parent household rose to 30% on average and up to 70% in some communities (Garland, 2001: 83).

References

Armstrong, S. and McAra, L. (eds) (2006) *Perspectives on punishment*. Oxford: Oxford University Press.

Beckett, K. and Murakawa, N. (2012) 'Mapping the shadow carceral state: Toward an institutionally capacious approach to punishment', *Punishment and Society*, 16(2): 221–244.

Bell, E. (2011) *Criminal justice and neoliberalism*. New York: Palgrave Macmillan.

Burchell, G. (1996) 'Liberal government and techniques of the self', in A. Barry, T. Osborne and N. Rose (eds), *Foucault and political reason*. Abingdon: Routledge.

Burchell, G., Gordon, C. and Miller, P. (eds) (1991) *The Foucault effect. Studies in governmentality*. Chicago: The University of Chicago Press.

Button, M. (2007) *Security officers and policing: Powers, culture and control in the governance of private space*. Aldershot: Ashgate.

Crawford, A. (1999) *The local governance of crime: Appeals to Community and partnership*. Oxford: Oxford University Press.

Dean, M. (2010) *Governmentality*. Second edition. London: Sage.

Foucault, M. (1977) *Discipline and punish. The birth of the prison*. London: Penguin.

Garland, D. (1996). 'The limits of the sovereign state: strategies of crime control in contemporary society', *British Journal of Criminology*, 36(4): 445–471.

Garland, D. (2000) 'The culture of high crime societies. Some preconditions of recent "law and order" policies', *British Journal of Criminology*, 40: 347–375.

Garland, D. (2001) *The culture of control*. Oxford; Oxford University Press.

Garland, D. and Sparks, R. (2000) 'Criminology, social theory and the challenge of our times', *British Journal of Criminology*, 40(2): 189–204.

Hayek, F. (1994) *The road to serfdom*. Chicago, IL: University of Chicago Press.

Hobsbawm, E. (1994) *Age of extremes*. London: Abacus.

Kaufman, N., Kaiser, J. and Rumpf, C. (2016) 'Beyond punishment: the penal state's interventionist, covert, and negligent modalities of control', *Law & Social Inquiry*, 43(2): 468–495.

Lea, J. and Hallsworth, S. (2013) 'Bringing the state back in: Understanding neoliberal security', in P. Squires and J. Lea (ed), *Criminalisation and advanced marginality*. Bristol: Policy Press.

Loader, I. and Sparks, R. (2007) 'Contemporary landscapes of crime, order and control: governance, risk and globalization', in M. Maguire, R. Morgan and R. Reiner (eds), *The Oxford handbook of criminology*, Fourth edition. Oxford: Oxford University Press, pp 78–101.

Miller, R. (2014) 'Devolving the carceral state: race, prisoner reentry, and the micro-politics of urban poverty management', *Punishment & Society*, 16(3): 305–335, http://dx.doi.org/10.1177/1462474514527487

Mudge, S.L. (2008) 'The state of the art. What is neo liberalism?' *Socio-Economic Review*, 6: 703–731.

O'Malley, P. (1999) 'Volatile and contradictory punishment', *Theoretical Criminology*, 3(2): 175–196, http://dx.doi.org/10.1177/1362480699003002003

Pierre, J. and Peters, B. (2000) *Governance, politics and the state*. Basingstoke: Macmillan.

Pratt, J. (1997) *Governing the dangerous*. Annandale: The Federation Press.

Reiner, R. (2007) *Law and order: An honest citizen's guide to crime and control.* Cambridge: Polity Press.

Rhodes, R.A.W (1995) *Understanding governance: Policy networks, governance, reflexivity, and accountability.* Milton Keynes: Open University Press.

Rose, N. (1999) *Powers of freedom.* Cambridge: Cambridge University Press.

Rose, N. (2000a) 'Government and control', in D. Garland and R. Sparks (eds), *Criminology and social theory.* Oxford; Oxford University Press.

Rose, N. (2000b) 'Government and control', *British Journal of Criminology*, 40(2): 321–339.

Rose, N. and Miller, P. (1992) 'Political power beyond the state: problematics of government', *The British Journal of Sociology*, 43(2): 173–205.

Smart, B. (2003) *Economy, culture and society.* Milton Keynes: Open University Press.

Stenson, K. (2001) 'The new politics of crime control' in K. Stenson and R.R. Sullivan (eds) *Crime, risk and justice.* Cullompton: Willan

Taylor, I. (1999) *Crime in context. A critical criminology of market societies.* Cambridge: Polity Press.

Turner, R.S. (2011) *Neo-liberal ideology, history, concepts, policies.* Edinburgh: Edinburgh University Press.

Von Hirsch, A., Garland, D. and Wakefield, A. (2002) *Ethical and social perspectives on situational crime prevention.* Oxford: Hart Pub.

Further reading

Barry, A., Osborne, T. and Rose, N. (eds) (2005) *Foucault and political reason.* Abingdon: Routledge.

Blackburn, R. (2008) *The psychology of criminal conduct.* First edition. Chichester: Wiley.

Blencowe, C., Brigstocke, J. and Dawney, L. (2013) 'Authority and experience', *Journal of Political Power*, 6(1): 1–7, http://dx.doi.org/10.1080/215837 9x.2013.774973

Borch, C. (2016) *Foucault, crime and power.* Abingdon: Routledge.

Button, M. (2016) *Security officers and policing.* London: Routledge.

Daems, T. (2008) *Making sense of penal change.* New York: Oxford University Press.

Davies, W. (2014) *The limits of neoliberalism. Authority, sovereignty and logic of competitiveness.* London: Sage.

Foucault, M. (1988) 'Technologies of the self', in L.H. Martin, H. Gutman and P.H Hutton (eds), *Technologies of the self.* Massachusetts: Massachusetts University Press.

Foucault, M. (1991) 'Governmentality', in G. Burchell, C. Gordon and P. Miller (eds), *The Foucault effect. Studies in governmentality.* Chicago: The University of Chicago Press.

Foucault, M., Senellart, M. and Burchell, G. (2009) *Security, territory, population.* New York: Picador.

Foucault, M., Burchell, G., Fontana, A., Gros, F. and Ewald, F. (2011) *The government of self and others*. New York: Picador/Palgrave Macmillan.

Garland, D. (1985) *Punishment and welfare*. Aldershot: Gower.

Garland, D. (1995) *Punishment and modern society*. Oxford: Clarendon Press.

Garland, D. (1997a) 'Probation and the Reconfiguration of crime control', in R. Burnett (ed), *The probation service: responding to change. Proceedings of the first Probation Studies Unit First Colloquium*, First edition. Oxford: Oxford University Press, pp 2–11.

Garland, D. (1997b) '"Governmentality" and the problem of crime: Foucault, criminology, sociology', *Theoretical Criminology*, 1(2): 173–214, http://dx.doi.org/10.1177/1362480697001002002

Garland, D. (2011) *The culture of control*. Oxford: Oxford University Press.

Garland, D. (2013) 'Penality and the penal state', *Criminology*, 51(3): 475–517. Available at: http://dx.doi.org/10.1111/1745-9125.12015

Garland, D. (2016) *The welfare state*. Oxford: Oxford University Press.

Garland, D. and Sparks, R. (2006) *Criminology and social theory*. Oxford: Oxford University Press.

Gordon, C. (1991) 'Governmental rationality', in G. Burchell, C. Gordon and P. Miller (eds), *The Foucault effect. Studies in governmentality*. Chicago: The University of Chicago Press.

Hannah–Moffat, K. and Lynch, M. (2012) 'Theorizing punishment's boundaries: An introduction', *Theoretical Criminology*, 16(2): 119–121, http://dx.doi.org/10.1177/1362480612443303

Hinds, L. and Grabosky, P. (2008) 'Responsibilisation revisited: from concept to attribution in crime control', *Security Journal*, 23(2): 95–113, http://dx.doi.org/10.1057/palgrave.sj.8350089

Hornqvist, M. (2010) *Risk, power and the state: after Foucault*. London: Routledge.

LeGrand, J. (1999) *Quasi-markets and social policy*. Basingstoke: Macmillan.

Lippert, R. and Stenson, K. (2010) 'Advancing governmentality studies: lessons for social constructionism', *Theoretical Criminology*, 14(4): 473–494.

Lynch, M. and Hannah–Moffat, K. (2017) 'Introductory editorial', *Punishment & Society*, 19(1): 3–4, http://dx.doi.org/10.1177/1462474516682437

Miller, R. and Purifoye, G. (2016) 'Carceral devolution and the Transformation of Urban America', in L. Abrams, E. Hughes, M. Inderbitzin and R. Meeks (eds), *The voluntary sector in prisons. Encouraging personal and institutional change*, First edition. Basingstoke: Palgrave Macmillan, pp 195–215.

Munck, R. (2005) 'Neoliberalism and politics and the politics of neoliberalism', in A. Saad-Filho and D. Johnston (eds), *Neoliberalism. A critical reader*. London: Pluto Press.

Pratt, J. (2000) 'The return of the wheelbarrow men; or, the arrival of postmodern penality?' *British Journal of Criminology*, 40(1): 127–145, http://dx.doi.org/10.1093/bjc/40.1.127

Rose, N. (1989) *Governing the soul*. London: Routledge.

Rose, N. (1993) 'Government, authority and expertise in advanced liberalism', *Economy and Society*, 22(3): 283–299, http://dx.doi.org/10.1080/03085149300000019

Rose, N. (1996) 'The death of the social? Re-figuring the territory of government', *Economy and Society*, 25(3): 327–356, http://dx.doi.org/10.1080/03085149600000018

Rose, N. (2009) *Inventing ourselves*. Cambridge: Cambridge University Press.

Smart, B. (2004) *Michel Foucault*. London: Routledge.

Wakefield, A. (2012) *Selling security*. First edition. London: Routledge.

Wickham, G. and Pavlich, G. (2001) *Rethinking law, society and governance*. Portland: Hart Publishing.

Winter, A. and Lumsden, K. (2014) *Reflexivity in criminological research*. Basingstoke: Palgrave Macmillan.

Wolch, J. (1990) *The shadow state*. New York: Foundation Center.

Zedner, L., Hoyle, C. and Bosworth, M. (2016) 'Mapping the contours of criminal justice. An introduction', in M. Bosworth, C. Hoyle and L. Zedner (eds), *Changing the Contours of Criminal Justice*. Oxford: Oxford University Press.

2

From a trained incapacity to professional resistance in criminal justice

Aaron Pycroft

Aims of the chapter
- To examine the impact of neoliberalism on social policy.
- To scrutinise the contract culture in criminal justice and its consequences for multi-agency working.
- To utilise theoretical developments in organisational sense making for criminal justice practitioners.

Introduction

The whole system of criminal justice in the UK is in an unprecedented crisis, in part due to its over-reliance on private capital. The purpose of this chapter is to explore that crisis, its economic and ideological origins and to examine its significance for criminal justice practitioners. Key theoretical links will be made with sense making in organisations to enable the practitioner to understand themselves, their work and service users within the wider multi-agency context of the organisation and its practices.

Context

When the first edition of this book was published in 2010 (Pycroft and Gough, 2010), my chapter focused on the development of the mixed economy of service provision (Pycroft, 2010) and the continuities between post war governments in developing the mix of public, private and charitable organisations in the development of public services. In preparing that chapter and editing the book as a whole we were in the midst of a worldwide economic crisis but we could not have foreseen the extent to which the incoming coalition government of the Conservatives and the Liberal Democrats (in 2010) would ideologically commit themselves to austerity policies across the public sector including criminal justice. Writing in 2018 the poorest sections of society have borne the brunt of the financial collapse brought about by casino capitalism and the decision by government to bail out financial institutions at the expense of some of the most marginal and vulnerable members of our society. The evidence for this assertion is stark. The Equality and Human Rights Commission (Portes, 2017: 30) states:

> Overall the impact of policy decisions taken between 2010 and 2017 is significantly regressive, and particularly so for policy decisions taken in 2015–17 Parliament (the impacts of which, are for the most part, still to come). These reforms will actually boost the incomes of the top two deciles, while reducing incomes substantially for the bottom half of income distribution. Our analysis, while subject to refinement, also shows clearly that a number of protected groups will be significantly adversely impacted, with particularly adverse impacts on disabled families. There is also a particularly strong adverse impact for lone parent families as well as families with three or more children.

These policies, being indicative of a neoliberal hegemony, are not specific to the UK and it is useful to consider the comparative research that reinforces the regressive nature of austerity measures. In considering the context of the UK and Europe, Stuckler and colleagues (2017) found that the choice of austerity to try and boost economic recovery either slowed this process or achieved the opposite through its impact on unemployment, homelessness, food insecurity, mental health, old age and mortality, and access to care.

Useful resource

See Warwick University reports on the impact of spending cuts across the UK: https://warwick.ac.uk/fac/soc/law/research/centres/chrp/spendingcuts/resources/reports-uk/#UK

These issues are important within the context of multi-agency working in criminal justice precisely because not only the justice system itself, but also the range of resources that are essential for building social and human capital in desisting from crime have been devastated by austerity. A key part of this austerity agenda is government focusing on bureaucratic waste and the need for greater efficiency in public sector organisations as a way of justifying reduced funding and the proclamation of ambitious targets in service delivery. The whole penal system in the UK is in crisis (see Pycroft, 2018), but that crisis is a systemic crisis of political economy due to an unquestioned commitment to neoliberalism from the institutions of the world economy including the World Bank and the International Monetary Fund.

What is neoliberalism?

'Neoliberalism' broadly means the project of economic and social transformation under the sign of the free market. It also means the institutional arrangements to implement this project that have been installed, step by step, in every society under neoliberal control ... The free market is the central image in neoliberal discourse, and deregulation of markets, especially capital markets, was among the earliest and most important neoliberal policies. Markets are hungry for new sources of profit, and under neoliberalism expand into new domains. Needs formerly met by public agencies on a principle of citizen rights, or through personal relationships in communities and families, are now increasingly likely to be met by companies selling services in a market. Neoliberals have had astonishing success in creating markets for things whose commodification was once almost unimaginable: water, body parts, pollution and social welfare among them. (Connell et al, 2009: 331)

New Public Management (NPM) is a key concept in neoliberalism through increasing cost effectiveness, in optimising outcomes and allocating scarce resources to sectors such as criminal justice. The use of outsourcing, key performance indicators (KPI), national standards, formulae for budget allocation, standardised training requirements and competencies are all indicative of this approach. NPM also seeks legitimacy through an appeal to scientific method and accurate measurement of inputs, throughputs and outputs from organisational activities. Reductive method (that is by breaking things down into their component parts and identifying key but isolated variables) positivism through seeking objectivity, predictability and ethical neutrality creates a number of significant problems which bely criminal justice as a project of humanity (see Arrigo and Williams, 2014). A challenging of the dehumanising effects of neoliberalism and NPM are central to concepts of resistance in professional practice.

A trained incapacity

Building on the work of Thorstein Veblen the philosopher Kenneth Burke (1954) develops the concept of trained incapacity,[1] which references the idea of right or wrong orientation. By utilising this concept as a tool of sense making in criminal justice practice we can begin to understand the wider contexts of practice, use professional voices to affirm what needs to be affirmed but also challenge what needs to be challenged. Trained incapacity refers to situations whereby one's abilities actually function as blindness. The example is given of business people '[w]ho through long training in competitive finance, have so built their scheme of orientation about this kind of effort and ambition that they cannot see serious possibilities in any other system of production and distribution' (Burke, 1954: 7). This is the attitude of politicians and policy makers that in their drive towards greater efficiency within reductionist economic considerations then a trained incapacity is blind to the consequences of those policies.

The argument of successive governments has been that the private sector provides efficiency, value for money and creativity in providing solutions to intractable social problems. It is argued by Heracleous and Johnston (2009) that the mantra has been that public services need to learn from private companies in achieving their objectives. They argue that the opposite can in fact be true, and I argue that given the spectacular failures in recent years then the opposite *needs* to be true. It is clear that the economic crisis and its consequences have been advantageous to capitalism (Petras and Veltmeyer, 2012) and also reinforce the neoliberal agenda for governments. In the UK it provided political and economic cover for the coalition government to engage in swingeing cuts to the welfare state in the name of common sense and 'good housekeeping' (to use a Thatcherite term) that would not have been possible in 'normal times'. In so doing the government not only reduced economic stimulus at a time when growth was slowly increasing but it also opened up spaces for private providers and capital to take over the running of services. This continued a process of transferring money from the poor to the rich through the commodification of social problems in the marketplace. There is a paradox here as in times of perceived economic crisis governments want to offload their own risk by outsourcing services, but when the market fails to deliver (as it frequently does and which was the whole rationale for the post war welfare settlement; see Pycroft, 2010) the state still has to pick up the pieces and the bail out; private capital is in a win–win situation.

Over the past two years alone, these failures of the marketplace and private capital in social policy are evidenced by the following examples, with all of them sharing similar themes with respect to a trained incapacity.

The Grenfell fire

On 14 June 2017 a fire spread throughout Grenfell Tower in London, killing 71 people with many more displaced. Concerns were raised about the design and materials used in the cladding systems used on this and other towers in the UK. One of the key issues was the sheer number of contractors involved in the refurbishment of Grenfell before the fire (see Davies, 2017). In her report to Parliament on the tragedy Dame Judith Hackitt stated that a new 'framework requires people who are part of the system to be competent, to think for themselves rather than blindly following guidance, and to understand their responsibilities to deliver and maintain safety and integrity throughout the life cycle of a building' (Secretary of State for Housing, Communities and Local Government, 2018).

The collapse of Carillion

Carillion was a major strategic supplier to the UK public sector, so much so that the government had to commit £150 million of taxpayers' money to keep essential services running when it collapsed in 2018. Rt Hon Frank Field MP, Chair of the Work and Pensions Committee, said:

> Same old story. Same old greed. A board of directors too busy stuffing their mouths with gold to show any concern for the welfare of their workforce or their pensioners. They rightly face investigation of their fitness to run a company again. This is a disgraceful example of how much of our capitalism is allowed to operate, waved through by a cosy club of auditors, conflicted at every turn. Government urgently needs to come to Parliament with radical reforms to our creaking system of corporate accountability. British industry is too important to be left in the hands of the likes of the shysters at the top of Carillion. (Commons Select Committee, 2018)

The inquiry also found that the government had continued to award public sector contracts to Carillion to the value of £45 million despite a profit warning having been announced for the company.

Transforming Rehabilitation (TR) in the National Probation Service in England and Wales

In 2014/15 the government re-engineered the structures and functions of the probation system. These changes included the supervision of offenders in the community who had served a custodial sentence of less than 12 months; introduction of a nationwide 'Through the Gate' resettlement service for those leaving prison; open up the market to range a probation providers from public, voluntary and private sectors; introduce payment by results mechanisms for those providers; split the delivery of probation based upon risk with the National Probation Service (NPS) supervising those offenders deemed as high risk and a range of Community Rehabilitation Companies (CRCs) supervising medium and low risk. The House of Commons Justice Committee (House of Commons Justice Committee, 2018) was scathing in its report on these arrangements, leading the government to announce that it will be ending contracts to CRCs two years early in 2020; but at significant cost to the taxpayer.

Crisis in UK prisons

In August 2018 and following a damning report by the Chief Inspector of Prisons the government announced an emergency takeover of HMP Birmingham which had been run by the private company G4S. The Chief Inspector stated:

We last inspected HMP Birmingham in February 2017, shortly after the major disturbances of December 2016. At the time, we found there was still a palpable sense of shock at what had occurred, but also a clear determination to move on from the disorder and re-build. This inspection, in sharp contrast, found that there had been a dramatic deterioration. The prison was in an appalling state. Against all four of our healthy prison tests – safety, respect, purposeful activity and rehabilitation and release planning – we judged outcomes for those detained to be 'poor,' our lowest assessment rating. This is only the second time the Inspectorate has given its lowest assessment score against all four of its tests, a fact that clearly shows the seriousness of my concerns. I was not surprised to find that of the 70 recommendations we made at our last inspection, only 14 had been achieved. None of the four main recommendations, concerning violence, staff-prisoner relationships, poor regimes and a lack of focus on education, training and work had been met. (HM Inspectorate of Prisons, 2018)

The Prisons Minister Rory Stewart admitted the government had to accept some responsibility for the failure of the prison and that another ten prisons were in similar situations. This was in no small measure due to the decision taken by the Ministry of Justice in 2012 to cut 7,000 jobs from the prison estate.

All of these are examples of governments trying to provide a diverse range of public sector providers and to introduce creativity and energy into systems that address the complex needs of people. However, in practice this diversity soon disappears (see DiMaggio and Powell, 1983) due to:

- organisations adapting themselves to business environments that constrain their ability to change further down the line – for example charities adopting business practices and competing for state contracts that may distort their institutional raison d'être;
- innovations linked to a desire for increased efficiency (such as payment by results mechanisms in the TR reforms) reach a limit beyond which legitimacy is attained rather than an ongoing and improved performance (so government continues to work with providers but changes the funding mechanisms involved thus undermining the original claim to innovation);
- because these strategies are seen as rational and are normatively sanctioned by the state then everybody adopts them thus leading to a lack of diversity in the organisational field.

It is argued by DiMaggio and Powell (1983: 149) that 'Organizations ... respond to an environment which consists of organizations responding to their environment, which consists of organizations responding to an environment of organizations' responses'. In practice this means that one organization among many competing for scarce resources forces organisations to resemble each other in the marketplace. With respect to criminal justice, Gough (2010: 30) states that

> as a result of the state's presence, increased managerialism, the narrowness of the contract culture, National Standards and the politics of punishment, the third sector in probation may result in conformity, control and reconfiguration of the voluntary sector in the image of the state.

Sense making and critical practice in organisations

In discussing trained incapacity, Burke (1954) also makes a linkage with mechanisms of scapegoating which is very similar to the cultural anthropology of René Girard (see Girard, 1978). Both of these thinkers identify the ways in which a scapegoat becomes a useful resolution to a crisis: we can blame someone for the problem and transfer our anger onto them; for example, George Osborne, the Chancellor of the Exchequer who was one of the architects of austerity policies, could assert 'that we are all in this together' but blame the 'feckless' poor for being a burden on limited resources. In a speech at a Conservative Party conference he asks 'Where is the fairness, we ask, for the shift-worker, leaving home in the dark hours of the early morning, who looks up at the closed blinds of their next-door neighbour sleeping off a life on benefits' (Jowitt, 2013). Burke (1954) argues that the scapegoat is an instance of trained incapacity and of a faulty means selection in resolving a crisis. Girard (1978) develops a similar line of thinking with respect to the transference of the crisis onto a random victim (anthropologically this is usually someone who is seen as an outsider by virtue of race, ethnicity, ability) by stating that the perpetrator/s cannot see that they are scapegoating. We can always identify people who are being scapegoated but cannot see our own scapegoating tendencies and therefore feel justified in our anger, meaning that we are all complicit in these processes (John Dewey would describe this 'occupational psychosis' as a pronounced character of mind that through habit pervades the cultural context; see Burke, 1954).

It is essential that criminal justice practitioners become aware of, resist and overcome trained incapacity that occurs through the bureaucratisation of criminal justice and its reduction to business transactions between organisations within the neoliberal marketplace. To start to achieve this, the criminal justice professional needs to understand their role(s) within the context of the team(s), the wider organisation, that organisation's relationship and responsibilities towards other organisations, funding and oversight bodies and legislation. This is a complex proposition. Sense making or process organisation studies are grounded in an understanding of the world in flux whereby organisations are in the process of becoming (for better or worse) not as things already made. It is argued by Langley and Tsoukas (2010: 2) that 'a process orientation prioritizes activity over product, change over persistence, novelty over continuity and expression over determination. Becoming, change, flux as well as creativity, disruption and indeterminism are the main themes of a process worldview.' The implications of this are the need for individuals to consciously engage with the processes that they are co-constitutive of rather than separate from; to stress the point further, a theoretical framework underpinning practice is required that eschews separateness and objectivity because such things are not possible, and where we seek to create such conditions then our actions become unethical. Sense making approaches do not eschew the existence of events, states or entities but seek to deconstruct them to understand the complex activities that take place of processes within processes.

In criminal justice, the concepts and practices of multi-agency working are 'taken for granted' and thus critically unexamined; they are a feature of an administrative criminology that remains descriptive rather than analytical of the dynamics of power and ideology involved in their delivery. It is argued by Polizzi and Draper (2013: 721) that we need to apply through phenomenology acts of consciousness but that in reality 'consciousness does not act upon many aspects of the experience of working in a correctional setting, leaving them phenomenologically unexplored and taking for granted the labels, the structure of the system, and the dehumanizing effects of the penitentiary.'

Phenomenology

[P]henomenology argues that reality and its objects are constituted by consciousness and are immanent in and inseparable from consciousness ... In this approach our consciousness structures what we experience on the basis of previous experiences and the context of our current experience. In discussing the ways in which our consciousness constructs reality Polizzi (2016) for example considers the fatal shooting of black teenager Trayvon Martin by Neighbourhood Watch volunteer George Zimmerman. In this situation Zimmerman's understanding of the world was '... framed by a set of contextually situated taken-for-granted expectations that are constructed or recognised as being most consistent or normal to that locality' (Polizzi, 2016: 30). In this case Polizzi argues that within all the accounts of this shooting no one questioned the basic rationale that was constructed of Martin being dangerous and criminal given that he was a black teenager and was present in that particular neighbourhood. (Pycroft, 2018: 8)

Competition and contestability are a key feature of the taken for granted nature of the contract culture, and which imbue the day to day practices of workers and directly impact on service users. To return to the example of the probation services in England and Wales and the TR fiasco, the government's response is striking for what it does not say in this respect. The Ministry of Justice (2018: 8) acknowledges difficulties in the delivery of the TR reforms and argues in its consultation document that

> We need to ensure that the NPS and CRCs work together more closely as part of a single, integrated system. In doing so we can improve the efficiency and effectiveness of local services, while creating the conditions for stronger partnership working.

The paper goes on to discuss yet another restructuring with the creation of ten probation regions in England to encourage this integration. Thus the complexity will remain with different organisations managing offenders and presumably on a competitive basis (this is not discussed). However, a completely different model for Wales in envisaged whereby the NPS assumes all responsibility for managing offenders and again presumably commissioning services from organisations as required (again not discussed). The question is why the arrangements for Wales cannot also apply to England, and why the Ministry of Justice would think that the continuation of a failed arrangement would be any better in its second iteration.

It is argued by Strier and Bershtling (2016) that social workers have been increasingly used to 'translate' state power and usually through being asked to justify the use of the private sector and the imposition of costs onto service users. In response to this Strier and Bershtling develop an argument for professional resistance that seeks to oppose the hegemony of neoliberal policies. Both social workers and probation workers are required to work within the confines of the law and receive their licence to practice from the state. Under the Rehabilitation of Offenders Act (2014) probation officers became civil servants, which restricts opportunities for resistance.

In considering the tools that practitioners have at their disposal then reflective practice is an engagement in acts of consciousness that have the potential to challenge and change the 'iron cage' of rationality that underpins punitive managerialism. It is argued by Whitehead (2010: 91) that 'Probation was once an integral component of the personal and professionalised social services, but it has become politically dominated and predominantly office-based bureaucracy in a business-orientated environment'. Whitehead (2010) also importantly makes a distinction between bureaucracy and management, as the latter is important and can (should) be a creative process in allocating scarce resources. However, bureaucracy particularly when standardised paperwork and sitting behind a computer come at the expense of personal relationships with service users actually mitigates again creativity (see Department of Education, 2011). The challenge for organisations is that high levels of conformity dampen creativity and also high levels of creativity work against conformity (see Pycroft, 2010, 2014).

Governments have sought both high levels of conformity while demanding creativity from practitioners. The key part of this argument that the private sector injects creativity and energy has clearly failed, but due to a trained incapacity on the part of policy makers this process continues. Strier and Bershtling (2016) argue that there are two core elements to resistance: first, actions that can be verbal or physical; second, opposition to policies or practices that affect the basic rights of those who resist. In the current environment probation workers and especially trainees find themselves in highly vulnerable situations with respect to job security (especially those employed by CRCs). Therefore, practitioners may be more inclined to engage in 'thin' resistance (everyday-life acts of resistance) rather than 'thick' resistance (overt, collective actions). The latter may be best achieved through joining a trades union.

In developing this argument within the context of probation practice I want to take Strier and Bershtling's (2016: 114) use of Foucault's thinking to develop the work of self-formation. They state:

> According to Foucault's work, society operates on individuals, groups or communities through social, economic, political and symbolic systems of oppression, instilling into them conceptions, norms and expectations, in ways by which people internalize those hierarchies of power and become compliant with them … Although the individual is never free, people have the ability to rework their relationships in established networks of power, thereby creating more flexible social arrangements, and in this process shape spaces of movement and legitimize multiple personal and professional options … the work of self-formation is embedded in the project of critique … [which] must operate consistently on two fronts. People must discern features within the present techniques of governance that would permit, and even enable, reflective resistance. This means transferring people's attention from the oppressed to the oppressor, delineating the generative core of the practices that shape the current modes of existence, and testing their limits.

It follows from the argument of this chapter that a core requisite of working within a multi-agented context such as criminal justice is to understand that context through a sense making approach and to subject it to high levels of scrutiny and analysis. It is argued by Veblen (Burke, 1954) that because of the dominance of business methods (for our purposes read NPM) then students are unable to see larger social concerns. One of the interesting dynamics that I experience in teaching students on probation officer qualifying awards and those who are already in practice is a significant under-appreciation of the importance of their own role within the multi-agency context. A trained incapacity represents itself as practitioners being invisible to themselves, brought about by the powerful myths of detachment and neutral observer status. Sense making and complexity theory (see Pycroft and Bartollas, 2014) demonstrate the need to be conscious of ourselves through reflection as well as being conscious of the connected whole, have a deep appreciation of person in context, and to understand that I am part of that context, but always with a limited view (see Pycroft, 2018); what I do and how I do it really impacts on the lives of the people concerned.

As a practitioner I may be concerned with for example trying to refer service users to a range of agencies that have long waiting lists and limited capacity due to being under resourced but the role of the professional is to both interpret and challenge why this is this case. Famously Karl Marx stated that 'Hitherto philosophers have only *interpreted* the world in various ways, the point is to *change* it' (see Bernstein, 1971). The process of reflection and sense making is then also about the ways in which the individual practitioner is in a process of becoming both professionally and personally.

Reflective exercise

Think about the following excerpt from David Garland (2018: 7) discussing the reprint of his seminal 1985 work *Punishment and welfare: a history of penal strategies* and consider what influence you might have as a practitioner in evolving attitudes towards crime, punishment and rehabilitation within your team, wider organisation and multi-agency context.

> Discursive transformations come about in and through the actions of agents whose interests and motivations can be inferred and whose struggles can be documented. The central theoretical claim of *Punishment and Welfare* is not that economic structures determine penal outcomes but rather that penal outcomes are consciously negotiated within the limits that economic, political and ideological structures impose. And these structures do not work all by themselves, somehow controlling outcomes with an unseen hand or an automatic functionalism. Instead it is a matter of situated, problem-solving, decision-making agents—in this case reformers, administrators, policymakers, and politicians—who consciously perceive the bounds of political possibility and adjust their actions accordingly, sometimes struggling to change the rules of the game, more often making compromises with the constraints that they face.

Reflection and resistance

The world of the professional criminal justice practitioner is in constant flux which is in itself a consequence of changing government priorities. Reflective practice has become a core component of training for practitioners working in these complex environments. The argument is made by Howard (2010) that reflection is essential in enabling us to broaden our horizons but that it is not and neither should be a comfortable process. Our processes of reflection should be challenging to ourselves but also the organisations in which we work. When I was a practice teacher for social work and probation students on placements one of the reasons that we as an organisation took students was to challenge our thinking by bringing a critique informed by fresh ideas. In an environment which focuses now largely on organisational competencies linked to administrative and business goals for trainees that kind of thinking is uncommon. In resisting the worst excesses of punitive managerialism driven by neoliberal policies practitioners will find that all public sector agencies are going through similar processes so it is worth engaging and collaborating with professionals from other organisations to negotiate spaces of resistance when working on joint cases. Our reflections as an individual need to move beyond the purely personal to that of the team level (see Pycroft and Wolf-Branigin, 2016) and then beyond that to the trans-disciplinary.

Useful resource

For a discussion on punitive managerialism, reflection and resistance in probation practice see Gregory (2010).

Despite the lack of designation of an inter-professional team for a particular case, the fact of a range of organisations involved with that case can be seen as a de facto or virtual team. In the case of probation, the Offender Manager (OM) will need to recognise that other professionals from other organisations may be more or less significant than themselves in achieving a positive outcome. Five principles in this inter-disciplinary approach have been identified by Hadorn et al (2010, cited in McDermott, 2014: 188):

1. Shared system-based thinking, whereby the whole and the parts of a problem are considered in relation to one another by a team.
2. Attention to problem-framing and boundary setting so that limitations to the scope of the problem addressed are set by the team.
3. Attention to values: these are identified by the team and reflected in the nature of boundaries set.
4. Understanding of ignorance and uncertainty: the systems perspective and the boundary setting initiated facilitate the team's recognition of areas about which nothing may yet be known, or what is known is recognised as partial.
5. Understanding the nature of collaborations: collaboration rests on the team's capacity to harness difference – in ideas, values, understanding, interests and personalities – such that difference enhances rather than destroys collaboration.

The trans-disciplinary approach requires a real shift in philosophy to a process and sense making approach that allows for the development of communication and innovative ideas that places outcomes for the service user at its heart. This is about finding a common ground of understanding between differing teams and organisations based upon mutuality rather than competition. As McDermott

(2014) states, what emerges from these interactions within the team and wider organisations is the material for reflection in and on action. This very reflection should challenge the ways in which an organisation works and which in itself should draw upon the underpinning research and debate that underpins professional practice. On the basis of this reflective practice practitioners from different agencies and teams can self-organise to make decisions for the cases they are working with and challenge management decisions that would reduce outcomes to a bureaucratic transaction.

Reflection

What opportunities or fora do you have as a practitioner to work creatively with professionals from other agencies? To what extent are you facing similar challenges? How can you self-organise and negotiate spaces of resistance in your joint work?

Conclusion

In considering changes to the probation service, both Skinner (2010) and Burke et al (2018) raise the question of whether constructive practice is possible within a competitive environment and point to the fact that the various changes that they are reflecting on were designed to bring innovation and creativity. Both research projects find a commitment from all practitioners to creative practice but who are constrained by the operating model itself. I take it that professional identity is more than what is owed to the state in return for a licence to practice, that a key part of that identity is to make a contribution to the integrity of foundational bodies of knowledge as applied to the 'common good'; to make voices heard in a legitimate and democratic way and to challenge and resist harmful practices enshrined in neoliberal operating models. After all, surely when David Cameron, the then leader of the opposition (and subsequent prime minister) re-stated the mantra that 'We are all in this together' (Cameron, 2009) to the Conservative Party Conference in addressing the financial collapse, he meant that we all have an equal voice, and that he would want us to use it in speaking truth to power? He would wouldn't he?

> **Summary of key learning points**
>
> • Practice within criminal justice organisations needs to be understood within the context of the dominant operating models.
> • Those operating models present both barriers and opportunities for creative practice.
> • Sense making helps us to understand those processes and the necessity of professional resistance to forms of trained incapacity.

Note

[1] It is beyond the scope of this chapter to discuss the relationship between Veblen and Burke's thinking but the reader is referred to Burke (1954) who outlines the debt that he owes to Veblen.

References

Arrigo, B. and Williams, C. (2014) 'Complexity, law and ethics: on drug addiction, natural recovery and the diagnostics of psychological jurisprudence', in A. Pycroft and C. Bartollas (eds), *Applying complexity theory: whole systems approaches to criminal justice and social work.* Bristol: Policy Press, pp 247–268.

Bernstein, R. (1971) *Praxis and action.* Philadelphia: University of Pennsylvania Press.

Burke, K. (1954) *Permanence and change: an anatomy of purpose.* Berkeley, CA: University of California Press.

Burke, L., Millings, M. and Robinson, G. (2018) 'Is constructive practice still possible in a competitive environment? Findings from a case study of a community rehabilitation company in England and Wales', in P. Ugwudike, P. Raynor and J. Annison (eds), *Evidence-based skills in criminal justice: international research on supporting rehabilitation and desistance.* Bristol: Policy Press, pp 57–78.

Cameron, D. (2009) Speech at the Conservative Party conference, www.theguardian.com/politics/2009/oct/08/david-cameron-speech-in-full

Commons Select Committee (2018) 'Work and Pensions and BEIS Committees publish report on Carillion', 16 May, www.parliament.uk/business/committees/committees-a-z/commons-select/work-and-pensions-committee/news-parliament-2017/carillion-report-published-17-19/

Connell, R., Fawcett, B. and Meagher, G. (2009) 'Neoliberalism, New Public Management and the human service professions', Introduction to the Special Issue, *Journal of Sociology*, 45(4): 331–338.

Davies, R. (2017) 'Complex chain of companies that worked on Grenfell Tower raises oversight concerns', *Guardian*, 16 June, www.theguardian.com/uk-news/2017/jun/15/long-builder-chain-for-grenfell-a-safety-and-accountability-issue

Department of Education (2011) *The Munro Review of Child Protection: Final report, a child-centred system.* London. HMSO.

DiMaggio, P. and Powell, W (1983) 'The iron cage revisited: institutional isomorphism and collective rationality in organizational fields', *American Sociological Review*, 48: 147–160.

Garland, D. (2018) 'Punishment and welfare revisited', *Punishment and Society*, https://doi.org/10.1177/1462474518771317

Girard, R. (1978) *Things hidden since the foundation of the world*. London: Athlone Press.

Gregory, M. (2010) 'Reflection and resistance: probation practice and the ethic of care', *British Journal of Social Work*, 40: 2274–2290.

Gough, D. (2010) 'Multi-agency working in corrections: cooperation and competition in probation practice', in A. Pycroft and D. Gough (eds), *Multi-agency working in criminal justice: control and care in contemporary correctional practice*. Bristol: Policy Press, pp 21–34.

Heracleous, L. and Johnston, R. (2009) 'Can business learn from the public sector?' *European Business Review*, 21(4): 373–379.

HM Inspectorate of Prisons (2018) 'Urgent notification: HM Prison Birmingham', letter and debriefing to the Justice Security, 16 August, www.justiceinspectorates.gov.uk/hmiprisons/wp-content/uploads/sites/4/2018/08/16-Aug-UN-letter-HMP-Birmingham-Final.pdf

House of Commons Justice Committee (2018) 'Transforming Rehabilitation: Ninth Report of Session 2017–19', House of Commons, https://publications.parliament.uk/pa/cm201719/cmselect/cmjust/482/482.pdf

Howard, J. (2010) 'The beauty of reflection and the beast of multi-agency cooperation', in A. Pycroft and D. Gough (eds), *Multi-agency working in criminal justice: control and care in contemporary correctional practice*. Bristol: Policy Press, pp 231–244.

Jowitt, J. (2013) 'Strivers vs shirkers: the language of the welfare debate', *Guardian*, 8 January, www.theguardian.com/politics/2013/jan/08/strivers-shirkers-language-welfare

Langley, A. and Tsoukas, H. (2010) 'Introducing "Perspectives on Process Organization Studies"', T. Hernes and S. Maitlis (eds), *Process, sensemaking and organizing*. Oxford: Oxford University Press.

McDermott, F. (2014) 'Complexity theory, trans-disciplinary working and reflective practice', A. Pycroft and C. Bartollas (eds), *Applying complexity theory: whole systems approaches to criminal justice and social work*. Bristol: Policy Press, pp 181–198.

Ministry of Justice (2018) *Strengthening probation, building confidence. Cm 9613*. London. HMSO.

Petras, J. and Veltmeyer, H. (2012) 'The global capitalist crisis: whose crisis, who profits', *International Review of Modern Sociology*, 38(2): 199–219.

Polizzi, D. (2016) *A philosophy of the social construction of crime*. Bristol: Policy Press.

Polizzi, D. and Draper, M. (2013) 'The therapeutic encounter within the event of forensic psychotherapy: a phenomenological hermeneutic of the givenness of the other within the therapeutic relationship', *International Journal of Offender Therapy and Comparative Criminology*, 57(6): 720–735.

Portes, J. (2017) *Distributional results from the impact of tax and welfare reforms between 2010–17, modelled in the 2021/22 tax year: Interim findings November 2017.* Equality and Human Rights Commission Research Report.

Pycroft, A. (2010) 'Consensus, complexity and emergence: the mixed economy of service provision', in A. Pycroft and D. Gough (eds), *Multi-agency working in criminal justice: control and care in contemporary correctional practice.* Bristol: Policy Press, pp 7–20.

Pycroft, A. (2014) 'Probation practice and creativity in England and Wales: a complex systems analysis', in A. Pycroft and C. Bartollas (eds), *Applying complexity theory: whole systems approaches to criminal justice and social work.* Bristol: Policy Press, pp 199–220.

Pycroft, A. (2018) 'Consciousness in rather than of: advancing modest claims for the advancement of phenomenologically informed approaches to complexity theory in criminology', *Journal of Theoretical and Philosophical Criminology*, 10: 1–20, www.jtpcrim.org/FEB2018/Pycroft.pdf

Pycroft, A. and Bartollas, C. (eds) (2014) *Applying complexity theory: whole systems approaches to criminal justice and social work.* Bristol: Policy Press.

Pycroft, A. and Gough, D. (eds) (2010) *Multi-agency working in criminal justice: control and care in contemporary correctional practice.* Bristol: Policy Press.

Pycroft, A. and Wolf-Branigin, M. (2016) 'Integrating complexity theory and social work practice; a commentary on Fish and Hardy (2015)', *Nordic Social Work Research*, 6(1): 69–72.

Skinner, C. (2010) 'Clients or offenders? The case for clarity of purpose in multi-agency working', in A. Pycroft and D. Gough (eds), *Multi-agency working in criminal justice: control and care in contemporary correctional practice.* Bristol: Policy Press, pp 35–50.

Strier, R. and Bershtling, O. (2016) 'Professional resistance in social work: counterpractice assemblages', *Social Work*, 61(2): 111–118.

Secretary of State for Housing, Communities and Local Government (2018) *Building a Safer Future: Independent Review of Building Regulations and Fire Safety: Final Report Presented to Parliament by the Secretary of State for Housing, Communities and Local Government by Command of Her Majesty: CM9607.*

Stuckler, D., Reeves, A., Loopstra, R., Karinikolos, M. and McKee, M. (2017) 'Austerity and health: the impact in the UK and Europe', *European Journal of Public Health*, 27(4): 18–21.

Whitehead, P. (2010) *Exploring modern probation: social theory and organisational complexity.* Bristol: Policy Press.

3

A time of change: the expanding role of Police and Crime Commissioners in local criminal justice delivery

Barry Loveday and Sue Roberts

Aims of the chapter

- To outline the arrangements for PCC governance.
- To critically evaluate the development of police and crime plans within the context of austerity funding.
- To discuss the impact on partnerships working with the Probation Services using the examples of MAPPAs and MARACs.

Introduction

This chapter provides an evaluation of Police and Crime Commissioner (PCC) governance and the adoption of a more intrusive police governance model in England and Wales since the passage of the Police Reform and Social Responsibility Act 2011. It considers the use, by PCCs, of local police and crime plans to shape local policing priorities and provides novel examples of this new engagement with police forces. It assesses the PCC role in relation to Multi-Agency Public Protection Arrangements (MAPPAs; see also Nash, in this volume), Multi-Agency Risk Assessment Conferences (MARACs); see also Tapley and Jackson, in this volume) and local partnerships through the authors' primary research undertaken for a conference paper in Tartu, Estonia on the role of partnerships (Roberts, 2016); further semi-structured interviews were undertaken during 2017 specifically for this chapter. Participants came from Hampshire, Sussex and Surrey including a former PCC, Office of the Police and Crime Commissioner (OPCC) staff and senior members of local partnerships with whom the joint author has current, working relationships (see Table 3.1). The role of PCCs is expanding to include responsibility for fire and rescue services along with probation. However, despite encouragement by central government and the planned assumption of responsibility for probation, PCCs have yet to exercise a coordinating role for other local criminal justice agencies.

Table 3.1: Interview participants, 2017

1–3	West Sussex and Hampshire community safety personnel
4–5	Probation Service (West Sussex) and former prison officer (HMP Pentonville)
6–9	Police commanders, including silver command, and officers in Sussex, Surrey and Hampshire
10–12	Community Safety Partners from Community Safety Partnerships in Hampshire and Sussex
13–14	Former PCC and officer from an OPCC
15	Councillor David Simmonds, West Sussex County Council
16	Former PCC Hampshire and Isle of Wight [Simon Hayes]

A new structure of police governance

In 2011 the Police Reform and Social Responsibility Act introduced a new model of police governance by replacing local Police Authorities with PCCs. Based on direct election, the PCCs were identified as potentially a more effective instrument in ensuring that local public priorities would be reflected in police priorities which traditionally and often had not proved to be the case (Operational Policing Review, 1990, sect.4 cited in Loveday, 2018). By way of the local crime and policing plan, drawn up annually by the PCC and the Chief Constable, primary concerns identified by the public could now be expected to be acted upon. This was because any failure on the part of the PCC might be tested at the next PCC election.

Reflection

What do you see as the strengths and weaknesses of having Police and Crime Commissioners directly elected by the public?

The Police Reform and Social Responsibility Act 2011 has also given the PCC significantly wider powers, which immediately differentiates this office from that of former Police Authorities. Thus, PCCs have been given a power of 'general competence', which enables the PCC to do 'anything that is lawful' (Loveday et al, 2014: (i); Police Reform and Social Responsibility Act 2011, Police Protocol Schedule 1. S.14). Along with this went an interest in encouraging the creation of a 'principal-agent' relationship between the PCC and the Chief Constable. This entirely reversed the situation which had pertained before where the Chief

Constable could often act as the de facto principal and the police authority as the agent.

These developments have impacted on the relationships between PCC and Chief Constable as now the PCC can both hire and fire the Chief Officer while also being solely responsible for renewing Chief Officer employment contracts where that option arises (Watts, 2019). The changed status was to be demonstrated early on with the non-renewal of a chief officers' contract (Avon and Somerset Constabulary) and the unexpected early retirement of chief officers following interaction with the PCC (Gwent Police: Northumbria Police). Later, following her retirement and in evidence to the parliamentary Home Affairs Committee, the former Chief Constable of Gwent referred to the 'unfettered powers of the PCC' (Loveday et al, 2014: (i)).

The relatively unique position now held by the PCC was to be reinforced by a decision of the then Home Secretary, Theresa May, to end the comprehensive system of performance management and central targets set for local police forces. These were given one target: to 'reduce crime' in their police force areas. The end of central intervention has also served to strengthen the position of the PCC, although recently the growing influence of Her Majesty's Inspectorate of Constabulary (HMIC) is viewed as a potential threat to local police governance (Interview 16). The increasing challenge of HMIC has only been underlined by a recent High Court judgement (R-v-PCC South Yorkshire QBD 2017). Here in an appeal made by the former Chief Constable of South Yorkshire against his dismissal, the court was to find for the appellant on the basis that the PCC had acted irrationally in not giving sufficient weight to HMIC's advice against the dismissal of that officer. The same judgement was, however, to discover that the PCC had much wider powers than assumed in relation to operational policing and that 'matters relevant to operational independence were not excluded from the scope of the PCCs power of scrutiny' (R-v-PCC QBD 2017: para 78).

Expanding the role of the PCCs

The increased power of PCCs has occasioned comment in a number of respects. In 2010 and 2011, articles appeared in the UK national press (Grimshaw, 2010; BBC News, 2012) which expressed concern that a long-held responsibility of the police to carry out their duties independently and free from outside interference could be compromised by bringing them into a politically led environment through the introduction of PCCs. Gravelle and Rogers (2011: 327) comment further prior to changes brought about by the 2011 Police Reform and Social Responsibility Act on the politicisation of the police and the possible implications of this. Concerns about emulating an American style politicisation of the police in Britain were echoed by Sampson (2012) where he argued that any similar political links with the police have, in the past, been 'eschewed' (p 4) by both the police service and the political establishment. The same article went on to argue that the introduction of political representatives to policing would herald the 'ruination' (p 4) of law enforcement in the UK. Joyce (2011: 5) has also expressed similar concerns and called the potential politicisation of the police a 'considerable danger'. Despite these concerns, the politicisation of the police appears to be seen as a reality by a number of commentators (Lister and Rowe, 2015: 368).

In The Police Foundation's Oxford Policing Report Forum papers for 2009 (p 5), it was recorded that the forum agreed with Professor Robert Reiner that policing 'should not be politicised in the sense that police could work for the advantage of a political party or sectional interest, or that party political interests could influence appointments'. Notwithstanding these concerns, the influence of PCCs continues to grow with discussions now taking place to widen their role to include, where appropriate, Fire and Rescue Services and Ambulance Services by way of the Policing and Crime Act 2017. In relation to the expanding role of the PCCs, one significant feature has proved to be that the PCC is responsible for both the police and crime in a force area. Having responsibility for crime has meant that PCCs have sought to establish effective relationships with the Community Safety Partnerships (CSPs) established under the terms of the 1998 Crime and Disorder Act. CSPs, as with local authorities across the country, have been circumscribed in terms of resources by the successive austerity policies and strategies undertaken by the coalition and Conservative governments from 2010. Yet it is still recognised, as this study shows, that local partnerships continue to be the most effective platforms to promote community safety and crime prevention programmes in local areas.

As a recent analysis of police and crime plans has highlighted, the overwhelming priorities identified within 19 of them relate to making communities safer and tackling crime (Crest, 2017: 5). Thereafter, antisocial behaviour and reoffending are identified as the priorities most frequently cited. However, given the local nature of governance, there are also widely differing priorities that reflect a more decentralised approach. In Sussex, for example, the PCC has a strong commitment to extending a restorative justice initiative in the police force area. This includes expanding the use of restorative justice in conjunction with the Sussex Restorative Justice Partnership and the Sussex Criminal Justice Board (Sussex Police and Crime Commissioner, 2017: 15).

It is also clear that many PCCs in developing their police and crime plans have also prioritised vulnerable people with specific focus on victims of crime. In Sussex, the Office of the PCC has expressed a strong commitment to reducing domestic abuse across the area. This involves close cooperation and interaction with the county MARACs. The PCC approach to supporting the MARACs in Hampshire is however more strategic. Here the perception is that these partnerships are operational or tactical meetings and where 'the day-to-day engagement' is left to agencies which are responsible for delivering services and interventions. Hampshire's PCC funds the IDVAs (Independent Domestic Violence Advisers) and ISVAs (Independent Sexual Violence Advisers) but continues to retain a strategic role. In the tradition of multi–agency working which has characterised local community safety arrangements since the 1998 Act (Crime and Disorder Act 1998) and established Crime and Disorder Reduction Partnerships (later the CSPs), MARACs have supported locally coordinated multi-agency action against domestic abuse.

The partnership approach to solving complex community safety issues is not new and has a long history in the delivery of public services since the advent of the Labour government in 1997. As delivery mechanisms aimed at tackling multi-faceted local issues in communities, multi-agency partnerships were in the vanguard of policy under New Labour (Ellison and Ellison, 2006: 338). Since the wide ranging cuts (Hastings et al, 2015: 4; Comptroller and Auditor General, 2014: 5) to local public services and the reorganisation and privatisation of services under the 2010 coalition, and then Conservative governments, the operation, practices and the resourcing of multi-agency partnerships have been adversely affected along with the agencies that support them, as is evidenced in this chapter (see also Pycroft, in this volume).

In policing, for example, there has been a 17% cut in funding since 2009 (Institute for Government, IfG, 2017) as demonstrated in Figure 3.1.

The same IfG report identifies a 14% loss in frontline police personnel, with the complete elimination in Norfolk of Police Community Support Officers (PCSOs). UNISON, the public sector trades union, stated that the community in Norfolk would be at greater risk of being victims of crime as a result (UNISON, 2017). In the light of these wide ranging cuts, strategic planning, such as that employed by the PCCs remains a challenge as does sustaining both greater efficiency and effectiveness. This not only applies to individual police forces that experience such cuts in funding, but also extends to PCCs who oversee them. Implementing local police and crime plans is likely, therefore, to be confronted in future with some serious resourcing obstacles.

Figure 3.1: Police officers in frontline roles, England and Wales

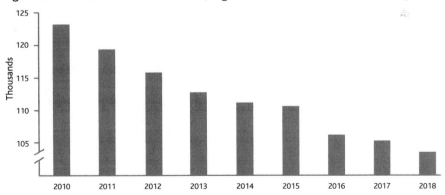

Source: Allen and Zayed (2018), p 13, Contains Parliamentary information licensed under the Open Parliament Licence v3.0.

Implementing local police and crime plans

The nature and extent of the change in governance and its efficacy can probably best be judged through the rollout by PCCs of their individual police and crime plans which set out strategic priorities for their areas. It is evident that given the differing backgrounds of PCCs, local provision can differ between jurisdictions. Some indication of the changing nature of the new governance has been most recently provided by a joint publication of Labour PCCs. In this they make it very clear that they intend to fully exercise the freedom of action provided within the 2011 Act in relation to implementing policing policy (Fabian Society, 2014).

Highlighting the significant role accorded PCCs in terms of strategic policy formulation, one PCC has argued that:

> We are required to consult our communities to ascertain what they want from the police and crime plans. These give a strategic direction to our Chief Constables and we then join the public in scrutinising how the plan is being delivered. This represents a significant shift of power towards the public. (Fabian Society, 2014: 3)

One further feature of the local police and crime plan identified by the PCC in Northumbria was that now an elected figure who could oversee the police 'obtrusively' could also counter any tendency within the police force to prefer institutional self-interest over popular need (Fabian Society, 2014: 3).

Examples of PCC engagement with service delivery

In the relatively short time since the introduction of the new police governance, there is clear evidence and examples of PCC engagement with the delivery of a range of services. This has largely followed on from direct consultation with the public or with issues that have arisen from operational issues involving police officers. In Northumbria, the PCC introduced a safeguarding programme for young women made vulnerable within the Night Time Economy. This programme subsequently became a compulsory element of the Security Industry Authority's new entrant course for all door staff. An additional initiative related to domestic violence where the police response would now automatically include a Women's Aid worker (Baird, 2016).

In Nottinghamshire the PCC commissioned a report to assess the personal experiences of policing in the BME community (Tipping, 2016). As the PCC has noted:

> The report made for uncomfortable reading and was the launch pad for improvements not only increasing transparency of the use of stop and search by the police, but also toughening procedures to ensure every use of these powers was fair, balanced and justified. (Tipping, 2016)

One consequence of the report and subsequent intervention by the PCC has been that currently Nottinghamshire Police now has one of the lowest uses of police stop and search powers while also experiencing one of the highest arrest and positive outcome rates. By 2015–16 the number of stop and search encounters had fallen by almost 40% from the previous 12 months (Tipping, 2016). In Wiltshire the PCC has identified the need to introduce, wherever possible, new technology to the police force. This has included the purchase of laptops, mobile phones and tablets and where 1,400 smart phones and 2,100 laptops are now available to staff. The PCC has also sought to integrate the police with other public protection departments. To that end the PCC has sold off police estate and moved the police into council offices in all the major towns (Macpherson, 2016).

Elsewhere, PCC engagement with service delivery has had national ramifications. In 2013, the Staffordshire PCC commissioned a review to evaluate how much time police officers spent responding to mental health issues in the community (see also Winstone, in this volume). This followed on from meetings with operational officers to discuss issues that most affected them. The review was to discover that in the previous year police officers had responded to 15,000 mental health incidents in Staffordshire, at an estimated cost of £600,000 and that at least 20% of police time was now taken up with such cases (Staffordshire OPCC, 2013: 15).

An Ethics, Transparency and Audit Panel established by the Staffordshire PCC was later requested to report on how a seriously ill man spent 64 hours in police custody despite not having committed a crime 'because NHS services were not available' (Staffordshire OPCC, 2016: 12). The work of the Staffordshire PCC in the mental health area is not an isolated example. In Greater Manchester, and Avon and Somerset, PCCs have been working to improve the way the police respond to people experiencing mental health problems through collaboration with the NHS, social care workers and the voluntary sector. In Avon and Somerset, it was noted that the PCC had aimed to reduce the number of people detained in police cells under the Mental Health Act from 646 in 2012 to zero in 2014 (Home Affairs Committee, 2014, para 19). These current and ongoing challenges to PCCs and police forces do, however, reflect a wider problem which has been identified by HMIC in his most recent report. As is noted within the report, while the police service is not the only public service charged with meeting the needs of vulnerable people, it is 'being used increasingly as the service of first resort [and] this is particularly true in respect of people suffering from mental ill-health' (HMIC, 2017: 8).

Reflection

To what extent is it appropriate for the police to be a service of first resort in dealing with vulnerable people?

Policing in a time of austerity

As identified earlier, the issue which has confronted all PCCs has been a significant reduction in funding and resources for the police service. PCCs and chief officers have been working to improve service delivery against a background of relentless cuts in spending on the police service. For the first time in decades the police service, previously a sacrosanct public service for the Conservative Party, was required to share the burden of 20% spending cuts.

One result of this has been noted most recently by HMIC: a police workforce which has been reduced from 243,000 officers, PCSOs and other staff in 2010 to 200,600 in 2016 – an 18% reduction (HMIC, 2017: 13). To this should be added a recent discovery by the Home Affairs Committee that a further 6,000 officers could be cut by 2020 in response to planned budget cuts (Forster, 2017).

The Chancellor's November 2017 budget did not suggest any significant change of direction for this service as it included no proposed additional spending for the police (Weaver and Elgot, 2017). Thus the fallout from cuts in spending on welfare has increasingly confronted a police service that is subject to significant reductions in resources. In this environment, it becomes ever more important but difficult for PCCs and police forces to respond to HMIC's demands for workforce modernisation, the adoption of new technology and the development of a skills base to meet future demand (HMIC, 2017).

An immediate problem confronting PCCs in light of austerity measures has been the steady erosion of neighbourhood policing strategies as police numbers, particularly PCSO numbers, continue to decline. Increasingly, police officers are now the 'response officers' for emergencies and as HMIC has stated, there has been a longstanding concern that the bedrock of neighbourhood policing 'is being eroded' (HMIC, 2017: 26). This will have an immediate impact on the police and crime plans developed by PCCs.

In the research for this chapter, police officer interviews 1–5 included a comment from a senior commander that "the loss of neighbourhood officers makes us all more vulnerable". PCSOs are officers who interact with communities, generate detailed information about local trouble spots, people already known to the police, along with individuals and families that are of concern within a local area. Thus the loss of PCSOs is a potentially worrying development in the gradual fragmentation of local information from communities upon which multi-agency partnerships dealing with local crime remain crucially dependent. While reducing PCSO numbers itself appears to represent a bid to preserve police establishment (Greig-Midlane, 2014: 7; UNISON, 2016) it has generated deep concern within all communities. This has occurred in the shadow of increased worries following the multiple terrorist attacks in the UK during 2017 about security and radicalisation (Home Office, 2012: 3) in many communities. There are also additional concerns over what are now termed 'County Lines' (National Crime Agency, 2016: 2), a drug-running operation using children, primarily from London and the big cities, to sell drugs in local areas.

The government's own advice (Gov.uk, 2015) on the Prevent Duty focuses on vigilance in community based schools where teachers are encouraged to identify signs of radicalisation (see also Grieve, in this volume). The issue here is that conversations about radicalisation and the sale of drugs in local areas do not take place in public where they can be monitored by law enforcement agencies. They take place covertly in neighbourhoods, requiring constant awareness from teachers, parents, friends, local leaders and the wider community. PCSOs and neighbourhood police have been well placed to capture and use and share this intelligence but this is now under threat.

In the introduction to the 2012 Strategic Policing Requirement (SPR) the then Home Secretary, Theresa May, argued when referring to threats from radicalisation and terrorism that:

> These threats have national dimensions but they cause harm locally as well ... they must be tackled not only by local policing, strongly grounded in communities, but also by police forces and other agencies working collaboratively across force and institutional boundaries. (Home Office, 2012: 3)

Yet, ironically, the capacity of the police to respond in this way has been significantly curtailed. A Silver Commander (Interview 7), for example, commented that he no longer had the latitude in his force to send officers to multi-agency partnership meetings unless legislation forced him to do so. Yet these partnerships are the very forums in which community issues of concern are raised and discussed.

With collaborative working across both force and agency boundaries, as set out in the SPR, there have also been cuts to local authority funding and resources across England. Altogether these cuts have involved an estimated loss of 1 million staff (Barej, 2017). This is a significant number, which has impacted on the ability of many local authorities to provide the staff to support multi-agency partnerships that deal with community safety. One County and District Councillor, retired police officer and currently chair of Adur Community Safety Partnership in Sussex has commented that it is multi-agency partnership working that supports community safety, where issues of local concern are debated openly between interested and participating agencies. All this is now seen to be at risk as a consequence of the government's current austerity strategy.

MARACs and MAPPAs

CSPs enable both the sharing of information about local issues and the potential for harm they might generate. These are discussed among partners including the police, health professionals, housing officers, probation, local authority Social Services representatives, support charities and local leaders. But MARACs, for example, also have a multi-agency approach to sharing both information and resources to help protect victims of domestic abuse and violence. Here, statutory, non-statutory and voluntary sector partners meet to pool information and produce coordinated plans to help protect victims of abuse. A Silver Command officer (Interview 6) has argued that the dialogue within these partnerships, often between trusted representatives from key agencies, enabled swift and timely action to tackle domestic abuse.

The MARAC profile comprises police, probation, children's services, health, housing, IDVAs and other relevant parties. Following a review in 2010, many were found to be very effective (Steel et al, 2011). In West Sussex, four MARACs now cover all of the districts in the county. The number of MARACs will usually be based on the levels or volume of referrals from sources including the police, from whom in fact around 50% of referrals to MARACs are made. Police in West Sussex then complete a DASH risk assessment (Domestic Abuse, Stalking and Honour based violence) to refer the victim to a MARAC. MARAC Plus in West Sussex deals with more complex cases that are of concern and these are chaired by a Detective Inspector. Each MARAC has a support officer or coordinator who is based in the local authority area. Although there have been many changes within the county since the government's austerity policy began to affect public sector resourcing, support for domestic abuse in West Sussex has remained strong and is a strategic priority for the PCC in Sussex (Sussex Police and Crime Commissioner, 2017: 20). This provides something of a contrast to many other areas where domestic violence services in the UK are charities.

In light of the austerity measures since 2010 it is important to reference the role of the Probation Service, which remains closely involved with the MARACs in all areas. Probation Service attendance at the important multi-agency partnerships has however proved to be sporadic in West Sussex and Hampshire despite their attendance being seen as vital. Counties report that probation is a major referral conduit for domestic abuse, yet since the engagement of Community Rehabilitation Companies (CRCs) in probation some significant developments have been made manifest (see also Gough, in this volume). The CRCs are private companies that have taken over the management of low to medium risk serious harm offenders following the introduction of the Offender Rehabilitation Act 2014. Most offenders in domestic abuse are categorised as low to medium risk, and therefore often become the immediate responsibility of the CRCs.

Since the Probation Service is now split between the National Probation Service and the CRCs, resources have been so reduced that attendance at multi-agency partnerships can only be achieved if a representative is in fact available and often this cannot be the same person for each meeting. The importance of a single point of contact was underlined by all the partnerships that were approached in the research for this chapter. It became clear, however, that case continuity, relationship building and trust depended on this in a partnership setting, especially in such sensitive areas as domestic abuse.

Interviewees 4 and 5 stated that the Probation Service had become severely fractured since the introduction of the CRCs to the National Probation Service

(NPS). The two sectors within the service now use separate computer systems, making the sharing of information difficult. One respondent (Interviewee 9) stated that the two sectors within the service rarely if ever communicate with each other. Although the NPS and the CRCs deal with different categories of offender, crime does not unfortunately remain in categories. Thus a low to medium risk offender may gravitate towards more serious crime, spanning both sectors of the service.

When the split occurred for the Probation Service in 2014, staff from probation who dealt with low to medium risk cases usually went to the CRCs while those dealing with high-risk cases were expected to remain with the NPS (Deering and Feilzer, 2015). Staff who remained with the NPS are usually fully qualified Probation Officers (POs) unlike those in the CRCs. These are more likely to be Probation Service Officers who are not qualified POs. Resource availability for attendance at the MARACs, where offenders are categorised as low to medium risk, can be drawn from the CRCs, yet their resource capacity is not sufficient to fully participate in multi-agency meetings at the MARACs.

Interviewees 4 and 5 referred to a lack of operational coordination between the two sectors of the service but also emphasised that this was not the fault of individuals in either the CRCs or the NPS. Rather this problem reflected a severe system design failure (see Pycroft, in this volume). The rationale behind the 2014 break-up of the Probation Service was claimed to be that those dealing with high-risk offences should be NPS staff, while lower to medium risk offenders could be dealt with by the CRC. This in effect meant a loss of consistent and informed resources for both sections of the service. This problem was further compounded by the use of different computer systems that did not communicate with each other. At local level the system design is therefore highly problematic as a result of the lack of shared information internally and externally generated within the multi-agency partnerships and which ostensibly provides community safety. Consistent information sharing is one of the key elements for successful partnership working (Roberts, 2016: 5), and provides each participating agency with a clear and mutually agreed sets of data relating to issues of local concern. Without a consistency of approach in the form of trusted representatives at multi-agency partnership meetings, this information, on which our security as a nation may well depend (Home Office, 2012), along with the ability to support victims of domestic violence and abuse and other offences, could be seriously impaired.

MAPPAs were set up to assess and manage the risks to society of sexual or violent offenders. These arrangements were initiated by way of the 2003 Criminal Justice Act (Schedule 15). MAPPAs are mechanisms through which statutory agencies discharge their responsibilities relating to violent offenders. MAPPA are chaired by the NPS and their involvement tends to be consistent in these partnerships because they hold all the MAPPA cases and chair the meetings. The PCCs are expected to interact with both the MARACs and the MAPPAs. PCC involvement in the MARACs is identifiable in both of the force areas surveyed (Hampshire and Sussex). However, it became apparent that there were clear strategic differences.

The Hampshire PCC maintains what is described as a 'strategic overview' of the MARACs while in Sussex the PCC is, in line with her strategic priorities, very closely involved. PCCs in both counties are of course politicians but engaging with multi-agency partnership working such as the MARACs and the MAPPAs is a strategic decision on the part of each PCC. Comments from interviewees 1–14 emphasised that consistent attendance at multi-agency partnerships by those involved in dealing with low to medium risk offending, including the representatives from the Office of the PCC, is critical in tackling local criminal offences within communities but this now could no longer always be expected.

However, the landscape for commissioning of services for probation may change and this could extend to a PCC role in the commissioning of the CRCs. Discussions have recently taken place (Lockyer and Heys, 2016: 7; IPPR, 2016) which suggest that the Probation Service will be included in the responsibilities of the PCCs. These are expected to commission the CRCs, which will be added to their already comprehensive commissioning responsibilities. It remains to be seen, however, if this will have any effect on developing the cohesive and sustained support needed for multi-agency partnership working through the MARACs, MAPPAs and other community safety partnerships.

The local and national picture

As has been identified following public consultations on PCC police and crime plans, a demand for more visible policing was a widespread public priority and one that was to be reflected in terms of local police priorities (Crest, 2017: 5). Yet reduced police budgets now threaten to undermine the locally determined strategies that the plans articulate and that the PCCs were statutorily required to devise. It is against this background that a major challenge confronts all police forces as they are increasingly required to respond to the changing profile of crime where fraud and cybercrime are fast overtaking traditional volume crime as identified in recent crime surveys (Office of National Statistics, 2016: section 6). Yet PCCs remain responsible for all major commissioning in their areas. These responsibilities also include sustaining local multi-agency partnerships on which most crime prevention and community safety initiatives are based. How PCCs respond to the decline in resources and the rise of the new crime profile remains a matter of speculation.

Conclusion

Most PCCs have done much to justify the reform of police governance but there is more to be achieved. One matter of concern remains for example the gender, age and class background of most PCCs (Mawby and Smith, 2013). It is evident, however, that while starting from a low base, public recognition of PCCs has increased and public awareness of the PCC role has improved (Home Affairs Committee, 2014: 4). Yet, rather like the police and crime plans, PCCs have yet to fully engage with the public and some local partners. This may reflect a deeper political and civic culture where early on commentators in England and Wales detected a strong deferential quality and where a clear respect was exhibited to independent authority (Almond and Verba, 1965: 315). As the evidence arising from voter turnout at PCC elections demonstrates there is still some way to go in cementing PCCs into the public mind.

This problem may have been compounded to date by the relative failure of PCCs to develop effective mechanisms to engage with the public. One element of this revolves around public consultation particularly in relation to police and crime plans. Here, as has been argued, the majority of consultations consisted of public meetings, invited submissions and online surveys, most of which simply asked the public to rank or agree/disagree with a number of earlier identified priorities. Evidence suggests that there is at best a very mixed picture in terms of PCC consultation with the public (Crest, 2017: 3).

It is also evident that while PCCs have proved able and willing to develop collaborative arrangements with other police forces and blue light services this has not extended in any real sense to 'partner agencies' in the criminal justice system. This is despite the fact that central government would support such a development. A number of factors may explain this limitation on PCC coordination of services. One might be that PCCs continue to exhibit rather limited horizons and this only reflects their own limited OPCC infrastructure and support services. However, as has been recently argued, another and deeper reason could be that if PCCs want to be able to join up the constituent elements of the criminal justice system and hold each agency to account they will only be able to do this 'by bolstering their own democratic credentials'. This becomes of increasing salience as the real power position of the PCC becomes apparent.

PCCs are ostensibly held to account by Police and Crime Panels (PCPs), but recent research demonstrates the startling limitations exhibited by the panels in exercising this role (Bailey, 2015, 2017). The lack of effective accountability of the PCC and OPCC between elections suggests the need, in fact, for a rapid review of the future role and structure of the panels. This matter becomes of even greater significance as the power position of the PCC and Chief Constable is now more widely recognised. Recently the National Police Chiefs Council has raised its concern about the changing status of the Chief Constable. That change has most recently been demonstrated in the significant decline in the number of senior officer applications for the position of Chief Constable (Orr-Munro, 2018). But this is not all. In an important and recent High Court judgement (Crompton, 2017) the court discovered that under the Police Reform and Social Responsibility Act (2011) the PCC had wider responsibilities than was at first assumed. The court found that the PCC role extends to all aspects of operational policing for which the PCC has ultimate responsibility. This may fatally weaken the earlier convention of constabulary independence on which contemporary policing was firmly based. The court has in effect overridden the earlier espoused operational independence of the Chief Constable based on common law, most notably that of the Metropolitan Commissioner ex parte Blackburn (1968 2QB 118 at 135). As stated by the court: 'It is in our judgement impossible to see operational independence as being beyond supervision of the PCC' (Crompton R–v–PCC South Yorkshire 2017 para 79).

Taken together these developments may increase the need to create an effective local accountability mechanism to provide a degree of balance to the assumed powers of the PCC and the OPCC.

As has been argued, PCCs may be democratically elected but one consequence of the very limited nature of local consultation exhibited to date by PCCs is that they do not enjoy a popular mandate to bring other criminal justice agencies to account (Crest, 2017: 13). Much therefore will depend on the ability of PCCs either singly or collectively to both significantly increase their public salience along with their commitment to both inform and educate the public. It may be the case, given these perceived limitations of PCCs, that the new directly elected city mayors could in future begin to better coordinate local criminal justice agencies based on the much higher public and media profile that these office holders can expect to enjoy.

Summary of key learning points

- Despite the changes that police governance has brought to the governance of policing more needs to be done in engaging with the public to give democratic legitimacy.
- PCC need to be more proactive in developing partnerships beyond immediate policing services.
- In part this is reflected in the need for PCC to reflect their constituencies in terms of gender and race.

References

Allen, G. and Zayed, Y. (2018) 'Police service strength', Briefing Paper Number 00634, London: House of Commons Library.

Almond, G.A. and Verba, S. (1965) *The civic culture-political attitudes and democracy in five nations*. Boston: Little Brown.

Bailey, R. (2015) 'Policing the Police and Crime Commissioner (PCCs): An examination of the current statutory and political frameworks for holding PCCs to account – A case study of the Surrey Police and Crime Panel', *Policing: A Journal of Policy and Practice*, 9(4): 305–313.

Bailey, R. (2017) 'Policing the PCCs: an evaluation of the effectiveness of PCPs in holding PCCs to account', unpublished PhD thesis, University of Portsmouth.

Baird, V. (2016) 'Sexual assault and the NTE-small idea make a difference', Police Foundation Blog, 21 October, www.police-foundation.org.uk/2016/10/sexual-assault-and-the-night-time-economy-small-ideas-make-a-difference/

Barej, A. (2017) 'GMB highlights 1 million public sector jobs lost since 2010', Public Finance, www.publicfinance.co.uk/news/2017/09/gmb-highlights-1-million-public-sector-jobs-lost-2010

BBC News (2012) 'Police crime commissioners: media reaction', 18 November, www.bbc.co.uk/news/uk-20376910

Comptroller and Auditor General (2014) *The impact of funding reductions on local authorities*. National Audit Office, www.nao.org.uk/wp-content/uploads/2014/11/Impact-of-funding-reductions-on-local-authorities.pdf

Crest (2017) 'PCCs: what's the plan?', 2 February, https://social.shorthand.com/CrestAdvisory/nyFLlyIKdT/pccs-whats-the-plan

Crompton, R. (2017) *Regina v PCC South Yorkshire*, QBD 2017.

Deering, J. and Feilzer, M. (2015) 'Probation officers feel betrayed by "shambolic" part-privatisation', Public Leaders Network, *Guardian*, 7 July, www.theguardian.com/public-leaders-network/2015/jul/07/probation-officers-betrayed-part-privatisation-service

Ellison, N. and Ellison, S. (2006) 'Creating "Opportunity for all"? New Labour, new localism and the opportunity society', *Social Policy and Society*, 5(3): 337–348.

Fabian Society (2014) *Letting in the light, lessons from Labour's Police and Crime Commissioners*, Policy Report. London: The Fabian Society.

Forster, D. (2017) 'Who'll suffer the most when the police retreat? Poor people', *Guardian*, 16 November, www.theguardian.com/commentisfree/2017/nov/15/suffer-most-police-retreat-poorer-people-crimes-communities

Gov.uk (2015) 'Protecting children from radicalisation: the prevent duty', 1 July, www.gov.uk/government/publications/protecting-children-from-radicalisation-the-prevent-duty

Greig-Midlane, J. (2014) *Changing the beat: the impact of austerity on the neighbourhood policing workforce*. University of Cardiff.

Gravelle, J. and Rogers, C. (2011) 'Commissioning accountability: change to governance and the police', *The Police Journal*, 84: 320–327.

Grimshaw, R. (2010) 'The danger of politicised policing', *Guardian*, 27 July, www.theguardian.com/commentisfree/2010/jul/27/danger-politicised-policing

Hastings, A., Bailey, N., Bramely, G., Gannon, M. and Watkins, D. (2015) *The cost of the cuts: the impact on local government and poorer communities*. University of Glasgow/Herriot-Watt/Joseph Rowntree Foundation, www.jrf.org.uk/sites/default/files/jrf/migrated/files/Summary-Final.pdf

Home Affairs Committee (2014) *Police and Crime Commissioners: progress to date, 16th Report of session 2013–14, HC757*. London: HMSO.

Home Office (2012) *The strategic policing requirement*. London: Home Office.

HMIC (2017) *PEEL: Police effectiveness, efficiency and legitimacy*. London: HMIC.

Institute for Government (IfG) (2017) 'Performance Tracker Autumn 2017', www.instituteforgovernment.org.uk/publications/performance-tracker-autumn-2017

IPPR (2016) 'A whole-system approach to offender management', www.ippr.org/files/publications/pdf/a-whole-system-approach-Dec16.pdf

Joyce, P. (2011) 'Police Reform: from police authorities to police and crime commissioners', *Safer Communities*, 10(4): 5–13.

Lister, S. and Rowe, M. (2015) 'Electing police and crime commissioners in England and Wales: prospecting for the democratisation of policing', *Policing and Society*, 25(4): 358–377.

Lockyer, K, and Heys, R. (2016) *Local commissioning, local solutions: devolving offender management*. London: Reform Research Trust.

Loveday, B. (2018) 'Police Scotland: challenging the current democratic deficit in police governance and public accountability', *Crime Prevention and Community Safety*, 20: 154–167.

Loveday, B., Lewis, C., Bayley, R. and Watts, S. (2014) 'Evidence to the Committee on Standards in Public Life: concerning public accountability structures of the police in England and Wales', www.gov.uk/government/uploads/system/uploads/attachment_data/file/414822/Police_Accountabillity__Evidence_A_-_D.pdf

Macpherson, A. (2016) 'How can PCCs better support innovative working within their communities?' Police Foundation Blog, 21 October, www.police-foundation.org.uk/2016/10/how-can-pccs-better-support-innovative-working-within-their-communities/

Mawby, R. and Smith, K. (2013) 'Accounting for the police: the new Police and Crime Commissioners in England and Wales', *The Police Journal: Theory, Practice and Principles*, 86(2), https://doi.org/10.1350%2Fpojo.2013.86.2.610

National Crime Agency (2016) *County lines, gang violence, exploitation and drug supply*. 0346 CAD National Briefing Report.

Office of National Statistics (2016) 'Crime Survey England and Wales', www.ons.gov.uk/releases/crimeinenglandandwalesyearendingjune2016

Orr-Munro, T. (2018) 'Chief Constable Recruitment: A PCC's behaviour can deter potential applicants', *Policing Insight*, 11 October.

Roberts, S. (2016) 'Just good friends. Can localism succeed through partnership?' ECPR Graduate Student Conference, University of Tartu, 10–13 July, https://ecpr.eu/Events/PaperDetails.aspx?PaperID=28250&EventID=98

Sampson, F. (2012) 'Hail to the chief?—How far does the introduction of elected police commissioners herald a US-style politicization of policing for the UK?', *Policing: A Journal of Policy and Practice*, 6(1): 4–15.

Staffordshire OPCC (2013) 'Mental Health Review', OPCC.

Staffordshire OPCC (2016) 'Report of the Ethics, Transparency and Audit Panel', OPCC.

Steel, N., Blakeborough, L. and Nicholas, S. (2011) *Supporting high-risk victims of domestic violence: a review of Multi-Agency Risk Assessment Conferences (MARACs)*, Research Report 55, London, Home Office, www.gov.uk/government/uploads/system/uploads/attachment_data/file/116537/horr55-report.pdf

Sussex Police and Crime Commissioner (2017) *Sussex police and crime plan, 2017–2022*, www.sussex-pcc.gov.uk/media/2428/spcc-crime-plan-2017.pdf

The Police Foundation (2009) 'Is the recession an opportunity to rethink the role of policing?' Oxford Policing Policy Forum, University of Oxford.

Tipping, P. (2016) 'Stop and Search – getting it right', Police Foundation blog, 10 October, www.police-foundation.org.uk/2016/10/stop-and-search-getting-it-right/

UNISON (2016) 'The future of our police', 7 April, www.unison.org.uk/news/article/2016/04/the-future-of-our-police/

UNISON (2017) 'Axing Norfolk's PCSOs will make the county a less safe place', 19 October, www.unison.org.uk/news/press-release/2017/10/axing-norfolks-pcsos-will-make-county-less-safe-place-says-unison/

Watts. S. (2019) 'Yes Minister. The Introduction and Police and Crime Commissioners and Relationship with Chief Officers', PhD thesis, University of Portsmouth.

Weaver, M. and Elgot, J. (2017) 'Autumn budget: the winners, the losers and the overlooked', *Guardian*, 22 November. www.theguardian.com/uk-news/2017/nov/22/autumn-budget-the-days-biggest-winners-and-losers

Further reading

Roberts, S. (2018) 'Detecting Radicalisation in Communities: The Role of Multi-Agency Partnership and the Power of Local Information', Research Association for Interdisciplinary Studies, DOI: 10.5281/zenodo.1244816, https://researchportal.port.ac.uk/portal/files/10708244/Proceedings_of_the_9th_RAIS_Conference.pdf

4

Integrated offender management: a brave new world or business as usual?

Andy Williams

Aims of the chapter
- To introduce and critically examine integrated offender management (IOM) within the UK.
- To discuss the origins and rationale behind the development of this 'new' philosophy by reviewing its core principles and focusing on targeting, selection and deselection, joined-up working, colocation and information exchange, support, intervention and disruption and the managing of compliance.
- To utilise empirical research into an IOM for high-risk offenders as a case study, to investigate the advantages and disadvantages that these schemes bring to the nexus of offender supervision, rehabilitation and the management of risk.
- To ask whether IOM is the panacea of offender management or if it is the rebranding of old ideas.

Introduction

In 2008 and 2009 the then Labour government put forward proposals for a new stage in the evolution of multi-agency working. Building on the policies that New Labour had championed since 1997, integrated offender management (IOM) was heralded by the government as providing, for the first time, a fully integrated response to offender management. Since then, IOM programmes have spread like wildfire throughout the police and probation services, with responsible authorities linking more closely with duty-to-cooperate agencies in a multi-agency setting. This chapter will introduce and critically examine IOM within the UK. Using empirical research into an IOM for high-risk offenders, it discusses the origins and rationale behind the development of this 'new' philosophy by reviewing the core principles that underpin IOM. It considers the common characteristics that constitute many IOM programmes across the UK, focusing on targeting, selection and deselection, joined-up working, colocation and information exchange, support, intervention and disruption and managing compliance. Finally, this chapter investigates the advantages and disadvantages that these schemes bring to the nexus of offender supervision, rehabilitation and the management of risk. In doing so, it highlights an issue that asks the important question: whether IOM is indeed the panacea of offender management or if it is simply the rebranding of old ideas.

Developing the IOM brand

IOM developed from a 2008 government proposal to create a fully integrated model of how to manage offenders in the community, which the then Labour government introduced in the *Punishing reform: our approach to managing offenders* paper (Ministry of Justice, 2008). The rationale behind the development of this 'new' philosophy was to move beyond the *coordinated* approach of end-to-end offender management that became the cornerstone of multi-agency working (Nash and Williams, 2008; Harrison, 2011; Annison et al, 2015), and develop a truly *integrated* approach. Its central aim was to integrate services and responses offered by all responsible authorities (such as prison, probation and police) and duty-to-cooperate agencies (housing, NHS/mental health, education, drugs and alcohol organisations, and so on) and deliver these services to those most in need of assistance. The 2008 paper outlines precisely the thinking behind IOM:

> For adult offenders, evidence shows that those sentenced to less than 12 months in custody are more likely to re-offend than those subject to either longer periods in prison or community punishments. We need to work together with partners to increase the supervision and support available to these offenders in order to benefit local communities and reduce reoffending. (Ministry of Justice, 2008: 13)

This increase in supervision and support was to be developed through IOM, and the Ministry of Justice announced a partnership with the Home Office to pilot IOM in five areas (eventually settling on Avon and Somerset, Lancashire, Nottinghamshire, West Midlands and West Yorkshire). In developing the pilots, the government set out a statement that IOM was to help local partners to achieve the following four aims (Ministry of Justice and Home Office, 2009: 3):

- Reduce crime, reoffending and improve public confidence;
- Address potential overlaps between existing approaches and programmes;
- Align and expand pre-existing criminal justice partner agencies' practice and make it more effective;

- Simplify and strengthen governance, leadership, roles and responsibilities, operational decision-making and the allocation of resources.

To focus on these four key areas, an IOM policy statement was developed that set out five principles that should underpin any IOM arrangement (Home Office and Ministry of Justice, 2010: 10):

- Principle 1 – All partners tackling offenders together;
- Principle 2 – Delivering a local response to local problems;
- Principle 3 – Offenders facing their responsibility or facing the consequences;
- Principle 4 – Making better use of existing programmes and governance;
- Principle 5 – All offenders are high risk of causing serious harm and/or re-offending are 'in scope'.

In short, IOM was designed to develop a localised and bespoke approach to reducing reoffending through enhanced multi-agency working with all relevant partners. The reduction of offending was to be achieved through the development of a 'managed set of interventions, sequenced and tailored response to the risks and needs of the individual' (Senior et al, 2011: i). The managed set of interventions was largely based upon the *Risk-Needs-Responsivity* (RNR) approach developed by Andrews and Bonta (2010), through numerous rehabilitation 'pathways' that was the core business of duty-to-cooperate agencies and other external organisations. For example, pathways helping offenders with accommodation, education, training and employment, alcohol and drug misuse and mental health problems were used to fit the RNR of each individual offender. Some have even argued that IOM fits the definition of a *brand*, and that this plays an 'important role for criminal justice practitioners seeking to (re-)construct their professional identity in the wake of substantial organizational change' (Annison et al, 2015: 403).

Drivers for change

In developing a managed set of bespoke interventions, the IOM approach was informed by a broad range of what have been labelled 'drivers for change' (Senior et al, 2011: 2). First, it was built upon *pre-existing public protection schemes* such as the Prolific and Priority Offender (PPO) and Drug Intervention Programmes (DIP), Youth Offending Teams (YOTs), Deter Young Offender Schemes (DOTs), and Criminal Justice Intervention Teams (CJIT). It also linked with current public protection processes such as Multi-Agency Public Protection Arrangements (MAPPA) (Senior et al, 2011: 2) (see Nash, and also Loveday and Roberts, in this volume). Second, *national drivers* such as the National Reducing Re-Offending Plans (Senior et al, 2011), the National Offender Management

Service Offender Management Model (NOMS, 2006), the PPO refresh document (Home Office, 2009) the loss of 'custody plus' arrangements (CJA, 2003) and the numerous policy reviews from Carter (2003), Casey (2008) and the Bradley Report (Department of Health, 2009) all influenced the creation of IOM. Finally, many *local drivers* underpinned the IOM charge. These included enhancement of pre-existing schemes, such as multi-agency partnerships and crime and disorder partnerships, concerns over serious acquisitive crime, crime reduction targets, and developing established information sharing and data exchange protocols. On the surface, it appears that the responsible authorities were using an 'everything-*and*-the-kitchen-sink' approach to tackling the most serious and persistent offending to reduce crime, which has led to wide variation in the types of IOM schemes that exist and their subsequent functioning and success in reducing reoffending. However, before discussing an example of an IOM model, it is useful to examine the wider criminal justice sector policy conditions in which IOM was born (see also Chapters 1, 2 and 3 in this volume).

The constant flux of offender management

Those in the know and working in the trenches of offender management have witnessed the constant flux in developments in their practice for the past 17 years, if not longer. For some time now, multi-agency working 'has been the default position for good practice in the "protection" aspects of social work and probation' (Nash and Williams, 2008: 108; also see Nash, 2006). The Crime and Disorder Act 1998 introduced a statutory requirement for relevant authorities (local councils, police and probation services) to develop joint crime and disorder strategies and work together in reducing crime (see sections 5–7); the multi-agency aspect was then reinforced by sections 67–69 in the Criminal Justice and Court Services Act 2000. These Acts were the precursor to the implementation of the Criminal Justice Act 2003, the then Labour government's flagship law and order policy that saw the implementation of the findings from the correctional service review undertaken by Patrick Carter, a businessman with experience of the private health care system (Nash and Williams, 2008: 120). The 2003 Carter Report shocked the system by suggesting that prison and probation services should be combined to form a new National Offender Management Service (NOMS). According to Carter, there was an 'urgent need for the different parts of the criminal justice system to work closer together' (Carter, 2003: 1). This claim was made at a time when multi-agency working, despite its somewhat veiled beginnings in 1998, had vastly improved by 2003 and was finally beginning to find its feet. Carter's vision was clear: focus on the managing of prison and probation services through a focus on the offender and the reduction of reoffending (2003: 1–4), eventually leading to the creation of NOMS in 2004. In 2007, the government formed the Ministry of Justice, when some functions of the Home Secretary were combined with the Department of Constitutional Affairs (the latter of which had replaced the Lord Chancellor's Department in 2003). In recent years, the Probation Service has also had to contend with the coalition/Conservative government's aggressive Transforming Rehabilitation policy (Ministry of Justice, 2013), which handed over anywhere between 60 and 70% of probation work to private Community Rehabilitation Companies (CRCs), created the National Probation Service in 2014 and created confusion as to which organisation oversaw IOM. NOMS was then disbanded and yet another new organisation was created in 2017 – Her Majesty's Prison and Probation Service (HMPPS). If the reader's head is spinning it is no surprise. To be clear, from its humble beginnings in 1998 and within the relatively short time span of 17 years, multi-agency partnership working has gone through so many changes and iterations it would make even the most loyal of civil servants raise a critical eyebrow. In addition, within ten years of Labour winning the election in 1997, there were over 30 new Acts (and over 3,000 new offences) of parliament relating to crime and criminal justice (HC Deb 7 November 2007, vol 467, col 103[1]). These new Acts, which included the Criminal Justice and Sexual Offences Acts of 2003, and the resultant changes to social and criminal justice policy and procedure, have also placed considerable strain on a system that is unable to cope (see Pycroft, in this volume). Figure 4.1 illustrates the major iterations and some of the more pertinent legislation.

Figure 4.1: A system in constant flux

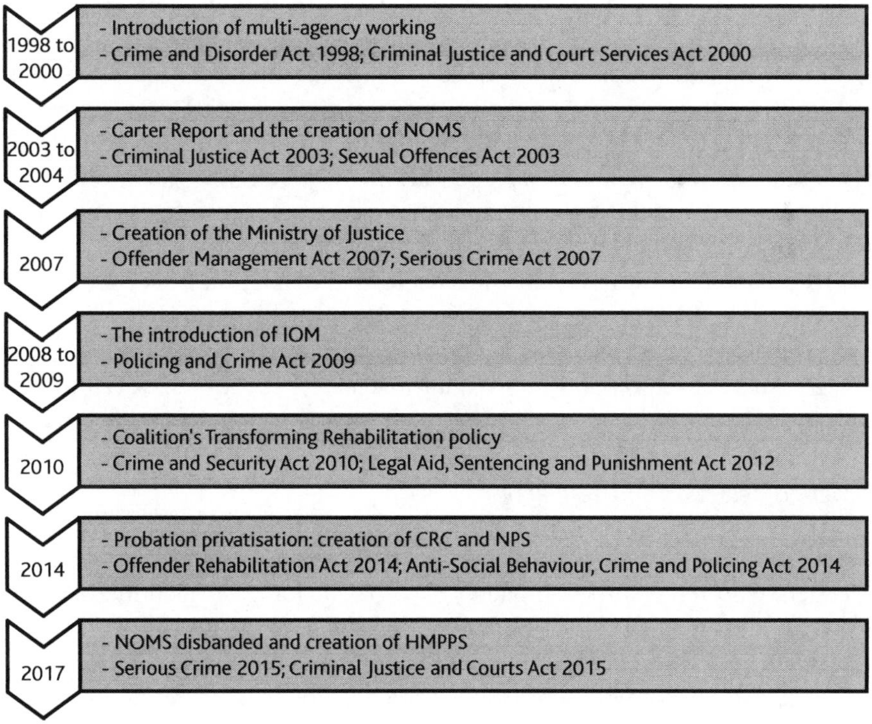

1998 to 2000	- Introduction of multi-agency working - Crime and Disorder Act 1998; Criminal Justice and Court Services Act 2000
2003 to 2004	- Carter Report and the creation of NOMS - Criminal Justice Act 2003; Sexual Offences Act 2003
2007	- Creation of the Ministry of Justice - Offender Management Act 2007; Serious Crime Act 2007
2008 to 2009	- The introduction of IOM - Policing and Crime Act 2009
2010	- Coalition's Transforming Rehabilitation policy - Crime and Security Act 2010; Legal Aid, Sentencing and Punishment Act 2012
2014	- Probation privatisation: creation of CRC and NPS - Offender Rehabilitation Act 2014; Anti-Social Behaviour, Crime and Policing Act 2014
2017	- NOMS disbanded and creation of HMPPS - Serious Crime 2015; Criminal Justice and Courts Act 2015

There are, of course, many more Acts that I could have included. While the speed and delivery of these dramatic changes have introduced important developments across the field of offender management, it should be questioned why these changes are made so quickly and before they have been properly embedded, evaluated and then revised where necessary. More optimistically, it does seem that out of the messy machinery of government bureaucracy there are some very innovative developments in offender management and rehabilitation happening at the local level. One such innovation was the development of IOM.

IRiS: an IOM case study

Because IOM is a localised approach to protecting the public, a typical model does not exist. Each IOM is potentially different because it forms and develops around the identified crime problems and geographical structure in which it is located (see Senior et al, 2011; Annison et al, 2015). There are, however, some core themes involved in each IOM. This section provides a brief case study using an evaluation that I undertook of one of the first IOMs for high-risk sexual and violent offenders in the country. Situated in central Bristol, IRiS – *Integrated Response, Integrated Services* – is a high-risk IOM scheme and built on an earlier IOM model called IMPACT. Located in Bristol, IMPACT is a multi-agency IOM team that is made up of drug workers, police, probation and prison officers who work together helping prolific offenders who commit high levels of acquisitive offences such as robberies, burglaries and thefts (see Senior et al, 2011 and Annison et al, 2015). Since IMPACT was launched in 2008, serious acquisitive crime in Bristol dropped by 51% by 2011 (Burgess and Jones, 2012: 5). IRiS is built on this pre-existing scheme by applying the key elements instrumental to IMPACT's success, for example, improved multi-agency working, information sharing, colocation, and developing relevant pathways and specialisms. As previously stated, one of the guiding principles of IOM was building on pre-existing structures. Because of the strong pre-existing framework, there were many structures and protocols in place that IRiS could borrow from and which were then adapted and incorporated into the overarching IRiS brand. Because of this, IRiS has characteristics common to many IOMs: targeting, selection and deselection; joined-up working and agency engagement; colocation and information exchange; support, intervention and disruption; and managing compliance.

Targeting, selection and deselection

A core principle behind IOM is the specific targeting and selection of those offenders who represent the highest risk of reoffending (as identified through actuarial measures such as Offender Group Reconviction Scale Version 3 (OGRS3)) and/or those who represent the highest risk of serious harm (through Offender Assessment System (OASys), Violence Predictor scores or assessments such as ARMS (Active Risk Management System)). Part of the targeting and selection of the right offenders requires localised intelligence of those most harmful to the public. Most early IOMs focused on persistent and serious acquisitive crime but more recently IOMs have been developed that focus on high risk of serious harm offenders, such as specific types of sexual and violent offenders. Therefore, any scoping exercise around the UK would find IOM teams that focus solely on crimes such as burglary and robbery (Senior et al, 2011), while others focus on sexual and violent offenders (Williams, 2014). Those meeting the criteria are assessed for their continued participation in the IOM, and this allows for deselection at any given time. There are clear processes in place that allow for the migration in and out of IOM, and this will depend on how well the risk is/has been managed. An offender may be deselected if their risk of reoffending and/or risk of serious harm has been reduced. Offenders may be selected to move from a standard Offender Management (OM) team to their local IOM, due to an increase in either their risk levels or because of concerning behaviour identified by any agency involved in their risk management. Selection/deselection criteria may vary between IOMs but there is usually a system that uses intelligence to make such decisions, for example, the dynamic Red Amber Green (RAG) system, which is a 'schema determining day-to-day actions driven by knowledge of intelligence concerns' (Senior et al, 2011: 7). Red equates to high risk and that the offender is known to be offending; amber suggests unknown or incomplete intelligence so further information is required; and green indicates that there is no intelligence that the individual is engaged in offending activity (diary observation, 25 January 2013). This type of system allows for a response to changes in static and acute dynamic risk factors, allowing for other more 'riskier' offenders to be selected for intensive help and support.

The initial IRiS cohort was selected using baseline criteria and in consultation with police, probation, YOT and prison agencies and involves both statutory and non-statutory offenders. The criteria consisted of three core factors and these were established to determine the relevant offenders chosen for inclusion (Burgess and Jones, 2012: 57):

1. Relevant Offence – where the offender has committed a relevant offence (i.e. sexual and violent offences, domestic violence, OCGs/gangs, IPP, PDP and MAPPA cases, repeat serious violence, domestic extremists, racially motivated violence, instrumental violence and so forth);
2. Risk of Serious Harm and Imminence – where the behaviour gives reasonable grounds for believing that there is a present likelihood of them committing a relevant offence and they pose significant and imminent risk of both re-offending and causing serious harm;
3. Medium and/or High Risk – where offenders have been assessed using actuarial measures used by relevant agencies and present as medium or high risk of reoffending and/or risk of causing serious harm.

As a result, 969 offenders were nominated for inclusion to the initial IRiS cohort, although 677 of these were removed as they did not meet the baseline criteria or there were other reasons for their exclusion (see Table 4.1, taken from Burgess and Jones, 2012: 58). At the problem profile and planning stage therefore, the IRiS cohort was approximately 292 and this was reduced to approximately 180 during the pilot phase, which ran between July 2012 and March 2014.

Table 4.1: Reasons for exclusion from IRiS cohort

Reasons for exclusion	Number	%
Not assessed as high risk on OASys	301	44.5
Not high risk based on professional judgement	155	22.9
Prison release date after 2014	56	8.3
Offender not living in Bristol	46	6.8
OGRS Score of <20	41	6.1
Lifer	37	5.5
Not assessed as high risk on ASSET	21	3.1
Pre-tariff IPP	7	1.0
Not assessed as high risk RSO	5	0.7
Deported	5	0.7
Deceased	3	0.4

Selecting the right clients for IRiS sat alongside the importance of selecting the right team to manage these individuals. At the very outset "selecting the right people who know for them, going the extra mile was really important" (quote from IOM worker). IRiS consisted of police and probation managers, probation OMs and administrators, police OMs, community psychiatric nurses, and forensic psychologists, all colocated in the same office and working together to develop and implement intensive supervision and management of their clients. Most of the probation officers had extensive experience and knowledge of dangerous, high-risk offenders and their risk management, while the police officers had high levels of experience with intelligence and public protection. This eclectic mix of experience and knowledge enabled all five of the IOM principles to be effectively implemented using pre-existing resources based on the relevant culturally embedded epistemologies. The importance of having an understanding and shared vision of what IRiS was trying to achieve can clearly be seen in the following quotes from the team:

> 'Managing the high risk cases in the Bristol area, in a multi-agency team with all the relevant agencies, to be able to manage their risk better.'

> 'It's a team that's taking the most complex cases, and the most complex cases that are high risk ... the cases where people have no idea what

to do next because everything has been tried ... we take the complex, the tricky and the difficult people ... and we bring them into a joint way of working ... joint within the team.'

'I think it's just a cohesive way of working with other agencies really, to manage risk. And I think it was sorely needed.'

Joined-up working and agency engagement

The creation of MAPPAs (see Nash, and also Loveday and Roberts, in this volume) through sections 67 to 69 of the Criminal Justice and Court Services Act 2000 introduced a statutory provision for responsible authorities (RA) to work together to create systems for managing the risk posed by violent and sexual offenders in the community (Nash and Williams, 2008). These RAs were the prison, probation and police services and since 2000, joined-up and multi-agency working has widened to include other agencies who aid in the risk management of dangerous offenders (Harrison, 2011). Section 325(3) of the Criminal Justice Act 2003 introduced the statutory provision that other agencies have a duty to cooperate with RAs. IOM is said to be effective due to its level of multi-agency partnerships and integrated agency working between RAs and duty-to-cooperate agencies. In the review of the five pilot sites, Senior et al (2011: 18) found that the 'joining up of the key agencies was an essential feature of all IOM sites'. Key stakeholders are therefore encouraged to put aside inter- and intra-agency conflict and 'silo working' and embrace cooperative communication and intelligence sharing. Despite this, there is some evidence across the IOM research that silo working and agency conflict still exists. Senior et al (2011: 17) found tensions because of police dominance of IOM. In my own research, I found the perception that the police were trying to widen their own organisational remit at the expense of probation (diary observation, 25 March 2013), for example through their involvement in pathways support and enforcement/disruption strategies. The core message is that joined-up working did not just happen and needs to be consistently worked at, although for the most part, many people within IOM embraced integrated approaches to working. Fundamentally, what makes joined-up inter-agency work effective in IOM is employing people who are willing to challenge and work beyond a silo mentality.

IRiS provides a high level of integrated inter- and intra-agency working practices. Although the core agencies involved were still the RAs, the structure of IRiS has close links with duty-to-cooperate agencies, as well as numerous voluntary sector organisations working with high-risk offenders through their 'pathways' programmes (such as local Sexual Assault Referral Centres, Circles of Support and Accountability, and domestic abuse organisations such as Splitz). IRiS also works closely with the MAPPA and standard OM teams, especially around the areas of migration to and from IRiS. The key aspects of this integrated work are within the areas of support, intervention and disruption to avoid future reoffending and reduce the risk of serious harm that the IRiS clients pose. The fieldwork identified strong processes regarding supporting clients (helping with accommodation through the agreement with Approved Premises), as well as high levels of intervention and disruption practices, especially through the intelligence work of the OMs and Field Intelligence Officers (FIOs). The number of recalls has been quite high (by February 2014 of the pilot, there were 71 recalls to custody), which has sometimes led to negativity from the OMs (some felt disappointed with so many recalls and somehow felt responsible for the clients' criminal behaviour). However, these recalls were necessary and provide evidence that there are robust intervention measures in place, meeting IOM principle 3 in that the offenders face the consequences of their actions.

Colocation and information exchange

A third commonality across the differing configurations of IOM is colocation and information exchange. It is generally accepted that colocation has many benefits including having direct interaction and contact with different agencies in the same office. This usually involves assigned probation and police officers working alongside prison representatives. Other agencies are also colocated part or some of the time, and this largely depends on the structure of the IOM which is determined by IOM principles 2 and 4 (Home Office and Ministry of Justice, 2010). Senior et al (2011: 20) highlight the core benefits of colocation as information sharing, a one-stop-shop, communication and cultural change. Being in the same office allows for the immediate exchange of intelligence on clients, access to other agencies' IT databases, which potentially lessens duplication and increases efficiency (Senior et al, 2011; Williams, 2014; Annison et al, 2015). A one-stop-shop allows for greater coordination between offender managers and pathway interventions and the support-disruption nexus. It also helps clients as they usually attend one main location. Finally, colocation allows for enhanced communication and the breaking down of agency cultural boundaries through knowledge exchange and what Senior et al call 'corridor conversations' (2011: 20). It has been identified that colocation through IOM allows for knowledge exchange and a positive environment where ideas and brainstorming take place (diary observation, 1 May 2014).

Even though colocation is seen in a positive light, a few concerns have been raised. For example, there have been cases where vetting has inhibited some individuals from Voluntary Community Sector (VCS) organisations 'being located in a police building' (Senior, et al, 2011: 19). The locating of the IOM at a police station also raised issues regarding clients having to attend the station for their meetings and interventions (Williams, 2014). Concerns have also been raised of the blurring of lines between line management of staff located in an IOM and their parent organisation. Another issue raised related to the IT systems used by each agency. While easier access to each agency's intelligence databases is a positive aspect, in reality this meant dealing with numerous different systems: 'In

Bristol, the information officer described 17 databases they had to track individuals through the systems' (Senior et al, 2011: 20).

As with other IOMs the high level of cohesiveness of the IRiS team was clearly a result of colocation. From its inception, multi-agency approaches have faced many barriers, especially when it comes to communication and information and intelligence sharing (Nash, 2006; Nash and Williams, 2008). Overall, the IRiS team responded positively to being relocated to another team and with different organisations. For example, one worker said "It has been really useful ... I've had some cases where I've got very little knowledge of, very little history in probation and I've been able to say 'look can you get me this information?'"; and another noted that having the community practice nurse (CPN) in the team

> 'has been absolutely fantastic ... It has been a really good, positive move, and it's really helped my understanding of some of the issues around mental health and just having her there to speak to people knowing what she's talking about, so that's been a real bonus.'

As I have previously shown in my work on serious further offences (see Nash and Williams, 2008), communication, information sharing and acting on the information in an appropriate and timely fashion are cornerstones to effective risk management and public protection. The two dominant themes that came out of the colocation of the IRiS team were more time for the supervision of cases and better information sharing between agencies. This was clearly a strength of the IRiS pilot as it offered a robust framework for IOM principles 1, 2, 3 and 4 to be anchored on and allowed managers to develop robust rehabilitation and enforcement systems. Figure 4.2 illustrates the core themes emerging from the IRiS research into colocation.

Support, intervention and disruption

It is argued that IOM is a unique and truly integrated approach as it is predicated on the intensity of the support and interventions it offers to clients, as well as its disruption strategies. When it comes to support, IOM is unique in its approach to offender management because the offender managers tend to have smaller caseloads. This, coupled with enhanced intelligence and direct access to the databases of other agencies and their personnel, allows for more support to be provided. Support activities include direct help upon release from prison, help with appointments, mentoring and home visits. While many of these support activities are undertaken in other OM structures such as MAPPA, the level and intensity of support is thought to be higher in IOM teams (Annison et al, 2015). Interventions relate to the customised care and risk management plans that create pathway interventions that suit the client's RNR assessment. Most IOMs are closely linked to numerous 'pathways' that provide rehabilitation programmes and protective factors to help clients desist from crime. The pathways most common

Figure 4.2: The benefits and challenges of colocation

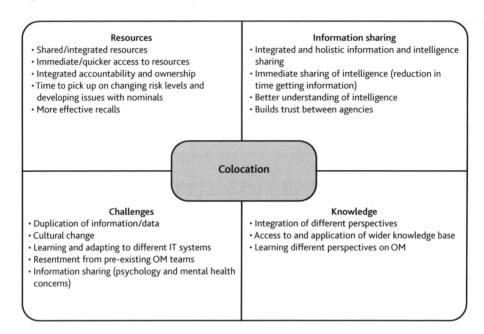

to IOM include drug and alcohol, accommodation/housing, mental and physical health, employment and education and finance benefit and debt management services (Williams and Ariel, 2013; Williams, 2014). Many IOMs have direct access to pathways' workers as many of them work part of their time at the IOM offices. If an offender disengages from the support and interventions provided to them, disruption strategies are identified and implemented, usually by the police to encourage re-engagement with IOM. These could include visits by uniformed police officers, to make the client aware that unless they re-engage, they will quickly resume a 'catch-and-control' mentality towards that individual. Many police and probation officers throughout the research recognise the need for this carrot and stick approach to managing risk in the community (Senior et al, 2011; Williams, 2014; Annison et al, 2015). For many officers, it is a key way to manage compliance.

There are many support, intervention and disruption aspects to the IRiS process and these have been developed, tested, and revised throughout the pilot process, ending in the creation of an IRiS offender protocol, which outlines the standard operation procedures for the team. These are tailored to fit IRiS and its clients and services, yet have similarities to IOMs across the UK. For example, cluster, migration and risk management plan (RMP) meetings are regularly held within the team and these are echoed across the other IOMs. Cluster meetings discuss clients/cases and they provide an opportunity for the relevant OM team to raise any concerns regarding their clients and discuss possible actions to take using the RAG system, reviewing any new intelligence they have and making appropriate decisions that may feed into the migration or RMP meetings. The migration meeting involves the deselection of IRiS clients whose risk has been reduced and can be migrated out of the team; and a selection process, which involves reviewing possible entry into IRiS from other OM teams or directly on release from custody. In the risk management plan meetings, RMPs are discussed and risk is revised where necessary and a reflective review of the restrictive, protective and rehabilitative factors are closely examined. Every IRiS client has an RMP based around the four key areas of risk management: (i) supervision, (ii) monitoring and control, (iii) interventions and treatment, and (iv) victim safety (Williams, 2014: 62–63). The aim of the RMP according to a worker within the scheme is to "reduce risk and re-offending, by supporting an offender's resettlement back into the community". The RMPs provide a comprehensive overview of the offender information, record of pre-release meetings, brief offence summary as well as the types of risks involved, who are the likely victims and/or targets of the client, and what relevant safeguarding measures have been put in place for victims (and clients).

Managing compliance

Even though IOM provides intensive supervision and intervention programmes to try to reduce the risk of reoffending and the risk of serious harm, it also has enforcement capabilities to try to manage compliance from clients. When asked, IOM clients are aware of the disruption tactics that help manage compliance. They accept this as part of 'the game' and that if they fail to attend meetings or ignore communications from their OM team they will be punished (Senior et al, 2011: 26). However, a key aspect uncovered in the pilot evaluations was choice: the feeling that it was the individual's choice to attend and engage, especially the non-statutory offenders. However, it has also been acknowledged that clients need to want to change so compliance is fully managed.

The work IRiS undertakes is primarily with statutory clients although they also manage several non-statutory clients. It has long been acknowledged that the end of statutory supervision does not equate to a reduction in risk of harm (Kemshall and Hilder, 2013; Nash, 2006; Nash and Williams, 2008). Therefore, it is important that risk management systems are still in place for non-statutory offenders who still pose a high risk of harm to the public. The police have the power to continue working with non-statutory cases and undertake a range of tactical options such as developing intelligence, surveillance and other covert methods, alongside the obvious powers of arrest, if they feel the risk of serious harm and/or reoffending has increased. IOMs tend to provide a more structured type of supervision and enforcement to cover the non-statutory loophole found in many standard probation structures. At any given time, any non-statutory client can be referred into IRiS through discussions at the cluster and migration meetings. This process is underpinned by the RMPs discussed above.

Summary

Ever since partnership approaches to crime and disorder were introduced in 1998, multi-agency approaches to offender management have been in constant flux. IOM has been designed to be a properly integrated approach that incorporates all RAs, duty-to-cooperate agencies with VCS organisations to deliver intensive supervision and rehabilitation programmes for prolific, priority and high-risk offenders living in the community. There are clear differences between this approach and standard OM systems, the most notable being colocation, enhanced intensity of supervision and intelligence and information sharing. There is a danger that IOM, as the latest form of joined-up working, promises too much and is viewed as the panacea of offender management. This is, of course, something which is difficult to deliver, especially given that successive governments on both the left and right have incessantly introduced changes to laws and policy even before previous systems have been properly tested. One question to perhaps ask is whether too many cooks spoil the risk management broth. With so many different agencies and organisations involved it can be difficult to truly ascertain which of those involved have the most useful impact on reducing recidivism and protecting the public. Furthermore, what still appears to be missing is OM input from the clients themselves (see Lewis, in this volume). Even though IOM in many places is a rebranding of what was already largely in place, the innovation seen in many IOM schemes up and down the country should be viewed as moving in the right direction for enhanced public protection and for helping offenders change over the long term.

Review questions

1. What were the key drivers for change that led the development of IOM?
2. List five key benefits of the IOM approach to offender management.
3. Name three elements of best practice for a typical IOM to engage in.
4. What makes IOM different from other types of offender management such as MAPPA?

> ## Summary of key learning points
>
> The philosophy underpinning IOM is that it is a fully integrated, localised approach to offender management and rehabilitation which is most effective when based on a problem profile analysis that identifies and understands the most prolific and/or dangerous offenders.
>
> - IOM can be viewed as another addition to the multi-agency approach to public protection and risk management that has a statutory footing requiring Responsible Authorities and Duty to Cooperate Agencies to work together to reduce reoffending.
> - The key characteristics of IOMs are: (i) efficient target, selection and deselection processes; (ii) effective joined-up inter-agency working; (iii) colocation and enhanced information exchange; (iv) intensive support, intervention and disruption practices; and (v) strong managing compliance conventions.
> - The case study of IRiS illustrates the benefits of using an IOM approach for high-risk offenders; specifically around colocation, their ability to immediately share information/intelligence on their clients and discuss cases in a more natural, organic way through 'corridor conversations'.
>
> As a result of Transforming Rehabilitation, IOM faces several challenges. For example, there is the potential to slip back into the 'silo-mentality' where communication and information sharing is lost between the police, NPS and CRCs.

Note

[1] https://publications.parliament.uk/pa/cm200708/cmhansrd/cm071106/debtext/71106-0016.htm

References

Andrews, D.A. and Bonta, J. (2010) *The psychology of criminal conduct*. Fifth edition. New Providence, NJ: Matthew Bender and Company Inc.

Annison, H., Bradford, B. and Grant, E. (2015) 'Theorizing the role of "the brand" in criminal justice: the case of integrated offender management', *Criminology and Criminal Justice*, 15(4): 387–406.

Burgess, L. and Jones, E. (2012) *Integrated offender management project development plan: version 1.16*. Bristol: IMPACT Board.

Carter, P. (2003) *Managing offenders, reducing crime: a new approach* (Correctional Services Review). London: Home Office.

Casey, L. (2008) *Engaging communities in fighting crime*. London: Cabinet Office.

CJA (2003) *Criminal Justice Act 2003*, www.legislation.gov.uk/ukpga/2003/44/contents

Department of Health (2009) *The Bradley Report: Lord Bradley's review of people with mental health problems or learning disabilities in the criminal justice system*. London: Department of Health.

Harrison, K. (2011) *Dangerousness, risk and the governance of serious sexual and violent offenders*. Abingdon, Oxon: Routledge.

Home Office (2009) *Prolific and other priority offender programme five years on: maximising the impact*. London: Home Office/Ministry of Justice.

Home Office and Ministry of Justice (2010) *Integrated offender management: key principles*. London: Home Office and Ministry of Justice.

Kemshall, H. and Hilder, S. (2013) 'Multi agency approaches to effective risk management in the community in England and Wales', in L.A. Craig, L. Dixon and T.A. Gannon (eds), *What works in offender rehabilitation: an evidence based approach to assessment and treatment*. Chichester: Wiley-Blackwell, pp 436–451.

Ministry of Justice (2008) *Punishment and reform: our approach to managing offenders: a summary*. London: Ministry of Justice.

Ministry of Justice (2013) *Transforming rehabilitation: a strategy for reform*. London: Ministry of Justice.

Ministry of Justice and the Home Office (2009) *Integrated offender management: government policy statement*. London: Ministry of Justice and the Home Office.

Nash, M. (2006) *Public protection and the criminal justice process*. Oxford: Oxford University Press.

Nash, M. and Williams, A. (2008) *The anatomy of serious further offending*. Oxford: Oxford University Press.

NOMS (2006) *The NOMS Offender Management Model*. London: NOMS.

Senior, P., Wong, K., Culshaw, A., Ellingworth, D., O'Keeffe, C. and Meadows, L. (2011) *Process evaluation of five integrated offender management pioneer areas*. Research Series 4/11. London: Ministry of Justice and Home Office.

Williams, A. (2014) *IRiS: an independent process and profile evaluation*. Final Report, June.

Williams, A.E. and Ariel, B. (2013) 'The Bristol integrated offender management scheme: a pseudo-experimental test of desistance theory', *Policing: A Journal of Policy and Practice*, 7(2): 123–134, doi.org/10.1093/police/pas053

5

MAPPA: sex offenders and managing 'the other' in the community

Mike Nash

Aims of the chapter
- To provide an overview of the policy context for the sentencing and management of sex offenders in England and Wales.
- To discuss the development of the MAPPA process.
- To evaluate these developments within a cultural context of 'othering'.
- To examine the ethical implications of these approaches.

Introduction

On 19 February 2018, former football coach Barry Bennell was sentenced to 30 years' imprisonment at Liverpool Crown Court for what was described as 'industrial scale child abuse'. Taking advantage of his role as a professional football coach he systematically abused young boys over a number of decades. The sentencing judge described him as 'the devil incarnate' and 'sheer evil' (Taylor, 2018). This case was reported alongside alarming disclosures concerning widespread sexual abuse of children by senior officials of the Oxfam charity, notably following the Haitian disaster (Cullen, 2018). In a remarkable sequence of serious sexual offenders coming to justice, Matthew Falder received 32 years imprisonment for blackmailing a string of vulnerable victims into performing depraved sexual acts. He was a computer expert, avoiding detection for four years due to his knowledge of the dark web. He was described by Judge Parker at Birmingham Crown Court as 'warped and sadistic', whose behaviour was 'cunning, persistent, manipulative and cruel' (Davies, 2018). The scale and scope of these crimes demonstrates the far reaching nature of sexual crime and underlines their power in creating a climate of fear among the public. Running parallel to these cases, and at the opposite end of the justice spectrum, is that of convicted serial sex offender John Worboys, commonly known as the Black Cab rapist. He had been convicted of 19 serious sexual offences on 12 victims, including rape. He was sentenced to an Indeterminate Sentence for Public Protection (IPP) in 2009 with a minimum tariff of 10 years. The tariff expired in February and the Board decided he no longer need be detained in December 2017.[1] A huge media storm followed this decision with a judicial review instigated by two women (one of whom was one of the 12 victims, the Mayor of London and News Group Newspapers. In essence the challenges concerned the lack of information provided by the Parole Board (PB), a lack of consultation, the secretive nature of its work and a large number of other victims coming forward saying that they had been assaulted by Worboys. In brief, the High Court upheld the challenge, saying that the PB should have conducted further inquiry into the circumstances and nature of his offending and that the principles of open justice should apply to the working of the PB when it is in the interests of the public to do so. In other words, there should have been more information and consultation. The final outcome was that a further PB review of Worboy's case denied him his release and he now has to wait two years before he can reapply. The chairman of the PB resigned and changes are underway in the way they work (see further reading section for more information). All of these cases demonstrate the power of sexual crimes to dominate the media agenda and also reflect the growing importance of victims in the making of justice decisions. These cases, reported over a few days, illustrate the context in which the assessment and management of offenders takes place. Not only is there considerable media interest but also, particularly in the cases of Bennell and Worboys, a much more proactive stance from victims. For example, the furore raised by the Worboys case is likely to lead to a significant change to Parole Board practice with their decision making possibly becoming much more transparent. This case is a perfect example of how, in the emotive world of sex offenders, high profile instances can lead to fundamental changes to legislation, policy and practice despite the existence of ongoing good practice.

Backcloths such as this have been repeated over the years, but perhaps most notably from the 1990s in both the UK and the USA. For example, the rape and murder of seven-year-old Megan Kanka in the USA and the abduction and murder of Sarah Payne in the UK, both by known and convicted sex offenders, led to huge public and media campaigns and shifts in legislation (Corrigan, 2006). It is not possible to rehearse the details of these cases but it is important to make the point that singular cases can and have had enormous impact on criminal justice. This chapter will largely describe developments in England and Wales (Scotland and Northern Ireland having similar but slightly different legislation) from the early 1990s. It will focus on the joined-up nature of assessing and managing convicted sex offenders, with the underlying caveat that the professionals involved in this process work within the context of ruthless media scrutiny when cases 'go wrong' (Nash and Williams, 2008).

A strong theme that will emerge in this chapter is that of 'difference'. Sex offenders have become 'otherised', in other words, they are not like 'us' (Garland,

1996: 461; O'Malley, 2000); they have become the 'new untouchables' (Janus, 2006). It therefore becomes legitimate, and indeed almost a requirement, to create new and different ways of dealing with the risks posed by this most reviled group of offenders, or what Simon (1999) described as 'managing the monstrous'. In the United States, for example, residency requirements may force offenders to live on the fringes of communities rather than within them. Personal privacy does not apply as widespread community notification advises of their details (Thompson and Greek, 2010: 295–315), with offender rights becoming almost a side issue (Agamben, 1998). Although less extreme in its scope, provision in the UK has nevertheless sought to underline the special status of sexual offending and the need to create targeted legislation and interventions, sometimes in opposition to countervailing orthodoxy. An example of this exceptionalism can be found in the 1991 Criminal Justice Act.

Policy development

The 1991 Act, the creation of a tax cutting Conservative government, aimed to reduce the numbers in prison as a way of saving money. The Act was based around the principles of proportionality and seriousness. The more serious the crime the more likely a lengthy custodial sentence would be passed and the less serious would be subject to 'punishment in the community' (a term itself designed to assuage Conservative party supporters that its leadership had gone soft). A key feature of the proposals was that past behaviour or convictions would not increase the seriousness of the current offence. Offenders would therefore not face increased punishment because of their previous behaviour, but would be proportionately punished for their current crime. There was, however, an exception to this and it occurred in the case of sexual and violent offenders. Here *previous* behaviour would be taken into account as an indication of *future* risk, offenders would therefore be punished for what they *might* do in the future as much as what they have done in the past. They could therefore receive a *disproportionate* sentence, up to the legal maximum for the instant offence, *even if it did not warrant it on seriousness terms* (Nash, 1999a). This process has been described as bringing the future into the present (Rose, 2000).

The risks posed by sexual and violent offenders were therefore regarded as greater than other offenders, resulting in a climate of fear (Furedi, 2002) even though, particularly in the case of sexual offenders, that risk is rather lower than many might expect. For example, one report recently recorded sexual offender recidivism at 13%, with 25% for violence against the person and 50% for theft (Ministry of Justice, 2017a). The predator myth, alluded to above, is frequently accompanied by a notion, again fuelled by elements of the media, that sexual offenders are dealt with too leniently by the criminal justice system. Yet sexual offending, at approximately 2.5% of all offending,[2] results in almost 17% of the total prison population in England and Wales (Sturge, 2018). Yet it is not just custodial sentencing which has marked out sexual offenders for special treatment;

their supervision in the community is also a different experience to many other offenders.

The 'war' against sex offenders was to take many forms. As noted earlier, there were to be longer than proportionate sentences with, during the 1990s, a dalliance with automatic life penalties in certain cases (1997 Crime Sentences Act) where a serious sexual offence was preceded by at least one other of a similar nature (this measure has now been repealed). There was also to be a strengthening of control in the community with one of the early measures being the development of the so-called sex offender register. Although registers as such did not exist, there was a requirement on nearly all sexual offenders, whether sentenced to imprisonment or a community penalty, to present themselves to their nearest police station and provide the police with certain information. This included: their names and any aliases, date and place of birth, national insurance number, address at time of conviction and current address, if living with a child under 18, if staying in a house where a child resides for more than 12 hours a day, passport details, bank account and credit card details. Offenders were required to update their details if there was significant change and to report to the police annually. Subsequent developments would also see sexual offenders receiving home visits from police officers. By 2000, what had been embryonic multi-agency public protection meetings developed during the 1990s, were formalised by the Criminal Justice and Court Services Act (CJ&CSA), which established the Multi-Agency Public Protection Arrangements (MAPPAs) (see Williams, and also Loveday and Roberts, in this volume). The Act required police and probation services, acting as Responsible Authorities, to cooperate in the supervision of potentially dangerous offenders (described as joined-up worrying by Lieb, 2003), of which registered sex offenders were to form a very substantial majority. The Act followed the abduction and murder of eight-year-old Sarah Payne in 2000 and two schoolgirls, Holly Wells and Jessica Chapman in Soham, Cambridgeshire, in 2002. Sarah was murdered by a man with previous convictions and Holly and Jessica by a man who, although not having previous convictions, had numerous allegations and was well known to police. At the time of the offences he was employed as the school caretaker. Both of these cases, leading to huge public disquiet and indeed massive media campaigns, highlighted the need for many to keep closer control over released sex offenders. The CJ&CSA established a framework for the management of MAPPA offenders, essentially based on their assessed risk levels, which in turn would determine their level of management oversight. Three levels of management were established: Level 1 would entail 'ordinary' or usually one agency oversight; Level 2 would be active multi-agency management; and Level 3 required senior managers to be involved. The choice of management oversight would be determined by assessed risk levels, ranging from low to very high. Adding to the overall classification system were categories of offenders: category one covered all registered sex offenders; category two, violent offenders; and category three, other potentially dangerous people not fitting into categories one or two. By 2003, the Criminal Justice Act extended the responsible authority to include the prison service and imposed on virtually every other agency a 'duty to cooperate' with that responsible authority. Public protection really was becoming the responsibility of everyone.

It is important to recognise at this juncture what a shift in agency culture this expansion of multi-agency working entailed. For example, agencies that had traditionally ploughed almost separate paths (police and probation services) were now collaborating on a daily basis. Indeed, some of the work required, for example, police officers to almost assume the role of probation officers (Nash, 1999b, 2014). MAPPAs, particularly the sex offender part of the caseload, produced significant amounts of extra work. This is because it brought some people into the system who were not in it previously and it kept many of them in for much longer than ever before. Sex offenders were to remain on the sex offenders register, and therefore part of MAPPA, for periods linked to the sentence they received. Those sentenced to 30 months or longer were to remain on the register for life. Sentences between 6 and 30 months resulted in 10 years' registration. Under 6 months produced as registration period of 7 years and a community penalty of 5 years. There was no appeal against this (see below for changes in lifelong registration) and, as a result, the sex offender MAPPA caseload (Ministry of Justice, 2017b) has grown year on year.

Growth of the MAPPA caseload

In 2016 the sex offender MAPPA caseload stood at 55,236, out of a total of 76,794. Sex offenders therefore constitute 72% of the total. The total figure for sex offenders has risen from 30,416 in 2006/07. Interestingly, out of the 55,236 registered sex offenders (RSOs), only 1,771 were at Level 2 management and 137 at Level 3, the highest level of multi-agency management and oversight. The overwhelming majority therefore are assessed as only requiring single agency oversight, perhaps somewhat belying the level of risk associated with this group of offenders in the minds of the public and the media. In 2016 there were just over 21,000 violent offenders on the MAPPA caseload (those serving more than 12 months in custody (Ministry of Justice, 2017b).

It should of course be remembered that the overriding outcome of MAPPA is relatively passive. Its aim is essentially crime prevention and particularly in the case of sex offenders, it offers the police an up-to-date source of information to aid in the investigation of new crimes. There are the aforementioned police home visits but at best these amount to little more than 1–4 per year, depending on risk levels. The police do not have a right to enter the offender's home as a result of registration and have to be invited in. Failure to do so would likely result in an application for a warrant and of course increase suspicion. Levels 2 and 3 cases have active multi-agency management based on risk management plans. These plans will establish the roles for the agencies involved, which might include frequency of visiting or reporting, restraints or constructive interventions (plans are not all negative). A range of orders can be imposed within the parameters of the risk management plan. These include Sexual Harm Prevention Orders (SHPOs), Sexual Risk Orders (SROs) and Foreign Travel Orders (FTOs). The first two orders are essentially negative: they prevent or ban the offender from engaging in certain activities which may escalate the risk of sexual harm. These behaviours might include restrictions on certain employments, visiting certain locations or staying at particular addresses. The main difference between the orders is that the SHPO is passed by the sentencing court at point of sentence and the RSO is at the request of the police and therefore usually when the offender is in the community. The FTO has the specific intent of protecting children outside of the UK from known sex offenders by placing restrictions on their ability to travel overseas; this order is again at the request of the police service.

Clearly the vast majority of RSOs are not subject to such restrictive measures, reflecting the lower risks they pose and the fact that so much of sexual offending is acquaintance rather than stranger based. Not that this should lower the seriousness of the crime but it clearly has an effect of muddying the waters if the case comes to trial. As stated earlier, the under-reporting of sexual crimes makes estimates of its prevalence and typologies very difficult. However, a recent report (ONS, 2017) suggests that 30% of rapes of a female are committed by an intimate partner and 10% by an acquaintance. There is a large percentage described as the perpetrator being unknown, but sub-set analysis of police data reveals that perhaps as many as 46% of this group are 'acquaintances' and only 14% are strangers (ONS, 2017: 133–134). The heavy focus on stranger danger in most public protection measures probably underestimates the risks posed by those known to the victim.

Regardless of the essentially skewed nature of public protection, the system itself would appear to be relatively successful. Overall figures for either non-compliance or further reoffending are low. Some 1,739 RSOs were cautioned or convicted for breaching their notification requirements and of these, 697 were returned to custody (15% of the total number registered). Perhaps of greater importance were the numbers of serious further offences recorded against MAPPA offenders. A total of 217 serious further offences (SFOs) were recorded in 2016–17; these offences are very serious violent and sexual crimes which carry lengthy periods of custody. The low number therefore suggests a relatively successful picture although there is a caveat; 200 of these SFOs were committed by Level 1 offenders. These are offenders subject to single agency oversight and therefore not part of a regular multi-agency review process. Risk is a dynamic process; it can change quickly in terms of escalation or de-escalation. The higher number of SFOs in the lower risk category might suggest that either risk is not well assessed, or that it moves and changes more quickly than the system designed to manage it. It might also suggest a degree of complexity in this offender group and that an over-fixation on levels and categories might in itself be a risky business.

Despite the introduction of MAPPA, the case for additional measures is frequently raised by the public and/or the media. Most notably demands have been made for more extensive controls over sex offenders. Much of this clamour centred on the murder of eight-year-old Sarah Payne by a known sex offender, Roy Whiting, in 2000. What perhaps elevated this murder beyond many others was the campaign run by her parents and notably her mother, Sara. Closely linking with the Sunday newspaper, the *News of the World*, the Paynes campaigned for sex offenders' details to be made available to members of the public, much as in the case of the USA.

Useful resources

For more about community notification, see Savage and Charman (2010) and Kemshall et al (2010).

However, the campaign was perhaps damaged by the *News of the World* deciding to name and shame a number of sex offenders. This resulted in some vigilante action, notably in Portsmouth and also indeed the wrong naming and shaming of some people (Williams and Thompson, 2004a, 2004b). A consequence of these disturbances was the growth of a fairly united professional opinion *against* widespread notification. The fear was that a more public process would have the effect of driving offenders underground, making their supervision and management all the more difficult. The compromise outcome was a limited form of notification and known popularly as Sarah's Law. The Child Sex Offender Disclosure scheme was rolled out across England and Wales in 2011 (see Kemshall et al, 2012), with similar measures in Scotland and Northern Ireland. This measure allows for members of the public to formally ask the police if someone with access to a child has a record of child sexual offences. This measure has though been criticised by the NSPCC (2012) as a 'postcode lottery' with variable responses from police forces. As a result of freedom of information request they found that only one in six applications resulted in information being disclosed.

It should therefore be clear that public protection processes have grown significantly over the past two or three decades. Sentences have been increased in severity with, for example, a short-term experiment with indeterminate sentences for public protection, introduced in the Criminal Justice Act 2003. These sentences allowed courts to pass an indeterminate sentence (rather like a life sentence) for serious offences specified in the Act. There was to be a risk calculation involved in the sentence and it meant that it was passed as much for risk of future offending as it was the instant offence. It was therefore essentially preventative but, of course, preventative of what might not actually happen. A real problem arose with these sentences in that they became extremely attractive to sentencers. This is perhaps not surprising as it ensured that any risk was passed to others, namely the Parole Board, who were charged with assessing the prisoner for release. From the start it was evident that offenders were receiving an IPP for crimes which might, in its absence, have earned only a short custodial sentence. The problem then arose that these prisoners found it enormously difficult to earn their release on licence. As the sentence was risk based then so was the release decision. To do this, prisoners were expected to take part in prison based programmes which aimed to reduce the prisoner's risk of offending on release such as alcohol and drug programmes, anger management courses and so on. The sudden influx of significant numbers of IPP prisoners meant that the programmes could not keep up with demand and prisoners were therefore being detained way beyond their recommended minimum release date. Between the IPP introduction in 2005 and its abolition in 2012, 8,771 sentences were passed. In 2017 the *Guardian* newspaper reported that 3,300 were still awaiting release, five years after abolition, with most considerably beyond their initial tariff date. The chairman of the Parole Board, Nick Hardwick, has suggested that the Board might reduce the numbers of IPP prisoners to 1,500 by 2020 by speeding up their processes and has said that, if government requires a faster outcome, it will need legislation saying the following could be considered:

- Revising the risk test so that prisoners only continue to be detained if there is evidence they remain a danger to the public.
- Introducing that measure just for 'short tariff' IPPs – those who received a tariff of two years or less but remain in prison long after their tariff has expired because they are unable to prove their risk has reduced.
- Taking executive action to release IPP prisoners who have now served longer than the maximum current sentence for their offence.

IPPs were abolished as a result of a European Court ruling that the sentence violated human rights. Unfortunately, in an attempt to both act tough and appease the media, successive governments have introduced populist measures that have needed to be reversed either because they are unworkable, unjust or just too popular and therefore over-used.

The current situation

So where are we now in dealing with sex offenders? Essentially they are governed by a risk-based matrix. They are by definition 'risky' because of the public and media response to their criminal activities. This covers almost all sexual offending; there is little discrimination over nature and type of offending although it does remain the case that domestic sexual offending still appears to be downgraded in terms of seriousness in the public consciousness. The focus on risk is both retrospective and prospective. It is retrospective because any previous sexual offending is regarded as automatically increasing the risk posed by the offender. They become more serious offenders by the nature of their previous actions. As a result of this, they become a much higher risk for future offending. Despite clear evidence that sexual offenders pose no greater risk of repeating their behaviour than other offenders – indeed that risk may well be lower – they are assumed to pose a much higher risk. This is a result of the *nature* of their offending rather than its likelihood of repetition. Therefore, they become prime candidates to be punished for what they might do in the future to a greater degree than other offenders.

This poses something of an ethical dilemma and of course touches on the principles underpinning the sentencing process. Should anyone be punished for what they have yet to do? This is not necessarily about increasing punishment for what has been done in the past (a lengthy criminal record, say) but for what might happen in the future because the defendant is a particular type of offender. Despite numerous attempts to improve the assessment and prediction of risk, it remains an elusive goal to tie it down with any degree of prediction, with numerous commentators suggesting that the prospects stubbornly remain at little better than evens (see for example the excellent short article by Scott, 1977). If it is therefore difficult to predict with accuracy what might happen in the future and with real evidence suggesting a lower reoffending rate, what is the justification for treating sex offenders so differently? Although their perceived level of risk is the underlying justification, their essential 'otherness' allows them to be dealt with in such different ways. Certainly the public, fed by a steady drip of sensational media stories, are unlikely to sanction any softening of the line. High profile SFOs (Nash and Williams, 2008) also stoke the fires of populist punitivism, despite their very low numbers. Sex offenders are therefore not only punished disproportionately at the beginning of their sentence but also find it 'extended' in the sense that they have to prove they have lowered their risk in order to secure an earlier release, a notable difficulty under the infamous IPP sentences. Equally, even if released at the normal point of their sentence or if subject to a community punishment, their assessed level of risk will determine the degree of control and supervision that they face. As already noted, in the United States this process might involve very widespread community notification and severely restrictive residency requirements. In the UK controls are more discreet and restrained but there is scope for limited public disclosure alongside potential restrictions on residency, employment and travel. If the risk is deemed to warrant it then satellite tracking or even constant surveillance may be authorised. However, such measures introduce us to another problem: resources. The higher the perceived risk and the greater the degree of control and monitoring, the greater amount of resources required. With the scale of public sector cutbacks in recent years, including the police and probation services (see Pycroft, in this volume), it is not difficult to see that, given the 'risk hype' associated with sex offenders, there would be a temptation to de-escalate risk as the resources are not available to service intensive supervision plans.

Another assumption underpinning the public protection process is that resources should be deployed to the greatest risk. Yet risk is fluid and dynamic and it is a moot point to suggest that resources and experienced and skilled professionals should 'follow the risk'. Figures for serious further offending (Ministry of Justice, 2017b) suggest that the vast majority of repeat serious crimes committed by known offenders are committed by those in the lowest tier of risk (Level 1 offenders). It may well be the case that, because by far the greatest number of MAPPA offenders are categorised as a Level 1 risk, these greater numbers are more likely to produce a greater number of SFOs. Even if the numbers of SFOs at each level of risk are skewed by their overall numbers, it remains the case that more than 200 offenders in 2016–17, assessed at the lowest level of risk, went on to commit a serious further offence. These offenders would have been subject to the least restrictive supervision plans and, as likely as not, with only one agency overseeing them in the community. Equally, it can be argued that the very small numbers of SFOs committed by Level 2 and 3 MAPPA offenders suggest that the additional attention to their monitoring is effective. That may well be the case but the continued and increasing numbers of SFOs committed by Level 1 offenders must be a worry and a warning that risk is not to be boxed off into categories that then determine punishment and supervision.

Conclusion

Sex offenders have driven the criminal justice agenda for over three decades. Indeed, they have succeeded in shaping a 'public protection' system with seriousness, risk and harm at the very forefront of the agenda. Violence related offenders have to a certain extent been dragged along in this process but sex offenders remain the drivers of punitive policies which themselves have knock on effects throughout the criminal justice process. Much of the legislation and policy has echoed that passed in the United States, although with degrees of restraint to curb the worst excesses. At the same time there have been beacons of hope such as Circles of Trust, a volunteer-based charitable organisation that aims to supervise and intensively support sex offenders in the community. Their success rates (in terms of their clients' reoffending rates) have been remarkably good but a lack of resources prevents a wider roll out of the programme. The structure devised to manage serious sexual and violent offenders, MAPPA, has grown into a large and amorphous grouping of agencies, many of whom would not have regarded themselves as part of criminal justice or public protection. On paper and in terms of reconvictions for the highest risk offenders, the system would appear to work. However, the numbers of problems occurring with those assessed at the lower end of the risk spectrum must raise questions about an overly simplified risk-based classification system.

MAPPA caseload numbers continue to grow, not least because the number of sex offenders increases each year as more are added than removed from the sex offenders register. With austerity measures ensuring efficiency savings are the order of the day in the Home Office and Ministry of Justice, it seems more a matter of when and not if another serious case is spread across the media, that will trigger demands for even tougher measures.

Case study

This fictional case study is designed to help you think through some of the issues raised in this chapter by asking you to assess and manage the risk posed by the offender. You should think about how he should be managed in the community; the level of intervention necessary to protect the public, balanced with his human rights; and any measures that might assist with his non-offending rehabilitation.

John is nearing the end of his 16-month prison sentence – he has served 8 months. He was convicted for five separate acts of indecent exposure; he exposed himself to mostly older female children (10–12) who he came across in quiet places. His penis was erect on each occasion. He did not speak to or threaten the girls... indeed, at the subsequent trial, it emerged that many simply laughed at him (although this is not to say this wasn't a fear-based response). However, he was reported to the police when one of the girls told her mother of the incident. John was quite well known in the community where he had lived all his life. He is now 23 years old, a large man who lived with his widowed mother. He has a patchy work record, mostly jobbing gardening. He did not achieve well at school and is generally regarded by those who know him as 'slow'.

He has a criminal record stretching back to age 18. He has three previous convictions for exposure but none, until the present sentence, has resulted in custody. He has been supervised by the Probation Service on one previous occasion where he was seen as a low risk, non-threatening individual. Most of the work carried out with him on that occasion was aimed at securing him employment and encouraging him to find friends of his own age. He has always felt comfortable in the company of those younger than himself.

He found his first experience of custody very difficult and was very worried that he would be beaten up for being a sex offender. During his sentence, which was spent on a sex offender wing, he was seen to befriend a number of known paedophiles, one of whom is due to be released at much the same time as John and to be returning to an adjacent area. This other offender has a long criminal history of child sex offending, including sexual assault.

John will return to live with his mother. She finds his behaviour difficult but does not see him as a serious risk. She believes he lacks confidence and does what he does because he is inadequate. He is her only child. He does not have any work to return to.

He will be supervised for a total of 12 months following release (8 months on licence and 4 on post release supervision). He will have to notify the police of his details under the sex offender registration requirements.

Issues for you
1. What do you perceive to be John's risk level in MAPPA terms? Are you thinking of risk of offending or seriousness of harm? Or both? On what do you base your assessment?
2. What would you include in his supervision plan based on your assessment of risk?

3. Is the plan inclined more towards restrictive measures? What might these be and why would you include them? Are there places, or people, from whom you would wish to restrict or forbid contact? What would be the purpose of this?

4. How frequently should he be seen by his probation officer?

5. How frequently should the police see him as a registered sex offender?

6. Are there any constructive measures that you would like to include in his supervision plan?

7. What might these be?

8. What period would you set before his risk level and the plan are reassessed?

Summary of key learning points

- The issue of sex offenders is emotive and this can lead to legal and policy developments which are often more geared towards media headlines than sound and effective practice
- The importance of victims is belatedly growing in importance and having an impact upon decision-making in criminal justice
- The risk posed by sex offenders is often inflated by their presentation as the 'other' or 'monsters'. The vast majority pose very few risks to the public but their perceived status ensures that elaborate and inclusive management processes are established which over-stretch scarce resources
- Risk assessment tools increasingly underpin decision-making but perhaps the lesson of Worboys should be that as much detailed consideration as possible needs to be obtained and that over-inclusive processes deny practitioners the time they need to undertake this task
- It should be understood that the 'exceptionalism' applied to sex offenders can drag along the whole criminal justice process to a much harsher place

Notes

[1]   The following web references are a summary of Parole Board and legal findings in the Worboys case: www.gov.uk/government/news/parole-board-welcomes-findings-from-moj-review-including-the-introduction-of-a-reconsideration-mechanism www.gov.uk/government/news/parole-board-statement-following-decision-of-judicial-review-in-the-case-of-john-worboys www.judiciary.uk/wp-content/uploads/2018/03/dsd-nbv-v-parole-board-and-ors-summary.pdf www.gov.uk/government/news/parole-board-welcomes-findings-from-moj-review-including-the-introduction-of-a-reconsideration-mechanism www.gov.uk/government/news/parole-board-welcomes-findings-from-moj-review-including-the-introduction-of-a-reconsideration-mechanism

[2]   Sexual offending is a very under-reported crime so the figure cited here is likely to be higher in reality.

References

Agamben, G. (1998) *Homo sacer; Sovereign power and bare life*. Stanford, CA: Stanford University Press.

Corrigan, R. (2006) 'Making meaning of Megan's Law', *Law and Social Inquiry*, 31(2): 267–312.

Cullen, E. (2018) 'Oxfam to appoint independent commission to investigate sex claims threatening charities future', *Independent*, 16 February, www.independent. co.uk/news/uk/home-news/oxfam-sexual-exploitation-crisis-independent- commission-investigation-winnie-byanyima-charity-a8213396.html

Davies, C. (2018) 'Sadistic paedophile Matthew Falder jailed for 32 years', *Guardian*, 19 February, www.theguardian.com/technology/2018/feb/19/dark- web-paedophile-matthew-falder-jailed-for-32-years

Furedi, F. (2002) *Culture of fear*. London: Continuum.

Garland, D. (1996) 'The limits of the sovereign state, strategies of crime control in contemporary society', *The British Journal of Criminology*, 36(4): 445–471.

Janus, E.S. (2006) *Failure to protect: America's sexual predator laws and the rise of the preventive state*. Ithaca, NY: Cornell University Press, pp 316–334.

Kemshall, H. and Wood, J. with Westwood, S., Stout, B., Wilkinson, B., Kelly, G. and Mackenzie, G. (2010) *Child Sex Offender Review (CSOR) Public Disclosure Pilots: a process evaluation*. Second edition. London: Home Office.

Kemshall, H., Kelly, G. and Wilkinson, B. (2012) 'Child Sex Offender Public Disclosure Scheme: the view of applicants using the English pilot disclosure scheme', *Journal of Sexual Aggression*, 18(2): 164–178, https://doi.org/10.1080 /13552600.2011.552987

Lieb, R. (2003) 'Joined-up worrying the multi-agency public protection panels', in A. Matravers (ed), *Sex offenders in the community: managing and reducing the risk,* Cullompton: Willan Publishing, pp 207–218.

Ministry of Justice (2017a) *Proven Reoffending Statistics Quarterly Bulletin*, October 2015 to December 2015, National Statistics, 26 October, www.gov.uk/ government/uploads/system/uploads/attachment_data/file/658379/proven- reoffending-bulletin-oct15-dec15.pdf

Ministry of Justice (2017b) Multi Agency Public Protection Arrangements Annual Report, 2016/7. https://assets.publishing.service.gov.uk/government/uploads/ system/uploads/attachment_data/file/655022/MAPPA-annual-report-2016-17.pdf

Nash, M. (1999a) *Police, probation and protecting the public*. London: Blackstone Press.

Nash, M. (1999b) 'Enter the Polibation Officer', *International Journal of Police Science and Management*, 1(4): 360–368.

Nash, M. and Williams, A. (2008) *The anatomy of serious further offending*. Oxford: Oxford University Press.

NSPCC (2012) '"Sarah's Law" postcode lottery may leave children at risk from sexual abuse', 30 July, www.nspcc.org.uk/what-we-do/news-opinion/sarahs- law-postcode-lottery/

O'Malley, P. (2000) 'Risk societies and the government of crime', in M. Brown and J. Pratt (eds), *Dangerous offenders: punishment and social order*. London: Routledge, pp 17–33.

ONS (2017) 'Office for National Statistics, Sexual Offences in England and Wales, Year ending March 2017', www.ons.gov.uk/peoplepopulationandcommunity/crimeandjustice/articles/sexualoffencesinenglandandwales/yearendingmarch2017

Rose, N. (2000) 'Government and control', *British Journal of Criminology*, 40 (2): 321–339.

Savage, S.P. and Charman, S. (2010) 'Public protectionism and: Sarah's Law': exerting pressure through single issue campaigns, in M. Nash and A. Williams (eds) *The handbook of public protection*, Abingdon: Willan Publishing.

Scott, P. (1977) 'Assessing dangerousness in criminals', *British Journal of Psychiatry*, 131: 127–142.

Simon, J. (1999) 'Managing the monstrous. Sex offenders and the new penology', *Psychology, Public Policy, and Law*, 4(1–2): 452–467, http://psycnet.apa.org/doi Landing?doi=10.1037%2F1076-8971.4.1-2.452

Sturge, G. (2018) 'House of Commons Briefing Paper, UK Prison Population Statistics', https://researchbriefings.parliament.uk/ResearchBriefing/Summary/SN04334

Taylor, D. (2018) 'Barry Bennell branded "sheer evil" as he is sentenced to 30 years', *Guardian*, 19 February, www.theguardian.com/football/2018/feb/19/barry-bennell-branded-sheer-evil-as-he-is-sentenced-to-31-years

Thompson, B. and Greek, C. (2010) 'Sex offender notification: policy imperatives, effectives and consequences in the United States', in M. Nash and A. Williams (eds), *The handbook of public protection*. Abingdon: Willan Publishing.

Williams, A. and Thompson, B. (2004a) 'Vigilance of vigilantes: the Paulsgrove riots and policing paedophiles in the community, part 1: the long slow fuse', *Police Journal*, 77: 99–119.

Williams, A. and Thompson, B. (2004b) 'Vigilance of vigilantes: the Paulsgrove riots and policing paedophiles in the community, part 2: the lessons of Paulsgrove', *Police Journal*, 77: 199–205.

Further reading

Karstedt, S. (2002) 'Emotions and criminal justice', *Theoretical Criminology*, 6(3): 299–317.

Kemshall, H. and Maguire, M. (2001) 'Public protection, partnership and risk penality: the multi-agency risk management of sexual and violent offenders', *Punishment and Society*, 3(2): 237–264.

Nash, M. (2006) *Public protection and the criminal justice process*. Oxford: Oxford University Press.

Nash, M.R. (2016) '"Scum cuddlers": police offender managers and the sex offenders' register in England and Wales', *Policing and Society: An International Journal of Research and Policy*, 36(4): 411–427.

Nash, M. and Williams, A. (2010) *The handbook of public protection*. Abingdon: Willan Publishing.

6

Protection and prevention: identifying, managing and monitoring priority perpetrators of domestic abuse

Jacki Tapley and Zoë Jackson

Aims of the chapter
- To provide a legislative and policy overview of responses to domestic abuse.
- To review responses to the problem of serial domestic abuse.
- To highlight the problems caused by a lack of agreed definitions and national responses to domestic abuse.
- To examine the development of MARAC and examples of good practice in multi-agency working.

Introduction

In the first edition of this book, the chapter by Tapley (2010) examined the historical and political context that contributed to the development of multi-agency partnerships to support and protect victims of domestic abuse. This chapter builds on that previous work to explore how a greater emphasis on prevention, in addition to and not *instead of* protection, could assist in improving and strengthening the multi-agency response to domestic abuse, and contribute significantly to reducing its prevalence. In particular, this chapter focuses on the need for a more robust management and monitoring of repeat, high-risk perpetrators and will consider the example of Multi-Agency Risk Assessment Conferences (MARACs).

Criminal justice responses to domestic abuse

The significance of the developments in criminal justice policy and practice in response to domestic abuse during the last three decades is indisputable. A combination of feminist campaigning and activism, an expansion of the crime-control landscape and the politicisation of crime victims has resulted in a salient shift from a non-interventionist approach towards domestic violence to the promotion of interagency collaborations and increasing powers to intervene, support and protect victims (Tapley, 2010; Hegemann-White et al, 2015). This shift is reflected in the growth of civil and legal remedies introduced to protect victims of domestic abuse and the increasing responsibilities placed on statutory and non-statutory agencies to improve the protection and safety of victims of domestic abuse (Strickland and Allen, 2017).

Earlier revisions to the non-statutory definition of domestic abuse to include young people aged 16 to 17 and an acknowledgement of coercive and controlling behaviour (Home Office, 2013) demonstrate an increased understanding of the nature of domestic abuse and recognition of its repetitive and pervasive nature. Previously, criminal justice responses to domestic abuse have been restrained and bound by a criminal justice system geared towards the prosecution of single acts. However, this approach has failed to reflect the reality of victims' experiences, often involving an ongoing pattern of multiple forms of abuse rather than one isolated incident. It is now hoped that, with the recognition of coercive and controlling behaviour as a criminal offence, as introduced by Section 76 of the Serious Crime Act 2015, we will move beyond perceptions of domestic abuse as predominantly one-off incidences of physical violence and towards a legal definition that recognises the persistent and insidious nature of domestic abuse, resulting in prosecutors bringing criminal charges that more accurately reflect the harm being done, and also provide greater clarity and consistency in convictions and sentencing.

There is now some optimism that sentencing in cases of domestic abuse may finally start to reflect the true extent of the harm caused, with the Sentencing Council proposing new guidelines for how people convicted of intimidatory offences, and offences involving domestic abuse, should be sentenced. These proposals are further evidence of a shift in attitude, proposing that abuse between people known to each other should be taken *more seriously* than abuse committed by strangers:

> It brings a distinct change in emphasis in relation to seriousness. Previously, guidelines stated that offences committed in a domestic context should be seen as no less serious than those in a non-domestic context, whereas the new guideline emphasises that the fact an offence took place in a domestic context makes it more serious. This is because domestic abuse is rarely a one-off incident, it is likely to become increasingly frequent and more serious the longer it continues, and

may result in death. It can also lead to lasting trauma for victims and their children. (Sentencing Council, 2018)

Importantly, the publication of the new guidelines takes into account new legislation introduced in recent years to address abuse undertaken within the context of an intimate relationship, including for the first time guidelines that have been produced for stalking, and for the offences of disclosing private sexual images, and controlling and coercive behaviour. The Council states that its aim in introducing the guidelines, subject to public consultation, is to provide consistent and comprehensive guidance for judges and magistrates in sentencing these related offences (Sentencing Council, 2018).

While still no specific criminal offence of domestic abuse currently exists, there has been a momentum towards the development of additional and significant legislative remedies, in addition to those already referred to above. Since the publication of the coalition government's strategy *Call to end violence against women and girls* (Home Office, 2010: 5), which set out a vision for a 'robust cross-government approach', such remedies have included the national implementation of the Domestic Violence Disclosure Scheme, the introduction of Domestic Violence Protection Orders in 2014, and the Protection of Freedoms Act 2012 created two new offences of stalking (CPS, 2017). In 2017, the government announced plans to draft a Domestic Violence and Abuse Bill, outlining plans for the Courts Bill to end the direct cross-examination of domestic abuse victims by alleged perpetrators in the family courts and to extend the use of virtual hearings (cited by Strickland and Allen, 2017). These plans were reiterated in 2018, when Theresa May launched a public consultation on the Bill, pledging to provide a statutory definition of domestic abuse and new Domestic Abuse Protection Orders, which could include the electronic tagging of perpetrators as a condition of the Order (Home Office, 2018). However, for these measures to have a meaningful impact on the lives of victims, it is essential that the government moves beyond the rhetoric and makes available sufficient funding and training. Continued cuts in funding for both statutory and non-statutory agencies have impacted negatively on the ability of agencies to implement reforms (HMIC, 2017) and their effectiveness as mechanisms to actually reduce domestic abuse continue to be challenged.

Measuring the effectiveness of responses to domestic abuse

While the introduction of legal remedies is largely seen as a welcome initiative, Walklate (2007: 111) described such criminal justice responses as 'tinkering with adversarialism', and argued that 'it is the adversarial system of justice itself that is frequently the barrier to the ultimate success or failure of the kinds of policy initiatives to be discussed here'. While criminal justice processes remain a barrier and commentators remain doubtful of the effectiveness of criminal justice approaches in reducing domestic abuse (Robinson, 2015), official data indicates that reforms are resulting in more arrests and successful prosecutions. The CPS (2016: 1) announced that it was 'prosecuting, and convicting, more defendants of domestic abuse, rape, sexual offences and child abuse in 2015–2016 than ever before'. However, whether an increase in arrests and prosecutions alone are having a deterrent effect on the extent of domestic abuse remains disputed, with commentators suggesting that a more targeted and consistent response by agencies has a greater impact:

> Overall the evidence suggests that a clear and decisive response by statutory agencies, condemning violence, along with good protection measures, is a more effective deterrent of re-offending than either arrest or incarceration alone. (Hegemann-White et al, 2015: 62)

Given the complexities and hidden nature of domestic abuse, the high levels of under-reporting, inconsistencies in criminal justice practices and the inherent biases associated with official data, it is difficult to conclude whether an increased criminal justice response is having a deterrent effect. In addition, evidence as to whether actual incidences of domestic abuse are declining is controversial and disputed. Data published by the ONS (2016) measuring domestic abuse in England and Wales, suggested that a cumulative effect of changes in recent years has resulted in 'significantly lower prevalence for the year ending March 2016 (6.1%) compared with the year ending March 2012 (7.0%), indicating a longer-term downward trend'. However, Walby et al (2015) challenge the methodology used and argue that the capping of incidents to five by official statisticians excludes the experiences of 'high frequency' victims, in particular, victims of domestic abuse, thereby challenging 'the ubiquity of the drop in violent crime' (Walby et al, 2015: 1204).

Further statistics published in 2017 reported an 18% rise in violent crime, with data from March 2015 to March 2017 demonstrating increases in crime accelerating from 3% to 10% in the last 12 months. Although it is argued that the rise is due in part to improvements in recording practices, increases in crime do factor in a number of categories (Flatley, cited by Travis, 2017). While police data indicates a 19% rise in offences involving violence against the person, it has been suggested that 40% of this increase is accounted for by the inclusion of certain types of harassment offences for the first time (Travis, 2017). However, a joint inspection undertaken by Her Majesty's Inspectorate of Constabulary (HMIC) and Her Majesty's Crown Prosecution Service Inspectorate (HMCPSI) (2017) found that, despite changes in legislation, police sometimes mis-recorded stalking offences or did not record them at all, thereby casting doubt that a 40% increase could be due to the inclusion of harassment offences. Instead it could suggest a significant under-representation of the number of cases being reported to the police, compared with those actually being recorded.

Given the difficulties in attaining an accurate picture of the extent of domestic abuse, taking into account the level of under-reporting, inconsistencies in criminal justice practices and the limitations of official data, it can confidently be argued that still greater efforts need to be made in order to ensure that the government's commitments outlined in the *Strategy to end violence against women and girls: 2016 to 2020* (Home Office, 2016) can be achieved.

Support, protection and prevention

Strategies to tackle domestic abuse typically focus on three key areas: measures to prevent abuse occurring in the first instance; timely and comprehensive support for victims; and holding perpetrators accountable for their behaviour. Following publication of the white paper *Justice for All* (Home Office, 2002: 4), with its aim to 'rebalance the system in favour of victims, witnesses and communities and to deliver justice to all', the government published 'Safety and Justice' (Home Office, 2003). This policy document identified three key elements for tackling domestic violence: prevention, protection and support for victims. Despite 'prevention' being one of the key elements, only a small section of the report focused on the perpetrator and reducing reoffending, while a greater focus was placed on changing public attitudes (particularly of young people) and providing help for victims of domestic violence as early as possible to prevent the violence recurring.

Although responses to the white paper (Home Office, 2002) called for the creation of a register of domestic violence offenders (along the lines of the register of sex offenders), in order to improve information sharing between agencies, inform risk assessments and alert new partners, it was decided that:

> The combination of a pro-arrest policy by the police with the new legal protection outlined in this consultation paper means that victims of domestic violence should receive significant extra protection from the law without establishing a register of offenders. (Home Office, 2003: 37)

The government's reluctance to track and monitor potentially high-risk domestic abuse perpetrators raises a number of concerns. In particular, its approach places greater responsibility on the victims of domestic abuse to take action to avoid domestic abuse and to seek the provision of support and protection if abuse occurs, rather than tackling the root causes of domestic abuse – that is, the repeated behaviour of the perpetrator. This is despite a specific recommendation to do so being supported by the Association of Chief Police Officers (ACPO) (2009) in a review commissioned by the Home Secretary on 'tackling perpetrators of violence against women and girls'.

In total, the ACPO Review (2009) made ten proposals, of which six have been wholly or partially implemented, including: Proposal 1, the introduction of MARACs nationally in 2011 (although they remain non-statutory); Proposal 2, the introduction of a Domestic Violence Disclosure Scheme in 2014, implementing a 'right to know'; Proposal 4, the criminalisation of coercive and controlling behaviour in 2015 (by acknowledging a 'course of conduct'); Proposal 6, the introduction of Domestic Violence Protection Orders in 2014; Proposal 8, the introduction of conditional cautions for domestic abuse, although these must be referred to a prosecutor due to concerns regarding the suitability of conditional cautions in cases of domestic abuse (CPS, 2013); and Proposal 9, an obligation for health professionals to report female genital mutilation (FGM), subsequently included in the Serious Crime Act 2015, which made further amendments to the Female Genital Mutilation Act 2003 to extend the protection of victims and potential victims.

Proposal 10 called for the introduction of a new homicide offence of 'liability for suicide' and while there has been no change in legislation, Nicholas Allen was found guilty of manslaughter in 2017 on a charge brought by the CPS of 'unlawful killing'. The victim, Justene Reece, a former partner of Allen, had left the relationship when his behaviour became obsessive and controlling. Following a sustained six-month campaign of intimidation, threats and stalking against Justene and members of her family, she committed suicide. The perpetrator, Allen, was a serial offender, having previous convictions for violence against women dating back to 1998. He was subsequently sentenced to a 15-year extended sentence with the judge indicating his belief that Allen had caused Reece to lose her life and that 'she committed suicide as a direct result of your sustained and determined criminal actions, actions which you knew were having a profound effect upon her' (Connett, 2017).

However, despite legal remedies now starting to acknowledge the repetitive and serial nature of domestic abuse, no action has been taken to implement the recommendation made by the ACPO Review for a wider recognition, and improved management, of serial perpetrators of violence against women and girls, in particular, Proposal 3 – 'This Review recommends that the law be changed to permit the registration and "tracking" of serial perpetrators of violence against women and girls' (ACPO, 2009: 15) – despite this echoing the earlier calls made in response to the white paper *Justice for All* (Home Office, 2002) discussed earlier.

This chapter will now go on to critically examine why there remains no consistent framework that provides for the tracking and monitoring of high-risk, prolific offenders, and explores calls for a national model to assist in a multi-agency approach to strengthen prevention strategies aimed at tackling domestic abuse.

Identifying, monitoring and managing 'priority perpetrators' of domestic abuse

The true pervasiveness of serial domestic abuse offending in the UK is unknown, and attempts to quantify this offender cohort to date have been relatively limited. In 2009, the ACPO estimated that there were as many as 25,000 serial perpetrators (defined as those who have used or threatened violence or abuse against two or more victims) in contact with police at any one time in the UK (ACPO, 2009: 28), while research by Hester and Westmarland (2006) suggested that up to 18% of domestic abuse perpetrators who reoffend do so against a different partner. Although these figures include both conviction and non-conviction data (arrests, cautions), they are nevertheless likely to represent a significant under-representation of the issue given that many incidents of domestic abuse never reach the point of a police report (Walby et al, 2015: 2, 6).

While an accurate assessment of the prevalence of serial domestic abuse offending remains elusive, it is nevertheless acknowledged as a 'sizeable problem' (ACPO, 2009: 8), both in terms of volume and presenting risk. At a base level, previous domestic abuse offending is the strongest predictor of future abusive behaviour, and as abusive behaviour repeats, it escalates – both in frequency and severity, thereby increasing the risk of serious further harm to the victim(s) concerned (Hester and Westmarland, 2006: 35; Sonkin, 1987 cited in Richards et al, 2008: 128–129.) Crucially, however, the risks posed by those who perpetrate repeated and/or high-risk domestic abuse are not confined solely to their ex/intimate partners, and those engaged in serial, serious or sexually abusive behaviours within their relationships often replicate this behaviour outside of an ex/intimate partner context (Richards, 2004: 7). Further, as their behaviour repeats, escalates and permeates outside of the home environment, these individuals tend to become increasingly adept at avoiding police and wider criminal justice system involvement (Richards, 2004: 14). Speaking about her work analysing serial and sexual offending in the Metropolitan policing area of London, Richards (2004: 27) summarises:

> Many are serial offenders, who go from one abusive relationship to the next, are violent to other significant women in their lives and other people. Two perpetrators had killed their first wives. Once a violent man leaves the partner, it does not mean the violence ends. Evidence suggests that many find new partners to abuse. This is why they need to be risk-assessed and managed. Information about specific abusers needs to be shared amongst professionals.

Serial perpetrators can therefore best be described as a subgroup of chronic, repeat offenders who present the greatest risk of physical harm not only to their partners, but also to women in general, and are likely to be known to the police for other offences (Scott et al, 2015: 274). On the basis that two women a week are killed by a current or former partner in England and Wales alone (ONS, 2015), the importance of tackling serial and high-risk abusive behaviour robustly and effectively is not just a public protection issue, but also a matter of homicide prevention.

Despite this, and a commitment by ACPO in 2009 to the 'wider recognition, and improved management, of serial perpetrators of violence against women and girls' (ACPO, 2009: 6), there still exists no consistent framework providing for the identification, tracking and management of serial domestic abuse perpetrators in England and Wales (HMIC, 2014; Paladin, 2014). Most police forces 'do not have a systematic approach to targeting repeat or prolific perpetrators of domestic abuse' (HMIC, 2014: 106), and few routinely include domestic abuse perpetrators within well-established offender management mechanisms, such as the Integrated Offender Management Process (HMIC, 2015a: 96). Equally, only a small number of policing areas incorporate a multi-agency element into their responses (Jackson, 2016), despite collaborative working and effective information sharing being recognised as best practice in the response to domestic abuse (Tapley, 2010; Home Office, 2014). In addition, despite recommendations by ACPO (2009) and many others (Richards, 2004; Paladin, 2014; Plaid Cymru, 2017) that a national register of serial domestic abuse perpetrators be established as a priority, in order to facilitate a more consistent and robust response to these offenders, no such mechanism currently exists.

Against this background of varied operational provision is an ever-growing body of learning from fatal cases, positioning this area of work as a pressing policy issue. Since their introduction in 2011, Domestic Homicide Reviews (DHRs) continue to identify perpetrators whose behaviour was known to agencies, well in advance of the fatal incident, to be serial in nature. In case after case, however, the way this behaviour has been drawn together and understood in terms of risk has been fundamentally flawed. This, in turn, has translated into ineffective offender management, absent in both effective information sharing and multi-agency working, with tragically fatal consequences.

> Mr L is a serial perpetrator; however, the developing systems of support and protection have understandably focused on victims. Tracking, responding to and dealing with serial perpetrators is less well developed as a method of protecting victims. This is just starting to change but the circumstances of this review underline the need for it. The learning from this review stems almost entirely from the knowledge of events and interventions in the perpetrator's 2 previous relationships. This is fitting as it contributes to a growing body of knowledge that suggests tracking and management of serial perpetrators has a significant role in protecting future potential victims. (Ashman, 2014a: 5)

Common to each analysis of the circumstances surrounding these deaths are calls for a more consistent, robust and multi-agency response to serial and high-risk perpetrators of domestic abuse (Davis, 2016; South and Vale Community Safety Partnership and Oxfordshire Safeguarding Children Board, 2016; Warren, 2015; Ashman, 2014a, 2014b; Lundberg, 2014). McAteer (2015: 76) asks:

> How are known perpetrators identified and how are the risks that they pose to others assessed? For example, an initial incident may not be serious, but if it is perpetrated by someone known to present high risks to partners, how can this be factored in and influence the overall risk assessment and risk management plan?

While there is a lack of national consistency in relation to this cohort of offenders, at the same time and in contrast, there are notable pockets of isolated good practice emerging. The Metropolitan Police Service (MPS), for example, has initiated Operation Dauntless, whereby it is actively tracking between 400 and 500 serial cross-border domestic abuse offenders (Duvall, 2017: 5). In Wales, the introduction of the WISDOM (Wales Integrated Serious and Dangerous Offender Management) model has sought to develop existing integrated offender management (IOM) provisions, in order to manage high-risk offenders, including potential serial perpetrators (North Wales MAPPA, 2015; South Wales Police, 2016). Across Sussex, Essex and South Wales, the Drive project, a partnership between national organisations Safelives, Respect and Social Finance, targets high-risk perpetrators through a multi-agency response with the aim of promoting long-term behavioural change (Safelives, 2016). In Hampshire, the DAPP (Domestic Abuse Prevention Partnership) model includes a specific focus on the identification, tracking and monitoring of serial/priority perpetrators, incorporating explicit provisions for multi-agency information sharing (Hampton Trust, 2016; Morgan and Parks, 2018).

Introduced in 2011, the purpose of the MARAC is to provide a multi-agency framework where a variety of representatives, from both the statutory and voluntary sectors, can share information about high-risk victims of domestic abuse, in order to produce coordinated plans to increase victim safety (Steel et al, 2011: 1). There are approximately 250 MARACs currently operating across England and Wales.

While the focus of MARAC is the safety of the (adult) victim, it is essential that these meetings also consider the risks posed by the perpetrator, and incorporate strategies to address their abusive behaviour effectively (Safelives, 2019: 1). This is particularly crucial in relation to priority offenders, and MARACs undoubtedly have a key role to play in the identification of these perpetrators and the safeguarding of their victims. Whether this occurs effectively, however, will depend on local responses: where an individual area takes a robust approach to the identification and management of priority perpetrators as a whole, so it follows that they are more likely to demonstrate effective MARAC action planning in this arena.

The importance of the links between victim safety mechanisms – like the MARAC – and strategies to tackle priority perpetrators is now being recognised, albeit only in some areas. The Drive project, for example, utilises MARACs as the vehicle by which high-risk perpetrators are identified for intervention in the first instance (Hester et al, 2017: 4), and makes use of the information shared via that process to obtain a comprehensive picture of the abusive behaviour, and enable case managers to challenge perpetrators effectively (Hester et al, 2017: 38). Given that the approach to priority perpetrators is not nationally standardised, these links will not always be established. This is, then, perhaps another area in which the introduction of a register – and the standardisation of responses that could result from it – has the potential to enhance current practice.

Reflection

• What do you see as the strengths and weaknesses of having a national and standardised approach to managing priority domestic abuse perpetrators?

• What do you think can be learnt from the experience of MAPPA in this respect?

The variation in responses to serial and high-risk perpetrators across England and Wales can, to a certain extent, be attributed to the decentralised nature of policing (see Loveday and Roberts, this volume for a discussion of the role of Police and Crime Commissioners): in a system whereby each force is led independently by its own Chief Constable, it is perhaps unsurprising that there are well-documented challenges in ensuring both consistency of standards, and an adherence to national guidelines/best practice, as HMIC have previously noted:

> I have concerns about the extent to which some chief officers allow their forces to disregard what is required of them and adopt systems, processes and practices which are not consistent with national requirements … It is therefore disappointing to reflect on the number of occasions when HMIC has had to report that the recommendations in its reports have not been implemented adequately or, in too many instances, at all. (HMIC, 2015b: 27)

To suggest that decentralised policing is the primary reason behind a significant lack of consistency in the response, however, is to side-step a far more fundamental issue, namely that in this area of work there exist no clear 'national requirements'. There is no overarching legal framework, policy guidance or national model that provides for or sets out a framework on which to base the identification, tracking and monitoring of serial domestic abuse perpetrators in England and Wales (Jackson, 2016; HMIC, 2014, 2015a, Paladin, 2014, ACPO, 2009). In the absence of any formalised process, the response to these offenders will, naturally, remain dependent on the commitment, leadership and drive of agencies at a local level, and be subject to potentially significant inconsistencies in practice as a result.

These inconsistencies are evident not only in terms of practice, but also at a more micro level in the use of terminology. Work conducted in Wales by Clancy et al (2014: 5), for example, highlights 'substantial variability' in the interpretation of the term 'serial' across different agencies including the police, probation service and third sector organisations. This inconsistency, they suggest, proves not only prohibitive in terms of building up any accurate picture of prevalence, but also almost certainly impacts on the ability of agencies to monitor and manage high-risk abusers in any consistent manner (Clancy et al, 2014: 5). Going further, they observe that there are limited differences in offending patterns between those perpetrators identified as serial, and those identified as non-serial (Clancy et al, 2014: 36), suggesting that maintaining a focus solely on 'serial' offenders (designated as such by the existence of a fixed, numerical number of victims) only serves to side-line the risks presented by 'multiple dimensions of offending' (Clancy et al, 2014: 39).

The Welsh research is significant for a number of reasons. First, in highlighting the absence of a consensus on the definition and scope of the term 'serial perpetrators', it identifies an additional and fundamental barrier to the consistent national identification and effective management of the individuals who present the greatest risk. Second, it emphasises the need for agencies to broaden their understanding of risk as it relates to perpetrators of domestic abuse, moving beyond more formulaic, fixed definitions and towards a focus on the context of the individual's behaviour in its entirety. Robinson et al (2014: 39) suggest, instead, that serial perpetrators are best assessed alongside both repeat and high-risk domestic abuse offenders, to identify a cohort of 'priority perpetrators', who should then be targeted for a more intensive and multi-agency response.

It is perhaps unsurprising, given such disparity in both policy and practice, that calls for a register of serial domestic abuse offenders continues to grow, as a vehicle by which to bring about both greater consistency and more proactive management requirements in relation to the highest risk individuals (Paladin, 2014; Plaid Cymru, 2017; Change.org, 2019). A register mandated at a national policy level offers both the potential to 'shift the emphasis away from victims and on to the perpetrators' (Paladin, 2014) and the possibility of creating a more consistent, cross-border approach, avoiding any potential 'postcode lottery' created by the wide variation in current responses on the ground. While the introduction of a register would have both cost and resource implications, this is an outlay likely to be more than offset by cost savings in relation to victim care and homicide (Paladin, 2014). Indeed, ACPO have already acknowledged that a register offers 'significant financial and moral benefits ... enough to outweigh the additional burden and duty which would inevitably fall on the police if the requisite law is made available' (ACPO, 2009: 33).

There is, of course, no suggestion that the introduction of a serial or priority domestic abuse perpetrator register will be a panacea. However, the increasing calls for its introduction are representative of a growing sense that more needs to be done in this vital area of protection work and that a more joined-up, national approach is required. While the safeguarding of victims via both the expansion of mechanisms available for their support and protection, and effective multi-agency working has advanced over recent years, the fact remains that responses to perpetrators of domestic abuse have not developed with the same momentum (Hester et al, 2006) or in keeping with the same collaborative principles. This lack of progress is particularly evident in relation to those individuals whose behaviour is serial or high risk in nature (ACPO, 2009; Paladin, 2014; HMIC, 2014, 2015a), and even more so when considered against the established mechanisms that exist to target other areas of prolific offending (HMIC, 2014: 107) (see Williams, and also Nash, this volume).

The current response to these priority domestic abuse offenders is both inconsistent and at odds with recognised best practice in a field where prevention, collaboration and consistency are key. Local policing areas have been left to develop identification and management mechanisms in the absence of any clear national model or overarching guidance resulting, predictably, in a response that is not nationally coherent or comprehensive, despite the existence of pockets of good and, in some cases, excellent practice.

Conclusion

This chapter has sought to make clear that, while supporting victims remains absolutely crucial, providing support and protection through multi-agency partnerships together with the development of legal remedies, the strengthening of prevention strategies needs to become a priority and requires a national policy intervention. Evidence suggests that a more coordinated approach is needed, mandated at a national level and robustly led locally, which focuses not only on ensuring high-risk perpetrators take responsibility for their own behaviour, but also crucially focuses on disrupting their offending. The literature and research reviewed in this chapter indicates that this could be achieved by the introduction of a national register of priority or high-risk domestic abuse perpetrators, through which their ongoing management and tracking can be facilitated. Central to this process, however, must be a commitment to learning from examples of existing best practice, and a response that is underpinned by effective information and intelligence sharing among multi-agency partners, in order to hold perpetrators accountable, protect current victims and assist in the prevention of future victims.

Summary of key learning points
- There needs to be greater emphasis on prevention strategies in tackling domestic abuse.
- Multi agency arrangements need to be strengthened to both monitor and manage high risk and repeat perpetrators
- MARAC should be developed to fulfil these functions

References

Ashman, J. (2014a) 'Domestic homicide review 001 (Executive Summary)', www.lambeth.gov.uk/community-safety-and-anti-social-behaviour/abuse-and-violence/domestic-homicide-review-001

Ashman, J. (2014b) 'Domestic homicide review 001 (Overview Report)', www.lambeth.gov.uk/community-safety-and-anti-social-behaviour/abuse-and-violence/domestic-homicide-review-001

Association of Chief Police Officers (ACPO) (2009) *Tackling perpetrators of violence against women and girls: ACPO review for the Home Secretary.* https://webarchive.nationalarchives.gov.uk/+/http:/www.acpo.police.uk/asp/policies/Data/FINAL_MASTERViolence%20Review.doc

Change.org (2019) 'Create a stalkers register', online petition, www.change. org/p/rt-hon-theresa-may-mp-create-a-stalker-s-register

Clancy, A., Robinson, A. and Hanks, S. (2014) *Defining and profiling serial domestic abuse perpetrators: an all-Wales feasibility review.* Cardiff: Cardiff University, http:// orca.cf.ac.uk/63750/

Connett, D. (2017) 'Stalker jailed for manslaughter of former partner who killed herself', *Guardian*, 28 July, www.theguardian.com/uk-news/2017/jul/28/ stalker-jailed-manslaughter-former-partner-killed-herself-nicholas-allen-justene-reece

Crown Prosecution Service (CPS) (2013) 'Conditional cautioning', www.cps. gov.uk/about/cautioning.html

CPS (2016) *Violence against women and girls crime report 2015–16.* London: Crown Prosecution Service.

CPS (2017) 'Legal guidance: stalking and harassment', www.cps.gov.uk/legal/s_ to_u/stalking_and_harassment/

Davis, M. (2016) *Child D: A serious case review overview report.* Sutton Local Safeguarding Children Board, www.suttonlscb.org.uk/lscb-serious-case-reviews. php#gsc.tab=0

Duvall, L. (2017) *Domestic abuse in London: addressing the problem.* London Assembly Labour, www.london.gov.uk/sites/default/files/domestic_abuse_report_final_ copy_correction.pdf

Hampton Trust (2016) *DAPP: Domestic Abuse Prevention Partnership*, www. hamptontrust.org.uk/our-programmes/dapp/

Hegemann-White, C., Humphreys, C., Tutty, L.M. and Diemer, K. (2015) 'Overview of current policies on arrest, prosecution and protection by the police and the justice system as responses to domestic violence', in H. Johnson, B.S. Fisher and V. Jacquier (eds), *Critical issues on violence against women.* London: Routledge, pp 47–65.

Her Majesty's Inspectorate of Constabulary (HMIC) (2015a) *Increasingly everyone's business: improving the police response to domestic abuse*, www.justiceinspectorates. gov.uk/hmicfrs/publications/increasingly-everyones-business-a-progress-report-on-the-police-response-to-domestic-abuse/

HMIC (2015b) *State of policing. The annual assessment of policing in England and Wales*, www.justiceinspectorates.gov.uk/hmicfrs/publications/state-of-policing-the-annual-assessment-of-policing-in-england-and-wales-2015/

HMIC (2014) *Everyone's business: improving the police response to domestic abuse*, www. justiceinspectorates.gov.uk/hmicfrs/wp-content/uploads/2014/04/improving-the-police-response-to-domestic-abuse.pdf

HMIC (2017) *PEEL: Police effectiveness 2016. A national overview*, www. justiceinspectorates.gov.uk/hmicfrs/publications/peel-police-effectiveness-2016/

HMIC and Her Majesty's Crown Prosecution Service Inspectorate (2017) *Living in fear – the police and CPS response to harassment and stalking.* London: HMIC.

Scott, K., Heslop, L., Kelly, T. & Wiggins, K. (2015). Intervening to prevent repeat offending among moderate to high-risk domestic violence offenders: a second-responder programme for men. International Journal of Offender Therapy and Comparative Criminology 59(3), 273-294. DOI: 10.1177/0306624X13513709.

Hester, M., Eisenstadt, N., Jones, C. and Morgan, K. (2017) 'Evaluation of the Drive Project – a pilot to address high risk perpetrators of domestic abuse. Year 1 feasibility study', University of Bristol, Centre for Gender and Violence Research, http://driveproject.org.uk/wp-content/uploads/2017/11/Evaluation-of-the-Drive-Project-Year-1-Feasibility-Study.pdf

Hester, M. and Westmarland, N. (2006) 'Domestic violence perpetrators', *Criminal Justice Matters*, 66(1): 34–35, DOI: 10.1080/09627250608553400

Hester, M., Westmarland, N., Gangoli, G., Wilkinson, M., O'Kelly, C., Kent. A. and Diamond, D. (2006) *Domestic violence perpetrators: identifying needs to inform early intervention*. Bristol: University of Bristol in association with the Northern Rock Foundation and the Home Office, www.bristol.ac.uk/media-library/sites/sps/migrated/documents/rj4157researchreport.pdf

Home Office (2002) *Justice for all*. London: The Stationery Office.

Home Office (2003) *Safety and justice: The government's proposals on domestic violence*. London: Home Office. https://webarchive.nationalarchives.gov.uk/20100408150510/http://www.homeoffice.gov.uk/documents/2003-cons-domestic-violence-cons/domesticviolence2835.pdf?view=Binary

Home Office (2010) *Call to end violence against women and girls*. London: Home Office, www.gov.uk/government/publications/call-to-end-violence-against-women-and-girls

Home Office (2013) *Guidance: Domestic violence and abuse*. London: Home Office.

Home Office (2014) *Multi agency working and information sharing project: Final Report*. London: Home Office, www.gov.uk/government/publications/multi-agency-working-and-information-sharing-project

Home Office (2016) *Strategy to end violence against women and girls: 2016 to 2020*. Policy paper. Home Office: London.

Home Office (2018) 'Government takes action to tackle domestic abuse', www.gov.uk/government/news/government-takes-action-to-tackle-domestic-abuse

Jackson, Z. (2016) 'Developing a consistent response: the identification and management of serial perpetrators of domestic abuse in England and Wales', unpublished MSc thesis, University of Portsmouth.

Lundberg, B. (2014) *Domestic Homicide Review under section 9 of the Domestic Violence Crime and Victims Act 2004. In respect of the death of a woman B-DHR2012/13-04*. Birmingham Community Safety Partnership, http://birminghamcsp.org.uk/admin/resources/bdhr-2012-13-04-final-published.pdf

McAteer, K. (2015) *Domestic Homicide Review executive summary (DHR NB01). Report into the death of a domestic homicide victim on 2nd January 2012*. Nuneaton and Bedworth Community Safety Partnership, https://apps.warwickshire.gov.uk/api/documents/WCCC-671-68

Morgan, S. and Parkes, J. (2018) 'The Hampshire domestic abuse prevention partnership 2016–2018: process and outcomes evaluation'. University of Southampton, https://eprints.soton.ac.uk/426401/

North Wales MAPPA (2015) *North Wales MAPPA Annual Report 2014–15*, www.gov.uk/government/uploads/system/uploads/attachment_data/file/471269/north-wales.pdf

Office for National Statistics (ONS) (2015) *Release: crime statistics, focus on violent crime and sexual offences 2013/14*, https://webarchive.nationalarchives.gov.uk/20160106112935/http://www.ons.gov.uk/ons/dcp171776_394470.pdf

ONS (2016) *Domestic abuse in England and Wales: year ending March 2016*, www.ons.gov.uk/releases/domesticabuseinenglandandwalesyearendingmarch2016

Paladin (2014) *Register for serial perpetrators of stalking and domestic violence*, https://paladinservice.co.uk/wp-content/uploads/2014/08/Overview-Briefing-Serial-Perpetrators-and-Register-BR15-14.pdf

Plaid Cymru (2017) 'Domestic Violence offenders register needed urgently', 27 July, www2.partyof.wales/cofrestr_dv_register

Richards, L. (2004) *Getting away with it: a strategic overview of domestic violence sexual assault and 'serious' incident analysis*. London: Metropolitan Police, https://webarchive.nationalarchives.gov.uk/+/http:/www.met.police.uk/csu/pdfs/Strat.Over_V3nonMPS1.pdf

Richards, L., Letchford, S. and Stratton, S. (2008) *Policing domestic violence*. Oxford: Oxford University Press.

Robinson, A. (2015) 'Pie in the sky? The use of criminal justice policies and practices for intimate partner violence', in H. Johnson, B.S. Fisher and V. Jacquier (eds), *Critical issues on violence against women*. London: Routledge.

Robinson, A., Clancy, A. and Hanks, S. (2014) *Prevalence and characteristics of serial domestic abuse perpetrators: multi-agency evidence from Wales*. Project report. Cardiff: Cardiff University, http://orca.cf.ac.uk/67542/

Safelives (2019) 'Guidance for multi-agency forums: addressing the abusive behaviour of perpetrators', www.safelives.org.uk/sites/default/files/resources/Perpetrator%20guidance%20for%20MARACs_0.pdf

Safelives (2016) 'New Project to hold perpetrators of domestic abuse to account', 17 February, www.safelives.org.uk/drive

Sentencing Council (2018) 'Sentencing Council publishes new guidelines on intimidatory offences and domestic abuse', press release, 30 March, www.sentencingcouncil.org.uk/news/item/sentencing-council-publishes-new-guidelines-on-intimidatory-offences-and-domestic-abuse/

South and Vale Community Safety Partnership and Oxfordshire Safeguarding Children Board (2016) *Child J – Domestic Homicide Review and Serious Case Review (combined). Report into the death of child J aged 17*, www.oscb.org.uk/wp-content/uploads/Child-J-OSCB-Overview-Report.pdf

South Wales Police (2016) *Domestic Abuse Action Plan*, http://swplive.blob.core.windows.net/wordpress-uploads/South-Wales-Police-Domestic-Abuse-Action-Plan-April-2016.pdf

Steel, N., Blakeborough, L. and Nicholas, S. (2011) *Supporting high-risk victims of domestic violence: a review of Multi-Agency Risk Assessment Conferences (MARACs)*, Home Office Research Report 55. London: Home Office, www.gov.uk/government/uploads/system/uploads/attachment_data/file/116536/horr55-summary.pdf

Strickland, P. and Allen, G. (2017) 'Domestic violence in England and Wales', Briefing Paper Number 6337. London: House of Commons Library.

Tapley, J. (2010) 'Working together to tackle domestic violence', in A. Pycroft and D. Gough (eds), *Multi-agency working in criminal justice: control and care in contemporary correctional practice*. Bristol: Policy Press, pp 137–153.

Travis, A. (2017) 'Violent crime rising in England and Wales, police figures show', *Guardian*, 27 April, www.theguardian.com/uk-news/2017/apr/27/violent-rising-england-wales-police-figures-ons

Walby, S., Towers, J. and Francis, B. (2015) 'Is violent crime increasing or decreasing? A new methodology to measure repeat attacks making visible the significance of gender and domestic relations', *British Journal of Criminology*, 56(6): 1203–1234, https://doi.org/10.1093/bjc/azv131

Warren, D. (2015) *Domestic Violence Homicide Review Overview Report into the death of Rosie (Pseudonym) on 18th February 2014*. Tewkesbury Borough Community Safety Partnership, www.tewkesbury.gov.uk/domestic-homicide-reviews/

Walklate, S. (2007) *Imagining the victim of crime*. Maidenhead: Open University Press and McGraw-Hill Education.

7

Policing a diverse society: the community based rationale for multi-agency working

Claudia Cox

Aims of the chapter
- To illustrate the development of policing models in England and Wales towards community based policing.
- To discuss partnership working between the police and the public, and how this has been integrated into policy in order to better represent the views of ethnic minority communities.
- To consider multi-agency working in highlighting and addressing issues impacting the policing of minority communities.

Introduction

The policing of ethnic minority communities is complex and, historically, events such as the Brixton Riots and the murder of Stephen Lawrence have drawn attention to multiple police failings and the enduring nature of institutional racism (see Grieve, 2014). The move towards a community based model of policing and calls for increased accountability and transparency as a result have often included rhetoric surrounding the need to effectively and fairly police all communities, not just the majority. As policy – and, it will be argued, good practice – requires the police to enlist the help of the public in creating safer communities, and the police recognise the value of working alongside other agencies, there is the potential for relations to the police and minority communities to improve. This chapter will examine the shifts in attitudes from the police through examining changes from a zero tolerance approach to crime control to a policing model which is centred on communities and partnership working. It will consider the impact this is having on the policing of ethnic minority communities and identify barriers which may prevent successful partnership working with minority communities.

Terminology

This chapter discusses issues relating to policing in England and Wales, with a particular focus on ethnic minority communities. Within this context, this terminology refers to individuals who do not identify as White British. This chapter will also use the phrase 'Black and Minority Ethnic' (BME) as this language is often used within policing discourse, such as in the College of Policing 'BME Progression 2018' programme, focused on the recruitment, retention and progression of ethnic minority police officers. It should not be assumed that the use of this term erases the experiences of those who identify as White Other, given the Institute of Race Relations (2017) note that 'BME' is commonly used to refer to those of non-white descent. The limitations of this chapter will not permit a critical discussion surrounding the complexities of such terminology (see Phinney, 1990), but it is important to recognise the impact that the improper or limited use of terminology can have on both data collection and, more importantly, the identities and cultural heritage of the individuals and communities being discussed

Policing in England and Wales: An academic overview

Academic research into policing began in the 1960s in the UK. Banton (1964) is credited with providing the first example of empirical research which focused on community policing. This offered a detailed insight into the day-to-day activities of a police officer, which was perhaps unknown to the public and other social science researchers. However, for the police, it was the first time an academic had observed and written about their role from a sociological perspective. Banton was largely positive about policing; however, research that followed became more critical. Consider, for example, work on police culture. Prominent scholars such as Skolnick (1966), Westley (1970), Cain (1973) and Banton (1973) became critical of the organisational culture that was seen to exist within policing. Previously, this had gone unknown to those outside of the policing bubble, yet now the police were finding themselves being scrutinised by those outside the profession. Reiner (1989) identified this as a period of controversy and conflict between academia and policing, with conflict becoming amplified after the Brixton Riots. The police faced calls to become more transparent and accountable, and becoming the subject of independent research certainly fits this agenda. However, the critical nature of research being published up until this point meant it was not particularly well received by the police, and academics wishing to research this field experienced resistance (Thomas et al, 2014). The resistance experienced during this time is in stark contrast to the role of academia in policing in the 21st century. Brown (1996) credits this shift to the need for senior officers to evaluate the effectiveness and cost efficiency of their approaches to crime control and community safety.

The eagerness of those outside of policing to conduct evidence-based research, often with the encouragement of academic institutions and research grants, now reflects the demand from within policing to develop evidence-based practice.

This had led to what Davies (2016) refers to as a collaborative stage whereby the boundaries between those inside and outside of policing have become increasingly blurred through partnership work. The evaluation of policing practices is made increasingly practical due to an increase in data recording by the police, for example through the recording of interactions with the public via body worn camera. Previously researchers would have had to accompany officers on patrol, whereas now incidents are recorded from start to finish to be viewed and scrutinised by the public and researchers. The Police Education Qualifications Framework (PEQF) also means that all police officers will soon pass through academic institutions in order to ensure they are educated to the level required for their rank (College of Policing, 2016a). The consultation document for PEQF highlights it as a strategy for professionalising the police and increasing the appeal of a career in policing to ethnic minority communities (College of Policing, 2016b).

This collaboration between the police and academia, as well as other research bodies, has undoubtedly benefited both parties. The police have become progressively more receptive to research conducted by those outside of the organisation, meaning research is more likely to impact police policy and practice (Davies, 2016). In terms of policing ethnic minority communities, academic research has shed a light on important issues such as police culture and discrimination (Chan, 1997). While the police may be open to scrutiny from the public, opportunities for public involvement are often lacking in diversity or representation from those who are over-policed. There is also the risk that ethnic minorities voicing their concerns directly to the police will be seen as 'crying racism' and not taken seriously (Barlow and Barlow, 2002). While this undeniably needs to be addressed internally, partnership working between the police and academia offers yet another opportunity for the voices of under-represented and marginalised groups to be heard by the police.

Since the Metropolitan Police was founded in 1829, policing in England and Wales has continuously evolved in its approach. This has often been guided by the political and economic climate, as well as the perceived needs of the public. These factors often focus on debates surrounding what the primary role of the police should be, and how those debates subsequently shape the policing model of the day. The two models of policing most commonly identified are 'zero tolerance' and 'community policing'. I will argue that the latter is the most relevant in relation to this chapter and the notion of policing within multi-agency contexts.

Zero tolerance policing

Zero tolerance policing is an example of an internal policing model that aligns itself with the crime control model of criminal justice. Packer (1964) describes how the crime control model seeks the repression of criminality and the maintenance of public order to ensure freedom and respect for legal authorities. Drawing upon 'broken windows theory' (Wilson and Kelling, 1982), there is an assumption that if minor crimes are not addressed (the broken window is not fixed) then further crimes will ensue (all the windows will end up broken) and be perpetuated in a criminogenic environment; thus zero tolerance policing and the maintenance of social order are seen to be inextricably related. Through the display of authority in reducing and preventing low level disorder, such as antisocial behaviour, it is anticipated that zero tolerance policing can prevent more serious crimes from occurring (Innes, 1999). Consequently, this model assumes the key role of policing is to reduce crime. Due to its broad definition and perceived support from the public, zero tolerance approaches to crime and disorder have featured regularly within political discussions (Cunneen, 1999). Theresa May, as Home Secretary in 2010, stated the 'mission' of the police was to "cut crime. No more, and no less" during her speech to the National Policing Conference.

The support for a zero tolerance approach appeared to come from both outside of and within policing (Manning, 1997). However, as highlighted by Innes (1999), zero tolerance policing failed to recognise that the notion of social order is likely to be prioritised differently and given differing levels of significance within different communities and across differing police forces with variable resource pressures. Therefore, zero tolerance approaches can lead to the criminalisation and discrimination of the minority to satisfy a majority view. This is of notable relevance in the context of policing increasingly diverse societies, where an intolerance of differing cultures, norms and values from the majority can result in the over-policing of these groups and communities.

Community policing model

Technology was a key feature of the zero tolerance approach as it permitted a fast-response and reactive policing style. But consequently the gap between the public and the police increased as the traditional 'bobby on the beat' became a far less common sight. The key concept of policing by consent was becoming untenable. Cars reduced the use of foot patrols, and personal radios reduced response times. A report by the Bureau of Justice Assistance (1994) raised concerns that isolating policing from the public in the United States had resulted in crimes being unreported and a reduction in the sharing of information and intelligence. Tilley (2008) notes that this signalled the need for a shift towards a policing model that incorporated the public and local communities.

Contrary to the zero tolerance approach, community based approaches to policing reflects the Peelian principle of 'the police are the public and the public are the police'. Although definitions of community policing are vast and varied, Oliver (1998) identifies the consistent themes as: interactions between the police and the public; partnership working with external agencies; neighbourhood patrols; and a focus on low level disorder and 'quality of life' offences. There is overlap between the two models with the latter being reflective of the concerns of zero tolerance policing. While it is still acknowledged that it is necessary to prevent more serious crimes, the community policing model is also concerned with improving community safety and, in turn, making the police more efficient through a reduced demand for their resources. Rather than the reactive nature of zero tolerance policing, a problem-oriented approach means that longer term solutions to such issues are likely to be identified. While the internal nature of zero tolerance meant the police would seek a solution themselves, this model sees the police working alongside members of the community to problem solve together, resulting in the role of the police becoming decentralised (Somerville, 2009).

However, the extent to which this approach can be effective is determined in part by the willingness of communities to engage with policing and in no small part determined by the perceived legitimacy of the police. While communities may support the idea of this approach, they may be unwilling to take personal responsibility for crime reduction or work alongside the police (Grinc, 1994). The police also need to be willing to be guided by members of the public. While the zero tolerance model seemed to reflect many elements of police culture, community policing does quite the opposite. The 'can-do' nature of police culture and institutional defensiveness (Holdaway, 1989) means that resistance to increased input and scrutiny from the public may be very real at an organisational and/or individual level.

Gill et al (2014) also concluded that while community policing models may be effective in improving police legitimacy, there is little evidence to suggest they contribute to the reduction of crime. While this is perhaps not the primary focus of community policing models, it is certainly one of the primary roles of the police. Although a community policing model may have its benefits, ever changing policing priorities in times of austerity are likely to determine its perceived importance and value. While it may not contribute directly to a reduction in crime, it may have other benefits for policing. Moore and Brown (1981) state that although effective community policing strategies are reliant on the community assuming partial responsibility for strengthening informal social controls, it can result in increased trust and confidence. This is likely whereby community policing has meant a localised approach which has reduced fear of crime. Ethnic minority communities in particular consistently report disproportionately low levels of trust and confidence in the police across a number of areas (IPCC, 2016a, 2016b; Ipsos MORI, 2016). This can reduce their willingness to cooperate with the police (Bradford, 2014) and is therefore likely to impact the extent to which they are willing to work alongside the police (Myhill and Bradford, 2011). Therefore, a community policing model which works to reduce fear of crime, improve the relationship between the police and communities, and subsequently improves trust and confidence, is likely to support the effective policing of ethnic minority communities.

Reflection

In what ways might the police work to overcome mistrust and low levels of confidence from minority communities?

Formalising the role of communities in policing

Partnership work between the police and the community takes many forms and is a defining feature of a community policing model. The introduction of Police Community Support Officers, dedicated neighbourhood policing teams, and therefore the continued use of foot patrols as a key feature of British policing may permit an increased visible presence and informal channels of information sharing. However, as the next section of this chapter will explore, the role of the community is now embedded in many areas of police policy and procedure. The Stephen Lawrence Inquiry (Macpherson, 1999) into the police handling of the racist murder of Stephen Lawrence called for processes that formed genuine partnerships with minority communities and encouraged their active participation within policing. Lay involvement does not require the public to be responsible for decision making and outcomes, but instead provides the opportunity for the public to offer observations and insights with a view to improving policing and community safety (Home Office, 2000). Three examples of this structured approach to working in partnership with the public are discussed below.

Independent advisory groups

Established in the 1990s, the concept of independent advisory groups (IAGs) evolved as a direct result of criticism within the Stephen Lawrence Inquiry that the Metropolitan Police had inadequate measures in place to consult with members of ethnic minority communities. Similar comments were also made by Lord Scarman (1981) in his report into the Brixton Riots which he identified as being, in part, due to a lack of communication between the police and minority communities. Following their introduction by the Metropolitan Police, their use was commended by a number of government reports: *Policing London: winning consent* (2000); *Let's get it right: race and justice* (2000); and *Winning the race: embracing diversity* (2001). Primarily it was acknowledged that their use offered the police and other criminal justice agencies greater transparency and accountability by allowing members of the public to contribute to decision making on matters that impacted them and their community.

The College of Policing defines the role of IAGs as follows:

> The role of an IAG is to help us to build insight into the needs, wants and assets of the groups who are under-represented in our normal decision making processes. We use this insight to shape our service for the benefit of all our communities and engender trust and confidence. (College of Policing, 2015: 4)

There are some important aspects of this definition to note here. First, it is widely acknowledged that ethnic minorities are under-represented in almost every criminal justice agency, and policing is no different. As of March 2017, only 6%

of all police officers identified as BME (Home Office, 2017). The reasons for and the impact of under-representation within the police workforce has been widely discussed within academia and elsewhere (see Stone and Tuffin, 2000). IAGs offer an alternative mechanism by which members of hard to reach communities can engage with policing while maintaining their identity as a member of the public. Therefore, while they may be under-represented in internal decision making processes, and unable to influence decision making in this way, IAGs could offer a meaningful alternative.

Second, IAGs are defined by their ability to engender trust and confidence as per the definition above. DC Rosemary Drewery of the Race and Violent Crime Taskforce at Scotland Yard, responsible for one of the first IAGs, stated that they are essential for improving relationships between the police and the community (Drewery, 2002). However, this trust and confidence must surely be dependent on the way in which advice is sought and responded to. Arnstein's (1969) 'Ladder of Citizen Participation' indicates that, in some instances, marginalised groups are afforded an input on the basis of tokenism. The impression is given that they are contributing to reform, but citizens lack the confirmation that the input they have offered will be acted upon. He notes that to merely listen to the views of members of the public equates to participation being just a 'window dressing ritual' (Arnstein, 1969: 219) with little meaning. Therefore, in the context of IAGs, a lack of transparency in relation to how advice has been utilised, or why it has not, has the potential to damage trust and confidence in policing. Consequently, the public's willingness to cooperate with the police may be reduced.

Best Use of Stop and Search Scheme: lay observers

Described by Bowling and Phillips (2007) as disproportionate and discriminatory, the improper use of stop and search is a common feature in discussions regarding the policing of ethnic minority communities. Of particular importance is again the Brixton Riots. Operation Swamp intended to combat street muggings, but stop and searches were targeted at young black men with few positive outcomes. While tensions between the police and the black community were already strained, this was the catalyst for the disorder which followed. The use of stop and search was again scrutinised following the murder of Stephen Lawrence. The subsequent report explicitly condemned disproportionality in the use of stop and search powers and rejected any attempts to justify such figures, stating that 'the perceptions and experiences of the minority communities that discrimination is a major element in the stop and search problem is correct' (Macpherson, 1999: 45.10). The Lawrence Inquiry also noted that discussions surrounding stop and search elicited strong reactions during consultations (Desol and Shiner, 2006). However, it did not suggest changes in stop and search legislation, but instead called for greater recording and monitoring of the use of stop and search powers (Macpherson, 1999).

In 2014, the Best Use of Stop and Search Scheme was introduced in order to 'achieve greater transparency, community involvement in the use of stop and search powers and to support a more intelligence-led approach, leading to better outcomes' (Home Office, 2014: 2). Key features of the scheme included changes to data recording and an attempt to reduce searches without grounds for suspicion. However, of particular interest for this chapter is the introduction of lay observer schemes and formalising the use of community scrutiny groups for complaints relating to stop and search.

The requirement to introduce a lay observer scheme is described by the Home Office (2014: 4) as an opportunity for 'two-way learning'. In theory, the public have the opportunity to witness the police carrying out a stop and search and provide feedback, and the police develop a greater understanding of their communities. This approach shifts the responsibility of community relations directly onto rank-and-file officers, rather than community engagement being managed elsewhere within the organisation. As noted by Bordua and Tifft (1971), effective community policing strategies require the integration of those responsible for everyday policing. They state that positive community relations are reliant not just on effective strategies, but the way in which these are executed by frontline officers. This is reflective of more recent discussions surrounding procedural justice and the need for the police to demonstrate fairness in the execution of their duties to secure trust and confidence and ensure legitimacy (Bradford et al, 2009; Hough et al, 2010).

As well as enabling an insight from members of the community on the use of stop and search, lay observer schemes may also result in the regulation of behaviour by police officers and act as a check mechanism to ensure powers are being used lawfully (Parpworth, 2014). Communities are also exposed to the realities of modern policing and are able to offer insights into their experiences of areas outside stop and search. In theory, it should be a unique opportunity to connect those who experience frontline policing with those who provide it. However, a report by Her Majesty's Inspectorate of Constabularies (HMIC, 2016) found that, despite every force signing up to the scheme, 11 were still failing to offer members of the public the opportunity to observe stop and search powers in use.

Best Use of Stop and Search Scheme: complaints triggers

The community complaints trigger clause within the Best Use of Stop and Search Scheme consists of three requirements: individuals stopped and searched must be aware of the complaints procedure; a threshold must be identified in terms of the number of complaints received; and if this threshold is breached explanations must be provided to a community scrutiny group. Prior to this scheme, police complaints procedures were complex and seen to benefit the police, thus reducing their use by the public and further disadvantaging those more likely to have a negative experience of policing (Kennison, 2002). This included ethnic minority communities, meaning the police were aware of their disproportionate use of stop and search powers but unaware of the impact this was having on individuals and their communities. In clarifying the complaints procedure and being held accountable to the public once a certain number are received, this appears to be an attempt to improve transparency and give more consideration to how communities experience policing.

However, referring again to Arnstein (1969) and his 'Ladder of Citizen Participation', while the police must explain a high volume of complaints to members of the public, this does not appear to involve opportunities for active participation. Instead the police are there to educate members of a scrutiny group about why they think a problem exists and what they will do to address it. In relation to stop and search, police forces have often tried to excuse disproportionate statistics which may point to the discriminatory use of powers (Bowling and Phillips, 2007). If the community trigger process does little more than require the police to offer an explanation, then the community are merely being manipulated into believing they are making a difference. This process is therefore at risk of becoming a ritual, rather than a useful opportunity for partnership working between the police and the public. This is in stark contrast to the 'two-way learning' approach adopted by the lay observer schemes, and instead is more reflective of a one dimensional approach to community involvement in policing.

Reflection

Each example provided here seems well meaning but there are flaws in how they have been executed. Why might this be? Consider both individual and organisational factors.

As already discussed, the effectiveness of community policing models is, in part, determined by the willingness of communities to work in partnership with the police and assume shared responsibility for crime reduction and community safety. Arnstein (1969) identified that citizen participation is, in theory, beneficial to all. Contributing to social reform should mean the active citizen will experience improved living conditions, and therefore it is an element of democracy which should be favoured by communities. On this basis, one would expect the police to have endless volunteers from all walks of life eager to attend community meetings, participate in observer schemes, help set police priorities, and challenge their decision making. In reality, this is not the case. If active participation in policing should benefit the public, one must then ask why this is? While many opportunities for the formal involvement of communities in policing have been shown to exist, it is crucial that those participating in this way are reflective of all communities so as not to further marginalise minority groups.

Reflection

What would you identify as the main barriers to community policing?

The role of external agencies

Another feature of community policing strategies is adopting a multi-agency approach. While this initially extends to involving members of the public, the role of other organisations should not be overlooked. The nature of crime has evolved, the demands on policing have increased, and public sector budgets have continued to be reduced. Therefore, a multi-agency approach to policing has been widely adopted to reflect the view that crime cannot and should not be the responsibility of the police alone (Berry et al, 2011). While evidence of a multi-agency approach to policing began to emerge in the 1980s, it was formally addressed within *Partnership in crime prevention*, a publication from the Home Office (1990) which supported multi-agency working. The focus on community safety supported by government saw a statutory obligation being placed on local authorities and other agencies to work alongside the police with a view to reducing disorder and fear of crime (Squires, 1997). This alternative approach to working was further evidence of the police 'opening up' to the public to become more transparent and accountable, thus moving away from the zero tolerance, internal policing model which had been favoured prior to the Brixton Riots (Squires and Measor, 2001). Multi-agency working has since evolved to be about more than managing quality of life offences and low level disorder within communities. As is being explored elsewhere in this edition, the police are now involved in multi-agency approaches to tackling hate crime (see Tyson and Hall, this volume), domestic violence (see Tapley and Jackson, this volume), terrorism (see Grieve, this volume) and more. The number of agencies involved and their contributions are varied dependent on the issue at hand. While the police may lead multi-agency approaches in some instances (such as Integrated Offender Management, see Williams, this volume), it is more commonplace to find them embedded within other groups and organisations (see discussions on MAPPA (Nash) and MARAC (Tapley and Jackson) in this volume) that are working to address issues experienced by hard to reach groups, such as ethnic minority communities (Jones and Newburn, 2001).

Reflection

What do you perceive as the barriers for the police in engaging in multi-agency arrangements?

Conclusion

Having previously favoured an internal approach to policing where the focus was on cutting crime, policing has undergone significant change since the 1980s to become more community focused. As a result, the police are more open to working alongside the public and other agencies to try and reduce crime, reduce the fear of crime, improve community safety, and police more effectively and efficiently. For communities which have historically been over-policed while their views remain under-represented, there are now opportunities to contribute to reforming policing. The police are accountable to more individuals and organisations than ever before, and their understanding about the importance of evidence-based practice suggests that they are more receptive to scrutiny and suggestions for change. However, while this may be written into policy, we must not assume that action is always being taken, or that the views of all communities are still represented, heard and acted upon. There is still work to be done if the police are to overcome the legacy of discrimination that often prevails and is undoubtedly preventing many individuals from fully participating in partnership working. The police must ensure that they are genuine in their desire to hear about the policing issues affecting all communities and be prepared to have some uncomfortable conversations with those who still feel marginalised. They must seek out the views of those who may not offer their support voluntarily and show a genuine commitment to change. They must continue to work in partnership with organisations who can help to bridge the gap further. The policing of ethnic minority communities is a complex issue, and while policing is unlikely to ever be perfect, partnership and multi-agency working is likely to contribute to improving trust, confidence and legitimacy.

> **Summary of key learning points**
> - A community policing model encourages multi-agency working and collaboration between the police and the public.
> - Collaborative working between the police and the public is often enshrined in policy and focused on improving transparency, trust, and confidence.
> - The police are now responsible for both leading, and participating in, multi-agency approaches to tackling a broad spectrum of offences, including those which are likely to disproportionately impact minority communities.

References

Arnstein, S.R. (1969) 'A ladder of citizen participation', *Journal of the American Institute of Planners*, 35(4): 216–224, https://doi.org/10.1080/01944366908977225

Banton, M. (1964) *The policeman in the community.* London: Tavistock Publications.

Banton, M. (1973) *Police–community relations.* London: Collins.

Barlow, D. and Barlow, M. (2002) 'Racial profiling: a survey of African American police officers', *Police Quarterly*, 5(3): 334–358.

Berry, G., Briggs, P., Erol, R. and van Staden, L. (2011) *The effectiveness of partnership working in a crime and disorder context*. Research Report 52. Retrieved from https://assets.publishing.service.gov.uk/government/uploads/system/uploads/attachment_data/file/116549/horr52-report.pdf

Bordua, D.J. and Tifft, L.L. (1971) 'Citizen interview, organizational feedback, and police–community relations decisions', *Law and Society Review*, 6: 155–182.

Bowling, B. and Phillips, C. (2007) 'Disproportionate and discriminatory: reviewing the evidence on police stop and search', *The Modern Law Review*, 70(6): 936–961, https://doi.org/10.1111/j.1468-2230.2007.00671.x

Bradford, B. (2014) 'Policing and social identity: procedural justice, inclusion and cooperation between police and public', *Policing and Society*, 24(1): 22–43.

Bradford, B., Stanko, E. and Jackson, J. (2009) 'Contact and confidence: revisiting the impact of public encounters with the police', *Policing and Society*, 19(1): 20–46.

Brown, J. (1996) 'Police research: some critical issues', in F. Leishman, B. Loveday and S.P. Savage (eds), *Core issues in policing*. London: Longman.

Bureau of Justice Assistance (1994) *Understanding community policing: a framework for action*. Washington DC: Bureau of Justice Assistance.

Cain, M.E. (1973) *Society and the policeman's role*. Abingdon: Routledge.

Chan, J. (1997) *Changing police culture: policing in a multicultural society*. Cambridge: Cambridge University Press.

College of Policing (2015) *Independent Advisory Groups: considerations and advice for the police service on the recruitment, role and value of IAGs*, www.college.police.uk/What-we-do/Support/Equality/Documents/Independent_advisory_groups_advice_2015.pdf

College of Policing (2016a) *Developing and delivering an education qualification framework for policing*, www.college.police.uk/What-we-do/Learning/Policing-Education-Qualifications-Framework/Documents/PEQF_2016.pdf

College of Policing (2016b) *Policing education qualifications framework: consultation*, www.college.police.uk/What-we-do/Learning/Policing-Education-Qualifications-Framework/Pages/PEQF-archive.aspx

Cunneen, C. (1999) 'Zero tolerance policing and the experience of New York City', *Current Issues in Criminal Justice*, 10(3): 299–314.

Davies, M. (2016) 'To what extent can we trust police research? Examining trends in research "on", "with", "by" and "for" the police', *Nordic Police Science*, 3(2): 154–164.

Desol, R. and Shiner, M. (2006) 'Regulating stop and search: a challenge for police and community relations in England and Wales', *Critical Criminology*, 14(3): 241–263.

Drewery, R. (2002) 'Independent Advisory Groups', *Criminal Justice Matters*, 49(1): 14, https://doi.org/10.1080/09627250208553488

Gill, C.E., Weisburd, D., Bennett, T.H. and Telep, C. (2014) 'Community-oriented policing to reduce crime, disorder, and fear and increase legitimacy and citizen satisfaction in neighbourhoods: a systematic review', *Journal of Experimental Criminology*, 10(4): 399–428.

Grieve, J. (2014) 'The Stephen Lawrence Inquiry: A case study in policing and complexity', in A. Pycroft and C. Bartollas (eds), *Applying complexity theory: whole systems approaches in criminal justice and social work*. Bristol: Policy Press, pp 141–158.

Grinc, R. (1994) '"Angels in marble": problems in stimulating community involvement in community policing', *Crime & Delinquency*, 40(3): 437–468, https://doi.org/10.1177/0011128794040003008

HMIC (2016) *PEEL: Police Legitimacy 2015: a national overview*, www.justiceinspectorates.gov.uk/hmicfrs/wp-content/uploads/peel-police-legitimacy-2015.pdf

Holdaway, S. (1989) 'Discovering structure: studies of the police occupational culture', in M. Weateritt (ed), *Police research: some future prospects*. Aldershot: Avebury, pp 55–75.

Home Office (1990) *Partnership in crime prevention*. London: Home Office.

Home Office (2000) *Policing London: winning consent*. London: Home Office.

Home Office (2001) *Winning the race: embracing diversity*. London: Home Office Communication Directorate.

Home Office (2014) *Best Use of Stop and Search Scheme*. London: Home Office.

Home Office (2017) *Police workforce, England and Wales, 31 March 2017*, www.gov.uk/government/uploads/system/uploads/attachment_data/file/630471/hosb1017-police-workforce.pdf

Hough, M., Jackson, J., Bradford, B., Myhill, A. and Quinton, P. (2010) 'Procedural justice, trust and institutional legitimacy', *Policing: A Journal of Policy and Practice*, 4(3): 203–210.

Innes, M. (1999) 'An iron fist in an iron glove? The zero tolerance policing debate', *The Howard Journal*, 38(4): 397–410.

Institute of Race Relations (2017) 'Definitions', www.irr.org.uk/research/statistics/definitions/

IPCC (2016a) *Police use of force: evidence from complaints, investigations and public perception*, https://s16878.pcdn.co/wp-content/uploads/2016/03/IPCC_Use_Of_Force_Report.pdf

IPCC (2016b) *Public Confidence in the Police Complaints System*, www.policeconduct.gov.uk/sites/default/files/Documents/statistics/IPCC_Public_Confidence_Survey_2016.pdf

Ipsos MORI (2016) *Public views of policing in England and Wales*, www.ipsos.com/sites/default/files/migrations/en-uk/files/Assets/Docs/Publications/sri-public-views-of-policing-in-england-and-wales.pdf

Jones, T. and Newburn, T. (2001) *Widening access: improving police relations with hard to reach groups*. Police Research Series Paper 138. London: Home Office.

Kennison, P. (2002) 'Policing diversity – managing complaints against the police', *The Police Journal: Theory, Practice and Principles*, 75(2): 117–135, https://doi.org/10.1177/0032258X0207500205

Macpherson, W. (1999) *The Stephen Lawrence Inquiry: Report of an Inquest*. London: The Stationery Office.

Manning, P. (1997) *Police work*. Second edition. Cambridge, MA: MIT Press.

Moore, C. and Brown, J. (1981) *Community versus crime*. London: Bedford Square Press.

Myhill, A. and Bradford, B. (2011) 'Can police enhance public confidence by improving quality of service? Results from two surveys in England and Wales', *Policing and Society*, 22(4): 397–425.

NACRO (2000) *Let's get it right: race and justice 2000*. NACRO Race Issues Advisory Committee. London: NACRO.

Oliver, W.M. (1998) *Community-oriented policing: a systemic approach to policing*. New Jersey: Prentice Hall.

Packer, H.L. (1964) 'Two models of the criminal process', *University of Pennsylvania Law Review*, 113(1): 1–68.

Parpworth, N. (2014) 'Reforming police powers of stop and search: voluntary action', *The Police Journal: Theory, Practice and Principles*, 87(4): 234–244, https://doi.org/10.1350/pojo.2014.87.4.677

Phinney, J.S. (1990) 'Ethnic identity in adolescents and adults: review of research', *Psychological Bulletin*, 108(3): 499–514.

Reiner, R. (1989) 'Race and criminal justice', *Journal of Ethnic and Migration Studies*, 16(1): 5–21, https://doi.org/10.1080/1369183X.1989.9976155

Scarman, Lord J. (1981) *The Brixton Disorders, 10–12th April (1981)*. London: HMSO.

Skolnick, J.H. (1966) *Justice without trial*. New York: John Wiley and Sons Inc.

Somerville, P. (2009) 'Understanding community policing', *Policing: An International Journal of Police Strategies & Management*, 32(2): 261–277, https://doi.org/10.1108/13639510910958172

Squires, P. and Measor, L. (2001) 'Rounding up the "usual suspects": police approaches to multiagency policing', in S. Balloch and M. Taylor (eds), *Partnership working: policy and practice*. Bristol: Policy Press, pp 223–243.

Squires, P. (1997) 'Criminology and the community safety paradigm: safety power and success and the limits of the local', *The British Criminology Conferences: Selected Proceedings*, 2: 1–19.

Stone, V. and Tuffin, R. (2000) 'Attitudes of people from minority ethnic communities towards a career in the Police Service', Police Research Paper Series 136, London: Home Office.

Thomas, G., Rogers, C. and Gravelle, J. (2014) 'Research on policing: insights from the literature', in J. Gravelle and C. Rogers (eds), *Researching the police in the 21st century: international lessons from the field*. Basingstoke: Macmillan, pp 1–19.

Tilley, N. (2008) 'Modern approaches to policing: community, problem–oriented and intelligence-led', in T. Newburn (ed.), *Handbook of policing*. Abingdon: Routledge.

Westley, W. (1970) *Violence and the police: a sociological study of law, custom and morality*. Cambridge, MA: MIT Press.

Wilson, J. and Kelling, G. (1982) 'Broken windows', *The Atlantic Monthly*, 127: 29–38.

Further reading

Aspinall, P.J. (2008) *Ethnic options of 'mixed race' people in Britain: a report for UK census agencies on preferences for terminology and classifications.* Swindon: ESRC.

Bowling, B. (1999) 'The rise and fall of New York murder: zero tolerance or crack's decline?', *The British Journal of Criminology*, 39(4): 531–554.

Bowling, B. and Phillips, C. (2003) 'Policing ethnic minority communities', in T. Newburn (ed), *Handbook of policing*. Devon: Willan Publishing, pp 528–555.

Clements, P. (2008) *Policing a diverse society*. Oxford: Blackstone's.

Greene, J.A. (1999) 'Zero tolerance: a case study of police policies and practices in New York City', *Crime & Delinquency*, 45(2): 171–187.

Hughes, G. and Rowe, M. (2007) 'Special Issue: Policing diversity/policing communities? Dilemmas and opportunities', *Criminology & Criminal Justice*, 7(4): 315–471.

Kirby, S. (2013) *Effective policing? Implementation in theory and practice.* Aldershot: Palgrave.

Ministry of Justice (2017) *Statistics on Race and the Criminal Justice System 2016*, www.gov.uk/government/uploads/system/uploads/attachment_data/file/663375/race-criminal-justice-system-2016.pdf

Sari, V. and Elli, H. (2017) 'Multi-professional work practices in the field of immigrant integration – examples of collaboration between the police and social work', *Migration Letters*, 14(2): 273–284.

8

The development of the police role in safeguarding children

John Fox

Aims of the chapter
- To provide an overview of the police's child abuse investigation approach in England and Wales.
- To evaluate the effectiveness of the Children Act 1989 with respect to investigating child abuse.
- To examine the strengths and weaknesses of joint working in carrying out child abuse investigations.

This chapter will examine how the police in England and Wales currently carry out their child abuse investigation function. This will include a discussion about whether the system introduced by the Children Act 1989, whereby police officers investigate child abuse crimes with local authority children's social care services, is working as well as it should. The strengths and weaknesses of this arrangement will be explored, together with an examination of the cultural or philosophical differences, the training methods, and information sharing arrangements, which might cause tension and inhibition among managers and practitioners. Along the way the chapter will discuss whether there is still any actual benefit in a joint investigative approach, or whether the differences between the core roles of two key agencies are so fundamental as to negate any benefit for the child.

In a recent report, Her Majesty's Inspectorate of Constabulary (HMIC)[1] reminded the Police Service that 'protecting children is one of the most important tasks the police undertake. Every officer and member of police staff should understand his or her duty to protect children as part of his or her day-to day business' (HMIC, 2015b: 5). This is impressive rhetoric but policing priorities are always changing, often as a reaction to great failures which have led to extreme reputational damage. There is evidence that the effectiveness of the police child protection function is at a low ebb, or at best inconsistent across England and

Wales. In late 2016, a major inspection of the Metropolitan Police child protection investigation capability was carried out by HMIC and the subsequent report was highly critical because a sample of 384 child protection cases were scrutinised and the inspectors found that three–quarters were substandard (HMIC, 2016). In an interview with the *Guardian* newspaper, Matt Parr, lead inspector for HMIC, was reported as saying, 'the failings were systemic and involved errors in leadership, training, organisation and judgment. They have really dropped the ball on child protection' (Dodds, 2016).

It is rare for the government to commission a statutory public inquiry to examine the failings in public services. Inquiries are expensive and take a long time to report. For example, the inquiry into the Bloody Sunday shootings in Northern Ireland was reported to have cost £400 million and it took ten years before the report was finally produced in 2010. Occasionally, however, a child abuse case is considered so abhorrent, and perhaps on the face of it so easy to have been prevented, that a major public inquiry is demanded. One such case was the inquiry into the death of Victoria Climbié. The report and recommendations by the chair, Lord Laming (2003), arguably led to the biggest shake up of child protection policing there has ever been. For a few years after the publication of Laming's report, child protection was afforded a very high priority within the police. Times change and memories dim, and there is evidence that 'the years of plenty' are over in respect of reactive, familial child protection work, perhaps because other great events have caused the Police Service to reassess their priorities.

The ball metaphor, used by a Detective Chief Superintendent to explain to the Climbié Inquiry why all the trained detectives had been stripped out of the two child protection teams he managed, is illuminating. He described the police as

> like an under 10 football team. The ball gets kicked to one part of the park and everybody rushes to the ball, no strategy or structure. If the concentration is on for example terrorist issues, all the resources are devoted to that. If it becomes murder issues, all the resources go into that. Whatever is the current issue takes priority and that is where the resources go. (Victoria Climbié Inquiry, 2002)

The officer went on to explain that, as a reaction to criticism by Sir William Macpherson (1999) in his report into the police failings in the Stephen Lawrence murder, the force decided to bolster up the squads tackling murder. There was no box of spare police officers to open up so they had to draw those detectives from elsewhere, and the Chief Superintendent claimed that all his trained detectives were transferred from the child protection teams to the murder investigation teams. This left in the child protection teams a group of police officers who were effectively uniformed officers (but in plain clothes) with no CID training, carrying out the investigations into child abuse across London. The officers and supervisors who failed to properly investigate the crimes against Victoria Climbié, fitted that description. Lord Laming remarked,

> It is wrong that victims of crime are disadvantaged in terms of the
> training and expertise of the investigating officer, simply because they
> are children. I heard worrying evidence to suggest that the culture of
> some police forces was such that child protection team work was seen
> as something less than the investigation of often very serious crimes.
> (Laming, 2003: 311)

In the aftermath, or perhaps aftershock, of the Climbié case, the ball was very
firmly kicked back towards child protection and many improvements and
investments were made, all over the country, some of which will be discussed later.
It seems that in respect of 'reactive' child protection things have regressed. The
chapter will later seek to identify current challenges which may, if not addressed,
contribute to further 'great events' down the road.

Origins of joint working between the police and social workers

With the passing of the Local Authority Social Services Act 1970, the then new
social services departments had the power to investigate cruelty and neglect,
but the emphasis was on early identification and non-punitive treatment. The
police had always found great difficulty in prosecuting child abusers as the rules
of evidence at that time made it virtually impossible to convict anybody on the
child's testimony alone. They were content therefore, to distance themselves from
the problem, leaving the social workers to try and prevent abuse by working with
the so-called problem families.

This state of affairs existed until the death of Maria Colwell in 1973. Maria
was murdered by her stepfather and the subsequent public inquiry identified,
among other things, a failure of the childcare *system*, as well as childcare *policy*
(Harding, 1991). As a result, child protection conferences, registers and manuals
were introduced (Parton, 1985). The focus was 'exclusively on how to recognise
child abuse, and manage cases, with particular emphasis on ensuring good
interprofessional communication' (Corby, 1987). The Colwell case also prompted
a House of Commons Select Committee report, *Violence to children* (1977), which
recommended that police and social workers should be given more training, and
that the police should be involved with the social services, in managing cases of
child abuse.

A fundamental weakness in the concept of a joint approach to investigation is
therefore that social workers and police officers are recruited generically. In other
words, their professions have represented completely opposing punitive/non-
punitive cultures which have been ingrained into their respective organisations
since their conception. However, during the 1980s, there came a milestone in joint
working arrangements, namely the Cleveland Inquiry (1988). This inquiry, chaired
by Justice Dame Elizabeth Butler-Sloss, came about after a series of children
were removed from their homes by Cleveland Social Services Department, after
being wrongly diagnosed by a paediatrician as having been sexually abused. The

management of these cases was compounded by a complete breakdown in the relationship between police and social workers.

For ten years, all around the country, these two agencies with very different viewpoints had been trying to paper over the cracks, but the events in Cleveland exposed just how deep the differences were. In her report, Butler-Sloss heavily criticised both agencies for their lack of cooperation and made several recommendations about joint working arrangements. These included:

- The police should develop, monitor and maintain communication and consultation with the other agencies concerned with child protection.
- The police should develop and practice inter-agency working, including joint planning and interviews of children in investigation of sexual abuse within the family or caring agency.
- The police should recognise and develop their responsibility for the protection of children as extending beyond the collection of evidence for court proceedings. This should include their attendance at case conferences and assistance to other child protection agencies.
- Social services departments should maintain an open and continuing relationship with the police to review areas of mutual concern.
- There is a need for inter-agency training and recognition of the role of other disciplines. For example, police officers and social workers designated to interview children should have joint training in their approach to this task.

Together with an elaborate model for ensuring inter-agency cooperation, the recommendations in the report led to the Children Act 1989 and the oft revised series of documents *Working together to safeguard children* (Her Majesty's Government, 1991–2017).

Immediately police forces began forming specialist child protection teams, but primarily many of these early teams were gatherers of evidence rather than investigators of the crime. The 'Bexley Experiment' (London Borough of Bexley, 1984) had been operating for three years prior to the publication of the Cleveland report, and many forces saw that as an example of good practice. This experiment, in an area of South London, introduced for the first time the idea of the two disciplines of police and social work operating together as a unit for the same end, and it paved the way for the joint interviewing of child victims using visual recording (Smith, 1992).

It seemed at the time to be an enormous strength for the two disciplines to work together, particularly in interviewing potential victims of abuse. The general perception around at the time was that police officers were not as skilled in talking to children as their social work colleagues, and this may indeed have been true. However, many police child protection teams were populated by officers who were selected for the skills in interviewing children rather than their detective expertise.

Until the publication of the Climbié Report (Laming, 2003) there was no national standard which required that trained detectives should be deployed to police child protection teams, and therefore although some forces did utilise at least some trained detectives it was hit and miss whether a crime against a child would be dealt with by someone who had been trained to investigate serious crime. The only training that did exist, and in some areas still exists today, involved the joint interviewing of child victims and witnesses. The rules of evidence made it virtually impossible to convict anybody on the child's testimony alone but changes introduced by the Criminal Justice Act 1988 meant that judges were no longer required to warn the jury about convicting someone on the uncorroborated evidence of a child. This effectively meant that for the first time children could give evidence in their own right, and the jury were entitled to believe their story over that of the defendant. The police therefore had to become proficient at gathering the testimony from a child because they now had the possibility of a viable prosecution even if there was no corroboration for the child's testimony.

Shortly after this legislation, the Pigot Report (1989) was published, which led to the introduction of visually recorded interviews and the playing of a DVD in court instead of the child's evidence in chief. To allow the recording to be used, however, the interviewers had to be careful not to lead the child or suggest answers; documents such as the *Memorandum of good practice* (Home Office and Department of Health, 1991), superseded by *Achieving best evidence* (Ministry of Justice, 2011), set the ground rules for these interviews. This necessitated specialist training for those social workers and police officers interviewing children, and that was the primary basis of what became known as joint interview training. The training had little, if anything, about investigation techniques for allegations of serious crime.

Developments in partnership working

In his report, Laming (2003) made it quite clear that he felt the training for child protection officers should adequately equip them to deal with the complexity and seriousness of the area of police work in which they were engaged. Clearly, in the context of serious child abuse this was a major shortcoming. The child protection units were simply not able to effectively tackle the most important cases within their sphere of interest. It was not until 2005, in response to a recommendation by Lord Laming (2003), that a national police training curriculum was created by the forerunner of the College of Policing. Known as the Specialist Child Abuse Investigators Development Programme (SCAIDP), this training includes a requirement that those attending must have already undertaken basic investigators training, and as well as the elements about interviewing children, the programme includes advanced training in investigating child abuse cases. It is now clear that the concept of joint training has in many areas fallen by the wayside and the reasons for this will be fully explored later. However, the fact that the police and social workers retained their own identity and cultural differences may well have contributed.

A logical and bold outcome of the Butler-Sloss (1988) recommendations might have been that integrated multi-agency teams were formed to tackle child abuse, whereby police officers and social workers worked together full time, and under single management, from the same building. In time, these teams might have formed their own occupational culture thereby alleviating some inhibitions in their professionalism. This idea was not taken up perhaps due to different employment and contractual conditions such as pay and overtime differences, but also probably due to senior managers having their cultural positions rooted in the historical development of their respective agencies. Indeed, when one progressive area in the south east of England did, in the early 1990s, decide to try and colocate police child protection officers and social workers in the same building, the local police managers insisted that they kept the adjoining door locked between their respective halves of the premises (see Williams, this volume for a discussion of colocation).

Although the Bexley Experiment led to most forces initiating a programme of joint interview training, it took a further 25 years before anything resembling true integrated working arrived. This came about because of constant criticism in serious case review reports (such as Brandon et al, 2016), as well as the Victoria Climbié Inquiry Report (Laming, 2003) that a failure to share information between agencies was one of the biggest factors leading to the failure to safeguard children.

One of the perceived benefits of multi-agency working is the sharing of relevant information held by the two agencies. Having examined and analysed hundreds of serious case review reports spanning three years, Marian Brandon and her colleagues concluded that despite 24 years having elapsed since the first edition of *Working together* (Her Majesty's Government, 1991),

> Communication is essential for collaboration but is inevitably one of the key points of breakdown. There is evidence of uncertainty amongst practitioners about how and when to share information, despite national guidance. (Brandon et al, 2016: 15)

Reflection

What would you identify as the key differences in practice between the police and social work and welfare organisations?

This sort of criticism led to the advent of something called the Multi-Agency Safeguarding Hub (MASH). Originating as a concept in Devon around 2004, the idea quickly spread throughout the country until currently most local authorities host a MASH. Although there are variations on the theme, the idea of a MASH is that professionals from police, social care and health sit together in the same room and receive and assess reports of potential child abuse, as well as share information held by their agency and plan a response to the referral. The Hampshire County Council website explains that their MASH provides 'triage and multi-agency assessment of safeguarding concerns in respect of vulnerable children. It brings together professionals from a range of agencies into an integrated multi-agency team' with an intended outcome of a 'faster, more co-ordinated and consistent response to safeguarding concerns' (Hampshire County Council, 2018).

Although an important step forward in terms of the assessment and planning of child safeguarding responses, in some areas the contributing agencies, the police in particular, appoint junior practitioners rather than managers to the MASH thereby limiting the MASH to little more than an information sharing hub rather than operational management of the case workers. In some areas the police provide a police staff member (in other words not a police officer) to the MASH which means they can access police intelligence systems but are not empowered to make tactical decisions about tackling individual cases. It is therefore a fallacy to believe that a MASH provides vulnerable children with a true multi-agency safeguarding response and, although they can often improve the sharing of information, the Multi-Agency Safeguarding Hubs may have little bearing on the operational cultural differences that have always dogged joint working. Indeed, in many MASH offices, each delegate will only be able to access the information held on their own agency database, so for example, a social worker or health worker will not be allowed the login details to access the Police National Computer or the Police National Database, the latter of which contains intelligence information rather than just convictions. In turn, no doubt the health agency will not allow a social worker or police officer access to patient health records. This means that, although information sharing is probably greater and more streamlined since the advent of the MASH, there is not necessarily a true, unfettered sharing of information, and each agency will no doubt instruct their MASH representative what sort of information may be shared with their partner sitting at the desk opposite and therefore a 'need to know' culture remains. The problem with this approach is that agencies may not know always what information another agency needs to fulfil its safeguarding role so it can be dangerous for them to be selective and make assumptions.

The MASH does not have any frontline deployable resources and in the main the working relationship is such that the frontline practitioners from police and social work are still located separately under separate line management, and in terms of the investigation the respective agencies often have different outcomes in mind.

Reflection

Make a comparison between the ways in which your local MASH or MARAC (see Tapley and Jackson, this volume) operates in comparison to Multi-Agency Public Protection Arrangements (MAPPAs) (see Nash, this volume). What is the significance of the statutory nature of the latter in how it works?

Research by Leah Fox (2018) reveals that social workers have a priority in maintaining a good relationship with the family of an abused child, whereas police feel that their role is to investigate a crime and if necessary prosecute that family. This is of course a simplistic view, and many social workers realise the need to protect children by using the criminal law; however, Fox (2018: 207) reveals that the different cultural starting point can lead to a feeling of mistrust between the agencies, particularly in the area of information sharing where she explains that police sometimes feel that 'boundaries can be blurred around friendship or familiarity [by social workers] with a parent, which can sometimes lead to police information being incorrectly shared with the parent'. This is a polite way of saying that police officers, at an operational level, sometimes feel that they cannot trust children's social care with sensitive information and intelligence because the frontline police generally struggle to accept the situation whereby social workers are *required* by their organisational culture to be transparent and open with families. This can cause the frontline police officers to pay lip service to the grand aspirations of their Chief Constable's commitment to partnership working and open and transparent information sharing, particularly when the information they hold is from a sensitive source such as a covert listening device or a covert human intelligence source (an informant). This claim is further supported by the author who, since 2010, has, on behalf of the College of Policing, trained hundreds of senior police detectives in child death investigation. It is invariably evident that during case study scenarios on information sharing with partners the police will generally feel they need to withhold or heavily sanitise any intelligence or sensitive information, rather than share it openly with social workers. This is even the case if the information might be perceived by their partners as important to allow them to safeguard a child, and crucially the police are making their own judgement about what information *they* think their partners need to know. When challenged as to why, many officers claim that they do not trust the ability of social work partners to be able keep the information confidential. It is fairly clear that 30 years after Dame Elizabeth Butler–Sloss (1988) knocked their organisational heads together, the two key organisations charged with protecting children are, in some respects, working together in name only, rather than in harmony.

Although at a strategic level the police and local authorities plan and communicate together through forums such as Community Safety Partnerships and Local Safeguarding Children Boards (see Loveday and Roberts, this volume), in frontline practice there are only a few stages when police officers will actually work alongside social workers. There may be a joint welfare visit to a home, there may be a strategy discussion to plan an investigation, and there may be a joint investigative interview with a child victim of crime. Social workers will never be involved in detaining or interviewing an alleged offender and will never be involved in taking statements from witnesses or preparing a file of evidence for the Crown Prosecution Service.

Victoria Climbié Inquiry Report

Things were not always that clear and in his Victoria Climbié Inquiry Report, Lord Laming (2003) expressed anger that the police were expecting social workers or even medical staff to conduct key elements of the criminal investigation. Victoria was admitted to hospital on two separate occasions. The first time she was noted to have bruised feet, arms, legs and buttocks; infected bruises on fingers; bloodshot eyes; a cut above her eye; and a healing wound on her cheek. On the second occasion, a few weeks later, she was admitted with facial burns and belt buckle marks. Despite recording both incidents as 'crime' the police officers carried out almost nothing by way of an investigation, and in particular Lord Laming's Report concludes that two of the most basic steps in investigating these crimes should have been the obtaining of statements from the doctors and nurses concerned and ensuring that Victoria's injuries were photographed, yet the police officers did neither. In his report, Laming wrote,

> I heard no satisfactory explanation from any of the officers who gave evidence to the Inquiry as to why at least basic investigative steps were not taken. The officer's response to the question of why they did not carry out basic tasks was simply to refuse to accept even their most obvious failings, saying that medical staff were responsible for identifying the crime scene and interviewing witnesses. (Laming, 2003: 318)

Laming went on to warn the police, 'I believe that although there should be a constant and thorough sharing of information between the agencies involved, it is the police who should keep sole responsibility for the evidence-gathering process' (p 313).

One criticism of this part of the 400-page Laming Report is that an unintended consequence was to entrench each of the key agencies into their respective core roles. The police were faulted for not taking responsibility for gathering the evidence and Laming felt the need to chastise them and recommend that:

> the police should carry out completely, and exclusively, any criminal investigation elements in a case of suspected injury or harm to a child, including the evidential interview with a child victim. This will remove

any confusion about which agency takes the 'lead' or is responsible for certain actions. (Laming, 2003: 382)

The word 'exclusively' was interpreted by some police and social care policy makers to mean that no longer should the two agencies carry out 'joint investigations' and this led to a reduction in joint child protection training offered to police and social workers. The author (who was one of Laming's four advisors on the inquiry) knows that it was never the intention that joint working or joint training should cease. On the contrary, throughout the report Laming extolled the virtues and importance of joint working. After the report was published, a letter was hastily sent out by the Home Office to all Chief Constables and Directors of Social Services stating that joint working and joint training should continue, but the views in some organisations were already entrenched and the joint training arrangements which had been in place since the 1990s started to diminish, often because social workers were not sent by their organisations to take part. Dr Liz Davies, an experienced social work lecturer, pointed out that

> there has been a reduction in the provision and availability of joint child protection training at advanced level between police and social workers in section 47 investigation and investigative interviewing of children. With few social workers now trained in these skills, it is not uncommon for police to conduct child interviews without social work involvement. (Davies et al, 2015)

This claim by Liz Davies is supported by the findings of a 2014 joint Criminal Justice Inspectorates report, which examined a number of investigative interviews of children which, under the *Working together* guidelines, should have been undertaken jointly by police and social workers, and found that of the 69 interviews analysed, only nine had actually involved a social worker while 60 had been conducted by the police alone.

Many police forces now have no provision for joint child protection training, although a notable exception is the Metropolitan Police, which recently re-introduced a two-week course for police officers and social workers that, using trainers representing each discipline, covers interviewing children and other aspects of child protection investigation.

Davies also highlighted another unintended consequence of the word 'exclusively' when she claimed

> This recommendation was interpreted by police as limiting their role in child protection cases to the investigation of crime resulting in less police involvement in the investigation of significant harm. It is now difficult for social workers to engage police in child protection matters which do not clearly constitute a potential or actual crime. (Davies et al, 2015)

Some police forces will allow their child protection officers to accompany a social worker on what is sometimes known as a 'joint visit' to a home when there is a referral of a child who may be at risk of harm. The crucial point here is that on the face of it, there may have been no report of crime, and the visit is partly an exploratory visit to see whether the child is safe and well and whether or not a criminal offence may have been committed. Other police forces take a different view on this and will not allow a police officer to take part in any inquiry until a crime has been confirmed. Anecdotally, some police managers feel that to allow their officers to take part in these welfare visits amounts to no more than providing an expensive security guard for a social worker.

It would seem that in some parts, the two agencies may be diverging in respect of operational practice and the whole concept of 'Working together'. Perhaps to some social workers that may be advantageous because arguably by participating in a process that is essentially within the police sphere of influence it may be undermining their professional relationship with the family, or certainly an abusing member of the family with whom they may need to work at a later stage.

The MASH system, while not perfect, has improved the initial sharing of information and in some cases where the MASH is a decision-making body it may have ensured that joint decisions are made by police and social work managers which improve the outcome for the child. It may, however, be time to recognise that outside the orbit of information sharing, each agency has an important, but quite separate role to play in the protection of children. A prominent social work academic once suggested,

> If child protection has become policing, and this in turn is skewing child welfare policies more generally, one option we need to consider is freeing up child welfare from its policing functions. The Police have become one of the investigatory agencies, perhaps now is the time to consider whether they should be the investigative agency. (Parton, 1995)

As has been discussed, the reality is that operationally police officers and social workers actually work together for a very small part of the whole process. As long as there is good communication from the strategic to the practitioner level, resulting in joint policies and shared information, each agency could perhaps stop trying to fight its history and work, not together, but rather alongside each other, with mutual respect and consideration for their differing professional roles.

For their part, the police appear to be regressing to a less than optimum response to safeguarding children. The evidence which emerged during the Victoria Climbié Inquiry showed overwhelmingly that prior to 2003 the police were confused about their role when dealing with potential child abuse cases, and that although there were child protection units in all police forces they were often staffed with inexperienced investigators with inadequate training and a lack of resources. Upon publication of the Victoria Climbié Report, a great deal of pressure was brought to bear on Chief Constables to radically overhaul their child protection units. More recent cases, such as the death in August 2008 of Peter Connelly (sometimes known in the media as Baby P), further underlined the importance, in policing circles, of dealing with potential crimes against children much more professionally and effectively than was the case in the past. Pressure came from the Home Office and HMIC, and major developments such as national child abuse investigation guidance (Association of Chief Police Officers (ACPO), 2005[2]) and the aforementioned new national training curriculum (SCAIDP), were introduced. In line with a recommendation by Lord Laming, a national standard was introduced by ACPO that child protection units would be predominantly staffed by detective officers and, indeed, since 2006 a prerequisite for becoming an accredited Specialist Child Abuse Investigator is that an officer must have successfully completed the Initial Criminal Investigators Development Programme, which is the minimum entry standard for anyone wishing to join the CID. In 2003 the Metropolitan Police formed a centralised child protection team known as SCD5, headed by a Commander, which included a dedicated 60 officer strong child homicide squad. This demonstrated the desire of that force to avoid any repeat of the Climbié type criticism. Many other forces made major investments in the four years post Climbié, such as Kent dedicating an extra £2.5 million towards child safeguarding, Hampshire making child protection a core CID role so that any vacancies would be filled as a priority with trained detectives, and Bedfordshire investing £500,000 on new child protection offices.

However, in the last few years something seems to have gone wrong. The Metropolitan Police is by no means the only force that has been found wanting during the round of National Child Protection Inspections being undertaken by HMIC. For example, in Surrey, the inspectors found that 'child abuse investigations are being undertaken by insufficiently skilled and knowledgeable staff and are often of a poor standard leaving children at significant risk' (HMIC, 2015a) and in Cumbria the inspectors found that 'some serious child abuse cases were allocated to non-specialist teams, and enquiries and investigations were undertaken by insufficiently skilled and knowledgeable staff' (HMIC, 2017). In fact, most of the forces in England and Wales were found to be wanting in respect of child abuse investigation and in a larger thematic report based upon the inspections in eight police forces the HMIC commented that,

> Overall, investigations of child protection cases were poor. Many of the cases that inspectors examined were superficial, with too few enquiries made about an incident, or leads not followed up. In some cases, even simple activities such as taking photographs of the scene, analysing mobile phones, or referring a child for medical attention or for a forensic examination were not undertaken. (HMIC, 2015b)

These comments echo those of Lord Laming in his 2003 report, so it is possible that the situation with police child safeguarding may have even regressed to that of the pre-Climbié era. .

Organised gangs and child sexual exploitation

The chapter thus far has predominantly focused on crimes against children who have been abused within their own home by a carer. However, in recent years the police have been exposed as failing children who have been sexually exploited and abused by organised gangs and by celebrities and other powerful people. Some of these cases, particularly in the latter category, involved historic or, as it is known by the police, legacy abuse.

Child sexual exploitation (CSE) is not a new phenomenon and it can include many different forms of abuse including online sexual grooming and child trafficking. What has changed is the level of professional and public awareness generated in the last few years by the media reporting of a series of high profile investigations and criminal trials. Cases in South Yorkshire, Rochdale, Derby, Oxford and other towns and cities have uncovered not only the previously hidden scale of the problem but also a particular pattern of abuse involving predominantly teenage girls as victims, and gangs of predominantly Asian or Eastern European heritage men as perpetrators. The various reports into these cases have shown many failings in the police investigation, not least a general theme that children were not considered to be victims. The report into the Rotherham CSE cases (Jay, 2014) indicates that approximately 1,400 children were sexually exploited from 1997 to 2013. The report criticised police by saying, 'At an operational level, the Police gave no priority to CSE, regarding many child victims with contempt and failing to act on their abuse as a crime' (Jay, 2014: 1). Because the victims were often girls considered by police to be 'on the run' from children's homes, and the gangs were considered to be organised crime gangs, the established child protection units may not have seen that type of abuse as their remit because they were focused on dealing with the sort of intrafamilial abuse like the Victoria Climbié case. Instead, the investigation, if there was one at all, might well have been conducted by uniformed patrol officers or general detectives with no specialist safeguarding training. Needless to say, the police received a huge amount of criticism both in the media and in Parliament for their failings and as such the ball was kicked towards improving the response to CSE. In some forces a dedicated CSE Team was formed; for example, Staffordshire now has 30 officers split into three dedicated teams dealing with CSE, including a Preventing CSE Team, an On-street Child Exploitation Team, and an Online Child Exploitation Team (Staffordshire County Council, 2017). The overall police establishment in Staffordshire has not been increased so it is likely that these 30 officers will have been re-deployed from other duties and it is also likely that some at least have been abstracted from the existing child protection teams. This response to the criticism relating to CSE will have been replicated in many police forces throughout England and Wales.

The public protection agenda

The concept of 'public protection' became prominent in policing at around the time of the creation of MAPPAs under the Criminal Justice Act 2003 (see also Nash, this volume). These arrangements made the police, probation and prison services responsible for managing dangerous offenders who lived in the community. The terms 'public protection' or in some forces 'protecting vulnerable people' have now become more widely used and are umbrella names for: child abuse; child sexual exploitation; hate crime; domestic abuse; female genital mutilation; forced marriage; honour-based violence; modern slavery; prostitution; serious sexual offences; stalking and harassment (College of Policing, 2018). It was identified, sometimes after cases went wrong or media criticism, that police forces were failing to effectively protect vulnerable people who were subject to crime in all these areas. Perhaps wanting to tap into the success of the intra familiar child protection teams, most police forces in England and Wales created omni-competent Public Protection Teams (in Hampshire, Northumbria, Surrey), or Protecting Vulnerable Person teams (in Thames Valley, Dorset). These larger groupings invariably subsumed the original child protection teams, and also consumed a lot of the detective resources from the whole police force. This has meant that the expertise in child protection as a dedicated area may have been watered down because officers are expected to deal with a wide range of incidents, some of which have little or no relation to intrafamilial child safeguarding.

Whereas some of these larger teams may work effectively, the evidence from many HMIC National Child Protection Inspections indicates otherwise. In one inspection in 2013 conducted in a force which a few years beforehand had subsumed the child protection teams into a multi-competent Public Protection Unit the results were bleak. Adverse comments included, 'currently there is insufficient capacity and capability within the team to consistently deliver the appropriate level of service to victims of child abuse' and 'there is a "rose coloured view" amongst staff of how things were before the days of omni-competence and a belief that "all will be well" if the force was to return to a specialist child abuse unit'.

Most police forces and Police and Crime Commissioners will claim that safeguarding children and protecting vulnerable people are top priorities. However, the police have had to deal with the emergence of many other 'priorities' not least counter terrorism (see Grieve, this volume) while at the same since 2010 overall frontline police officer numbers declined by around 20,000 (Home Office, 2015). With this background, it is difficult to see how any improvement in safeguarding children is going to arise. HMIC regularly criticise forces for failing vulnerable children, but a review of their inspection reports reveals that they do not seem to come up with many solutions.

Conclusion

It is reasonable to conclude that the role of the police in safeguarding children like Victoria Climbié, who have been abused in the home by a carer, has been detrimentally affected by the perceived need to increase resources in the many other areas of policing now sheltering under the umbrella name of public protection. Perhaps the ball has been kicked to the other end of the park and it will take another high profile tragedy to bring it back.

Summary of key learning points

- Working Together has existed as a concept since The Cleveland Inquiry in 1988, yet despite the advent of the MASH system there are still tensions and inhibitors in information sharing between key safeguarding agencies, sometimes caused by a simple lack of trust.
- Most police forces and children's social care departments have no provision for joint training. The concept of "Working Together" is in fact restricted to a very small part of the overall process of safeguarding children. There is no such thing as a fully organised joint agency team which manages a case from start to finish.
- The Police have a finite number of officers. If a 'new' team is formed to deal with a problem of apparent high importance, such as the Savile case, the officers are removed from other important duties in order to form that team. There is evidence that the police sometimes react disproportionately to political or media pressure, or a fear of organisational criticism, thereby diverting resources from some important areas of their safeguarding response.

Notes

[1] In summer 2017, HMIC took on inspections of England's fire and rescue services and the name changed to Her Majesty's Inspectorate of Constabulary and Fire & Rescue Service (HMICFRS).

[2] ACPO is now known as the National Police Chief's Council (NPCC).

References

Association of Chief Police Officers (ACPO) (2005) *Investigating child abuse and safeguarding children*. London: Centrex.

Brandon, M., Sidebotham, P., Bailey, S., Belderson, P., Dodsworth, J., Garstang, J., Harrison, E., Retzer, A. and Sorensen, P. (2016) *Pathways to harm, pathways to protection: a triennial analysis of serious case reviews 2011 to 2014*. London: DfE.

Butler-Sloss, E. (1988) *Report of the inquiry into child abuse in Cleveland*. London: HMSO.

College of Policing (2018) **Authorised professional practice major crime and public protection**. Retrieved from https://www.app.college.police.uk/app-content/major-investigation-and-public-protection/

Corby, B. (1987) *Working with child abuse: social work practice and the child abuse system*. Milton Keynes: Open University Press.

Criminal Justice Inspectorates (2014) *Achieving best evidence in child sexual abuse cases.* London: HMIC.

Davies, L., Douieb, B. and Kline, R. (2015) 'Revision of Working Together, response to consultation', unpublished paper.

Dodds, V. (2016) 'Met police heavily criticised over child protection failings', *Guardian*, 25 November, www.theguardian.com/uk-news/2016/nov/25/met-police-heavily-criticised-over-child-protection-failings

Fox, L. (2018) 'The paralysis of practice in child safeguarding', unpublished PhD thesis, University of Portsmouth.

Hampshire County Council (2018) www.hants.gov.uk/socialcareandhealth/childrenandfamilies/safeguardingchildren/childprotection/mash

Harding, L.F. (1991) *Perspectives in child care policy.* London: Longman.

Her Majesty's Government (1991–2017) *Working together to safeguard children.* Various editions. London: TSO/HMSO.

Her Majesty's Inspectorate of Constabulary (HMIC) (2015a) *Surrey – National child protection inspection.* London: HMIC.

HMIC (2015b) *In harm's way: the role of the police in keeping children safe.* London: HMIC.

HMIC (2016) *Metropolitan Police – National child protection inspection.* London: HMIC.

HMIC (2017) *Cumbria – National child protection inspection.* London: HMIC.

Home Office and Department of Health (1992) *Memorandum of good practice on video recorded interviews with child witnesses for criminal proceedings.* London: HMSO.

Home Office (2015) *National Statistics: Police workforce, England and Wales: 31 March 2015.* London: Home Office.

Jay, A. (2014) *Independent Inquiry and Child Sexual Exploitation in Rotherham.* Rotherham: Rotherham Borough Council.

London Borough of Bexley (1984) *Child sexual abuse: joint investigation programme – Bexley Experiment.* London: HMSO.

Laming, Lord (2003) *The Victoria Climbié Inquiry Report.* London: TSO.

Macpherson, W. (1999) *The Stephen Lawrence Inquiry Report.* London: TSO.

Ministry of Justice (2011) *Achieving best evidence in criminal proceedings.* London: TSO.

Parliament UK (1977) *First Select Committee Report on Violence in the Family, Violence to Children.* London: HMSO.

Parton, N. (1985) *The politics of child abuse.* London: Macmillan.

Parton, N. (1995) 'Child protection: welfare and policing', paper for Rethinking Child Protection: Research Leading the Way (Conference), University of Lancaster.

Pigot, H.J.J. (1989) *Report of the advisory group on video evidence.* London: Home Office.

Smith, A.C. (1992) 'Police reforms in child abuse investigation: their success and limitations in the struggle to uphold children's rights', *Children and Society*, 6(2): 104–110.

Staffordshire County Council (2017) *Update on work to address child sexual exploitation (CSE) in Staffordshire*, Safe and Strong Communities Select Committee, 16 January, http://moderngov.staffordshire.gov.uk/documents/s90465/Update%20 on%20work%20to%20address%20child%20sexual%20exploitation%20CSE%20 in%20Staffordshire%20to%20include%20progress%20agai.pdf

Victoria Climbié Inquiry (2002) Archived oral evidence. Retrieved from https://webarchive.nationalarchives.gov.uk/20130130095758/http://www. nationalarchives.gov.uk/ERORecords/VC/2/2/P2/Evidence/Archive/ Jan02/140102latestp2.htm. Page 53, Line 15.

Further reading

Curtis, M. (1946) *Report of the Care of Children Committee*. London: HMSO.

Heald, H. (ed) (1992) *Chronicle of Britain and Ireland*. Farnborough: Chronicle Communications.

Hendrick, H. (1994) *Child welfare, England 1872–1989*. London: Routledge.

Kelly, L. and Regan, L. (1990) 'Flawed protection', *Social Work Today*, 21: 13–15.

Nardinelli, C. (1990) *Child labour and the industrial revolution*. Bloomington, IN: Indiana Press.

Reder, P., Duncan, S. and Gray, M. (1993) *Beyond blame – child abuse tragedies revisited*. London: Routledge.

Townsend, P. (1970) *The fifth social service: a critical analysis of the Seebohm proposals*. London: Fabian Society.

Wattam, C. (1992) *Making a case in child protection*. Longman: London.

9

Hate crime, policing and multi-agency partnership working

Jemma Tyson and Nathan Hall

Aims of the chapter
- To define hate crime.
- To review the evolution of responses to hate crime.
- To evaluate the strengths and weaknesses of partnership working in addressing hate crime.

Introduction

As academics working in the field of hate crime, we have collectively been involved in multi-agency partnership working as independent advisors to government, police and prosecutors at local, national and international levels over a period of 20 years or so. We have also worked with a variety of advocacy groups and third sector organisations. Over that time, we have witnessed considerable change in the nature, extent and activity of partnership approaches to hate crime, but also shared the frustrations of many others at the persistence of the challenges that this type of working inherently possesses. A simple online search using the term 'multi-agency partnership working in hate crime' instantly produces a plethora of strategies and plans from a multitude of agencies from a range of geographical locations – a testament to the development and the importance of this type of approach. In this chapter, we introduce the reader to a range of relevant issues relating to hate crime and multi-agency partnership working, including its history and evolution, and in particular the benefits and challenges involved. The chapter refers to *some* of the available and relevant literature, but also refers to our own personal reflections of working in this area.

Defining hate crime

Providing a definition of hate crime is not as simple as it may seem. It is not necessarily, as one might assume, just a crime motivated by hate. The concept is far more nuanced than that. Crime itself is a social construct and hate crime is therefore no different. While there are debates within academia about what hate crime actually is (see Bowling, 1999; Hollomotz, 2012; Perry, 2001), there is a shared, common definition of both hate crime and incidents in England and Wales: 'any crime or incident where the perpetrator's hostility or prejudice against an identifiable group of people is a factor in determining who is victimised' (College of Policing, 2014: 3).

The above is a working definition used across the criminal justice agencies of England and Wales. This definition evolved from that of a racist incident provided by the Stephen Lawrence Inquiry, which states that: 'A racist incident is any incident which is perceived to be racist by the victim or any other person' (Macpherson, 1999, para. 47.12).

The shared criminal justice system (CJS) definition therefore mirrors the intention to be purposefully broad and inclusive by concentrating on perception based reporting, and by drawing on motivations far less nuanced than hatred. The underlying rationale is to encourage the reporting of these incidents by victims and others in an attempt to reduce the dark figure of under-reporting that characterises hate crime. One can also see that there is no mention of *hate* in the definition, therefore hate crimes are, for the most part, not about hate at all. Rather, the focus is placed on *prejudice* and *hostility*. These terms are themselves not clear cut and 'everyday' interpretations are often applied.

The extent and nature of hate crime

Since the Macpherson Report (1999), hate crime has received increased attention from politicians, academics and activists. However, the extent of this problem remains unclear. The most recent publication of hate crime statistics states that in 2016/17 there were 80,393 hate crimes recorded by the police (O'Neill, 2017: 1), an increase of 29% when compared to the previous year. This is the largest percentage increase since the Home Office Statistical Bulletins on hate crime began in 2011/12, and is believed in part to be a product of increased offending following the EU referendum. Five strands of hate crime are centrally monitored, and there are clear variances in each of the recordings:

- 62,685 racially aggravated hate crimes (78%)
- 9,157 homophobic hate crimes (11%)
- 5,949 religiously aggravated hate crimes (7%)
- 5,558 disablist hate crimes (7%)
- 1,248 transphobic hate crimes (2%)

Despite over 80,000 hate crimes being recorded by police, hate crimes are considerably under-reported, with the Crime Survey of England and Wales estimating that there are more than 220,000 hate crimes per year (Corcoran et al, 2015: 1). Therefore, as a best guess, just over a third of hate incidents come to the attention of the police. There are a number of possible explanations for this, which will be considered throughout this chapter. It is, however, worth noting here that the size of the dark figure of hate crime varies by identifiable characteristic and is not uniformly distributed. There are also variations in the type of offence committed, with the majority either (relatively low level) public order offences (56%) or violence against the person offences (33%) (O'Neill, 2017: 5). These percentages are much higher for hate crime than they are for overall crime, but again the prevalence varies for each monitored strand. Recorded disablist hate crime, for example, involves much lower levels of public order offences but higher levels of violence against the person without injury, compared to, say, race hate crimes. The implication here is that such variables command different and appropriate responses from the authorities – a point noted by the Stephen Lawrence Inquiry when it highlighted the need for police services to treat individuals according to their *needs*, rather than treating them the *same*.

Reflection

What might be some of the reasons for the under-reporting of hate crime?

This is evidenced, for example, when exploring the specific needs of disablist hate crime victims. *Disability* is itself an umbrella term and can refer to physical and learning disabilities, of varying degrees. The accurate identification of a learning disability can often be challenging, with some easily hidden unless an individual discloses their disability (Jacobson, 2008: 37). Failure to identify, or for a victim to disclose their disability, can result in inappropriate responses from the police and other agencies, but also impacts on the knowledge available on the extent of disablist hate crime.

Furthermore, there are some forms of bullying and antisocial behaviour that may not be considered a criminal offence, but the suffering experienced by the victim may not be less than that inflicted by offences that are labelled as criminal (Rieter et al, 2007: 373). The cumulative effect is evidenced in the case of Fiona Pilkington, where a combination of persistent hostility and a failure of organisational responses ultimately led to the death of Fiona Pilkington and her disabled daughter Francecca in 2007. In other disablist cases, however, the perpetrator may be a carer or have a close personal relationship with the individual with learning disabilities, who may be dependent on them in their day-to-day life. This can therefore reduce the likelihood of victims reporting their abuse and victimisation. In short, this brief consideration of just a few of the variables contained within just one strand of hate victimisation is illustrative of the complexities facing those seeking to challenge its occurrence.

The impact of hate crime

A growing volume of academic literature has increasingly made the case that the impact of victimisation is often significantly worse for hate crime victims than for victims of comparable crime without the hate element (Corcoran et al, 2015; Hall, 2013; Iganski, 2001). Research has demonstrated that hate crime victims experience multiple impacts for a longer duration than victims of crime overall. Hate crime victims are also more than twice as likely to experience fear, anxiety or depression and have lower levels of confidence and greater feelings of vulnerability than victims of crime overall (Corcoran et al, 2015: 22). Crucially, hate crime also has the potential to impact beyond the individual victim, with its effects permeating the wider community (see Hall, 2013, for a wider discussion of the effects of hate crime).

In addition, and key to the focus of this chapter, hate crime victims are also more likely to be dissatisfied with the police response they receive. The Crime Survey of England and Wales (CSEW) reported that hate crime victims are less likely to think the police treated them fairly or with respect than victims of crime overall. In only 59% of hate crime incidents did victims think the police treated them fairly, compared to 81% of incidents of crime overall (Corcoran et al, 2015: 21). As with crime types and reporting levels, satisfaction rates also vary across the monitored strands. While the constraints on this chapter prevent a full examination of these variances, it is important to reiterate the point made by Macpherson (1999) and recognise that hate crimes are not homogenous and therefore the responses cannot, and should be not, be uniform.

Perpetrators of hate crime

The following two quotes from Ben Bowling, which still resonate today, illustrate the relative novelty of research concerning hate offenders. Moreover, it arguably provides an additional explanation for the situation we describe in the following section of this chapter – namely that effectively addressing hate crime through partnership working has historically proved to be extremely difficult and has produced uncertain and inconsistent outcomes. Referring to race hate offenders, Bowling argued that:

There has been almost no research on perpetrators. Whilst the most basic of descriptions have been formulated, they remain something of an effigy in the criminological literature ... The perpetrator is unknown and, consequently, the possibility for any understanding or interpretation of his or her behaviour becomes impossible. (1999: 163)

He further argued that:

What is needed for the purposes of explaining violent racism is for attention to be turned away from an analysis of the characteristics of victims to focus on the characteristics of offenders: their relationship with those they victimise; the social milieux in which anger, aggression, hostility, and violence are fostered; and the social processes by which violence becomes directed against minority groups ... Criminologists operate with scant evidence about what is going on in the lives of these people. Instead, we have only a devilish effigy for symbolic sacrifice. (1999: 305)

The potential for multiple motivations for hate offenders more generally was also made in one of the early seminal pieces of research in this field. Although limited by a methodology that drew only on police files in Boston (McDevitt et al, 2002) nevertheless suggested a typology of hate crime offenders that involves four categories of motivation. The first category – and by far the most common – relates to offenders being motivated by a desire for excitement and *thrill*; the second suggests offenders are *defensive*; the third suggests that offenders are *retaliatory*; and the final category – and thankfully the rarest of them all – refers to offenders who view themselves as fulfilling a *mission* to rid the world of the object of their hatred. Further discussions of these motivations are beyond the remit, and purpose, of this chapter; however, it is important to note for the purposes of this chapter that the motivations behind hate crime differ, and therefore the required response to occurrences of hate crime should also vary.

This position is further reinforced by Craig (2002) in her review of the socio-psychological literature relating to hate offenders. She identified specific issues that relate to the characteristics of hate crime perpetrators, and in doing so noted the difficulties associated with seeking to explain why hate crime occurs:

Although several explanations may be applicable to hate crime occurrence, no existing one can fully account for all types of hate crime. This is because the factors that contribute to hate crime (i.e. perpetrators' motives, victims' characteristics, and cultural ideologies about a victim's social groups) differ markedly for each incident ... Thus, in order to explain hate crimes, a consideration of all potentially relevant explanations is necessary. (Craig, 2002: 120)

Simply then, hate crime perpetrators can effectively be motivated by one or more of a wide range of social, psychological, political, cultural and other factors. On the basis of Craig's statement, searching for a single, universal causal factor for hate crime will be fruitless. Rather, it is the interplay of a number of different factors prevalent in the lives and social circumstances of individuals that produces perpetrators. The implications of this for the subject of this chapter are therefore significant. Craig's conclusions identify multiple causal factors in the commission of hate crime, which in turn implies the need for tailored solutions to local problems that draw on the expertise and knowledge of a range of relevant individuals, agencies, and organisations.

The historical context of multi-agency partnership working in hate crime

Iganski (2008) notes that the importance of cooperation between the police and other statutory agencies in tackling race hate crime, and between the statutory agencies and non-government organisations, has long been recognised in European countries, reflecting the principles of multi-agency cooperation enshrined in the European Constitution. Article III-257 states that:

> The Union shall endeavour to ensure a high level of security through measures to prevent and combat crime, racism and xenophobia, and through measures for coordination and cooperation between police and judicial authorities and other competent authorities ...

The evolution of hate crime multi-agency partnership working in England and Wales, meanwhile, has its roots in responses to racist offending and victimisation dating back to the 1980s. As Iganski (2008) correctly states, the reference point commonly used in policy literature for the origins of multi-agency working in the UK is the 1986 House of Commons Home Affairs Committee report *Racial attacks and harassment* (HM Government, 1986) This regarded a multi-agency approach as critical for effectively addressing problems associated with race hate crime, and thus cemented multi-agency working as one of the dominant official state responses for tackling race hate crime over the following two decades and beyond (HM Government, 1986); Iganski, 2008). In its report, the Home Affairs Committee recommended that police forces and local authorities, where the need existed, should develop a multi-agency response that included local authority departments (including education, housing and social services), together with the police, Crown Prosecution Service (CPS), the local Race Equality Council (REC), and other non-statutory voluntary organisations involved in supporting victims of race hate crime.

Following the Home Affairs Committee report, the government of the day established the *Racial Attacks Group* – an inter-departmental working party chaired by the Home Office and tasked to consider the potential for increasing cooperation between the police and other agencies in preventing and responding to race hate crime and the provision of support for the development of local multi-agency working (Bowling, 1999; Iganski, 2008). The group produced three key reports, in 1989, 1991 and 1996. Chronologically and collectively, the reports found limited examples of effective multi-agency working, and documented the difficulties and challenges encountered by those seeking to implement such approaches. Key among these difficulties were issues of trust and confidence and a lack of understanding and appreciation of the roles and priorities of partner agencies. Later on, in 1999, the *Racial Incidents Standing Committee* (in effect the successor to the Racial Attacks Group) added the crucial issue of leadership (or the lack/ weakness of, to be more precise) to the list of factors that significantly limited the effectiveness of partnership working, noting the importance of having, but vulnerability of relying on, a small number of committed individuals in ensuring the success of partnership approaches.

Despite the plethora of instructional guidance concerning effective multi-agency partnership working published throughout the late 1980s and 1990s, the principle and the process, while widely accepted as good practice, was plagued by problems, the need to overcome which was reflected by the introduction of a legal requirement in the Crime and Disorder Act 1998. Indeed, the significance and urgency of the issue had become indisputably apparent in Part Two of the Stephen Lawrence Inquiry (Macpherson, 1999; emphasis added), which categorically stated both with alarm and optimism that:

> 45.18. Another much canvassed topic during our meetings was the importance of and the need for genuine multi-agency partnership and co-operation to combat racism, and to bring together all sections of the community with this aim. Such partnership between the police, local Government, Housing and Education officers, Probation Officers and many others is a vital part of the necessary co-operation which is required. Again there is evidence of promising good practice. We heard of encouraging advance in Lambeth, Collyhurst (Manchester), Bristol, and elsewhere. But there is plainly a need for much more co-operation, both in directly combating racism and in the vital arrangements which must be made for the collection, recording and exchange of information between agencies. Racist incidents in schools or between tenants may provide most useful intelligence for the police, and vice versa.

And:

> 46.40. First and foremost and fundamentally we believe that there must be a change so that there is genuine partnership between the police and all sections of the community. This cannot be achieved by the police alone. The onus is upon them to start the process. All

other agencies, particularly those in the field of education and housing must be involved. Co-operation must be genuine and vigorous. Strategies to be delivered under the new Crime and Disorder Act will provide an opportunity in this respect. Training will play its part. The active involvement of people from diverse ethnic groups is essential. Otherwise there will be no acceptance of change, and *policing by consent may be the victim.*

The importance of these issues was reflected in Recommendation One of the Inquiry, that a Ministerial Priority be established for all police services: 'To increase trust and confidence in policing amongst minority ethnic communities'.

Legal duties and obligations

The Crime and Disorder Act 1998

The Crime and Disorder Act 1998, referred to by the Stephen Lawrence Inquiry with considerable optimism and expectation, places a statutory duty on a number of responsible authorities to work in partnership to reduce crime and disorder (see also Loveday and Roberts, this volume). Community Safety Partnerships (CSPs) are made up of representatives from the responsible authorities, which include:

- the police
- local authorities
- fire and rescue authorities
- the probation service
- health services

The statutory duty requires these authorities to work together to address local crime and disorder problems and in doing so protect local communities from crime. As part of this process, local crime priorities should be reassessed annually and community safety plans are required to be developed in consultation with partners and the local community (note the link to Macpherson's observations, above, here).

The Equality Act 2010

In addition, and of particular relevance to hate crime, is that public authorities and organisations all share the same legal duties under section 149(1) of the Equality Act 2010. These duties state that a public authority must, in the exercise of its functions: have due regard to the need to eliminate discrimination, harassment, victimisation and any other conduct that is prohibited by or under this Act; foster good relations between persons who share a relevant protected characteristic and persons who do not share it; and advance equality of opportunity between persons who share a relevant protected characteristic and persons who do not share it.

The Police Reform and Social Responsibility Act 2011 and the role of Police and Crime Commissioners

Police and Crime Commissioners (PCCs) are not a responsible authority for the purpose of membership of the CSP. However, they are required to work together with their local CSP to develop local approaches to reduce and prevent crime. Section 10 of the Police Reform and Social Responsibility Act 2011 sets out a flexible framework for partnership working between CSPs and PCCs, allowing for the adoption of locally meaningful arrangements:

> Section 10(2) The elected local policing body for a police area, in exercising its functions, and a responsible authority, in exercising its functions conferred by or under section 6 of the Crime and Disorder Act 1998 in relation to that police area, must act in co-operation with each other.

Both the PCC and the relevant authorities are also required to have regard to each other's priorities when developing their respective plans (Section 10(1)).

The challenges of effectively policing hate crime

Article 47 of the Charter of Fundamental Rights of the European Union states that individuals have the right to an *effective remedy* and a fair trial. In its consideration of 'effective remedies' available to victims of hate crime across the member states of the EU, the European Union Agency for Fundamental Rights (FRA, 2017) notes that while it is essential to prevent such crimes, it is equally important to ensure that victims have access to justice. For FRA (2017: 1) this means enabling victims to report their experiences to competent institutions, and then providing them with the support they need. At the same time, FRA insists, hate crimes must be promptly and effectively investigated, and the perpetrators punished.

However, in concluding its review, FRA (2017: 8) notes that:

> Efforts to counter hate crime can only succeed if victims report the wrongs they endure, and the various responsible actors all do their part to ensure that perpetrators are brought to justice. As the report underscores, a variety of factors prevent this from happening. These include weaknesses in the applicable legal frameworks, difficulties in grasping and working with the concept of hate crime, uncertainties as to the concept's significance and meaning to the organisation in which a professional works, and risks of institutional discrimination,

which can have a devastating impact on the trust of victims and their readiness to report their victimisation.

FRA's report brings to the fore a number of challenges that exist that affect the effectiveness of criminal justice responses to hate crime. There is not the space here to examine each of these issues in any real detail, although their importance is deserving of considerable attention. However, in seeking to identify the issues that impact upon the effectiveness of police responses to hate crime in England and the United States, Hall (2009, 2010, 2012, 2013) concluded that a multitude of interrelated factors exist, but they can ultimately be reduced to issues relating to *ability* and *desire* on the part of law enforcement agencies, and to *knowledge*, *ability* and *desire* on the part of the public.

Hall's research suggests that while there is inevitably considerable overlap between those factors that impact upon the ability and the desire of the police to respond to hate crimes, the key factors impacting upon the *ability* of the police to respond are broadly as follows:

1. The operational definition and conceptualisation of hate crimes and incidents
2. The volume of hate crimes and incidents
3. The nature and legal ambiguity of hate crimes and incidents
4. The extent and nature of personal and organisational resources
5. The exercise of discretion
6. The content and propriety of both strategy and policy instruction
7. The investigative process and case construction
8. Quality of training
9. Internal and external pressures
10. Organisational goals and visions of 'success'

In addition, the key factors impacting on the *desire* of the police to respond to hate crimes are as follows:

1. Organisational culture
2. State of staff morale
3. Levels of officer confidence in dealing with hate crime incidents
4. Extent of understanding and appreciation of the issues relating to hate crime
5. Calibre of leadership
6. Nature of formal rules and sanctions

Crucially, as also noted by FRA above, law enforcement agencies are largely dependent on the public to invoke the services on offer (primarily by reporting incidents to them), which in turn is dependent on both the *ability* and the *desire* of the public to do so. Furthermore, these two caveats are themselves dependent on the public first having a degree of *knowledge* about hate crime and the services available to respond to it. The ability and desire of the police to respond effectively to hate crimes are therefore crucial in influencing the ability and desire of the public to engage with the police, and the relationship is reciprocal. For Hall, it is this relationship that is central to 'success' in the effective policing of hate crime.

As both Pound (1917) and Cotterrell (1992) have rightly claimed, and in line with FRA's observation above, citizens' willingness, and having the trust and confidence, to invoke law is therefore essential for effective service delivery by state agencies. In Hall's view, therefore, the three interrelated areas of *knowledge*, *ability* and *desire* within and between relevant parties are of central importance in developing and delivering effective responses to hate crime including, of course, partnership working. Indeed, factors relating to each of these broad principles are reflected in the guidance on multi-agency partnership working in the area of hate crime produced by the College of Policing (2014), discussed below.

The benefits of multi-agency partnership working in responding to hate crime: the perspective of the College of Policing

The College of Policing (2014: 64–65) states that the benefits of statutory partnership activity to tackle hate crime are clear. The College's Operational Guidance for Hate Crime outlines the key benefits of such activity, which include: the ability to facilitate information and intelligence sharing, thereby helping to quantify the hate crime geographically or within a specific section of a local population; the ability to prompt agencies with community safety responsibilities to develop and deliver a coordinated safety package for actual and potential victims of hate crime; preventing the duplication of service delivery by different agencies; and producing a consolidated approach to accessing additional resources.

The College also highlights the importance of extending activity beyond statutory partnerships to include communities and third sector partners, who are not part of statutory arrangements, in order to encourage wider collaborative working. The key to success, it suggests, is the imagination and innovation to secure a spread of partners. Involving groups and individuals that other agencies cannot reach will, the College suggests, helps to achieve sustainable relationships between the police and minority communities to: address local hate crime problems; enhance trust and develop confidence in the ability and commitment of the police to deal with hate crime; create an ongoing dialogue to increase community confidence and generate a flow of community intelligence; produce openness and transparency, which they suggest will provide the police with a better understanding of the impact that hate crime has on the community while simultaneously assisting the community to better understand the constraints and legal requirements that can hamper police action and prevent successful prosecutions; and through the joint ownership of problems and solutions provide an opportunity for partners to share in the success of hate crime initiatives, thereby promoting further collaborative effort.

In further espousing the benefits of multi-agency partnership working, the College also points out the importance of continually appraising the impact of hate crime on the day-to-day quality of life of victims and communities, which in turn will help to identify where adjustments to policing policy, priorities and operational practice are necessary. Effective partnership working therefore ensures that individual and collective needs are not only captured but that, more importantly, positive action is (at least in theory) taken.

The result of this, the College (2014: 65) suggests, should be to produce an environment where individuals feel free to live, work and move around freely. It follows, they suggest, that such an environment will be less tolerant of hate crime and those who commit it. The importance of this very point was articulated by Bayley, back in 2002. While arguing that the police cannot directly reduce hatred, Bayley (2002) insists that they can significantly contribute to the creation of an environment that lessens the likelihood that hatred will result in interpersonal violence by acting in ways that create bonds of citizenship. This, he suggests, will be the result of being fair, effective and open in all policing activity, and protecting the human rights of *all* members of a diverse society.

The College further recommends that through effective partnership arrangements the opportunities for joint training and the provision of secondment opportunities can enhance the understanding of all stakeholders and thereby improve the effectiveness of the police response to hate crime. This type of approach, it suggests, may offset a lack of experience within some statutory partnerships. In line with the observations of the Stephen Lawrence Inquiry, the College insists that the police service is ideally placed to assume a leadership role to expand and extend partnership networks and develop joint working protocols to enhance local service provision. Ultimately, it suggests, the police need to invest effort to support partners to improve the service provided to victims.

The need for multi-agency partnership working in combating hate crime: the UK government's Hate Crime Action Plan

Although there is not the space here to discuss the document in any detail, the government's Hate Crime Action Plan itself is a demonstration of a commitment to partnership working between government departments, criminal justice agencies and other statutory bodies, the third sector and members of diverse communities (HM Government, 2016: 10). Indeed partnership working is one of the central underpinning themes of the action plan, and a significant number of the 119 action points specifically refer to the need to work with partners when responding to hate crimes in order to reduce their occurrence across a whole range of hate crime issues.

For example, action point 48 specifically refers to the need to work with community groups when responding to hate crimes in order to reduce their occurrence. This engagement with community organisations is seen throughout the action plan and there is also a recognition that organisations with specific knowledge and experience of particular characteristics must also be involved. For example, action point 50 refers to the engagement with community based organisations that can meet the needs of those affected by hate crimes motivated by homophobia or transphobia, and point 89 places importance on the organisations that are already present within the Gypsy, Traveller and Roma communities.

Effective partnership working therefore involves a wide range of partners and this is evidenced in the variation of agencies that are discussed throughout the action plan. The Department for Culture and Local Government, Department for Education, CPS, the National Holocaust Centre and Museum, Police forces, the College of Policing, the Director of Public Prosecutions, the Sophie Lancaster Foundation, Tell MAMA, the Community Security Trust, and the Fire and Rescue Service are just some of the organisations mentioned, in addition to the government's own hate crime independent advisory group.

The challenges of multi-agency partnership working in hate crime

We have already identified a number of historical challenges to effective multi-agency partnership working. There is no doubt that these are stubbornly persistent – a clear indication of the complexity of the issue. Having reviewed a range of international strategies from around the world aimed at preventing hate crime, the International Centre for the Prevention of Crime (ICPC, 2002) identified a number of common challenges pertaining to partnerships and consultations. While reflecting the theme of this chapter, namely that partnership working is essential in effectively responding to hate crime, the ICPC also recognised that they can be very difficult to develop, work and sustain, not least because of the sensitive nature of the issues in hand.

These difficulties, the ICPC research (2002: 28) suggested, can be because of a reluctance by individuals, local authorities or organisations to acknowledge racial and other minority harassment; a reluctance on the part of minority communities and victims to report incidents or trust other groups; and over-ambitious expectations, unforeseen constraints and mistaken assumptions. The ICPC (2002: 28) also identified a range of other common problems, including: insufficient resources and finance; organisational constraints, such as difficulties in changing existing policies; inflexible internal structures, ideologies and working practices; procedures and legal frameworks outside the control of local agencies; lack of full – rather than token – representation of minority communities; and inequalities in power and decision making between, for example, the police and other agencies, and minority or community representatives. Experience shows, the ICPC suggests, that there need to be very clear and specific objectives laid down for consultations between the police or other agencies and community groups.

Concluding comments

As is the norm with a chapter such as this, we have tried to provide a wide-ranging overview of what we believe to be the key issues in hand. Undoubtedly, forming, managing and sustaining meaningful partnerships that produce effective responses that in turn deliver improvements to the lives of victims of hate crime is a complex, challenging and vulnerable process. We fully expect that practitioners working in this area will readily recognise some or all of the challenges that we have outlined from their own experiences.

Summary of key learning points

Drawing on both the available literature and our own professional experience, we believe that the following points, although not exhaustive, are central to effective partnership working:

- clear organisational goals and priorities;
- terms of reference that include *clear and realistic* aims and objectives and that are regularly reviewed in line with changing local priorities;
- clear actions and associated accountability for delivering those actions;
- strong moral leadership and commitment both to legal and moral duties from all levels of the agencies involved;
- ensuring that the partnership has the correct representation (and therefore the correct knowledge, expertise, experience and agendas) from both statutory agencies and the communities affected;
- an appreciation of the roles, priorities and capabilities of others in the partnership;
- empathy, understanding, and an ability to metaphorically 'walk in the shoes of victims';
- an evidence-based approach to understanding (not just identifying) local problems;
- creativity, imagination and flexibility in the creation of solutions to problems that go beyond simply viewing hate crime in silos (that is, just as race, or disability, or gender identity, and so on, and recognising the impact of intersectionality); and
- measurement and evaluation of processes, deliverables and outcomes to assess effectiveness and progress.

While the need to achieve the above might seem obvious to some, but perhaps unrealistic to others, it is our view that these issues should serve as the aspiration of multi-agency partnerships in seeking to effectively respond to hate crime. We recognise the complexities involved here, but at the same time we are drawn to Lord Laming's words in his report of his Public Inquiry into the failure of statutory agencies in West London to prevent the murder of 8-year-old Victoria Climbié in 2000. In seeking to learn the lessons from Victoria's death for responding to, and preventing, future incidents of this kind, Lord Laming concluded by stating that 'I am convinced that the answer lies in doing relatively straightforward things well' (2003: 13).

References

Bayley, D.H. (2002) 'Policing hate: what can be done?', *Policing and Society*, 12(2): 83–91.

Bowling, B. (1999) *Violent racism: victimization, policing and social context*. New York: Oxford University Press.

College of Policing (2014) *Hate crime operational guidance*. Coventry: College of Policing Limited.

Corcoran, H., Lader, D. and Smith, K. (2015) *Hate Crime, England and Wales, 2014/15*. Home Office Statistical Bulletin 05/15, www.gov.uk/government/uploads/system/uploads/attachment_data/file/467366/hosb0515.pdf

Cotterrell, R. (1992) *The Sociology of Law*. Second edition. London: Butterworths.

Craig, K.M. (2002) 'Examining hate-motivated aggression: a review of the social psychological literature on hate crimes as a distinct form of aggression', *Aggression and Violent Behaviour*, 7: 85–101.

European Union Agency for Fundamental Rights (FRA) (2017) *Ensuring justice for hate crime victims: professional perspectives*. Vienna: FRA Publications Office, http://fra.europa.eu/en/publication/2017/ensuring-justice-hate-crime-victims-professional-perspectives-summary

Hall, N. (2009) 'Policing hate crime in London and New York City', unpublished PhD thesis, University of Portsmouth.

Hall, N. (2010) 'Law enforcement and hate crime: theoretical perspectives on the complexities of policing hatred', in N. Chakraborti (ed), *Hate crime: concepts, policy, future directions*. Cullompton: Willan Publishing.

Hall, N. (2012) 'Policing hate crime in London and New York City: reflections on the factors influencing effective law enforcement, service provision and public trust and confidence', *International Review of Victimology*, 18(1): 73–87, https://doi.org/10.1177%2F0269758011422477

Hall, N. (2013) *Hate crime*. Second edition. Abingdon: Routledge.

Hollomotz, A. (2012) 'Disability and the continuum of violence', in A. Roulstone and H. Mason-Bish (eds), *Disability, hate crime and violence*. Abingdon: Routledge.

HM Government (1986) *Racial attacks and harassment*. London: Home Office.

HM Government (2016) *Action against hate: The UK Government's plan for tackling hate crime*. London: Home Office.

Iganski, P. (2001) 'Hate crimes hurt more', *American Behavioural Scientist*, 45(4): 626–638.

Iganski, P. (2008) *Hate crime and the city*. Bristol: Policy Press.

International Centre for the Prevention of Crime (ICPC) (2002) *Preventing hate crime: international strategies and practice*. Montreal: ICPC.

Jacobson, J. (2008) *Police responses to suspects with learning disabilities and learning difficulties: a review of policy and practice*. London: Prison Reform Trust.

Laming, H. (2003) *The Victoria Climbié Inquiry*. London: The Stationery Office.

Macpherson, W. (1999) *The Stephen Lawrence Inquiry*. Cm 4262. London: The Stationery Office.

McDevitt, J., Levin, J. and Bennett, S. (2002) 'Hate crime offenders: an expanded typology', *Journal of Social Issues*, 58(2): 303–317.

O'Neill, A. (2017) *Hate Crime, England and Wales, 2016/17*. London: Home Office.

Perry, B. (2001) *In the name of hate: understanding hate crimes*. New York: Routledge.

Pound, R. (1917) 'The limits of effective legal action', *International Journal of Legal Ethics*, 27: 150–167.

Rieter, S., Bryen, D.N. and Shachar, I. (2007) 'Adolescents with intellectual disabilities are victims of abuse', *Journal of Intellectual Disabilities*, 11(4): 371–387, https://doi.org/10.1177/1744629507084602

10

The complexity of partnerships in the UK Counter Terrorism Strategy. What might we learn from contemporary efforts to counter hate crime?[1]

John Grieve

Aims of the chapter

- To provide an outline of the current UK Counter-Terrorism Strategy and its complex nature, with a particular focus on the 'Prevent' element within that strategy.
- To assess its impact on community relations and multi-agency working.
- To consider whether UK governmental approaches to hate crime might provide a better framework.

Introduction

The UK Counter Terrorism Strategy[2] is called CONTEST and has four constituent pillars: 'Prepare, Pursue, Prevent and Protect'. This chapter looks at the complexity of partnership working across CONTEST[3] and in the 'Prevent' pillar in particular, and some of the perceived problems associated with it. It will be argued that much might be learnt from the joined-up thinking, community engagement and involvement in the UK cross government action plan on hate crime. Given the nature of, and concerns about the terrorist threat in the UK it is difficult to engage in research and therefore much of the discussion that follows will rely on speeches by key stakeholders, reputable media accounts and policy documents.

Terrorism in context

BBC News published a very useful highly detailed analysis on 30 August 2017 entitled 'Who was behind jihadist attacks in West and North America?'

A series of attacks in Europe over the summer months has raised the number of people killed in the West by jihadists during the past three years to more than 420 ...The deaths of 16 people in Barcelona and Cambrils earlier this month highlighted the continued threat posed by Islamist militants. The summer months have also seen new attacks in Belgium, France, Austria, Germany and the UK, as well as the first in Finland and one in the US. We identified 63 attacks between September 2014 and late August 2017 ... A relatively limited number of countries were affected: nine in Europe – those named above, plus Denmark and Sweden – along with the US and Canada. Regardless of country, most attacks were in large towns and cities – including Barcelona, London, Manchester, Paris, Nice, Berlin, Brussels, Stockholm and Orlando. In total, the 63 attacks caused 424 deaths and left almost 1,800 people injured. The perpetrators are not included in these figures. The Paris attack of November 2015 was the deadliest, with 130 people killed, including 90 at the Bataclan theatre. France also saw the Nice lorry attack, which left 86 people dead. There were many other attacks that left many people dead and others injured. In Orlando, 49 people were killed in an attack on a gay nightclub. Bombings at Brussels airport and at a metro station left 32 people dead; 14 people were killed at a Christmas party in San Bernardino, California; 12 people died when a lorry was driven into a crowded Christmas market in Berlin; 12 people died when the Paris offices of Charlie Hebdo were attacked in January 2015; Five people were killed in the Westminster attack in April. The Manchester Arena bombing in May led to 22 deaths: The London Bridge attack in June left eight people dead: The attacks in Barcelona and Cambrils left 16 people dead. In total, these 11 attacks were responsible for 386 deaths... Although the number of young people being radicalised has caused concern, the average age of the attackers – 27.5 – is not unusually young. The two youngest were 15 – an unnamed boy who attacked a Jewish teacher with a machete in Marseille, and Safia S, a girl who stabbed a police officer at a Hanover train station. Of the five who were under the age of 18 at the time, four were in Germany. The vast majority of the attackers were in their 20s, with about one in four attackers above the age of 30 and six aged 40 or older. Despite women becoming increasingly active in jihadist networks, only two out of 85 individual perpetrators were female. Fewer than one in five perpetrators was a convert to Islam, with a significantly higher percentage in North America than in Europe. However, the converts were significantly more likely to have a criminal background and to have served time in prison. Overall, half of the attackers had a prior criminal background. The relationship between terrorism and migration is a complex one and has been at the centre of extremely polarising debates, particularly during the European migrant crisis. However, the number of attackers who were illegally in a country or who arrived as refugees is small. Two-thirds were citizens of the country they attacked, with others either legal residents, or legal visitors from neighbouring countries. However, individuals who were in the West illegally also carried out deadly attacks. At least two of those involved in the November 2015 Paris attacks are thought to have posed as refugees to enter Europe through Greece. Three other individuals were refugees or asylum seekers at the time of attack, while seven were in the country illegally or awaiting deportation. There is also one case of 'terrorist tourism', involving Egyptian citizen Abdullah Hamamy, who lived in the United Arab Emirates and attacked soldiers at the Louvre in February 2017. Two of the four most lethal attacks – those in Paris in November 2015 and in Brussels in 2016 – are believed to be well orchestrated multiple attacks directed by IS [Islamic State]. They were also executed in part by former foreign fighters. However, the two other most deadly attacks – those in Orlando in June 2016 and in Nice in July 2016 – were carried out independently by individuals without operational connection to a jihadist group. *These episodes demonstrate that terrorist sympathisers who never travelled to conflict areas and who act independently can be as dangerous as a team of highly trained militants.* Overall, links between attackers and jihadist groups operating overseas are not always easy to determine. Of the attacks that have hit the West since June 2014, *fewer than one in 10 was carried out under direct orders from the leadership of IS*. In some cases, it can be difficult to tell, for example IS said it was behind both the Las Ramblas and Cambrils attacks, but it did not provide any evidence. Nevertheless, the influence of IS can be clearly seen. During or before the attack, six out of 10 perpetrators pledged allegiance to a jihadist group, almost always IS – which frequently claims responsibility. Unsurprisingly, given the frequency of attacks and the number of deaths and injuries, jihadist terrorism has come to the fore of political debates in the West and receives widespread news coverage. *The threat is not expected to wane in the near future, with policymakers, counter-terrorism officials and the public all being asked to take action.* There are huge implications for domestic and foreign policy throughout Western countries. It is hoped that knowing more about the attacks and the people who carried them out will help us all have a more informed debate about what action is needed. (BBC News, 2017a[4], emphasis added, permission to quote kindly given by BBC)

CONTEST

In responding to, or preventing such attacks from happening the four pillars of the CONTEST strategy are as follows:

1. Prevent means stopping people becoming terrorists and supporting violent extremism (which in itself includes a thread called 'Channel', a counter radicalisation project to provide considerable resources to divert people identified as crossing a threshold of threat and risk).
2. Pursue involves stopping terrorism by investigation, disruption, arrest, prosecution.
3. Protect is concerned with strengthening defences against terrorists.
4. Prepare deals with resilience in communities, to be able to mitigate the impact and after-effects of any attack.

The roles of the police in the four pillars of CONTEST

Police,[5] policing and partnerships with other agencies have a role in all of the four pillars. The arrangements in the CONTEST roles are multiple and complex but nonetheless includes the lead for the Police in any investigation.

- Other government departments such as the security services, secret intelligence service, Foreign and Commonwealth Office, and Home Office have the lead role of intelligence gathering. The Police act as the executive arm of the lead intelligence agencies and also have a major role in gathering street level and community intelligence.
- The Police investigate if an attack takes place (Pursue).
- They gather evidence with forensic scientists, arrest suspects, and aid Crown Prosecution Service (CPS) prosecutions (Pursue).
- They aid with counter terrorism prevention and target hardening (Protect and Prepare) and of course they have their traditional task of working with communities and creating public confidence in the protection of citizens (see Cox, this volume).
- At street level the Police help with multiple community involvement projects (Prevent/Protect). This involves the Department of Communities and Local Government and Department of the Environment to help to reduce risk by stopping terrorists for example by licensing boundary security guards at crowded events (Protect) or by identifying warning signs in young people and hence minimise their vulnerability (Protect/Prepare/Prevent). (PNLD, 2013; Pearse, 2015)

The contested nature of the policy and practical environment of 'Prevent'.

The policing partners and Police role is complicated by elements in the environment in which the threat takes place. The first element is the scale and tempo of the contemporary attacks and the fear they spread (Basu, 2018; BBC, 2017a). The second element is legal: the UK Terrorism Act 2006 defines terrorism as 'acts designed to intimidate the public to advance political, religious, racial, ideological agendas'. This includes preparatory acts, to finance, incite, encourage, induce, urge or persuade, possessing items or disseminating publications. These acts can be inside or wholly or partly outside the UK and concern the commission, preparation, encouragement, training and instigation of acts of terrorism (PNLD, 2013). The third element is the interrelationship of Prevent with the other pillars of CONTEST, for example the intelligence gained during Prevent shared with the partners in Pursue (the part of the strategy aimed at collecting evidence to put individuals before the UK Criminal Justice System). The fourth element is the international dimension: a global set of partners, ranging for example from USA officials and diplomats and some aspects of the Syrian conflict (non-governmental organisations for example), to the geographic origins of some immigrants. Fifth is the economic environment, the poverty of some in the Muslim community, the absence of standards of critical thinking in some education that would enable challenges to the purveyors of violent extremist ideology. Sixth is the difficulties of narratives and complex dialogues involving religions, varieties of faiths, race, culture, social background and geographic origins. Seventh is the mass of information, alleged as facts, immediately available on the internet on all the six preceding elements.

The problems with 'Prevent' pillar of the strategy are that some people view it as 'toxic' to social cohesion (Basu, 2018; Warsi, 2018: 87, 109–110; Cole, 2016). This group may be broken down into those who actively and vocally undermine and denounce it, including some academics, some religious leaders and some who have experienced it. Another group might be those who are anxious and cautious about it including some politicians, teachers, community leaders and parents. In taking on board some of these criticisms, the development of the programme from 2018 includes an emphasis on improving the understanding of which people are truly vulnerable and how partnerships can be strengthened to meet these needs. This includes strengthening and learning from all the safeguarding issues and applying the more generalised safeguarding duty to young people directly to counter terrorism; this includes for example learning from responses in respect of online child sexual exploitation and grooming or other issues.

The US Open Society Justice Initiative, after studying 17 cases, concluded Prevent was 'flawed and potentially counterproductive' (Cobain, 2016). The report highlighted lack of evidence for referrals to Prevent and Channel and concluded there were 'multiple, mutually reinforcing structural flaws ... and serious risks human rights violations' (in respect of discriminations and freedom of expression). The structural flaws alleged included targeting pre criminality, nonviolent extremism, interference with day-to-day lawful discourse. Cobain also quotes Rights Watch UK with similar conclusions. Alan Travis (2017) pointed out that 80% of Prevent referrals led to a decision of no risks nor threat and only 5% were referred for specialist help.

A particularly trenchant critical analysis by Tariq Ramadan, Professor of Contemporary Islamic Studies at Oxford University, heavily criticised Prevent and drew robust responses from Ben Wallace MP the Security Minister, as well as CC Simon Cole cited above. Ramadan concluded many referrals were created by an overemphasis on religious grounds, targeted on communities on specific religious profiles while ignoring the role of social status, unemployment, drug use, psychological imbalance or views on the role of foreign policy (Ramadan, 2016). Ramadan goes on to attack the securitisation and surveillance aspects in Prevent and especially what he identifies as the subjective, highly selective emphasis in local community partnerships. He argues that many of the latter are with non-credible organisations and are suspicious of and antagonise nonviolent Muslims. Ben Wallace (2016) took him to task in forthright terms.

A similar critical challenge to that of Ramadan was made by the Muslim Council of Britain in respect of what they claimed was a strand of 'ideological purity' required of Muslim partners in Prevent whereby, for instance, UK foreign policy could not be criticised. This therefore excluded from debate some Muslim scholars who were against violence in any form, which in turn precluded their potential engagement in Prevent action at a local level. They did acknowledge, however, that there was a very real threat of radicalisation to violent extremism for young Muslims (Dodd, 2016). This alleged exclusion of critics is exactly the opposite of what the Hate Crime Action Plans have proposed. This inclusion of critics could be addressed in the three-year planning and activity proposed in CONTEST (Home Office, 2018). A principle of democratic safeguarding and governance is at the heart of some of Home Secretary Sajid Javid's response to what he describes as robust challenges from current and former independent reviewers of counter terrorism strategy. Javid (2018) conceded that it is not always possible to agree but that this was part of the liberal, tolerant, pluralistic society we live in. He did not, however, conclude that other serious critics of policy, strategy and tactics should be included in those discussions as they are in the hate crime forums (Hate Crime IAG Minutes, 2009–2018).

A BBC News website report (2017b) stated that:

> Thousands of children and teenagers were referred to the government's anti-terror programme in England and Wales last year, Home Office figures show. Of the 7,631 referrals in 2015–16, a quarter of which were ... under-15s, but only 381 required specialist help.

Reflection: the Prevent pillar of CONTEST

Given the number of referrals and the proportion who required specialist help, how do you interpret those figures?

Do you agree with Labour MP Naz Shah who said the figures reinforced her concerns about the scheme? What concerns might you have?

Or do you agree with Conservative security minister Ben Wallace, who said it had got 'real results'? What are those results and might there be any unintended consequences?

Or do you agree with Chief Constable Simon Cole, the national policing lead for Prevent, who said the number of referrals showed that 'trust and support is growing' for the programme? How is this statement supported by the data?

Despite the difficulties there are different views on the issues raised, with for example Dean Haydon (Senior National Coordinator for Counter Terrorism) being very positive about the community relationships that have been developed through the Prevent process (Bentham, 2018). I would argue that criticisms of the policy tend to be instantly repeated while often sub judicial rules prevent examples of good practice with respect to community support and robust counter measure reaching the public. Different people have very different and honest opinions about these issues but, as Simon Cole writing in the *Guardian* (Cole, 2016) argues, there may be an unwillingness to listen to the positives of the policy before adopting a negative attitude and engaging in a confirmation bias. Successes of approaches like Project Servator[6] tend to be ignored. One of the issues with identifying the development of successful community relationships in Prevent is that there is no agreed profile nor identified pathway into terrorism that people take (Home Office, 2018: 32). Effective partnerships in this latest iteration of CONTEST are therefore identified as working as widely as possible with schools, local authorities, local communities, health groups and professionals, social care, NHS and psychiatrists (Home Office, 2018: 36, which also cites examples of best practice but which are anonymous for obvious reasons). These have been achieved by the increasingly skilled Prevent Coordinators and the Prevent Education Officials. Simon Cole, the NPCC Lead for Prevent, has said 'I know Prevent is not perfect … Prevent needs to improve' (Cole, 2016). By 2017 Cole was saying 'This notion of Prevent as toxic brand is simply incorrect and born from misunderstanding. what I would like to hear more of is constructive dialogue … [it] feels like people are sniping for the sake of it … [it] doesn't reflect the reality of local delivery of the voluntary safeguarding' (Dodd, 2017).

Possible lessons from the Hate Crime Strategy

As noted above the Prevent aspects of CONTEST are seen as problematic through it being racist, post-colonial and patronising. When seen within the context of the Home Office Hostile Environment Policy that Theresa May created as Home Secretary this would make some sense. The real problem here is that the approach has been driven by a top down strategy rather than engaging with local communities to build from the bottom up. Approaches such as complexity theory demonstrate that it is precisely the lower order interactions which drive a system, and that these 'problems' cannot be controlled out from the top down (see Pycroft, this volume; Grieve, 2015). In a detailed and extremely thoughtful exception to the limited information rule, Metropolitan Police Deputy Assistant Commissioner Neil Basu (addressing the Police Superintendents' Association annual conference in September 2017) said the risk posed to the UK from terrorists was 'an unknown threat in our midst' and the authorities could not 'arrest their way' out of terrorism because there would be a 'revolving door' of suspects. He warned isolated communities and unregulated schooling in the UK were a 'breeding ground' for extremism. He went on to say:

Prevent is the hugely controversial part of the strategy. Government will not thank me for saying this, but an independent reviewer of Prevent ... would be a healthy thing ... Prevent is, as a Prevent officer who used to work for me said, five percent of the budget but 85 percent of the conversation. Prevent is the most important pillar of the four pillar strategy. There is no doubt in my mind about it. Prevent is the key... There is still this hangover of toxicity around the Prevent campaign that we need to stop, because people need to understand that this about stopping people in the pre-criminal space ever getting anywhere near criminality. And Prevent needs to concentrate on how it does that. That cannot be a job for the police and security services. That has got to be a wider societal pillar... There will always be a role for policing because we are a frontline. But actually the big responsibility is how do we get everyone else interested and involved and talking positively about some of the brilliant work that is going on. Prevent, at the moment, is owned by the government, but I think it should be outside central government altogether. I think people who are running their local communities should be taking the lead... Communities should be talking about protecting themselves from the grassroots up. When you see Prevent working on the ground brilliantly, that's where it's working, and largely unsung and un-talked about. Substantial community resilience is produced by that sort of work, and giving people that resilience is important and communities have to help each other do that... We have gotten all of that messaging the wrong way around, it should be grassroots up. Previously, this was not being done. But there are increasingly some phenomenal voices who've got real gravitas in their communities who are beginning to talk about the issues. The Mayor of London, Sadiq Khan, is a really good example of that. He is not central government, he runs a city, and the protection of the city is his concern, he should be doing that, not MI5. Not the Cabinet, and the National Security Council and New Scotland Yard." (Basu, 2018, permission to quote kindly given by BBC)

I have selected one aspect of the UK response to hate crime and some partnership roles within it to illustrate the potential partnership learning from the 'bottom up'. It has been argued by Paul Giannasi, the intergovernmental programme lead, that hate crimes are sometimes the foothills of terrorism (Giannasi, 2018). Key activities in the 2018 Hate Crime Action Plan for the programme have been the detailed, continuous involvement of a wide range of different perspectives and narratives from an independent advisory group (IAG) with an independent chair. This is an example of partnerships in a complex environment involving community organisations both statutory and non-statutory, single interest support and advocacy groups. The Stephen Lawrence Family campaign produced in turn a public inquiry and recommendations that included community, local and national IAGs with a considerable diversity of participants and a variety of concerns. It also, of course, introduced many other activities – for instance, hate crime legislation and the important national introduction of Police Family Liaison Officers. These latter actions had their origins in Avon and Somerset Constabulary but also, relevantly for the argument in this paper, in national counter terrorism policing. The advisory groups set up for monitoring the recommendations of the Stephen Lawrence Inquiry have representative members currently on the Intergovernmental Hate Crime IAG and are monitoring progress with recommendations nearly 20 years later. This demonstrates the importance of continuity (Hall et al, 2015).

The Sophie Lancaster Foundation is another example of the diversity of interests and perspectives on an IAG. Named after the victim of a vicious attack based on identity, the Foundation has produced teaching packs about very early interventions in blocking the formation of irrational likes and dislikes that can produce bias and arguably later prejudice in very young children, by considering their likes and dislikes.

The joint working of the Jewish Community Security Trust (CST) and the Muslim organisation that learnt from them – Tell Mama – illustrates widely holistic strategic partnerships of direct relevance to the arguments introduced here. CST has developed innovative protection measures and the analysis of anti-Semitic incidents, for example their location and other patterns, and shared their methodology with the Islamic organisation. Both groups are represented at senior level on the IAG. Together they contributed to creative, calm and practical responses to 'Punish a Muslim' Day (Minutes of Hate Crime IAG, 2009–2018).

The approach adopted for hate crimes is for a detailed partnership learning approach across government departments and integrated by an action plan and a programme largely driven at local, even neighbourhood, level. It is an acknowledgement of the power, impact and interaction of some families within their communities, and directs attention to proximate causes from family issues and other social problems. Most importantly, it recognises and focuses on understanding how communities are seeking their own solutions. The programme has been internationally admired and commended as best practice (Hall et al, 2015). Changes to the programme in 2018 included the re-introduction of a strategy board of senior officials on which the IAG has permanent membership. Above that group it is being mooted that there should be a regular meeting of ministers to discuss, among other things, the interaction of hate crimes and terrorism and the so called 'spikes' in hate crime following the 2017 Westminster, Manchester and London Bridge attacks. This development, provided it does not supersede local and neighbourhood activities, would go a long way to address the learning suggested here (Hate Crime IAG Minutes, 2009–2018).

Reflection

What is your experience of involvement with Prevent and with other agencies? To what extent do you think that this could be a genuinely 'bottom up' initiative or is it hampered by 'top down' narratives of control?

Further thinking and resource

Read Simon (2009) and consider the extent to which Prevent can be considered a part of his governing through crime thesis.

Conclusion

This chapter has looked at the complexity of partnerships across the counter terrorism arena and what might be learnt from the cross government programme and action plan on hate crime. It has been argued the UK Counter Terrorism Strategy and the variety of partners is one cause of complexity. Another is strategic role of policing (in its widest senses including the roles of all partners) and Policing in the sense of the 43 services, NCA and other public bodies. So one task here has been to articulate how the government can achieve a joined-up strategy. This task needs to be examined in the light of current threats, including that from the extreme right wing.

There are commonalities to be learnt in how to deal with this partnership complexity from the UK hate crime programme. Community organisations like Stephen Lawrence Family campaign, Sophie Lancaster Foundation, CST and Tell Mama have all identified the importance of addressing racism, listening to experiences of the people involved, and the role of women in mediating and impacting on issues through a widely diverse partnership approach largely driven at local (even neighbourhood) level and supported by government. The programme also emphasises the power, impact and interaction of some families within their communities, the role of very early intervention with young people and attention to proximate causes from social problems. Government needs to provide support and resources at the grassroots level to tackle extremism and terrorism to ensure that top down control mechanisms do not bring about the very things that they want to prevent.

> **Summary of key learning points**
> - The policing of counter terrorism is complex given the range of partners and their functions that are involved.
> - A strategy that encourages a bottom up approach that actively works with communities is required.
> - To achieve this much can be learned from the development of the UK hate crime programme and the grass root initiatives that have followed from it.

Notes

1. An early version of this chapter was presented at the University of Delft in Den Haag in September 2017 and another version in central England with some practitioners in February 2018. I am grateful to both groups for their feedback. Other ideas were developed with master's and undergraduate students and with teachers in training all of whom helped. Responsibility for this version is mine alone.

2. See Lawrence Freedman (2013): nearly 750 pages on the complexities of strategy, pages x, xi and 32 on allies as partners are especially useful.

3. The context is further complicated by ongoing policy developments in this field, not least the 2018 appointment of a government commissioner for countering violent extremism (CVE) and the recent advertisement for an advisor on CVE to the Mayor of London (City of London Step Change Summit, 2017).

4. This analysis piece was commissioned by the BBC from an expert working for an outside organisation. Dr Lorenzo Vidino is the director of the Program on Extremism at the George Washington University and of the Program on Radicalisation and International Terrorism at the Italian Institute for International Political Studies (ISPI) in Milan. This research is part of a report by ISPI, George Washington's Program on Extremism and the International Centre for Counter-terrorism in The Hague, conducted by Dr Vidino, along with Dr Francesco Marone and Eva Entenmann. Full report: *Fear Thy Neighbor. Radicalization and Jihadist Attacks in the West.* An earlier version of this piece was published on 14 June 2017. This version provides updated figures, based on the attacks that have subsequently taken place (BBC News, 2017a).

5. This chapter uses the distinction between 'Police' with a capital 'P' denoting the public sworn police and their civil service colleagues in for example the Metropolitan Police; 'policing' with a small 'p' relates to all the bodies concerned with keeping the peace, for example partnerships in schools or local government. See Grieve et al (2007) or Haberfeld et al (2018).

6. www.cityoflondon.police.uk/community-policing/project-servator/Pages/Project-Servator.aspx

References

Basu, N. (2018) 'A view from the CT foxhole: Neil Basu, Senior National Coordinator for Counterterrorism Policing in the United Kingdom', Combating Terrorism Center at West Point, https://ctc.usma.edu/view-ct-foxhole-neil-basu-senior-national-coordinator-counterterrorism-policing-united-kingdom/

BBC News (2017a) 'Who was behind jihadist attacks in West and North America?' 30 August, www.bbc.co.uk/news/world-40000952

BBC News (2017b) 'Prevent scheme: anti-terror referrals for 2,000 children', 9 November, www.bbc.co.uk/news/uk-41927937

Bentham, M. (2018) 'Counter-terror chief praises tip-off that led to conviction of IS recruiter', *Evening Standard*, 12 February, www.standard.co.uk/news/london/counterterror-chief-praises-tipoff-that-led-to-conviction-of-is-recruiter-a3764381.html

City of London Step Change Summit (2017) Notes of a Workshop, 17 July.

Cobain, I. (2016) 'UK's Prevent counter-radicalisation policy "badly flawed"', *Guardian*, 19 October, www.theguardian.com/uk-news/2016/oct/19/uks-prevent-counter-radicalisation-policy-badly-flawed

Cole, S. (2016) 'Hear us before you knock Prevent', *Guardian*, 31 October, p 23.

Dodd, V. (2016) 'UK Muslims to go it alone with rival terror prevention strategy', *Guardian*, 20 October, p 1.

Dodd, V. (2017) 'Police consider making Prevent Scheme compulsory', *Guardian*, 10 August.

Freedman, L. (2013) *Strategy*. Oxford: Oxford University Press.

Giannasi, P. (2018) Lecture July 2018 at London Metropolitan University Cross Government Hate Crime Program Action Plan and Role of Independent Advisory Group. See also True Vision Website.

Grieve, J., Harfield, C. and MacVean, A. (2007) *Policing*. London: Sage.

Grieve, J. (2015) 'Thinking about peace', in J. Pearse (ed), *Investigating terrorism. Current political, legal and psychological issues*. Chichester: Wiley, pp 239–258.

Haberfeld, M., Lieberman, C. and Horning, A. (2018) *Introduction to policing. The pillar of democracy*. Carolina: Carolina Academic Press.

Hall, N., Corb, A., Giannasi, P. and Grieve, J. (2015) *The Routledge international handbook on hate crime*. Oxford: Routledge.

Hate Crime IAG (Independent Advisory Group) (2007–2018) Minutes of meetings, conferences and workshops, unpublished.

Home Office (2018) *Counter-terrorism strategy (CONTEST) 2018*, www.gov.uk/government/publications/counter-terrorism-strategy-contest-2018

Javid, S. (2018) 'Our response is to terrorism is balanced not Orwellian', Opinion Journal, *Guardian*, 11 June, p 4.

Police National Legal Database (PNLD) (2013) *Blackstone's counter-terrorism handbook*. Oxford: Blackstone.

McAulay, J.W. and Spencer, G. (eds) (2011) *Ulster loyalism and the Good Friday Agreement, history identity and change*. London: Palgrave.

Pearse, J. (ed) (2015) *Investigating terrorism. Current political, legal and psychological dimensions*. Chichester: John Wiley and Sons.

Ramadan, T. (2016) 'The politics of fear: how anti-extremism strategy has failed', *Guardian*, 5 September, p 21.

Simon, J. (2009) *Governing through crime: how the war on crime transformed American democracy and created a culture of fear*. Oxford: Oxford University Press.

Travis, A. (2017) 'Only 5% of those referred to Prevent get specialist help', *Guardian*, 10 November, p 17.

Wallace, B. (2016) 'Prevent strategy has more pros than cons', *Guardian*, 6 September, p 28.

Warsi, S. (2018) *The enemy within. A tale of Muslim Britain.* London: Penguin.

Further reading

Brown, J. (ed) (2014) *Future of policing.* London: Routledge.

Cobain, I. (2016) 'UK far right: fractured, dispirited, violent', *Guardian*, 25 November, p 19.

Cook, T. and Tattersall, A. (2014) *Senior investigating officer handbook.* Oxford: Blackstone Oxford University Press.

Cronin, A.K. (2009) *How terrorism ends.* Princeton: Princeton University Press.

English, R. (2009) *Terrorism: how to respond.* Oxford: Oxford University Press.

Hall, N., Grieve, J. and Savage, S. (2009) *Policing and the legacy of Lawrence.* Devon: Willan.

Huntley, B. (1977) *Bomb squad.* London: W.H. Allen.

Independent Monitoring Commission (2003–2011). Reports 1–26. Northern Ireland and London: The Stationery Office.

Khalil, T. and Zeuthen, M. (2016) *Countering violent extremism and risk reduction.* Whitehall Report 2-16. London: RUSI.

Omand, D. (2010) *Securing the state.* London: Hurst and Co.

Ratcliffe, M. and Rabinstein, C. (2013) *Counter terrorism handbook.* Third edition. Oxford: Blackstone Oxford University Press.

Rea, D. and Masefield, R. (2014) *Policing in Northern Ireland. Delivering the New Beginning.* Liverpool: Liverpool University Press.

Ridley, N. (2014) *Terrorism in East and West Africa.* Cheltenham: Edward Elgar.

Rowley, M. (2018) 'Extremism and Terrorism: The need for a whole society response', The Colin Cramphorn Memorial Lecture. 26 February, https://policyexchange.org.uk/pxevents/the-colin-cramphorn-memorial-lecture-by-mark-rowley/

Royal United Services Institute (2015) *A democratic licence to operate. Report of the Independent Surveillance Review.* London.

The Times (2017) 'Editorial: Burnham's Myopia. The government deradicalisation program is working though you would not know it', 27 May, p 29.

11

Interviewing children as suspects: the need for a child-centred approach

Lesley Laver

> **Aims of the chapter**
> - To consider how young people experience the criminal justice system as a suspect.
> - To review (briefly) the policy and provisions that exist to protect children when they first come into contact with the police.
> - To analyse the roles that different parties and agencies play in the interviewing of young suspects.
> - To discuss the need for effective strategies for the assessment and proper inclusion of young suspects in the police station.

Introduction

Of the 779,660 million arrests conducted by UK police in 2017, around 10% were of children aged 10–17 (Home Office, 2017). Young people make up a noteworthy proportion of the crime suspects passing through police custody each year yet, in the UK, there is technically no separate criminal justice system for children. Instead, a number of adaptions to the adult system have developed over the course of UK history, in an attempt to account for the difficulties young people are likely to face accessing justice (Taylor, 2016). Despite some modifications, the youth justice system is still complex and requires a young suspect to deal with many complex concept and processes, as well as a number of different adults and agencies along the way. Involvement in the criminal justice system as a suspect can be perplexing enough for adults: for children, it can be confusing to the point of paralysis. Young suspects often bounce between services disorientated, not really that aware of who does what or where they are going (Bevan, 2016).

The police arrest and interview are often the earliest moments of interaction between a young suspect of crime and the justice agencies. They form a very central element of the criminal justice system. The interview is the point at which crucial evidence may be gathered and the suspect of crime is offered an opportunity to state their case. It is the moment when a suspect, under threat of prosecution and potentially life-changing consequences, must make important decisions; such as whether to cooperate, exercise rights and answer questions. During these moments of stress and important decision making, the juvenile must interact with a number of different adults from a number of different agencies, all the while trying to work out which ones they should trust. It can be argued that the interview places a greater burden on a young suspect of crime than any other aspect of the criminal justice process. It requires a child to understand their rights, understand the roles and responsibilities of others, listen, remember, communicate and resist pressure. It requires a number of mature cognitive and social skills, which are not yet fully developed in a young person. The interview places a young suspect in a position of inferiority and vulnerability but, despite this, more than 70,000 young people are subject to investigative interview each year (Home Office, 2017).

International laws and treaties recognise the difficulties that children will face navigating complex legal systems and require member states to make provisions to assist them. The Convention on the Rights of the Child (1989) and the European Convention on Human Rights (1950) stress the importance of enabling young people to express their views in any matters affecting them. They also emphasise that respecting the dignity of children in conflict with the law requires *all professionals* involved in the legal process to have knowledge of child development, knowledge of the dynamic and continuing growth of children, and knowledge of what is appropriate to their wellbeing. There is a global expectation that individual countries provide laws to protect the interests of children when they are interviewed by the police, and an expectation that the interests of the child remain the primary consideration of all agencies involved (UN General Assembly, 1989). This chapter explores the multi-agency dynamics of the police interview with child suspects and looks at whether this process can actually be considered 'child-centred' in the UK.

The child-centred approach

In March 2015 the UK Government published *Working together to safeguard children: A guide to inter-agency working to safeguard and promote the welfare of children*. The guidance outlines the legislative requirements and specific duties of different UK agencies to protect children. Within its definition of children who are at risk or in need, the guide refers to 'children who are unlikely to achieve or maintain a reasonable level of health or development without the provision of services' (in accordance with the Children Act 1989). Children who have committed (or are suspected of committing) a crime are explicitly included within this definition and the guidance highlights how early intervention is critical to the future wellbeing of such children. The guidance also makes specific reference to the police as an agency with such a duty. They are considered to be particularly well placed to identify risk in the young people they encounter and are expected to work closely with other agencies to safeguard the futures of such children.

The guidance describes effective early intervention for at risk children as being reliant on a 'child-centred approach' (the approach also supported by the Children Act 1989, the Equality Act 2010 and the United Nations Convention on the Rights of the Child). It states that 'Failings in safeguarding systems are too often the result of losing sight of the needs and views of the children within them, or placing the interests of adults ahead of the needs of children.' Organisations with effective safeguards are described as promoting 'a culture of listening to children and taking account of their wishes and feelings'. The guidance states that:

> Children want to be respected, their views to be heard, to have stable relationships with professionals built on trust and to have consistent support provided for their individual needs. This should guide the behaviour of professionals. Anyone working with children [including police] should see and speak to the child [including suspects]; listen to what they say; take their views seriously; and work with them collaboratively when deciding how to support their needs.

While suspects' needs are often an afterthought in the prosecution of crime (Jacobson, 2008), the arrest and subsequent interview of a young person may provide some of the first insights into the risks a young person is facing. The arrest and interview themselves, if perceived negatively by the child, can *contribute* to their risk of reoffending. Research has demonstrated that the attitudes individuals develop towards police in childhood exert a lasting effect on their judgement of police as adults (Easton and Dennis, 1969). Involuntary contact with the police is likely to have a detrimental effect on this attitude (Skogan, 2005) and any perceived procedural unfairness is likely to negatively influence a child's future compliance with the law (Fagan and Tyler, 2005). Offending before age 14 has been identified as a primary risk factor for serious and/or persistent violent offending in adulthood (Mclean and Beak, 2012) and it is therefore extremely important for the police and other agencies involved in the arrest and interview process to consider their approach to young suspects very carefully. The Crime and Disorder Act (1998, s37) establishes a duty on all agencies involved in the youth justice system to prioritise the *prevention* (rather than *prosecution*) of offending by children. It is therefore very important that principles of procedural fairness are upheld and that agencies work together to give the child suspect a voice. The police interview is one of the few points in the criminal justice process at which a child is afforded the opportunity to speak, but their ability and willingness to take this opportunity can be largely dependent on the type of tactics used by the police and other agencies involved.

First contact

When we consider legal processes and policies, it can sometimes be easy to neglect the impact of the real-life context in which they operate. It can be intuitive to presume that when a suspect is questioned by police, their focus will be on the police process and possible legal consequences. This is not always the case though, and for many young suspects, relationships, home life, school, or a number of other concerns can be a preoccupation while in custody. Fears of punishment from parents, carers or headteachers can be a priority and may have a significant influence over the way in which a child responds to questions. Arrests, by their nature, tend to happen suddenly without warning and with limited opportunity to make any arrangements. Contact with others is immediately limited and in the technological communication age we live in, this alone can be quite distressing for some suspects. This distress may be further heightened where a suspect feels an urgent need to 'deal' with whatever circumstances have led to arrest. Juvenile suspects describe having quite different experiences of the police when being arrested. Some juveniles describe the police coming to their homes and politely escorting them to the station, while others complained of being "grabbed" and immediately "treated as though they were guilty". Some of these children described "kicking off" in custody in direct response to what they perceived as "bad treatment" from officers (Panzavolta et al, 2016). The manner in which police or other agencies approach a young person is likely to have a direct influence on whether a child chooses to speak; intimidation, lack of trust and resistance to procedural unfairness are cited as common reasons to invoke the right to silence (Quirk, 2016).

Custody and questioning

When a young person is suspected of a crime, the police may arrange to speak to that young person about their involvement in one of two ways: arrest, followed by an interview in custody, or voluntary interview.

Arrest

Police can arrest young people where it is necessary to allow prompt and effective investigation of a crime, provided that they have reasonable grounds to suspect that young person of being guilty. Children under the age of criminal responsibility (ten years of age) are conclusively deemed to be incapable of committing a criminal offence, so cannot be arrested. Police must take into account the age of a young person when deciding whether grounds of arrest apply and should particular attention to the timing of arrests and that children are held no longer than needed (Police and Criminal Evidence Act, PACE, 1984).

Custody

Once arrested, a suspect should be taken to a police station as soon as is practical (they may also be 'street bailed' and asked to return to the station at a later date). Once at the station, the suspect is presented to a custody officer. The custody officer must then assess whether there is a necessity for detention. Unless there is sufficient evidence for a charge, or detention is *necessary* for questioning or preservation of evidence, the young person must be bailed (released). If the decision is made to detain the suspect, the custody officer becomes responsible for the oversight of the young person's detention and must ensure that they are questioned in accordance with a number of safeguards (which are set out in the paragraphs below). The custody officer has a duty to inform the person(s) responsible for the child's welfare of their arrest and, in most cases, will request that they attend the police station for the child's interview. Once a young suspect is detained at the police station, the 'PACE clock' begins and officers have 24 hours in which to conduct their investigations. This can be extended up to 36 hours with permission of a superintendent, but once elapsed, the child must be released (PACE, 1984). This 'clock' puts a number of operational pressures on police, not least of which is the pressure to get a number of necessary parties together (parent, solicitor, interpreter) in order to interview the child. These pressures have been attributed to a rise in voluntary interviews in place of arrest and, in some cases, breach of the young person's rights (such as the discouragement of legal advice) (Ashford et al, 2006).

Voluntary interview

If an arrest is not deemed *necessary*, the police may interview a young suspect voluntarily 'outside of custody'. In practice, such interviews might take place at a police station, satellite suite, the suspect's home, school or even in the back of a police car. Where a suspect voluntarily accompanies an officer to a police station (or any other location) for the purposes of assisting an investigation, he or she is entitled to leave at any time (unless subsequently placed under arrest) (PACE, 1984). However, research shows that this is not always made clear to the juvenile. Some child suspects describe being told that they can leave, but if they do they might be taken into custody, or that their freedom to leave will end at any time the officer feels the need to arrest them (Panzavolta et al, 2016).

When interviewed on a voluntary basis, information gained from a suspect will have the same admissibility in court as information gained under arrest. The suspect's rights are also identical to those as when they are questioned under arrest; however, this may not be immediately obvious to a young suspect – especially if asked to provide information in an informal location (PACE, 1984). Suspects are less likely to be informed of their rights effectively in voluntary interviews, as it is the interviewing officer, rather than custody officer, who falls responsible for explaining them. The interviewing officer is not independent from the investigation in the same way that the custody officer is, and does not have a set custody procedure to follow to ensure that all entitlements are made clear. Some solicitors state that their clients declined legal advice for a voluntary interview because the police officer informed them that they would need to be taken into custody for a lawyer to attend (Panzavolta et al, 2016). Young suspects may feel obliged, under such pressures, to answer 'informal' police questions quickly and may not realise that this can still very much lead to prosecution. Surprisingly, many professionals from other agencies involved in the youth justice process report being unaware of this danger (Panzavolta et al, 2016). A recent government consultation on the revision of the PACE (1984) Code C has seen a number of charities involved in the protection of vulnerable groups request that the oversight of voluntary interviews become independent (Bath, 2017). This appears a necessary step if the legal rights of young suspects are to be clearly explained and respected.

Rights

When in custody, all suspects have the right to:

- have a person informed of their arrest;
- obtain legal advice (for free); and
- consult a copy of the Codes of Practice.

These rights must be explained to a suspect and may be exercised at any time while the suspect is held in custody. In practice these rights are read to child suspects a number of times over the course of an investigation, but many claim that these are read out too quickly for them to understand (Panzavolta et al, 2016). Suspects also have the right to remain silent (both inside and outside of custody) and the implications of this right are explained in the police caution (which must be given before any interviews are conducted). This reads:

> You do not have to say anything. But it may harm your defence if you
> do not mention when questioned something which you later rely on
> in court. Anything you do say may be given in evidence.

This complex legal position can be very difficult to understand, especially for young people or vulnerable adults (Gudjonsson, 1994), which is why a number of specific safeguards are in place for these groups. These safeguards are conferred by Code C of the Police and Criminal Evidence Act ('PACE' 1984), which considers all children, by nature of age, to be vulnerable in interviews. Most PACE safeguards apply to all suspects under the age of 18 (though a few small provisions apply only to those under 17 years of age). The key safeguards relevant to interviewing and custody are:

- the requirement for presence of an 'appropriate adult' (AA) during questioning or searches; and
- the provision of local authority accommodation where a child is charged with an offence but is not released from custody.

The appropriate adult

The requirement for an 'appropriate adult' (AA, independent from the police) to be present in interviews is perhaps the most significant difference between the interview process for child suspects and adults. The AA is an additional party to the interview (not the police, lawyer or interpreter) and is designed to act as a procedural safeguard for the juvenile. Their purpose is to:

- support and assist the child;
- ensure the police act fairly and respect the child's rights; and
- help the child communicate with the police.

Their presence in police interviews with juveniles is mandatory (unless an 'urgent' interview is authorised by a superintendent) and they are intended to provide an independent safeguard and assistance for the child. In practice, however, their ability to act independently and effectively has been questioned: Research has shown that the intentions and behaviour of the AA can vary considerably depending on who has been chosen to fulfil the role and that their influence on interviews is not always positive (Pearse and Gudjonsson, 1996a). Such controversy surrounding the AA role raises important questions about the motives of each of the adults sat in the interview room and questions who (if anyone) is really best placed to know what the best interests of the child are.

The AA is arranged (and therefore usually selected) by the police and is permitted to be:

- the child's parent or guardian (or care authority if the child is in care);
- a local authority social worker, or, failing this;
- another responsible adult over the age of 18 who is not a police officer or employed by the police.

Estranged parents and solicitors are not considered appropriate and nor are any parties 'interested' in the proceedings, such as the victim, witnesses or anyone to whom the child has admitted the offence. The first port of call for police is usually the child's parent or guardian, but where parents or social workers are not available to perform the AA role, dedicated AA services with paid or volunteer staff are often on hand to provide a suitable adult. Such adults have usually received some training on PACE and the child's rights and have been advised on how to perform the AA role in advance.

On arrival at the police station, the AA is entitled to meet with the suspect to help them understand their rights and the police process. Trained AAs will often explain the roles of the other parties that will be involved in the interview, such as the police officers and legal representative. Trained AAs will usually request the presence of a solicitor, although it is ultimately up to the child if they wish to speak with them. Parents may be learning about this role for the first time and might not be as knowledgeable about police procedure or what is expected from them (Palmer and Hart, 1996). They have been shown to be less likely to ask for legal representation for the child suspect (Panzavolta et al, 2016). Once in the interview room, the AA should be reminded by the police that their role is not to be a passive observer, but to actively facilitate communication. Research has demonstrated, however, that there is often confusion between AAs and police about what constitutes 'appropriate facilitation'. In an example from one study, an officer stated to an AA: "Your role is to facilitate communication and not to answer questions or talk to your son. If you do, we will stop the interview and get another AA" (Panzavolta et al, 2016). It is not clear from this statement whether the police thought the AA (a parent in this case) should be actively involved in the interview or not, but it is possible to see where this sort of confusion could arise: while a parent may be well placed to gauge their child's level of understanding, they might also experience a temptation to answer questions on their child's behalf, especially if they feel it is in their child's best interest to do so.

Research into the effectiveness of the AA as a safeguard has illustrated that they can serve as both a protection and also a possible source of jeopardy for the juvenile. The mere presence of an AA in the interview room has been shown to influence the behaviour of police in interviews, with less leading questions being asked and less interruptions or challenges of the child's account being made. In this respect, the AA role can be considered an important safeguard for the child's right to fair evidence and fair trial. It has been suggested that the presence of the AA may draw police attention to the potential vulnerability of their suspect and result in selection of a more cautious interviewing strategy (Medford et al, 2003). For this reason, the AA has been considered to strengthen the reliability and fairness of evidence given by children. The danger of this, however, is that their mere presence can legitimate the interview process even in situations where the manner of the interview might be less than suitable. The AA's presence may be seen to 'bestow a degree of respectability' on what could in some cases constitute a false confession (Pearse and Gudjonsson, 1996b). The suitability of the approach, behaviour and intervention of the AA is therefore very significant to the fairness of a child's interview.

Studies that have examined the particular contributions made by AAs to suspect interviews have found that AAs are not always that active in supporting the child or ensuring fair procedure (Evans, 1993). They are frequently described as passive observers by police and in some studies as having intervened in inappropriate ways (Brown, 1997). In one particular analysis of inputs made by AAs in interview, they were seen to have answered questions on the behalf of the suspect, sometimes incriminating them, or took on the role of the investigating officer by asking questions, challenging the truth of the suspect's account or insisting the suspect tell the police the truth (Medford et al, 2003). These activities are contrary to the advice usually given by a legal representative and are rarely considered to be in the best interests of the child's case (Cape, 2011). While the role of the AA is not to provide legal advice to the young person, it is to ensure that the child is supported to act in their legal interests during an investigation. The majority of parents may intend to act in their child's best interests, but they are not necessarily best placed to know what this constitutes in the legal arena. Parents are rarely legally trained and may not appreciate the full legal implications of providing a detailed account to the police, despite this perhaps seeming preferable in a moral sense.

With no formal screening process in place, it has been suggested by some members of trained AA services that police tend only to reject parental AAs where they are prolific offenders, involved in the offence or heavily substance dependent (Panzavolta et al, 2016). There is no fixed system to ensure that a parent who takes on the AA role understands the legal process. There is also, arguably, no possible way in which a parent could be seen as an 'independent' party to proceedings, whatever their approach to their child's arrest. Trained AAs are also not above the influence of personal and political opinion and may differ considerably on their interpretation of what is 'best' for a child. While less 'connected' to an individual case, trained AAs also receive only a small amount of instruction for what can be considered a very active, complex and onerous role (Medford et al, 2003). Most AAs remain confused about the requirements of their role (Palmer and Hart, 1996) and even some social workers, solicitors and custody officers are not clear about the primary function of the AA (Bean and Nemitz, 1994). The responsibility for the procedural fairness of an investigative interview is a considerable one and perhaps none of the providers listed in the PACE can reasonably be expected to meet such high demands. One of the most crucial elements of the criminal investigation process should possibly be overseen by a professional with considerable training in child development, law and procedure.

The legal representative

Suspects of crime in the UK have an unequivocal right to consult with a legal representative (LR/solicitor/lawyer) free of charge and in private at any time in the police station (or elsewhere if being interviewed voluntarily). The police are required to inform a suspect of this right when they enter custody and again before the commencement of an interview (where the suspect is entitled to have his/her lawyer present). The lawyer's role is solely to protect and advance the rights of their client (Ashford et al, 2006). They have extensive training on the law and the duty solicitor accreditation scheme in the UK also requires legal representatives in police stations to undertake training on the special treatment of juveniles. This has been shown to improve the quality of advice given to child suspects (Panzavolta et al, 2016) and is a practice also compulsory in many other

European states – where AAs are not mandatory and many lawyers take on this welfare role themselves (Bridges and Choongh, 1998).

An important element of the suspect–lawyer relationship is 'legal privilege' – a doctrine which dictates that discussions between the two parties are completely confidential. Neither the suspect nor the lawyer can be obliged to divulge the contents of their conversations to the police, courts or anyone else. This gives the child a unique opportunity for openness and honesty that is not available with any other adults at the police station, as information divulged to any other party can be used against the child in court. This also puts the lawyer in a unique position in relation to other agencies, as they may be the only adult with which a child chooses to share information about risk. The lawyer is therefore in a good position to signpost the child to other forms of support, should they consent to this. The lack of legal privilege in all other contact with adults puts the child in a problematic and paradoxical situation. Conversations that include the AA (or an interpreter) are not protected, meaning that the AA (the child's 'support') can technically be called to testify in proceedings *against* the child. The child should therefore be wary of sharing their full situation with the AA (the person tasked with protecting them) and it is difficult to see how this situation could really be said to assist with communication. As the AA often meets with the child *before* the legal representative arrives, the child needs to understand the roles and relative interests of the different parties *before* choosing whether to speak to the AA who is tasked with explaining them. While it is not *compulsory* for either the AA or interpreter to attend the solicitor's consultation with the child (and it is arguably discouraged by PACE Code C) it is clear that as an aid to communication, both parties should be present if they are useful. Both legal privilege *and* effective opportunity for communication are considered necessary conditions for a fair trial under Article 6 of the Human Rights Act 1998, meaning that this conflict effectively removes a child's legal entitlement to justice.

Given the potential for a young suspect's openness to be used against them, is it perhaps unsurprising that they describe being suspicious of nearly all agencies' intentions (Panzavolta et al, 2016). Young suspects can even be prosecuted using conversations had in corridors and police cars – a predicament that can leave even the most knowledgeable adult feeling somewhat persecuted. In the large part, juveniles report finding their lawyers most helpful, and describe them as protective when officers attempt to 'twist their words' or try to 'trip them up' (Panzavolta et al, 2016). However, this trust of lawyers does not necessarily extend to the courtroom, where the dynamic between agencies changes yet again. Some juveniles describe their lawyers 'cosying up to' judges to make deals and trying to make them plead guilty. It is difficult to see how the young suspect can establish trust in any agency when their intentions seem to be constantly changing based on their relative positions and wider societal and political forces.

The police

In the UK (and most of the world) there is no specific legal requirement for police officers working with juvenile suspects to receive any specialist training. This is despite there being a plethora of evidence to demonstrate that young people have considerable difficulties with interviews (see Gudjonsson et al, 1993). While an 'Achieving Best Evidence' model (Ministry of Justice, 2011) exists to guide the appropriate interviewing of young *witnesses* and *victims*, no such document or guidance exists for the interviewing of young suspects. This position is at odds with the UN Convention on the Rights of the Child, which states that respect for the dignity of children in conflict with the law requires *all* professionals involved in the legal process to have knowledge of child development, the dynamic and continuing growth of children and knowledge of what is appropriate to their wellbeing. An independent parliamentary inquiry into the effectiveness of the youth justice system in 2014 has made a specific recommendation that the training and specialisation of officers that work with child suspects become a legal requirement (Carlile, 2014). Such a requirement is yet to come into force.

As an agency, the police have a specific duty to safeguard the wellbeing and future outcomes of all children with whom they come into contact (The Crime and Disorder Act, 1998, s37; HM Government, 2015). Their primary purpose, however, is arguably public protection and enforcement of the law. The Home Office Statement of Common Purpose and Values for the Police Service (adopted by the police in 1990) states that:

> The purpose of the police service is to uphold the law fairly and firmly; to prevent crime; to pursue and bring to justice those who break the law; and to keep the Queen's Peace; to protect, help and reassure the community; and to be seen to do all this with integrity, common sense and sound judgement. (House of Commons, 2007–08)

The UK operates an adversarial legal system (one in which two opposing parties argue their positions before an independent judge), rather than an inquisitorial one (where judges directly investigate the facts in search of 'the truth'). In this UK system, police work in conjunction with the Crown Prosecution Service to provide evidence *against* suspects, while lawyers work to *defend* suspects (Cape, 2011). In this sense, the police can be seen to act in what is defined (by the government of the day) to be 'the public interest'. Despite their complex and multi-faceted statement of purpose, the police force's position in the adversarial system sees them having to prioritise the needs of the public over those of the individual suspect. This aim makes it difficult for police to cater for the interests of the child suspect and provide the many different preventative and welfare roles expected of them.

The introduction of prosecution targets for police in the 1990s saw police work grow ever more punitive in nature and the influence of such targets on the motives of officers was the subject of much controversy (Curtis, 2015). Numerical prosecution targets were abolished by the UK Home Office in 2010, but an increase in police powers and out of court disposals over the past 30 years still sees a burden on the police to focus on sanctioning offenders (Cape, 2011). For some young suspects, the entire criminal justice process can now be completed at the police station, making the need for a 'defender' in the interview room all the more important. Not all of the intentions of the police and lawyers are in opposition, however. The admissibility of evidence obtained in interview is largely dependent on the manner in which it was acquired, so it pays for officers to prioritise fair treatment of the juvenile too. Oppressive interview tactics are not beneficial for the prosecution once evidence reaches the courtroom. Multi-agency focus groups discussing the juvenile interview have demonstrated that all agencies feel that closer working relationships and better knowledge of each other's roles would improve their work. Some officers admitted to holding back evidence in the hope of utilising it mid-interview, while lawyers responded to this lack of disclosure by advising their clients not to answer police questions (Panzavolta et al, 2016). This interaction renders both parties unable to achieve their aims and the child is left in the middle, sceptical of the entire process.

Case study: The blurring of roles in the child's best interests?

In 2012 a 14-year-old boy, Rob, was arrested and held in custody at a police station in the south of England. Rob seemed to be a polite young boy and had been arrested for playing the look-out for a domestic burglary performed by a number of older boys.

On arrival in custody, the police could not reach Rob's parents, so after a long wait, an AA was called from a local service. On arrival at the police station, the AA requested a solicitor on behalf of the child. While waiting for a solicitor to arrive, the AA accompanied Rob from his cell to a side room where Rob and the AA discussed his rights and how the AA would be able to help him. The AA returned to the custody desk after the meeting and informed the police that Rob's general understanding seemed very low and that he likely had considerable problems with communication. He seemed to take a lot of things very literally and did not seem to understand his rights or their implications. The AA requested an assessment of his suitability for interview, but the police responded that there was no provision for an assessment and that the child was deemed old enough to understand what was going on.

On arrival at the station, the solicitor met with Rob in private. Following their consultation, the interview went ahead. In the interview room, Rob was read the police caution concerning his right to silence and asked if he understood, to which he responded 'yes'. The AA interjected, stating that it was not clear whether Rob had fully understood the caution. The police officer repeated the caution and asked the child to explain what it meant. Rob stated 'I don't have to answer your questions'. This seemed satisfactory to the officer, and he continued with his interview. The police officer asked his first question and Rob promptly responded. The solicitor then interrupted and spoke to Rob: 'I've advised you to make no comment in this interview, do you understand what that means?' Rob responded 'Yes, I don't have to answer questions'. The officer then proceeded with his next line of inquiry. Rob promptly answered the next question, stating who was with him in the street at the time of the burglary. Unsure whether Rob was really understanding the advice of his solicitor, the AA asked the officer to stop the interview to give time for Rob and his solicitor to speak in private. After speaking alone, the interview re-commenced and Rob answered 'no comment' to the next question the officer asked. The officer then asked Rob a different question, to which Rob provided a detailed response. The AA interjected again and stated that Rob did not seem to be able to understand or follow the advice from his solicitor. The solicitor attempted (in the interview room) to explain to Rob in simple steps, that whatever the officer asked, he should only say the words 'no comment'. The solicitor practised this in the interview room with the suspect with the officer and AA present. Rob said no comment in the 'practice interview' and said he understood what he had to do now. The officer re-commenced the interview and Rob responded 'no comment' to the next question. The officer asked another question, and Rob began to answer. It became clear to the officer at this point that Rob was unable to follow his solicitor's advice under the pressure of questioning. As a last attempt at completing the interview, even the officer himself tried to explain the solicitor's advice to the suspect, but it was clear that no evidence would be admissible and the interview was terminated. The AA and solicitor both made a statement to the tape that in their opinion, the child was unable to understand their rights or the legal advice provided to them.

Consider the following questions:

- To what extent were Rob's rights infringed?
- How could Rob's understanding of his right to silence have been better tested?
- Each agency had more power to protect Rob than they utilised. Why do you think they did not exercise this?
- What could each agency have done better to improve Rob's ability to engage with the interview process?

Conclusion

The evidence set out in this chapter illustrates the need for agencies involved in suspect interviewing to work together more closely. While statute and guidance continue to increase the duty to cooperate, in practice, some examples of agencies separating are troubling. Recent research suggests that the quality of advice from lawyers, for example, has dropped in police stations where the legal advisors have been excluded from custody suites (Kemp, 2013). News of trained AAs in-situ at stations (TAAS, 2017), however, is promising, so positive results from such ventures could re-ignite a movement towards a more inclusive station environment.

When considering how agencies can work together to promote the best interests of the child suspect, we must contemplate whether there is really any objective position on what is 'best'. Parents want their child to be honest, police want their suspect to face consequences for wrongdoing and legal representatives want their client to be free of incarceration. All of these are legitimate aims that can be considered in the child's best interest, yet in the interview context, they are not all possible. No single agency has grounds to claim that their objectives should be the priority, as there is nothing to govern which of the child's interests should be considered superior. Nothing, that is, but the child themselves. We afford adults in custody the right to make decisions for themselves, so despite children needing assistance with communication, patience and forethought, perhaps they are the most suitable party to dictate their best interests. Perhaps the 'best' thing we can do for the young suspect is to focus the efforts of all agencies on a child-centred approach that aims only to increase the understanding and autonomy of the child. In this way, it becomes nobody's place but the child's to decide what is 'best' for their life, but with adequate support to make that decision rationally. To achieve this, there is a necessity for agencies to learn more about one another, and this can be realised through the provision of inter-agency training. There is also an argument for the 'neutral' delivery of information to a child suspect in custody. By providing interactive electronic resources from which the suspect can inform themselves about the police process, children could autonomously boost their understanding of their rights and the complex multi-agency dynamic they are about to enter.

Further consideration might also be given to the structure of a youth justice system that contains so many 'competing' interests in the first place. While we safeguard the right to silence and employ solicitors to 'protect' the interests of the child, we also imply that cooperation with the police is sometimes not good for the child. It is possible to see how this state of affairs could lead a young person to suspect the motivations of police, the law and perhaps even society. Such an outlook is unlikely to assist a young person with their development into a thriving, law-abiding citizen. The UK criminalises the acts of children at a much younger age than many other nations and it is perhaps this somewhat 'cold' approach to the difficulties faced by young people that justifies some of their anger and rebellion against the state. Adoption of a multi-agency welfare-based approach in practice, rather than just on paper, might go a long way towards the reduction of offending by young people in the UK.

> **Summary of key learning points**
> - Around 80,000 young people are arrested each year. Most are interviewed and many are tried - in a justice system designed by adults, for adults.
> - The right to a fair trial (Article 6 of the Human Rights Act 1998) requires an individual to be able to engage with proceedings against them. Many national and international conventions, laws and policies recognise the need for a child-centred approach when dealing with young people accused of crimes.
> - The current arrest and questioning process for young people in the UK is developmentally inappropriate, not child-centred and not fit for purpose. It requires young people (often from disadvantaged backgrounds or with additional communication needs) to possess the understanding and communication skills of an adult in order to access their rights.
> - The 'safeguards' in place to support young people in police custody (such as the 'Appropriate Adult') do not really work as intended by the Police and Criminal Evidence Act 1984.
> - The many adults and agencies working with child suspects are not sufficiently trained to deal with the needs of the young suspect. Furthermore, they often work at cross-purposes, with little understanding of each other's roles.
> - To improve the engagement of young people in the criminal justice process (or ensure their appropriate diversion from it), agencies need to take a child-centred approach and require child-suspect-specific training. Only by working closely with one-another to empower the young person, will they be able to support child suspects in accessing their right to a fair trial and the services they may require for their rehabilitation.

References

Ashford, M., Chard, A. and Redhouse, N. (2006) *Defending young people in the criminal justice system*. Legal Action Group.

Bath, C. (2017) *Police and Criminal Evidence Act Consultation*. National Appropriate Adult Network.

Bean, P. and Nemitz, T. (1994) *Out of depth and out of sight*. London: MENCAP.

Bevan, M. (2016) *Investigating young people's awareness and understanding of the criminal justice system: an exploratory study*. The Howard League for Penal Reform.

Bridges, L. and Choongh, S. (1998) *Improving police station legal advice: the impact of the accreditation scheme for police station legal advisers*. London: Law Society.

Brown, D. (1997) *PACE ten years on: a review of the research*. Home Office Research Study 155. London: Home Office, London.

Cape, E. (2011) *Defending suspects at police stations: The practitioner's guide to advice and representation*. Legal Action Group.

Carlile (2014) *Independent Parliamentarians' Inquiry into the Operation and Effectiveness of the Youth Court*. https://yjlc.uk/lord-carliles-independent-parliamentarians-inquiry-into-the-youth-court/

Council of Europe (1950) *European Convention for the Protection of Human Rights and Fundamental Freedoms, as amended by Protocols Nos. 11 and 14*, 4 November 1950.

Curtis, I. (2015) *The use of targets in policing*. London: Home Office.

Easton, D. and Dennis, J. (1969) *Children in the political system: origins of political legitimacy.* New York: McGraw-Hill.

Evans, R. (1993) *The conduct of police interviews with juveniles.* Royal Commission on Criminal Justice Research Report No. 8. London: HMSO.

Fagan, J. and Tyler, T.R. (2005) 'Legal socialisation of children and adolescents', *Social Justice Research*, 18(3): 217–241.

Gudjonsson, G.H. (1994) 'Psychological vulnerability: Suspects at risk', in D. Morgan and G. Stephenson (eds), *Suspicion and silence: The right to silence in criminal investigation.* London: Blackstone Press, pp 91–106.

Gudjonsson, G.H., Clare, I., Rutter, S. and Pearse, J. (1993) *Persons at risk during interviews in police custody: the identification of vulnerabilities.* Royal Commission on Criminal Justice. London: HMSO.

HM Government (2015) *Working together to safeguard children: A guide to inter-agency working to safeguard and promote the welfare of children.* [This guidance is, at the time of printing, under review in order to reflect changes brought about by the Children and Social Work Act, 2017.]

Home Office National Statistics (2017) *Arrest statistics data tables: Police powers and procedures.* www.gov.uk/government/statistics/police-powers-and-procedures-england-and-wales-year-ending-31-march-2017

House of Commons (2007–08) Home Affairs – Seventh Report HC 364-I.

Jacobson, J. (2008) *No one knows: police responses to suspects with learning disabilities and learning difficulties: a review of policy and practice.* London: Prison Reform Trust.

Kemp, V. (2013) '"No time for solicitor": implications for delays on the takeup of legal advice', *Criminal Law Review*, 3: 184.

Medford, S., Gudjonsson, G.H. and Pearse, J. (2003) 'The efficacy of the appropriate adult safeguard during police interviewing', *Legal and Criminological Psychology*, 8(2): 253–266.

Mclean, F. and Beak, K. (2012) *Factors associated with serious or persistent violent offending: findings from a rapid evidence assessment.* National Policing Improvement Agency.

Ministry of Justice (2011) *Achieving Best Evidence in Criminal Proceedings: Guidance on interviewing victims and witnesses, and guidance on using special measures.* www.cps.gov.uk/sites/default/files/documents/legal_guidance/best_evidence_in_criminal_proceedings.pdf

Palmer, C. and Hart, M. (1996) *A PACE in the right direction? The effectiveness of safeguards in the Police and Criminal Evidence Act 1984 for mentally disordered and mentally handicapped suspects: A south Yorkshire study.* Sheffield: Institute for the Study of the Legal Profession.

Panzavolta, M., de Vocht, D., Van Oosterhout, M. and Vanderhallen, M. (eds) (2016) *Interrogating young suspects: procedural safeguards from an empirical perspective.* Cambridge: Intersentia.

Pearse, J. and Gudjonsson, G.H. (1996a) 'How appropriate are appropriate adults?' *Journal of Forensic Psychiatry*, 7: 570–580.

Pearse, J. and Gudjonsson, G.H. (1996b) 'Understanding the problems of the appropriate adult', *Expert Evidence*, 4: 101–104.

Quirk, H. (2016) *The rise and fall of the right of silence: principle, politics and policy.* Taylor & Francis.

Skogan, W.G. (2005) 'Citizen satisfaction with police encounters', *Police Quarterly*, 8(3): 298–321.

Taylor, C. (2016) *Review of the Youth Justice System in England and Wales.* Ministry of Justice.

The Appropriate Adult Service (TAAS) (2017) Personal communication, 14 December.

UN General Assembly (1989) *Convention on the Rights of the Child,* 20 November 1989, United Nations, Treaty Series, vol. 1577, p 3, available at: www.refworld. org/docid/3ae6b38f0.html.

Further reading

Gudjonsson, G.H. (2003) *The psychology of interrogations and confessions: A handbook.* Chichester: John Wiley & Sons.

12

Culture Club Assemble! The powerful role of multi-agent relationships in prison habilitation

Sarah Lewis

> **Aims of the chapter**
> • To critically examine the significance of relationships in prison habilitation.
> • To examine the possibilities of institutional growth through the use of a case study.
> • To identify new approaches to multi-agency working in a prison environment.

Introduction

This chapter critically examines the role of relationships in prison habilitation and growth. It draws on the academic literature and experiences of an habilitative journey in an English prison, as it embarks on co-constructing an environment which promotes personal and institutional growth. Pat Carlen (2013) highlights that 'offenders' are rarely habilitated let alone rehabilitated and yet there seems to be an assumption that prisons were once an effective habilitative arena, which has lost its way. Carlen (2013, para 6) presents her arguments against rehabilitation, stating:

> The majority of criminal prisoners worldwide have, prior to their imprisonment, usually been so economically and/or socially disadvantaged that they have nothing to which they can be advantageously rehabilitated.

Comparatively, prison has historically lacked the investment and social support it is starting to receive, following high publicity regarding prison conditions, and the financial burden and high recidivism rates that incarceration brings. The historical context of prisons indicates the seemingly inferior goal of rehabilitating for those that enter prison rather than other philosophies of punishment that support the perspective of popular punitivism. Prison in some ways shows signs of de-habilitation, whereupon those that experience prison (both staff and residents) come out in a worse state than when they entered (Nurse et al, 2003) or, at best, prison effects have been conceptualised as a deep freeze for 'prisoners', whereupon they come out the same as they went in. This state of affairs was only exacerbated through austerity (Allen, 2013; see also Pycroft, this volume), as prison staff were extracted from the broken vessel, leaving those who remained to bail out the water of a slowly sinking ship.

The appetite for prison reform has dominated the recent government agenda, following a recent exposure to the difficulties prisons are facing in England and Wales (Ministry of Justice, 2016). Reports of violence, harm and drug use continue to litter inspection reports and the rate of imprisonment remain the highest in Western Europe (see Aabi et al, 2017). With the focus on rehabilitating 'the prisoner' remaining significant, analysing contextual issues and how the prison climate might influence desistance and the problems of unrest and harm (see Ackerman and Needs, 2018 for a detailed examination) is essential. The desistance paradigm links strengths-based work, positive psychology and environmental factors together, to aid 'the offender' to reinvent their identity (Maruna, 2001; Burnett and Santos, 2010). In a similar vein, this chapter explores this approach on a larger scale, considering which aspects of prison promote growth and build prison capital, exploring how environmental factors and relational practice might alter the way in which an individual experiences their incarceration. Up until now multi-agency literature within health and social science has focused on improving the lives of the 'service user' through an integrated approach (Atkinson et al, 2007). This chapter instead explores the role of relationships within multi-agency working (between multiple agents) and how relationships provide the foundations of reforming the prison environment, through an all-prison approach. Relationships are central to the effectiveness of multi-agency working and examining these relationships can be both enlightening and valuable to the development of multi-agency working. In light of the inherent problems associated with prison, a consideration into how agencies can work together to nurture a new culture holds both hope and value. But first, an exploration into the processes that feature within relational practice on an individual level is necessary to set the context.

The dynamic model of therapeutic correctional relationships

The dynamic model of therapeutic correctional relationships breaks down how relationships move and shift over time and influence processes of positive change (Lewis, 2016). It starts with two individuals or players: the practitioner and the 'prisoner'. Both of these individuals share many things; each have their own set of attachments and rules around relationships, their own set of values and their own past experiences of each other. These variables influence the bond between the two players and the psychological distance between them. The practitioner may have some pre-conceived ideas connected with an individual's crime, their history in the criminal justice system or may even know the 'offender' or know of him/her. While this knowledge can assist the practitioner in making sense of the individual who stands before them, it may also encourage the practitioner to see that individual in a specific light, through a different lens than others. These pre-conceptions can both hinder or help the practitioner as they embark on a professional relationship and, indeed, influence the distance between the two players. If pre-conceptions are negative, the practitioner may inadvertently distance themselves from the 'prisoner'; if the pre-conceptions are positive, the practitioner may provide a welcoming environment where respect can be nurtured more readily. Safran and Muran (2003) argue that within relationships, there is a constant negotiation (and therefore movement) between the desire to relate and the desire to be autonomous, independent and have agency.

As the relationship develops, both players can move closer or further apart, in response to their experiences of one another or events that might happen. For example, as trust is developed, the bond between the two players brings them together. Alternatively if trust is broken, this can create a rupture (a tear in the relationship, see Safran and Muran, 2003) which contributes to a psychological separation. The relationship is therefore fluid and shifts throughout its life cycle. From the work of Bordin (1979) a therapeutic relationship is developed by a bond between two people and through the creation of shared goals and tasks to achieve these goals. Therapeutic relationships within a correctional setting have been found to be similar and can be developed in this way, alongside the shared understanding of the 'prisoners' needs (see Lewis, 2016).

From this framework, it can be useful to consider three key spaces, which are occupied by both players during their relational journey: an exclusionary space, an inclusive space and collusive space. First, if both individuals are distant from each other (characterised as disengaged, disinterested, mistrustful, cynical and/ or disrespect), they are situated in an exclusionary space where little is gained and no interpersonal growth can thrive through the relationship. If enough trust and respect is built, the players can move into a therapeutic, inclusive space whereupon honest conversations can be sought and the conditions can facilitate personal growth. Finally, if the two relational players become too close, they may instead focus on each other's needs and move away from those shared goals and tasks that are necessary for growth, leaving them in a collusive space which can increase the likelihood of manipulation on either side. It is proposed that deep, authentic knowledge and understanding can only be achieved when both players are in the inclusionary position. In the event that either player occupies the exclusionary or collusive spaces, the knowledge that is received is not grounded on trust and is more likely to hold inaccuracies and distortions. For example, a 'prisoner' may find it easier to lie to a practitioner because they are 'distant-far' from the practitioner and not invested in the relationship. Between each relational space are boundaries which are depicted as 'lines of power'. These boundaries signify thresholds between the spaces and how power might shift, as bond varies. When power is imposed on one of the players, this can be a catalyst which can influence the players to either draw close or become distant. This may be observed during a rupture, when a practitioner 'puts their foot down', with the 'prisoner' consequentially moving from the inclusive and engaged position, to the exclusionary space. The model in Figure 12.1 outlines how these variables may look and how valuable knowledge can be gained from developing a therapeutic correctional relationship.

The key learning from this model is the appreciation that relationships shift depending on the events and conditions that exist within their interpersonal space. It sheds some light on the processes of relationships and why change might emerge over the course of a professional relationship. Examining these processes within a multi-agented context could illuminate the mechanisms of change and what conditions might nurture prison habilitation, on a multidisciplinary level.

Figure 12.1: The dynamic model of therapeutic correctional relationships

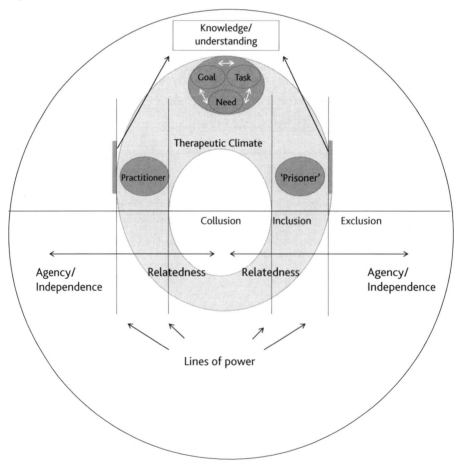

Case study: Co-constructing a rehabilitative culture in an English prison

This case study presents an example of how this knowledge was applied to a prison, within its habilitative journey. In October 2016, I was contracted to deliver a Growth Project in an English training prison, to assess the prison environment and consider how a rehabilitative environment might be achieved. The aim of the Growth Project initially was twofold:

1. To examine the root causes of the problems that were being experienced at the prison.
2. To examine which elements of practice promote rehabilitation.[1]

To do this I recruited nine 'prisoners' and trained them as growth champions and, together, we formed the first English Growth Team. Previous to this project, my research experience as an academic was centred upon unearthing the principles of growth within a Norwegian prison environment. During the research, Growth Teams were created, with staff and 'prisoners' joining me in researching rehabilitative environments. This English project was informed by this experience and adopted the same values of inclusion, bottom–up reform and a personalisation of the criminal justice system, as promoted by Weaver (2011).

For six months the Growth Team considered the 'as is' environment, carrying out projects that uncovered the key issues experienced by the 'prisoners' and staff at the prison and those aspects of practice that promoted a rehabilitative climate. We had created the Growth Project at a time when the prison was suffering from bad publicity and a poor inspection report, which highlighted failings in resettlement, safety and drug use. Talking with the staff it was clear that they had experienced incredibly difficult times, and presented as let down, helpless and exhausted. Non–operational staff conveyed feelings of isolation and silo-based working was day-to-day practice. This environment played out in numerous ways: violence was high and assaults on staff were regular. Further to this, spice use was rife and tension was invariably felt on the majority of the house blocks. That said, from the analysis it was found that there were pockets of growth within the establishment and beneath the tiredness and relentless challenges, there lay a group of staff that were dedicated to their work and wanted to improve things.

To capture elements of quality practice, a photo–essay research project was undertaken by the Growth Team and the findings were displayed at a two–day exhibition. This project was an appreciative inquiry and aimed to build hope and inspire those who worked and resided at the prison. A photo-book was designed after the exhibition and shared with the staff and 'prisoners' to promote the key messages, which were associated with a rehabilitative climate. This provided the staff and 'prisoners' the opportunity to 'see' which aspects of their current practice were rehabilitative and promoted growth. The project also allowed staff to consider their prison identity and the extent to which rehabilitation features within it. Both staff and 'prisoners' stated that the project brought hope in the face of adversity and identified an educational opportunity whereby their prison's rehabilitative culture had been captured, making it personal and real. From the research, the following principles were identified by the 'prisoners' and staff.

Principles of growth

Meaningful relationships: Developing respectful and positive relationships with fellow 'prisoners', staff, family and society. This includes drawing on similarities, working together and creating opportunities for quality relationships.

Meaningful work: Aligning the strengths of an individual to provide a framework to work in a purposeful manner. This is focused on the individual and matching their talents/skills/ interests to work opportunities.

Finding pro-social ways of coping with prison: Developing healthy coping strategies to manage the difficulties of imprisonment, rather than resorting to unhealthy strategies. This may include art, music, gym or spending time with positive peers.

Tasting freedom: Feeling free promoted a sense of ease, which enabled people to consider and reflect on their own identities. This included spaces in the prison where 'prisoners' could free themselves from prison and think for themselves. It may be places where people can use their imagination, carry out activities where the mind can escape, or be given the freedom to make decisions.

Experiencing normality: Doing 'normal things' built confidence and allowed the 'prisoners' to feel, and be, responsible and 'normal'.

Promoting wellbeing: The focus on a healthy mind and body seemed to produce a number of positive consequences, building strength and overcoming obstacles successfully.

Experiencing joy and peace: Spending time in quiet spaces was one of the key opportunities to provide peace and ease, within a challenging environment.

Connecting with nature: Engaging with nature provided a sense of privilege, to a world bigger than oneself.

Constructing a positive climate: This finding suggested that staff and 'prisoners' were co-constructing an environment which focused on ownership, peace and belonging. Community based activities like cooking and sharing promoted this as well as physical changes to the environment, like flowers in the house blocks.

Authentic Leadership: The need for courageous, authentic leaders that are pro-social, respectful and decent. Leaders with a strong vision and pro-active attitude are paramount to growth, as well as leaders that embrace the growth principles and advocate them in all that they do.

Investing in people and learning new things: The investment in staff and 'prisoners' were deemed important, as it highlighted that people were seen and deserved investment. This encapsulated learning skills, gaining insight into one's problems and taking positive risks.

Using these principles as a simple framework, proposals were suggested which brightened these practices to build a growth-centred identity. To help achieve this habilitative vision, the Growth Team promoted the nurturing of trust and carried out a number of events, which were evaluated and fed back to staff efficiently. For example, wellbeing days were organised within each house block whereby 'prisoners' and staff carried out team building activities, sports, games and cooking. These were evaluated and a briefing report was created to highlight the benefits of the days on the house block and the prison as a whole.

From a multi-agented perspective it was surmised that the relationships across the estate lacked cohesion and the 'glue' which holds a whole team together. Horizontally, relationships did not flow well between house blocks and across the estate (between departments such as health care, education, charities or workshops) and vertically, the management lacked visibility as they were consumed with reactive measures. Returning to the dynamic model of therapeutic correctional relationships, a shared goal was not clear nor were the tasks each member of staff needed to undertake to achieve the goal or vision. On an organisational level the relationships could be represented generally as 'distant-far', with little hope, trust or shared understanding. Different agents worked together on their allocated targets but looking sideways to find connections was neigh on impossible due to the conditions which had emerged. Instead, silo-based thinking was maintained and reactive management was not sustainable, leading to exhaustion and exasperation. During these distant times, certain practices flourished. For example, scapegoating bred happily in such conditions, with little trust and consequently, fragmentation throughout the system (see Pycroft, this volume). Instead of collectively understanding problems that arose, identifying the sole individual to blame seemed more comforting. These effects only lead to greater distancing and anxiety, with control and the need to retrieve 'operational grip' dominated discussions, rather than the notion of building trust.

The relationships between the community and the prison were also low. There was a dedicated and committed group of volunteers who visited the prison, but due to few ROTLS (release of temporary licence), the relationship between the inside and outside was piecemeal. This reduced the likelihood of progression and the overwhelming pressures experienced by all staff left some not knowing where to begin. The processes of incentivisation became swamped by the reduction of trust–nurturing opportunities and as one 'prisoner' stated: "it is easier to be bad in here than good". The prison was on survival mode, adapting to the dominant culture that had developed over years of cutting back. The 'them and us' culture was easy to maintain and the dominant goal was to get through a day without being assaulted, belittled or hurt.

Using the dynamic model of therapeutic correctional relationships, Figure 12.2 depicts how one might conceptualise this 'as is' position, with the majority of departments presenting as 'distant–far' in connection with the new organisational vision of creating a safer, more cohesive, growth–centred prison. The majority of agents were positioned within a distant–far position, due to the difficult conditions which had developed over many years.

Following a collaborative analysis stage of the 'as is' environment, the Growth Project then began to facilitate the co-construction of a rehabilitative climate. This focused heavily on personalising reform, whereby the prison ('prisoners' and staff) were creating the future together, using the ideas from Weaver (2011) and Weaver and Nicholson (2012) by considering co-production on a broader scale. The aim of this phase was to use the knowledge gained from numerous research projects to assist in engaging and empowering the staff and 'prisoners', to shape their future practice, identity and culture. Improvement boards were constructed on each area of the prison and events were designed by the Growth Team to promote the key principles of growth and evidence-based practice.

Figure 12.2: The dynamic model of multi-agent relational practice at the 'as is' stage

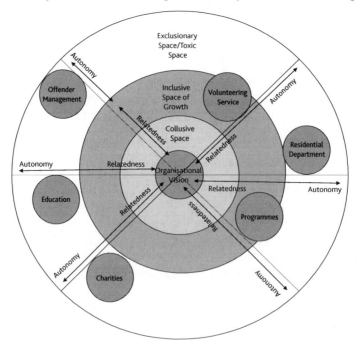

Note: The organisations named here are for illustrative purposes only and does not depict reality.

This provided an evidence-based improvement strategy, which was visual and transparent: anyone could place a suggestion on the boards, so long as it aligned to the principles of growth.

Engagement grew over the course of the project, and as voices were appreciated and magnified, staff and 'prisoners' began to cooperate, to drive reform. This project was participatory in nature, driving innovation by including both staff and the 'prisoners' to, as a team, address the challenging issues they experienced in the day to day. This interconnection between 'prisoners' and staff built greater cohesion and begun to break down the 'them and us' culture that hampers current prison culture.

As 'oneness' throughout the organisation slowly grew and a new found legitimacy of a rehabilitative culture started to emerge, the importance of nurturing this approach and sustaining any progress was vital. Early indicators of this culture shift were seen in the language being used in everyday practice, referring to 'prisoners' as 'men' and talking about change with greater hope in the future. This developed into greater engagement from the staff and 'prisoners' and the motivation to collectively move the prison forward. The work of Richeson (2014) around healing environments highlights the need to critically consider how maintaining an environment is paramount for sustainable growth. A healing environment is defined by Richeson (2014: 27) as follows:

> The Healing Environment is purposefully created by the way we work together and treat each other while encouraging all to use their initiative to make positive, progressive changes to improve lives. It is safe, respectful and ethical — where people are both supported and challenged to be accountable for their actions.

Richeson (2014) recognised that through this approach, a shift in paradigms can be best achieved within a correctional context. In order to achieve a healing environment, it is proposed that there is a need for all players/agents to share the same goal and fully embrace this 'oneness' so that safety, respect and support can be utilised and grown. Returning to the case study, the process of bringing people together with a shared goal seemed unattainable at first and both the staff and 'prisoners' were cynical of this new approach due to their experiences of past approaches which have failed, thus isolating themselves further from the prison habilitation debate. Through perseverance and dialogue it became clear that under this mask there were individuals who felt let down and disappointed. Further to this, there were new conversations that emerged which talked about redemption, 'not giving up' and support, similar to the redemption scripts described by Maruna (2001) in his work on desistance.

Examining relational practice through a multi-agent lens

From a multi-agency perspective, it is recognised that there is a relational matrix that exists, whereupon multiple agents occupy differing spaces. Within the criminal justice system there are numerous connections between players but also connections between different practitioner groups within the system. Some may be close (for example, within integrated offender management; see Williams, this volume), some distant and, like any climate, these can change and shift over the course of time. This may influence the rate of growth, readiness to change or the (re)habilitation of an individual, as they manoeuvre their way among relationships, engaging more heavily in those relationships that bring them greater connectivity and avoiding or resisting those that frustrate or threaten their worth. The relationships between agents depend on those same characteristics of a therapeutic correctional relationship: sharing an appreciation for an organisational goal or vision, where tasks are outlined and a shared understanding of the needs of each organisational agent is sought. The likelihood of success could therefore be determined by the conditions that are experienced on both a micro, interpersonal level and on a macro level; making desistance difficult and, as described by Glaser (1964), a 'zig zag path'.

On an organisational level, relationships between staff groups may similarly be positive or negative. Communication, trust, empowerment, appreciation and inclusion are forces that may build these relationships and are considered conducive to effective multi-agency work (Vangen and Huxham, 2003; Kramer and Taylor, 1996; Atkinson et al, 2002). In contrast, removing key culture carriers from the growth arena, prioritising competition or cooperation, building up a wall of control and exclusionary practice only distances organisations from one another and those they are supporting to habilitate. Due to the contextual nature of relationships, the growth environment brings with it an energy and feeling that is hard to articulate, and the benefits infuse throughout a prison. As the Growth Project began to develop some staff would say that "the prison feels different" but they were not able to fully articulate what this 'feeling' was or why they felt this way. On reflection, I believe it was a sense of hope that was knitted into the fabric of the prison. One staff member stated "the prison has a new spirit" and those invested in the changes seemed to 'see' it more readily than through fighting against the change. The view here is that people, both 'prisoners' and staff, were adapting to a slowly shifting climate and growth was not limited to the 'prisoner' alone but to all that entered into the prison.

With this is mind, the context in which relationships sit holds real significance. These virtues are at odds with the current climate outside of the prison wall. With neoliberalism breeds competition (Robinson, 2013) and the need to prove impact and to reach targets may distance groups of individuals away into their silo towers. Further to this, prison is immersed more broadly within a risk society (Beck, 1992) and decisions to trust and provide 'prisoners' with agency and power is in conflict with the forces exerted on the prison from above. The interplay between this risk culture, the politicisation of the prison service and the new drive to create a rehabilitative culture in prisons is interesting and hard to grasp at this time, though it is surmised that a revival of hope slowly gains momentum.

Unpacking the conditions of success in multi-agent relational practice

As recognised by Mitchell (1988), identity is a dynamic process, which requires an individual to interact and connect with others. Mitchell (1988: 30) states:

> The development of a sense of self is a complex process, an intricate and multifaceted construction that is a central motivational concern throughout life, which we are deeply dependent on other people.

If this were considered on a larger scale, across an organisation, it is fair to deduce that the negotiations between a 'prisoner' and multiple agencies, magnify the complexity and intricacy of the sense of self further.

The role of multi-agency relationships holds real significance to the distance prisons can travel in creating a (re)habilitative culture. In order for this to take place a number of conditions can be seen as conducive to this venture. Echoed in the work of Bryan et al (2015), a collaborative approach is recognised as valuable in order to free up flows of communication, increase hope and encourage the notion that a collective impact may provide some new answers to inherent problems. A new collective consciousness and sense of responsibility seems to be a more responsive approach to this historically disconnected system. Therefore, at the heart of governmental prison reform there could be what McLaughlin et al (2001: 307) describe as an 'emphasis on developing and employing incentives and levers to promote strategic co-ordination and collaboration via "joined-up" partnerships'. While there is a clear strap line that prisons need to do better and address the 'penal crisis' that has developed (see Gough, this volume), the need for an organisational vision, with shared goals and tasks, would be the first step in establishing a multi-agented relationship across a prison environment. Continuing a silo-based mentality may threaten this necessary ingredient of relational practice. Glaister (1999) suggests that cooperation between public, private and voluntary organisations and departments is in high demand. Nurturing this attitude to change goes against the protectionism that dominates prison culture at present. Carley and Christie (1992) state that considerable effort is needed in order to nurture collaborative relationships at the initial stages of change. Sadly, there does not appear to be any quick wins when applying this philosophy to prison habilation. Instead, Huxham and Vangen (2000) highlight the need for a 'continuous process of nurturing' through small changes that lead to incremental gains.

The development of trust across the prison service could be considered a foundation block in the co-construction of a (re)habilitative culture. The trust between staff and 'prisoner' is more likely if it is embedded in a network of trust-focused agents. Granovetter (1992) highlighted that trust emerges from 'structural embeddedness' as systems provide opportunities to build social and human capital. From this platform, growth and lessons of prison habilitation are learnt and reinforced through continuous feedback, specific to the climate. Burt and Knez (1996) acknowledge that trust enables different staff groups within an organisation to be more adaptive in changing. Vangen and Huxham (2003) differentiate between two ways in which trust can be created: through an anticipation of something that will materialise (Vansina et al, 1998) or drawing on past experiences, which have been seen to hold legitimacy (Das and Teng, 1998).

From individual relational practice, a consistent message that an individual is trusted provides a strong backdrop for personal growth. On an organisational level, repeated trust-nurturing interactions over time can build what Rousseau et al (1998) refer to as 'relational trust'. The need to inform practice as and when these interactions bear fruit allows an organisation to learn and validate this approach. Vangen and Huxham (2003) rightly accept that power relationships can contribute to mistrust and act as an inhibitor for trust building practices to be validated. Similarly, therapeutic correctional relationships on a micro level are hampered by power struggles, which increase the likelihood of ruptures (Lewis, 2016). It is suggested that ruptures also operate on a macro level across organisations, both vertically (between frontline staff and management) and horizontally (between departments that work on the frontline). It is noted by Vangen and Huxham (2003) that when trust is low within an organisation and uncertainty is high, trust building needs to be incremental and taken a step at a time.

In the event that trust is built and nurtured within a prison environment, a collective impact becomes a possibility. This is, however, dependent on a number of variables, as stated here, by Kania and Kramer (2011: 36–37):

> The social sector is filled with examples of partnerships, networks, and other types of joint efforts. But collective impact initiatives are distinctly different. Unlike most collaborations, collective impact initiatives involve a centralized infrastructure, a dedicated staff, and a structured process that leads to a common agenda, shared measurement, continuous communication, and mutually reinforcing activities among all participants.

To transform an organisation successfully, Bryan et al (2015) highlighted the need for a collective impact to involve product, processes, a model and a movement, which spreads across an organisation with an energy that is difficult to ignore. On establishing the Growth Project, some staff were identified as those who were resisting the cultural shift that was being encouraged. Comments such as "you are not the silver bullet, you won't ever make a difference" were conveyed alongside expressions of doubt to even the possibilities of change. The relentless search for the 'missing intervention' echoed that of 'programme fetishism' (Lewis, 2009: 113) that dominated the What Works Era: the notion that only one intervention will be the answer to all of the problems associated the prison crisis and desistance. The dominant discourse at the prison was initially "it never changes and it never will". Invariably these conversations were only spoken between like-minded staff, as they remained anchored to a 'distant-far' position. As time passed and opportunities for dialogue began, the concerns shifted, moving the focus and language in a different direction. This led to a different strategy of praising quality practice, immediate performance recognition for good work and managers being more visible and accessible.

While inclusivity remained at the heart of the Growth Project, it was a difficult task in such a large organisation and conveying this heartfelt message was challenging and ultimately led to some staff feeling left out. As communication flows were examined and developed, connectivity improved and the Growth Project was able to reach more of the prison staff. The consistent message that decision making and problem solving began on the frontline slowly disseminated into the prison, creating a force and energy in its own right. Staff began to share their difficulties more openly and hope in change began to be restored. Prilleltensky and Prilleltensky (2007) proposed that worker participation in decision making and communication marks the degree of organisational wellbeing and this was relentlessly nurtured over the course of the Project.

That said, the Growth Project has not been without its difficulties. Many mistakes were made during the course of the work with staff criticising the 'prisoners' that were selected for the Growth Champion roles. Cynicism remained and some staff felt the focus on a rehabilitative culture was both unrealistic and idealistic. Learning was regularly sought throughout the course of the implementation and collaborative problem solving seemed to create greater ownership of the changes and ease resistance. The need to comprehensively approach difficulties through collaborative working and opportunities of dialogue was recommended by Prilleltensky and Prilleltensky (2007) and this brought about the support and empowerment that was needed. Considering social and human capital on an organisational scale and linking up shared interests and projects lead to greater cohesion and participation, as predicted by Prilleltensky and Prilleltensky (2007).

By embracing Vince's (2001) idea of a learning organisation, constant evaluation and adaptation was promoted. This had negative consequences in terms of energy depletion and a relentless obsession to always find a better way to communicate and drive change. Multi-agency steering groups made up of staff from numerous departments including residential staff, probation, drug services, health care, education and activities helped to alleviate these feelings through relational support within the prison and an opportunity to share doubts and difficulties in a safe environment was greatly received. This group was nicknamed the 'culture club' and brought with it a sense of togetherness that helped maintain motivation and hope, through humour and positivity. This developed into the notion of multi-agency teams allocated to each house block, to form and strengthen connections horizontally between education, the gym, health care and drug services (S. Robertson, personal communication, 5 January 2018).

Trust was also a significant driver during the Growth Project. Building trust within any prison environment that is dominated by mistrust, was difficult. The prison environment has historically questioned, observed, controlled and restricted other people. This trust was diminished further by the immediacy of blame when mistakes were made and blanket punishments invariably fell over all 'prisoners' when an 'incident' took place. The fear connected with more poor media coverage or an inquest only fuelled this air of anxiety and the need to 'screw down the place', both physically and psychologically. From the extensive efforts to determine the root causes associated with prison problems, a lack of trust was concluded. This coincides with Liebling's (2004) extensive work associated with the importance of relational trust and its links to radicalisation and unrest. "So we just have to build trust", one researcher concludes, presenting it as a simple and easily solved task. The reality was that such a task remained overwhelmingly challenging if it is seen as an outcome. Instead, creating small achievable opportunities for the development of trust remained the strategy of the Growth Project throughout its time at the prison.

A key learning point associated to prison reform and habilitation was that positive change cannot take place as a bolt-on project. This simply creates another silo, which works in isolation. Prison habilitation benefits from articulating habilitation into every level of practice. This starts on the shop floor, where officers are working alongside other staff and the 'prisoners'. The new keyworker scheme recognises the necessity and significance of working with 'prisoners' in a motivational and desistance-focused manner. The power of this approach extends to how officers work and communicate with civilian staff, recognising where each player fits within this rehabilitative vision. This horizontal spread of (re) habilitation has the potential to increase the power of relational work.

Lewis (2017) highlights how positive correctional relationships can be stunted when an individual experiences exclusion or negative relationships within another pocket of their prison reality. Therefore, the flow of relationships needs to operate horizontally among all agencies of prison practice as well as vertically within management structures, from the frontline to the senior management and beyond. For some forward-thinking governors, workstreams dedicated to rehabilitation have been created and working groups have been established to consider how rehabilitation can be laced into all practices across the prison. Group discussions, relational training for both operational and non-operational staff and an exploration into prison values have also started to set the new expectations of the staff. These strategic changes could not have been accomplished without a brave management team who trusts the theoretical underpinnings of the vision. Without them, the project would have received little traction and remained an unsustainable bolt-on.

Currently the notion of prison habilitation is gaining some support as staff and leaders recognise the need for prison investment and growth, though operationally it is hard to see and measure what an environment might look like, or even where to start. By considering prison (re)habilitation through a multi-agency lens, it is helpful to recognise that all prison agents, from health care to volunteering, are striving for the same thing through a collegiate effort. To achieve this, leaders are required to relinquish some of their power to empower those below them to provide sustainable solutions and begin new discussions. The notion of a 'silver bullet' was abandoned as it was recognised and celebrated that the answers did not lie in the echelons of government, but behind the cell doors and with the frontline staff. The rationale for this approach led back to the view that any future changes need to hold a new legitimacy, which was centred on those who were in the thick of it. The aim was that no one was excluded from the job in hand, a goal which was difficult to achieve and remains a challenge even now.

The 'them and us' culture has historically been linked to officers and 'prisoners' and yet, it is observed that this is shifting as culture carriers for rehabilitation are convincing some staff and 'prisoners' of the need for a paradigm shift. The aim is to create an 'us', with all staff and 'prisoners' holding a membership to the Growth Project and its view on punishment. As Day et al (2014) acknowledged, potential barriers of effective multidisciplinary practices arise when different agents hold competing attitudes about those that are in their care. This can account for some of the differences and questions that are arising within this journey to a growth environment in prison.

From reflecting on the academic literature and experiential findings, the aim for organisations can be constructed as in Figure 12.3.

This figure does not attempt to accurately depict all of the variables that are at play within multi-agency relationships, but instead provides a simple framework

Figure 12.3: The ideal dynamic model of multi-agent relational practice with promoters and inhibitor forces depicted

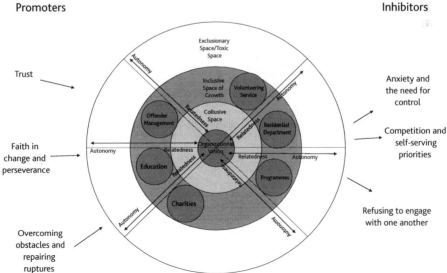

to enable reflections to take place when examining the position of agencies, in relations to one another and the organisational vision.

Similar to therapeutic correctional relationships, this figure highlights the ideal position, though it is acknowledged that this is incredibly difficult to achieve due to the natural occurrence of ruptures within the system. Ruptures may take place within an agent's department (such as a security breach) or across the prison as a whole. Agents may be blamed by other staff and encourage them to retreat into the exclusionary space, as that agent withdraws away from others. The importance here is twofold: to provide a positive environment where ruptures are reduced to a minimum; and to respond to ruptures in a rehabilitative way, engaging in dialogue and promoting inclusion. If this is achieved, the organisation as a whole, with full force, can move forward and have a collective impact on those that reside and work in the environment, as outlined in Figure 12.4.

Figure 12.4: Agent connectivity and movement toward the organisational vision

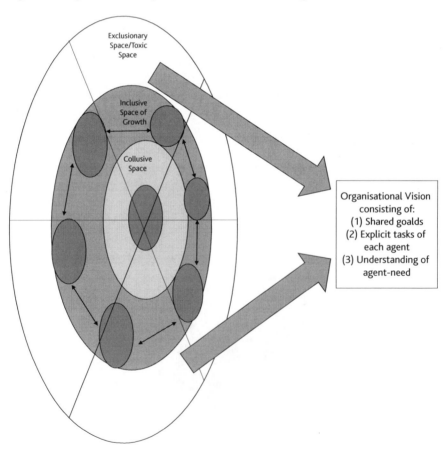

Conclusion

While it has been articulated by Copsey (2011) that relationships can be powerful vehicles through which people can change, this is now extended by stating that all-prison relationships are a force that can provide transformative conditions for growth. These relationships need to be centred on trust and respect, connected together and anchored in evidence-based practice. Our prisons need to hold intellectual capital and apply this within all facets of our work. It is proposed that by creating a pro-social, rehabilitative environment behind the prison wall, the 'prisoner' has the space to consider and evaluate their identities, staff can grow within their job, with meaning and purpose central to their work and organisations can heal and grow through open communication and connectivity.

Up to this point, prison reform has been solely ordained to those in positions of power. The autonomy of governors and political discourse associated with prison reform dominants discussions and agents have been allocated and tasked to address the 'prison crisis'. But there are multi-agencies that have both experience and a worthy contribution to this challenge task. These include staff, including officers that work on the 'shop floor', and non-operational staff who have a wealth of experience of prison from chaplains to librarians. There are then those that come into the prison and operate on the outskirts, including contractors and visitors, volunteers or programmes or employment opportunities such as Key4life, Unlock Drama and Fine Cell work. Finally, and of significant importance, are those that reside in prison. Those that have, between them, served decades of years in prison both nationally and internationally. Both long serving staff and 'prisoners' have seen cycles of changes to regimes and political ideologies play out, time and time again. They have experienced the problems at a detriment to their wellbeing, continue to live with the consequences of them and suffered through this period of disorder and chaos. And yet these collective views are not always sought, not considered, not captured. The Growth Project created a structure whereby all voices were welcomed, all perspectives were valued and all ideas were explored. This was through organised discussion groups, informal conversations and more formal avenues, like visible improvement boards throughout the prison estate. Embracing multiple voices in this way, with courage, openness and persistence is required to drive this agenda. It is not enough to only build human capital and resource within organisations; there must also be opportunities for voices to be heard. If these virtues are present and this is achieved, it is fervently believed that slowly but surely the function of prison will be transformed from one that is focused on punitivism to one that centred on habilitation and growth. It is recognised that in order for this to take place, such changes need to challenge the current culture of prison and embed a new and sustainable culture, gradually and sensitively. If unity is achieved, this multi-combining form can be anchored within the organisation and change might be more likely to ensue. The need to join forces and pool resources hopes to form an alliance that moves forward with transformational gain. Culture carriers exist within the nooks and crannies of our prison system, often hidden from view but strong in dedication and drive. Assembling these individuals (and organisations) together and joining up quality practice will not only influence the prison environment inside the prison wall, but will also create connections between prisons that are necessary for a sustainable system, which adopts a growth mindset.

Summary of key learning points
- Prisons need investment and trust to habilitate and grow into places of personal growth.
- Therapeutic Correctional Relationships provide the vehicle by which reform and rehabilitation is possible.
- An all-prison, research informed approach is instrumental to a rehabilitative prison, recognising the value of academic knowledge and the need to strive for continuous improvement.
- Prison identity can be re-imagined if strong cohesive relationships are developed through integrative and collaborative efforts. We all have a part to play towards a shared rehabilitative vision.

Note
[1]   See www.penalreformsolutions.com for more details.

References

Aabi, M.F., Tiago, M.M. and Burkhardt, T.C. (2017) *Council of Europe Annual Penal Statistics SPACE I – Prison Populations*, http://wp.unil.ch/space/files/2017/04/SPACE_I_2015_FinalReport_161215_REV170425.pdf

Ackerman, G. and Needs, A. (eds) (2018) *Transforming environments and rehabilitation*. Oxon: Routledge.

Allen, R. (2013) 'Paying for justice: prison and probation in an age of austerity', *British Journal of Community Justice*, 11(1): 5–18.

Atkinson, M., Wilkins, A., Stott, A., Doherty, P. and Kinder, K. (2002) *Multi-agency working: a detailed study*. National Foundation for Educational Research, www.researchgate.net/profile/Alison_Stott/publication/44827561_Multi-Agency_Working_A_Detailed_Study/links/0deec5236caefb1524000000.pdf

Atkinson, M., Jones, M. and Lamont, E. (2007) *Multi-agency working and its implications for practice: A review of the literature*. EfBT Education Trust, www.nfer.ac.uk/publications/MAD01/MAD01.pdf

Beck, U. (1992) *Risk society: towards a new modernity*. London: Sage.

Bryan, J.L., Haldipur, J., Martin, M. and Ullrich, S. (2015) 'Envisioning a broader role in philanthropy in prison reform', *Society*, 52(6): 572–579.

Bordin, E. (1979) 'The generalizability of the psychoanalytic concept of the working alliance', *Psychotherapy: Theory, Research & Practice*, 16(3): 252–260.

Burnett, R. and Santos, G.H. (2010) 'Found in transition? Local inter-agency systems for guiding young adults into better lives. Final report of the formative evaluation of the T2A pilots', Centre for Criminology University of Oxford, www.t2a.org.uk/wp-content/uploads/2011/09/Oxford-CfC-Final-Evaluation-Report-2011.pdf

Burt, R. and Knez, M. (1996) 'Trust and third part gossip', in R.M. Kramer and T.R. Taylor (eds), *Trust in organisations: frontiers of theory and research*. London: Sage, pp 68–90.

Carlen, P. (2013) 'Against rehabilitation: for reparative justice', *Criminal Justice Matters*, 91(2): 32–33, https://doi.org/10.1080/09627251.2013.778760

Carley, M. and Christie, I. (1992) *Managing sustainable development*. London: Earthscan Publications.

Copsey, M. (2011) The Offender Engagement Programme: An Overview From Programme Director, Martin Copsey. London: NOMS.

Das, T.K. and Teng, B-S. (1998) 'Between trust and control: developing confidence in partner cooperation in alliances', *Academy of Management Review*, 23(3): 491–512.

Day, A., Boni, N., Hobbs, G., Carson, E., Whitting, L. and Powell, M. (2014) 'Professional attitudes to sex offenders: implications for agencies and collaborative working', *Sexual Abuse in Australia and New Zealand*, 6(1): 12–19.

Glaser, D. (1964) *The effectiveness of a prison and parole system*. Indianapolis: Bobbs-Merrill.

Glaister, S. (1999) 'Past abuses and future uses of private finance and public private partnerships in transport', *Public Money & Management*, 19(3): 29–36.

Granovetter, M.S. (1992) 'Problems of explanation in economic sociology', in N. Nohria and R. Eccles (eds), *Networks and organizations: structure, form and action*. Boston: Harvard Business School Press, pp 25–56.

Huxham, C. and Vangen, S. (2000) 'Leadership in the shaping and implementation of collaborative agendas: How things happen in a (not quite) joined-up world', *Academy of Management Journal*, 43(6): 1159–1175.

Kania, J. and Kramer, M. (2011) 'Collective impact', *Stanford Social Innovation Review*, 9(1): 36–41.

Kramer, R.M. and Taylor, T.R. (1996) *Trust in organisations: frontiers of theory and research*. London: Sage.

Lewis, S. (2009) 'The probation service and race equality', in H.S. Bhui (ed), *Race and criminal justice*. London: Sage, pp 102–121.

Lewis, S. (2016) *Therapeutic correctional relationships: theory, research and practice*. Routledge: London.

Lewis, S. (2017) 'A campaign for climate change', in G. Ackerman, A. Needs and C. Bainbridge (eds), *Transforming environments and rehabilitation: a guide for practitioners in forensic settings and criminal justice*. London: Routledge, pp 150–167.

Liebling, A. (2004) *Prisons and their moral performance: a study of values, quality and prison life*. Oxford: Clarendon.

Maruna, S. (2001) *Making good: How ex-convicts reform and rebuild their lives.* Washington: American Psychological Association.

McLaughlin, E., Muncie, J. and Hughes, G. (2001) 'The permanent revolution: new labour, new public management and the modernization of the criminal justice', *Criminology and Criminal Justice*, 3(1): 301–318.

Mitchell, S.A. (1988) *Relational concepts in psychotherapy: an integration.* London: Harvard University Press.

Nurse, J., Woodcock, P. and Ormsby, J. (2003) 'Influence of environmental factors on mental health within prisons: focus group study', *British Medical Journal*, 327: 1–5.

Prilleltensky, I. and Prilleltensky, O. (2007) *Promoting wellbeing: linking personal, organizational and community change.* London: Wiley.

Ministry of Justice (2016) *Prison safety and reform*, Cm 9350, www.gov.uk/government/uploads/system/uploads/attachment_data/file/565014/cm-9350-prison-safety-and-reform-_web_.pdf

Richeson, S. (2014) 'Can corrections heal? Reducing re-offending and increasing public safety in Virginia', *Corrections Today*, 26–29.

Robinson, A. (2013) 'Transforming rehabilitation: Transforming the occupational identity of probation workers?', *British Journal of Community Justice*, 11(2–3): 91–101.

Rousseau, D.M., Sitkin, S.B., Burt, R.S. and Camerer, C. (1998) 'Not so different after all: a cross-discipline view of trust', *Academy of Management Review*, 23(3): 393–404.

Safran, J. and Muran, J. (2003) *Negotiating the therapeutic alliance: a relational treatment guide.* New York: Guildford Press.

Vansina, L., Taillieu, T. and Schruijer, S. (1998) '"Managing" multiparty issues: Learning from experience', in R. Woodman and W. Pasmore (eds), *Research in organizational change and development*, Volume 11. Greenwich, CT: JAI Press, pp 159–181.

Vangen, S. and Huxham, C. (2003) 'Nurturing collaborative relations: building trust in organisational collaboration', *Journal of Applied Behavioral Science*, 39(1): 5–31.

Vince, R. (2001) 'Power and emotion in organisational learning', *Human Relations*, 54(10): 1325–1351.

Weaver, B. (2011) 'Co-producing community justice: The transformative potential of personalisation for penal sanctions', *British Journal of Social Work*, 41(6): 1038–1057.

Weaver, B. and Nicholson, D. (2012) 'Co-producing change: resettlement as a mutual enterprise', *Prison Service Journal*, 204: 9–16.

13

Integrated secure care pathways for people with complex needs: service user, policy and practice perspectives

Graham Noyce

Aims of the chapter

- To review the use of out of area care pathways for mental health patients at risk of offending.
- To evaluate the use of these pathways where more than one agency is involved.
- To consider good practice in inter-agency working.

Introduction

This chapter will review the practice of using 'out of area' care pathways for mental health patients who are at risk of offending. It will start by reviewing the practice for mainstream acute mental health patients. The chapter will then review the causes, experiences and difficulties associated with the use of out of area pathways for patients who have more complex needs – that is, those who are 'managed' by more than one agency or care provider in an out of area secure care setting. The chapter will conclude by looking at the practice of placing women in secure services and will discuss consequent considerations for good inter–agency practice.

Definition: out of area placement

A person with assessed acute mental health needs who requires adult mental health acute inpatient care is admitted to a unit that does not form part of the usual local network of services. By this, we mean an inpatient unit that does not usually admit

> people living in the catchment of the person's local community mental health service
> and where the person cannot be visited regularly by their care co-ordinator to ensure
> continuity of care and effective discharge planning. (Department of Health, 2016: 1)

The extent of the use of out of area placements

The 'scandal' of placing acute patients in out of area placements (OAPs), under compulsory detention via Part II of the Mental Health Act (2007), is now well documented (BMA, 2017a; NHS Confederation, 2016). These patients are placed nationally in hospitals either via independent sector hospital providers or in NHS hospitals. Due to potential geographical distance and constraints on staffing and travel costs, often the care coordinator cannot regularly visit the person placed. This is often also the case for family visitors and additional external support networks such as friends and peer group members. The significant majority (over 90%) of these OAPs will be considered as 'inappropriate', as the guidance states that 'patients should be treated in a location which helps them to retain the contact they want to maintain with family, carers and friends, and to feel as familiar as possible with the local environment' (Department of Health, 2016: 1).

It has not been uncommon for patients to travel over 500 miles from their own area of residence, with over 6,000 patients being placed away from home annually, a rise of 40% between 2014–15 and 2016–17 (Marsh, 2017). These figures have now become an established trend (NHS Digital, 2017a) that remains contrary to local and national commissioning policy (NICE, 2016a). The media coverage of mental health patients and families in some considerable distress has prompted a government pledge to eliminate acute OAP placements by 2021 (Department of Health, 2016). Other than acknowledging the scale of the problem, better recording and more robust datasets, together with a 'decision tree' of considerations when having to commission to such placements, there is a paucity of information with regards to how the NHS and government will physically achieve a reduction in the use of OAPs. NHS England is currently engaging in pilot work on the issue, which will be discussed at the end of this chapter.

The effects on family and patients when using OAPs

There has been very little academic research covering this specific issue, however, there is clear anecdotal distress communicated by patients and families via the media and service user supported websites. This has been specifically related to the highly negative experience of being placed significant distances away from home. Recognition of considerable distress caused to patients is recognised by the British Medical Association (2017a: 1) which argues that 'the government need to get a handle on this situation because patients are being routinely failed by a system at breaking point, with tragic consequences'. There have already been documented coroner reports, such as the case of David Knight, directly attributing avoidable cases of suicide to the use of OAPs (Courts and Tribunals Judiciary, 2016).

Existing research has tended to focus on the needs of patients detained in secure services in relation to their anxieties around discharge planning and a return home (Parry-Crooke et al, 2012). However, this has not covered concerns about patient and family involvement in the use of OAPs per se. There has been some research covering the use of OAPs for adults with intellectual disabilities; for example, the thematic analysis of 17 patients in OAPs with an intellectual disability revealed strains on maintaining family relationships and themes of loss when asked about how they felt when unable to visit (Chin et al, 2011: 56).

The contributory causes for the increased use of OAPs

The reasons for the rise in the use of OAPs are complex. We know for example that there are linear commissioning patterns that are likely to have promoted the rise in OAP use. The number of learning disability and mental health acute hospital beds has fallen by 72.1% and 96.4% respectively between 1987 and 2017 (King's Fund, 2017). This was due to a combination of policy changes brought about by the National Health and Community Care Act (1990) initiated by the Griffiths Report (1988). The discharge of long stay acute patients with learning disabilities and mental health issues back into community residential care settings occurred gradually but was sustained in the medium term due to the transition of funding responsibilities for residential services from the NHS to local authority social care budgets. 'Long stay' hospital service users have reflected that these hospital closures were because 'the over-riding fundamental reason was that it was the right thing to do' (King's Fund, 2017: 1).

While there has been a corresponding increase of 26.2% in social care beds since 1998, there has also been a complex combination of factors that have contributed to the increased commissioning of OAP hospital beds (Laing Buisson, 2017). The effects of government austerity policies over the last ten years may also have been an influence on reductions in locality NHS services, but this is a complex national picture and is open to debate. While governments have pledged to protect and ring fence reductions in NHS spending, citing a real term spending increase in 2015–16 of £1.28 billion, 40% of mental health trusts had reported budget cuts in the same period (King's Fund, 2015). These have resulted in NHS multiple sustainability and transformation plans (STPs) across 44 areas in England which have been brought about by the need to 'rationalise' services (NHS England, 2017d). These have not been without controversy with recent austerity cuts undermining the practicalities of these STPs (BMA, 2017b) (see Pycroft, this volume).

We also know that there are broader changes in demographic presentations for mental illness that are likely to increase the likelihood of severe and enduring mental health issues occurring. This may have an impact on the increased use of

OAPs. In 1993, in any given week, 6.9% of the UK population reported severe symptoms of common mental disorders; this figure had risen to 9.3% by 2014. We know that women are now more likely to be affected by mental health issues, particularly during their late adolescent period (NHS Digital, 2014) and that one in ten children have a diagnosable condition; that half of all mental health problems are established by the age of 14 years and that 75% of all mental health issues are established by the age of 24 years (Mental Health Taskforce, 2016).

These trends have emerged over time and we know that early treatment and intervention have been a priority for commissioners of adult and community adolescent services for some time as obvious treatment savings can be made (NICE, 2016b). The shift in funding towards psychological talking therapies with a target waiting time of 18 weeks, with 2 weeks for people experiencing their first episode of psychosis, is an NHS priority (NHS England, 2015b). This is offset by a pharmaceutical explosion where medicines dispensed for anxiety, depression, obsessive-compulsive disorder and panic attacks have increased by 108.5% from 31 million to 65 million prescriptions between 2006 and 2016 (NHS Digital, 2017b).

The complexity of factors that coalesce and contribute to an increase in the use of OAP hospital beds is difficult to untangle. It is further complicated by emergent trends and commissioning complexities in the Child and Adolescent Mental Health Services (CAMHS), which have created some recent cause for alarm and speculation. Large cohort studies are now evidencing marked rises in self-harm of up to 68% among girls aged 13–16 years (Morgan et al, 2017). The causes of this are being hotly debated in the media with charities such as Young Minds who are vigorously lobbying for accountability and transparency in CAMHS budgetary processes (Young Minds, 2015). Government capital funding for CAMHS has increased by an extra £250 million in the period 2015–20, and politicians have cited the practice of using OAPs for children as 'institutionalised cruelty' (*Guardian*, 2015). With the practice of OAP commissioning for children still in evidence, this has forced the government to commission and publish additional services, namely additional funding for 150–180 new adolescent beds in 'under-served' areas of the country (NHS England, 2017c).

Key learning point

In itself 'single service' commissioning whereby a patient is 'managed' by a single agency in a case management framework is complex. This complexity is compounded where a patient is 'managed' by both criminal justice and mental health service providers.

The chapter has so far illustrated the policy of commissioning OAPs, highlighting potential causes of their increased use in the patient 'care pathway' in mental health service provision. While the experience of being placed a long distance from home can be very distressing, for the patient, their peer support group and their family, clinical commissioning groups bear the costs of these services. Subsequently there is some impetus to return 'single agency managed' patients home, as soon as practicable. This is borne out by the high 'turnover' of placements. As an example, for the month of July 2017, 540 OAPs were commissioned and 446 were ended; that is, either discharged or returned to a local area bed (NHS Digital, 2017a).

We must bear in mind that nearly every commissioned OAP represents a failure of national and local mental health and commissioning policy (Chaudhry and Pereira, 2009: 15; The Reed Report (Department of Health, 1992: iii); The Bradley Report, 2009: 140; The Corston Report, 2007: 48, 69; Care Programme Approach, 2008: 21, 27; and Mental Health Act (2007: s118(c))). In response to lobbying and media pressure, a recent national dataset directive has been requested by government which now provides more accurate recording statistics for the use of OAPs including data on the length of stay, diagnostic category and reasons for admission (Department of Health, 2017). Data 'shaming' of offending NHS Trusts effectively coalesce with high profile legal hearing such as the case of *ZX*, where prominent judges state that the nation will have 'blood on their hands' unless urgent hospital beds are found ([2017] EWHC 2036 (Fam)). This provides an effective 'stick and stick' approach to ending the use of OAPs. The case of *ZX* highlights the additional complexity of caring for a patient when more than one 'managing agency' is involved. It also highlights the complexity of developments in the adolescent population.

Case study: *ZX*

The judgement involved a 17-year-old girl at high clinical risk of suicide who was due to be released from a secure youth custody unit within 11 days, following a Detention and Training Order, imposed by the Youth Court in the late summer of 2017. With the clock ticking, she needed urgent provision of an acute hospital bed. She had a diagnosis of Emotionally Unstable Personality Disorder and ADHD with Conduct Disorder. She was considered to be at immediately high risk to self as she would ingest anything around her, would use hair, clothing or fabrics to tie a ligature around her, would self-harm by banging her head, biting herself or by punching herself in the face or body. She would secrete items within her clothing to ingest or self-harm with later and would self-harm by inserting staples and her own fingers into existing wounds. She required constant 1:1 nursing supervision and support in a secure environment. She was effectively nursed in a stripped bedroom in order to make it secure, with only a mattress; she had to be dressed in anti-ligature clothing. The proposed care plan was to send her back home which care staff considered to be 'a suicide mission to a catastrophic level'. [2017] EWHC 2036 (Fam)

The assessment process and commissioning issues

There was no doubt that *ZX* would have been eligible under the criteria for detention to hospital under Part II or III of the Mental Health Act (1983) and medical recommendations for detention were also available. Therefore, the provision of a hospital bed was the only procedural sticking point. Following assessment, it was considered that her behaviours were too severe for admission to a psychiatric intensive care unit (PICU; see Green and Pycroft, this volume) as her needs were considered to be too complex. She was considered inappropriate for admission to a medium secure hospital as the criteria for admission were too high. In order to satisfy this criterion, she would need to 'demonstrate behaviour relating to direct or serious violence to others, sexually aggressive behaviour, or the life threatening use of fire' (NHS England, 2017a: CAMHs form 1). However, this is only guidance, and individual admission criteria for medium security varies considerably from hospital to hospital (CMH, 2011: 24).

Given the circumstances of her referral she would only have been considered appropriate for CAMHS (Tier 4) low security hospital provision, which could have been provided in the independent or the private sector. This would have been funded and commissioned via NHS England, rather than at cost to her home clinical commissioning group. The dearth of bed availability was the reason for 150–180 recently commissioned new adolescent beds in 'under-served' areas of the country (NHS England, 2017c). In recording his judgement on the case of *ZX*, Justice Sir James Munby said:

> The lack of proper provision for [ZX] – and, one fears, too many like her – is an outrage. If, when in eleven days' time she is released from [X], we, the system, society, the State, are unable to provide [ZX] with the supportive and safe placement she so desperately needs, and if, in consequence, she is enabled to make another attempt on her life, then I can only say, with bleak emphasis: we will have blood on our hands. [2017] EWHC 2036 (Fam)

In the event, he addressed his direction for a hospital bed to the Secretary of State and the Chief Executive of NHS England. At the time of the judgement, there were six potentially suitable beds available nationally, none of which were due to expect vacancies within at least two months. NHS England did finally find a suitable bed for her prior to the expiration of the 11-day release. This was following extensive pressure from judicial services and reporting from the local and national media.

The complexity of transitioning between institutions

The case highlights 'agency interface' issues; these create serious 'service tensions' and individual distress, to the extent that she almost 'fell through the gap' between services. For around 90% of OAP beds, the referrals are considered to be 'inappropriate' (NHS Digital, 2017a). As reiterated, most acute patients will be returned to their locality area within a short time frame, frequently in less than a period of a month. This is because OAPs are funded by the patient's locality CCG so there a budgetary locality impetus, together with pressure via national drivers and key data sets which are attempting to end the use of OAPs for acute mental health patients. This is not necessarily the case for ZX who, at 17 years of age, is likely to be transferred to adult secure care services within a relatively short time frame. In the case of ZX and all adults who enter the secure hospital estate, their beds are commissioned and paid for by NHS England at no cost to their locality CCG (NHS England, 2014). The same funding streams apply for adult patients admitted to secure services under part III of the MHA (1983), which include hybrid hospital orders and 'disposals' via crown court proceedings through the criminal justice system. Adults who enter secure service provision via these routes are not subject to the monitoring and service targets that are now scrutinised via the datasets that are designed reduce OAP admissions (NHS Digital, 2017a). This is because these datasets apply to acute inpatient admissions only.

The point above is critical because the 'default position' for transfer from prison or court services via the Mental Health Act (1983) is usually via medium secure hospitals (CMH, 2011: 11). This means that most adult patients who are admitted to secure hospital OAPs under the Mental Health Act (1983 as amended 2007), via non-acute multi-agency routes, will be subject to different funding processes, datasets and alternative local and national policy frameworks. These different and often competing factors do not necessarily prioritise the need to repatriate patients back to their home area at the earliest opportunity.

While there are multiple routes for admission to hospital, all patients detained in OAP secure hospital provision are placed nationally via mental health case commissioners and the Ministry of Justice in placements which are funded by NHS England (JCPMH, 2013: 11). These patients frequently remain detained at a significant distance from their own locality area at no direct cost to their responsible locality clinically commissioned area (for discharge); this reduces the opportunity and incentive for timely, well planned and effective reintegration back to their locality home communities (Parry-Crooke and Stafford, 2011: 29). Extensive waiting times can be counter-therapeutic, are likely to increase the effects of long-term institutionalisation and reduce personal hope in terms of positive outcomes for recovery (Drennan and Wooldridge, 2014: 10; Lart et al, 1999: 33). Ineffective and poorly planned transitions can increase avoidable re-admission rates for patients who are subject to high-cost secure hospital provision, and are the point of highest risk for patients (JCPMH, 2013: 4).

Key learning point

The complexities for tracking, caring and discharge planning for mentally disordered offenders in OAP secure hospitals are substantial and significant. The situation is further compounded for minority groups within the secure system. This includes adults with a learning disability and women, who are at risk of isolation and marginalisation within the secure hospital system.

We have established the complex nature of the commissioning of OAPs generally; and while there are additional complexities with regards the adolescent acute mental health population, we have seen how national key drivers and datasets are attempting to improve commissioning arrangements. To some degree this has been assisted by intense media coverage which has spurred government to return patients to their home area at the earliest opportunity. However, we have also seen how the 'adult secure population', who are at risk of offending, can escape the gaze of such national datasets and key national drivers; this despite the reality that mental health patients who are 'managed' by multi-agency processes due to complex needs are those who are frequently at risk of offending and most likely to be 'cut-off' from mainstream services once they enter the world of out of area commissioned secure hospital placements.

The reality for women in secure settings

The situation is compounded for minority groups within the OAP secure estate. One example is through gender separation which has created specific anomalies for women in secure services. Practice evidence suggests that waiting times for women in secure services can be extensive and can last for many months, and in some cases, years (Parry-Crooke and Stafford, 2011: 72). Research demonstrates that discontinuities around 'transition' are being seriously undermined for this client group and that the care 'pathway' system is not functioning as intended (Parry-Crooke et al, 2012: 34; Somers and Bartlett, 2014: 8).

While there is some evidence to suggest that regional secure specialised services may have adapted effectively to meet the therapeutic needs of this specific female patient group (Long et al, 2008: 304), there has also been 'increasing disquiet' about the placement of women at a significant distance away their home area for substantial periods of time. (Parry-Crooke et al, 2012: 19). For the past 15 years there has been a critical view that these patients have been viewed as 'out of county, out of sight and out of mind' (Page and Dix, 2007: 82). Many of the commissioning complexities and practices relating to the use of OAPs apply to males as well as females, but the isolation and marginalisation of female patients in OAP secure services are significant due to a number of systemic factors which relate to the evolution of service provision.

Bartlett and Hassell (2001) first questioned the validity of detaining women in conditions of high security especially when their specific needs are more in line with the need for 'relational security' rather than 'physical security'. 'Relational security is the knowledge and understanding we have of a patient and of the environment, and the translation of that information into appropriate responses and care' (Royal College of Psychiatrists Centre for Quality Improvement, 2015). Mental health secure provision is primarily focused on the needs of men who occupy 80% of available secure beds, with a lack of specialised provision for females. Females have traditionally been considered part of a homogenous group when it has come to secure mental health provision and as such have been 'admitted as a category' (Parry-Crooke et al, 2012: 210). This is despite a significant and growing body of dated academic research that has identified female offenders with mental health issues as a heterogeneous and vulnerable group with a highly diverse range of needs (Bartlett and Hassell, 2001: 304).

A flurry of associated policy initiatives over the past 15 years has occurred in growing recognition of the different needs of female offenders with mental health issues in secure health provision. This included the closure of high security female hospitals for women (Rampton and Broadmoor) and the subsequent development of regional enhanced medium secure provision for women (WEMS). Parallel to this was the government's intention to eliminate all mixed sex hospital ward provision (Department of Health, 2009), together with the added requirement of specified standards for women in medium secure care (CCQI, 2008). This has resulted in a suspected and subsequent reduction in the number of female low secure beds in a patient's own locality commissioned areas, and the consequent rise in the use of secure OAP provision. The increase in the use of female OAPs has been partly fuelled by a lack of appropriate facilities for this client group in their own locality areas, but also due to the need to develop specialised dedicated services for female only patients. At a time when the number of NHS beds for learning disability long stay patients has been halved (NHS England, 2015a) and the use of NHS long stay beds for older persons has been virtually eradicated, this increase in the use of OAPs for female offenders with mental health problems represents a significant commissioning anomaly within the current national policy objectives and related practice guidance.

Until 2012 there was no national dataset that could even provide us with the numbers of women in OAP secure care. We were unaware of the numbers, how women were admitted, why they were admitted, their length of stay or intended route of discharge. We now know that approximately 1,625 women are in secure hospital services across England and Wales and that the independent sector is the main service provider. We also know that it is 'a population that is steadily increasing; once in secure settings women stay longer than men and for up to four times longer than women in prison' (Harty et al, 2012: 15; Bartlett et al, 2014).

The latest research studies provide us with a rich dataset for minority groups in OAP secure provision and this should provide a valuable area of consideration for commissioners and practitioners of secure services for minority populations which we know by definition are hard to reach and easily side-lined by the service and target driven pressures of mainstream NHS service provision. As Bartlett et al (2014: 303) highlight,

> Some women appear detained in secure settings without easy evidence of risk to others. Many women are located outside of their home region. The independent sector is the main provider of these services, it is thought by their own analysis to be more expensive and yet the NHS services are not fully occupied. There is a need to consider carefully how and why this pattern of care has arisen, the extent to which it is appropriate and whether there is scope for improvement in the light of a national data-set.

Implications for commissioners and practitioners

This chapter has highlighted the complexity of OAP provision and the negative service implications for patients. It has also highlighted the tendency for minority groups in OAPs to fall off the radar and potentially 'get lost' in a commissioning process that should lead to patients being discharged and repatriated back to their own locality community.

The obvious solution would be to avoid their use in the first place. There are local and regional policy initiatives to avoid the use of OAPs with a particular emphasis on locality acute mental health services as a catalyst to prevent avoidable hospital admissions. One notable example is Bradford, where the local mental health trust reduced a £2m OAP spend (106 beds) from 2015–16, to zero beds with an 18-month period. It achieved this by joint inter-agency working forums, improved responses in A&E places of safety and the provision of an emergency social care service called 'the Sanctuary', which took over 600 referrals during those 18 months (McNicoll, 2016).

On a national level there are also commissioning developments that are currently attempting to address and reduce OAP provision. NHS England has launched 11 test sites worth £640 million that aim to incentivise local managers and clinicians to take some control of specialist centralised NHS England budgets and use the money to develop strong locality services. This will be with a view to a hoped for cost-saving of over £50 million by avoiding unnecessary OAP treatment provision (NHE, 2017). Any savings will be used to increase funding for existing community mental health projects. This is exciting work and the projects will cover not only CAMHS (Tier 4) services but also eating disorders services and adult secure care provision. The two wave test pilots will need to be fully evaluated, and will need to include innovative design and implementation that mirror those such as Bradford in order to be a success.

The golden thread of through-care

This chapter has reviewed the difficulties in commissioning services for individuals with complex needs who straddle the interface between criminal justice, health and social care agencies. The challenge for multi-agency practitioners that work across mental health and criminal justice settings has always been to promote inter-agency working as a key to successful client outcomes via the promotion of shared outcomes. This is reflected in policy initiatives such as 'My Shared Care Pathway' across the secure hospital estate. These have been adapted from service user led initiatives in response to dissatisfaction with available 'non-recovery based' mental health services (NHS England, 2017b; Callaghan, 2014). While policy initiatives such as this must be lauded, they represent a response to the fragmentation of services that have had the unintentional outcome of severing the longer-term relationship between the practitioner and the service user, offender or patient. This relationship was originally designed to enhance collaboration with service users, and valued the importance of shared pathway planning. The increased use of the OAP hospital bed represents the epitome of the fragmentation of this process. The process is neither 'shared' nor voluntary as the patient has been forced into a treatment often hundreds of miles from their own home. The sooner services are re-designed around locality models of need, the stronger the relationship between practitioner and service user will be. This can only result in better outcomes in the delivery of care.

Summary of key learning points
- Single service commissioning becomes problematic when a patient is 'managed' by more than one statutory supervising agency.
- Monitoring the quality of through care and discharge planning is complex for mentally disordered offenders in secure hospitals. It is made highly complex if patients are in out of area placements.
- This complexity is exacerbated further if you are female or have a learning disability; these patients risk becoming isolated and marginalised within the secure hospital estate.

References
Bartlett, A. and Hassell, Y. (2001) 'Do women need secure services?', *Advances in Psychiatric Treatment*, 7: 302–309.
Bartlett, A., Somers, N., Fiander, M. and Harty, M.A. (2014) 'Pathways of care of women in secure hospitals. Which women go where and why?', *British Journal of Psychiatry*, 205(4): 298–306.

British Medical Association (BMA) (2017a) 'BMA figures show startling rise in mental health out of area placements', press release, 26 June, www.bma.org.uk/ news/media-centre/press-releases/2017/june/bma-figures-show-starling-rise-in-mental-health-out-of-area-placements

BMA (2017b) 'Delivery costs extra: can STPs survive without the funding they need?', Committee Report.

Bradley, Lord (2009) *Lord Bradley's review of people with mental health problems or learning disabilities in the criminal justice system.* London: Department of Health.

Callaghan, I. (2014) 'Putting recovery first in secure care', Rethink Mental Illness, 18 January, www.rethink.org/news-views/2014/07/putting-recovery-first-in-secure-care

Care Programme Approach (2008) *Refocusing the care programme approach – policy and positive practice guidance.* London: Department of Health.

CCQI (2008) *Quality Network for Forensic Mental Health Services: standards and criteria for women in medium secure care.* London: Royal College of Psychiatrists.

Centre for Mental Health (CMH) (2011) *Pathways to unlocking secure mental health care.* London: National Mental Health Development Unit.

Chaudhry, K. and Pereira, S.M. (2009) 'A comparison of NHS and private low secure units: Unit and patient characteristics', *Journal of Psychiatric Intensive Care*, 5(1): 15–23.

Chin, D., Hall, I., Ali, A., Hassell, H. and Patkas, I. (2011) 'Psychiatric in-patients away from home. Accounts by people with intellectual disabilities in specialist hospitals outside their home localities', *Journal of Applied Research in Intellectual Disabilities*, 24: 50–60.

Corston, J. (2007) *The Corston Report: The need for a distinct, radically different, visibly-led, strategic, proportionate, holistic, women-centred, integrated approach.* London: Home Office.

Courts and Tribunals Judiciary (2016) *Coroner Report – Regulation 28: Report to Prevent Future Deaths – David Knight deceased*, 14 November, www.judiciary.gov. uk/wp-content/uploads/2017/02/Knight-2016-0414.pdf

Department of Health (1992) *Review of health and social services for mentally disordered offenders and other requiring similar services.* Final summary report. London: HMSO.

Department of Health (2009) 'Eliminating mixed sex accommodation', Chief Nursing Officer and the Director of NHS Finance, Directive PL/CNO/2009/2.

Department of Health (2016) *Out of area placements in mental health services for adults in acute inpatient care.* London: Department of Health.

Department of Health (2017) 'Direction on out of area placements data collection', Department of Mental Health Policy, Dementia and Disability, 19 October, www.gov.uk/government/uploads/system/uploads/attachment_data/ file/656504/DH_Direction__Extension_of_the_interim_OAPs_in_Mental_ Health_Services_data_collection_FINAL.pdf

Drennan, G. and Wooldridge, J. (2014) 'Making recovery a reality in forensic settings', Centre for Mental Health and Mental Health Network, NHS Confederation, London.

Guardian (2015) 'Clegg announces extra £1.25bn for child mental health services at Lib Dem conference: Politics Live blog', www.theguardian.com/politics/blog/live/2015/mar/14/nick-cleggs-qa-at-the-lib-dem-conference-politics-live-blog

Griffiths, R. (1988) *Community Care: Agenda for Action*. London, HMSO.

Harty, M., Somers, N. and Bartlett, A. (2012) 'Women's secure hospital services: national bed numbers and distribution', *Journal of Forensic Psychiatry Psychology*, 23 (5–6): 590–600.

Joint Commissioning Panel for Mental Health (JCPMH) (2013) *Guidance for commissioners of forensic mental health services: practice mental health commissioning*, www.jcpmh.info/wp-content/uploads/jcpmh-forensic-guide.pdf

King's Fund (2015) 'NHS spending: squeezed as never before', 20 October, www.kingsfund.org.uk/blog/2015/10/nhs-spending-squeezed-never

King's Fund (2017) 'Case Study 1: Deinstitutionalisation in UK mental health services', www.kingsfund.org.uk/publications/making-change-possible/mental-health-services

Lang Buisson (2017) 'County care markets update 2017, Financial challenges in the light of proposals for long term care funding reform', County Councils Network, p 30. www.countycouncilsnetwork.org.uk/download/1179/

Lart, R. Payne, S. Beaumont, B., MacDonald, G. and Mistry, T. (1999) 'Women and secure psychiatric services: a literature review', NHS Centre for Reviews and Dissemination, University of York.

Long, C., Fulton, B. and Hollin, C. (2008) 'The development of a "best practice" service for women in a medium-secure psychiatric setting: treatment components and evaluation', *Clinical Psychology and Psychotherapy*, (15): 304–319.

Marsh, S. (2017) 'Almost 6,000 mental health patients sent out of area for care last year', *Guardian*, 27 June, www.theguardian.com/society/2017/jun/27/almost-6000-mental-health-patients-sent-out-of-area-for-care-last-year-nhs-treatment-england

McNicoll, A. (2016) 'How one area's mental health teams are tackling the 'scandal' of out-of-area care', Community Care, 20 May, www.communitycare.co.uk/2016/05/20/one-areas-mental-health-teams-tackling-scandal-area-care/

Mental Health Taskforce (2016) *The five year forward view for mental health: a report from the Independent Mental Health Taskforce to the NHS in England*, www.england.nhs.uk/mental-health/taskforce/

Morgan, C., Webb, R.T., Carr, M.J., Kontopantelis, E., Green, J., Chew-Graham, C.A., Kapur, N. and Ashcroft, D.M. (2017) 'Incidence, clinical management, and mortality risk following self-harm among children and adolescents: cohort study in primary care', *BMJ*, 359:j4351, https://doi.org/10.1136/bmj.j4351

National Health Executive (NHE) (2017) 'NHS England launches £640 million test sites to redesign mental health services', 23 June, www.nationalhealthexecutive.com/Health-Care-News/nhs-england-launches-640m-test-sites-to-redesign-mental-health-services#

National Institute for Clinical Excellence (NICE) (2016a) 'Transition between inpatient mental health settings and community or care home settings', NICE Guideline NG53, August.

NICE (2016b) 'Implementing the early intervention in psychosis access and waiting time standard: guidance', NHS England Publications Gateway Reference 04294.

NHS Confederation (2016) *Improving Acute Inpatient Psychiatric Care for Adults in England, Interim Report*. London: NHS Confederation.

NHS Digital (2014) 'Adult psychiatric morbidity survey: survey of mental health and wellbeing, England, 2014', http://digital.nhs.uk/catalogue/PUB21748

NHS Digital (2017a) 'Out of area placements in mental health services, July 2017', http://digital.nhs.uk/catalogue/PUB30088

NHS Digital (2017b) 'Prescriptions dispensed in the community – statistics for England 2006–16', http://digital.nhs.uk/catalogue/PUB30014

NHS England (2014) 'NHS Standard Contract for Medium and Low Secure Mental Health Services (Adults) – Schedule 2, The Services, A Service Specification', Co3/S/a, NHS Commissioning Board.

NHS England (2015a) 'Homes not hospitals for people with learning disabilities', 30 October, www.england.nhs.uk/learningdisabilities/2015/10/30/homes-not-hospitals/

NHS England (2015b) *Improving Access to Psychological Therapies (IAPT) Waiting Times – Guidance and FAQs*, www.england.nhs.uk/wp-content/uploads/2015/02/iapt-wait-times-guid.pdf

NHS England (2017a) 'NHS standard contract for Tier 4 Child and Adolescent Mental Health Services (CAMHS): Children's Services: Schedule 2 – The services – A. Service specifications', C07/S/b, www.england.nhs.uk/wp-content/uploads/2013/06/c07-tier4-ch-ado-mh-serv-child.pdf

NHS England (2017b) 'My shared pathway – involving service users of secure mental health services', www.england.nhs.uk/participation/why/public/my-shared-pathway/

NHS England (2017c) 'Next steps on the NHS Five Year Forward View: NHS acts to cut inappropriate out of area placements for children and young people in mental health crisis', 3 March, www.england.nhs.uk/2017/03/nhs-acts-to-cut-inappropriate-out-of-area-placements-for-children-and-young-people-in-mental-health-crisis

NHS England (2017d) 'Sustainability and transformation partnerships – local partnership to improve health and care', www.england.nhs.uk/integratedcare/stps/view-stps/

Page, M. and Dix, J. (2007) 'Supply versus demand: market forces in low secure and psychiatric intensive care units', *Journal of Psychiatric Intensive Care*, 3(02): 79–83.

Parry-Crooke, G. and Stafford, P. (2011) *My life: In safe hands? Dedicated women's medium secure services in England*, commissioned NHS National R&D Programme on Forensic Mental Health, www.ohrn.nhs.uk/resource/policy/WMSSEvaluationFinalReport.pdf

Parry-Crooke, G., Robinson, C. and Zeilig, H. (2012) *Stepping out – The needs of women discharged from secure mental health services*, NHS East of England Specialised Commissioning Group, London Metropolitan University.

Royal College of Psychiatrists Centre for Quality Improvement (2015) *Your guide to relational security – See, Think, Act*. Second edition.

Somers, N. and Bartlett, A. (2014) 'Women's secure hospital care pathways in practice: a qualitative analysis of clinicians' views in England and Wales', *BMC Health Services Research*, 14: 450.

Young Minds (2015) 'Children's mental health funding not going where it should be', https://youngminds.org.uk/about-us/media-centre/press-releases/children-s-mental-health-funding-not-going-where-it-should-be

Further reading

Bonell, S., Ali, A., Hall, I., Chinn, D. and Patkas, I. (2011) 'People with intellectual disabilities in out-of-area specialist hospitals: what do families think?', *Journal of Applied Research in Intellectual Disabilities*, 24(5): 389–397.

14

Removing the 'dual' and working with the presenting diagnosis: core processes of change

Anita Green and Aaron Pycroft

Aims of the chapter

- To outline and explore the profile of the secure and forensic population with respect to dual diagnosis.
- To examine the importance of the therapeutic relationship in secure and forensic settings.
- To review how a motivational interviewing informed intervention can be applied to secure and forensic settings.
- To explore the importance of the service users' voice as an integral part of education planning and training in multi-agency working.

Introduction

The concepts of 'dual diagnosis', 'co-morbidity' and 'complex needs' are still sources of consternation and confusion in psychiatric medicine and community services, despite a significant amount of research and policy making over the last 30 years. We have argued elsewhere (Pycroft and Green, 2015) that the effective void still exists in policy terms and to the significant detriment of people who experience dual diagnosis; this despite the Bradley Report (Department of Health, DOH, 2009) saying that:

> Throughout the course of this review it has become apparent that the issue of dual diagnosis ... is a vital component of addressing the issue of mental health and criminal justice. In fact ... stakeholders (have) sent out a clear message that no approach to diverting offenders

with mental health problems from prison and/or the criminal justice system would be effective unless it addressed drug and alcohol misuse. (DOH, 2009: 21)

In this chapter, we briefly revisit the structural challenges in working with service users who have a dual diagnosis and come into contact with the secure and forensic (S&F) services, to make and reinforce the argument that people working within a fractured and fragmented system have to hold the tension of working with vulnerable people while at the same time making the arguments for systemic change. In particular with respect to supporting people who have concurrent mental health and drug/alcohol problems we argue that every practitioner should have the core skills to work with service users experiencing these problems, including in the forensic population; this is especially important within case management models where a number of different agencies might be involved in the supervision of one service user. We argue for an approach grounded in reflective practice that recognises an evidence base for working with dually diagnosed persons that incorporates the psychological processes of self-efficacy and building motivation. This is in effect taking the 'dual' out of 'dual diagnosis', and working with the presenting individual, irrespective of whether they present to mental health services with substance use problems or substance misuse services with mental health problems. We will make our argument by reviewing the research literature on the effectiveness of these approaches, provide and discuss a case study, and then make suggestions for further reading.

The secure and forensic population

People with serious mental health problems have higher rates of co-morbid problematic substance use (drug and/or alcohol use) compared with the general population (Regier et al, 1990; DOH, 2002). Studies of forensic service users in the UK show that rates of substance use are higher still within this population (Scott et al, 2004; Derry and Batson, 2008). Rates of problematic substance use among people admitted to S&F units are typically between 50 and 90% (Derry and Batson, 2008; Oddie and Davies, 2009). Ongoing use of substances following admission has also been shown to be a common problem within S&F units (Whyte and Harrison, 2004; Durand et al, 2006). Until recently, the predominant substance of choice was cannabis and alcohol and to a lesser extent poly drug use (the regular use of three or more substances) though with the increase in use of legal highs this picture has been changing over the past few years (see Bartholomew, 2015) providing further challenges for S&F practitioners because of the training requirements to understand these relatively new and evolving substances while also ensuring that the problem of legal highs is recognised in policies and procedures.

Substance use among the forensic population is a challenge for the S&F practitioner for a number of reasons: drug and/or alcohol use tends to exacerbate the mental health symptoms, and increases physical health concerns; for example, we know in relation to physical health that diabetes, coronary heart disease and hepatitis B or C increases. This has been highlighted recently by the King's Fund and Centre for Mental Health (Naylor et al, 2012). Though not focusing specifically on dual diagnosis, the authors of the report state the strong link between long-term physical health conditions and co-occurring mental health problems resulting in: poorer health outcomes so reducing the quality of life; increased admissions to hospital; poor medication concordance; and increased contact with the criminal justice services. Overall, the cost of care and treatment is increased (NICE, 2011). The potential risk of violence by people with a complexity of mental health and drug and/or alcohol misuse is stressed by the National Confidential Inquiry into Suicide and Homicide by People with Mental Illness (Centre for Suicide Prevention, 2010) which states that 36% of homicides are committed by people presenting with drug and/or alcohol use and a mental health diagnosis. Forensic service users who use drugs and/or alcohol have also been found to be at higher risk of violent reoffending (Maden et al, 2004) and reconviction following discharge (Scott et al, 2004). Risk to self in the dual diagnosis population has been well documented; though evidence of self-harm among those with a forensic history is less extensive, though there is evidence of an increased risk (Shaw et al, 2004). The Bradley Report (Department of Health, 2009) highlights the problems of care pathways within the criminal justice system and the key point to make is that persons dually diagnosed and who are involved with the criminal justice system are significantly disadvantaged, in terms of the overall treatment they receive and the potential outcomes from those services. There has been an increased recognition of the importance of service user participation in developing effective and responsive services in prisons and forensic secure units, but with the evidence demonstrating huge variability in how this is implemented (see National Survivors Users Network, 2011).

Evidence to inform interventions used within secure and forensic services

There is very little substance use guidance for practitioners who work in S&F environments based on methodologically sound research (Weldon and Ritchie, 2010). More important is the need for longitudinal intervention studies that reflect the service user's journey through the S&F services (see Noyce, this volume). Over the past ten years, standards and guidance for medium secure units have been published to reflect the growing concerns relating to forensic service users who have problematic drug and/or alcohol issues. The Royal College of Psychiatrists Centre for Quality Improvement (2006) stipulated the importance of medium secure units (MSUs) having access to a substance use or dual diagnosis specialist and that there should be policies specific to the control of illicit substances covering: 1) treatment of substance use; 2) education on the dangers of substance misuse; 3) advice to visitors on the dangers of passing illicit/unauthorised substances; 4) a protocol in collaboration with the police when drugs are discovered; and 5) a policy on 'searching with cause' for drugs. The guidance also states that teams should have access to local drug and alcohol services to support the needs of the service user. Even though this guidance does not provide any clear direction on assessment and therapeutic interventions, and is somewhat 'medical' in its approach – and it could be argued punitive in style – it highlights the importance of having access to a practitioner to support, guide and educate staff about drug and alcohol use.

A best practice guidance specification for adult medium secure services was published a year later by the Department of Health (DOH, 2007) which focuses on MSUs having a policy on the control of illegal substances and health promotion to support individuals in line with what would be offered to the individuals outside S&F services. The key recommendations of these two documents underpin the standards published later in 2013 by The Royal College of Psychiatrists (Clark and Sandbrook, 2013). The scoping exercise from this later document emphasised the importance of using structured assessment tools and having a variety of dedicated interventions run by well trained staff to address substance misuse, including the use of group work interventions.

Along with the lack of empirical research studies in S&F services specifically, there are hardly any studies examining the effectiveness of assessment processes and care planning linked to drug and alcohol use, with the few there are focusing on treatment interventions. A small number of studies have been published evaluating the use of psychosocial intervention programmes in S&F units (Miles et al, 2007; Derry and Batson, 2008; Oddie and Davies, 2009), though these studies were small and do not include longitudinal components as part of the follow ups.

What becomes apparent in a number of these studies based on inpatient facilities is the challenge of incorporating realistic approaches to evaluating interventions when the forensic service user is living in an environment where they can be detained for long periods of time and have limited unescorted leave (which usually limits their access to drugs and alcohol). Monitoring and measuring abstinence in relation to an intervention can provide a false picture during the service user's admission because they are not exposed to their drug of choice and cannot realistically use the insight, knowledge and skills they may have gained through being involved in an intervention or psycho-education programme. It may also mean that assessing a person's motivation to change their behaviour may be more of a challenge for the practitioner as the service user may believe, due to the period of time unexposed to their drug of choice, that they may perceive themselves as not having a problem and reluctant to be involved with programmes which prepare them for community living (for example, relapse prevention or harm reduction programmes). Swain et al (2010) describe this challenge particularly with service users who have been detained for long periods of time with limited or no access to drugs and alcohol. This is understandable from the service user perspective because motivation to change is usually assessed within their psychosocial and economic context. Inevitably, being in a locked environment can provide a false or at least an unclear picture for the practitioner and service user.

Core processes of change

The literature consistently demonstrates that in the population of those with a mental health problem diagnosis, a dual diagnosis or a forensic diagnosis they still have the same aspirations for their lives with respect to recovery and housing, employment and lifestyle (Rössler, 2006; Hipolito et al, 2011, Pycroft et al, 2015). Likewise, the processes of recovery include the importance of practitioners utilising reflective practice to develop their own skills that focus on supporting service users to build their self-efficacy and motivation. While dual diagnosis has been a basis for service exclusion, the evidence in contrast demonstrates that skills sets linked to core processes of change which are typically found in both forensic and non-forensic settings to address substance misuse and mental health problems are suitable for working with dual diagnosis (see Handmaker et al, 2002).

The following case study was informed by the principles used in the seminal works of Prochaska and DiClemente (1982) on the transtheoretical model of intentional behavioural change (but focusing on the stages of change part of the model), which incorporates the core psychological processes of motivation and self-efficacy (situational confidence; see Bandura, 1977); and motivational interviewing, which has developed as an adjunct to the model (Miller and Rollnick, 2012). Both motivation and self-efficacy are linked with the importance of positive feedback loops, non-confrontational approaches, building confidence and reducing the risk of relapse. Importantly, both processes are situationally determined and link biological, psychological and environmental factors.

Case study: Using motivational interviewing in locked facilities

This case study describes an intervention that was introduced as a feasibility study on a Psychiatric Intensive Care Unit (PICU); however, the intervention format with some adaption could be used in S&F units or S&F community services. Although the focus is on cannabis use, the intervention could be used for other substance use, including new psychoactive substances (NPS; see Green and Joy, 2013, for the full text).

The authors designed a set of motivational interviewing (MI) informed template interventions that could be used by qualified and unqualified practitioners at the point of providing the service user with their urine screening result. This is a particularly sensitive issue as there are specific consequences and sanctions imposed should the urine test reveal ongoing drug use. This, therefore, could be an opportunity for practitioners to provide a consistent therapeutic approach to a sensitive procedure and to reflect upon their own interventions and their outcomes.

The intervention

The aims for the service users engaged in the intervention were to:

- help to engage the service user in talking about their cannabis use at the point of receiving the result of their cannabis urine screening;
- support the service user to talk specifically about concerns they have about using cannabis;
- to provide the service user with the experience of MI as an opportunity to review their motivation to change their cannabis using behaviour; and
- complete the post MI informed intervention feedback questionnaire for evaluation purposes.

The aims for practitioners applying the intervention were to:

- be consistent in using a MI informed therapeutic dialogue with service users when providing them with a negative or positive cannabis urine screening result;
- be opportunistic in using a MI informed approach to assess motivation to change;
- document the comments made by the service user when providing the cannabis urine screening result using the MI informed templates as part of the data collection;
- help the service user to complete the post MI informed intervention feedback questionnaire for the evaluation.

The ethos, structure and process of the intervention were adapted from work by Rees, Copeland and Swift at the National Drug and Alcohol Research Centre in Australia (Rees et al, 1998), the work of Bonsack et al (2011) and from guidance produced by the Centre for Substance Abuse Treatment in America (Steinberg, 2005; Sampl, 2001). The intervention was a brief (10 to 15 minute) MI one-to-one confidential dialogue between a practitioner who had received MI training from one of the authors and the service user. The intervention was undertaken at the point when the service user received their urine drug screen results, which in some cases was weekly depending on whether or not they had been given unescorted leave from the unit. The practitioners were provided with an intervention prompt guidance sheet to support the MI informed dialogue. Two guidance sheets were created, one for positive urine drug screen results for cannabis and one for negative results with the practitioner working through the appropriate guidance sheet depending on the urine screening results. The guidance sheets for negative results included: positive feedback; discussion about the pros and cons of using and not using cannabis to assess ambivalence; discussions about protective and promoting factors for cannabis use; problems and difficulties (such as cravings and triggers); strategies for managing relapse situations, including refusal skills); goals and current behaviour (discrepancies). For positive results: reassurances about lapses; review of the circumstances (where, when, who, why, how much?); feelings before use (bored, upset); feeling after use; positive and negative consequences; discussion about the pros and cons of using and not using cannabis to assess ambivalence; goals and current behaviour (discrepancies); strategies for managing relapse or trigger situations. Using the guidance sheets ensured consistency between the content of dialogue. This was an important safeguard as the interventions could potentially have been administered by a number of different practitioners. The intervention included strategies for managing situations away from the hospital (self-efficacy) when unescorted leave commenced which included contact with drug dealers and drug using associates. In this way, weekly urine drug screens, carried out as standard on the ward, became positive opportunities for service users providing protected one-to-one time with practitioners to explore their cannabis use, rather than being a potentially unhelpful experience which could be viewed as intrusive and punitive by the service user when a positive urine drug screen result is given.

Evaluation

The intervention was evaluated with some provisional positive qualitative results. The evaluation provided an opportunity for the authors to modify the intervention format based on feedback from the service users and practitioners and assess its application to other clinical areas, including inpatient and community settings.

Method of evaluation

The evaluation of the process was undertaken over five months. Service users consented to weekly urine drug screens and the concurrent one-to-one intervention and their anonymised details (demographic information and analysis of one-to-one sessions) being used as part of the evaluation process. The consent was provided through the intervention being included in the care plan and signed by the service user. Before the service user left the unit they were asked to complete a short evaluation questionnaire in order to gather feedback on their experience of the intervention.

Findings

All of the participants stated that the intervention should continue to be offered on the PICU after the feasibility project had finished. The following themes emerged from the participants' comments on the open-ended feedback questionnaires about their experience of taking part in the intervention:

- the discussion helped me to understand and focus my thoughts;
- the talk was helpful; I did not feel judged or pushed into doing anything;

- it was a positive experience;
- it helped me to think about my cannabis use; and
- good, as I am nearing the end of my hospital admission.

Limitations to using the intervention

There are potential limitations to using this approach in a S&F unit and there may be more scope to using it in S&F community services to help support service users who require an intervention after discharge as part of a relapse prevention strategy. Perhaps more significantly is the need within a multi-agented context for all the stakeholders to be working to a motivational agenda. The interpretation and application of the non-confrontational and non-punitive ethos of MI (collaboration, acceptance, evocation and compassion) can be problematic within S&F services (Mezey et al, 2010) for both practitioners, because of having to meet both care and custody requirements, and service users, who may experience control, power and compliance as the dominant model leading to a lack of trust in therapeutic process (see Lewis, this volume). Ideally a good case management system would span the bridge from inpatient to community, but of course this is not always the case (see Gough, this volume). In addition, a positive drugs test has different connotations for differing agencies depending on their remit. This case study demonstrates the sensitivities of drug testing and the need to build it in (where required) to the recovery process (working with relapse) rather than using it to exclude people from recovery services. This approach we argue needs to be at the heart of good multi-agency liaison and working and in no small measure driven by the service user.

Addressing education and training requirements

The 2001 Health and Social Care Act required all NHS organisations to engage with service users in service planning and evaluation as well as providing opportunities for inclusion in treatment decision making. It is essential that this is also true for S&F settings where risk factors and security protocols are very much to the fore (see National Survivors Users Network, 2011). Enabling and empowering all relevant practitioners to work with forensic service users who have a history of drug and/or alcohol use is vital with a fundamental need to ensure that professional training meets these needs. The addition of attitudinal work and the exploration of prejudice and stereotyping will help to ensure the complex needs of the forensic service user's social, psychological, physical and economic needs are considered. An approach based on motivational principles is entirely commensurate with service user participation and increased democratisation of service delivery. In addressing drug use and dependency there is an acceptance that relapse is the norm rather than the exception (see Tiquet, this volume), and that relapse rates increase in the dual diagnosis population (see Handmaker et al, 2002). Ongoing drug and alcohol use is a common problem in S&F units (Durand et al, 2006) despite the ideal of eradicating all illicit substances from those services thus presenting challenges in the use of drug testing and checking for contraband to meet risk and security requirements. A democratic approach to achieving the goals of a drug free environment for therapeutic purposes, and the maintenance of a motivational ethos is a consistent way to address this issue (drug free wings in prisons and the development of variations of democratic therapeutic communities might provide some interesting models). (See Barnes and Bowl, 2001, for a discussion concerning consultation and participation and their relationships to therapy and democracy.) It also raises the question of the ways in which treatment goals are negotiated and agreed on with respect to abstinence, controlled use (alcohol) or harm reduction (substitute prescribing and needle exchange) and whether dually diagnosed people within the S&F population have access to the same choice of services.

It is clear that the voice of the service user must be heard and viewed by those providing the training as integral partners in developing a comprehensive and realistic training curriculum (Pycroft and Green, 2015) that is underpinned by recovery principles that meet individual needs and treatment goals. Their voices and 'lived experience' can play an important part in exploring stereotypes and prejudice (see Webb, 2010) and in the co-production of training.

Robust forensic service user informed training can help aspects of practice that include being more drug and alcohol use aware, and sensitivity and confidence to improve clarity in what needs to be prioritised in assessment, care planning, treatment and care (Pycroft and Green, 2015). Practitioners working in a S&F service must be able to competently assess someone's mental health, drug and/or alcohol use (or previous use) and their criminal behaviour and the complex relationship between these three aspects of a person's presentation. A drug and alcohol assessment alongside mental health and forensic assessments can provide information to help make sense of the association between drug and/or alcohol use, mental state – including a diagnosed mental illness (and an alteration in mental state due to drug and/or alcohol use) – and criminal activity and the associated risks. The service user's concerns and needs may also be different from what the practitioner perceives as important; for example, abstinence (the practitioner's view); an attempt at controlled drinking (the service user's view) (Green, 2015). Additional training to include MI would help practitioners understand what is meant by a meaningful therapeutic alliance, the manifestations of ambivalence and recovery principles. Accessing appropriate training and education that includes service user input would support this shift to reflect more collaborative ways of working.

The implementation of effective interventions requires good multi-agency collaboration, clear care and service pathways and opportunities for shared learning and networking (Guest and Holland, 2011). Shared learning and education across professional groups may help to address some of these challenges. This, combined with good, consistent and sustainable clinical supervision as a model for learning in practice, will help to ensure that practitioners develop a knowledge base that informs their practice and encourages them to be more service user centred in their interactions with forensic service users with drug and/or alcohol issues. Care assistants are exposed to the same types of stressors and dilemmas as other practitioners and should be included in clinical supervision provision. Cromar–Hayes and Chandley (2014) suggest the use of group reflective practice sessions (though they do not specify whether these sessions are with or separate from the other team members); and training and supervision has shown to improved staff attitudes towards people who use drugs (Moore, 2013).

Conclusion

Being dually diagnosed has historically and in the main excluded service users from services for a number of reasons: stereotyping and stigmatising of individuals who do not 'fit' the mainstream accepted 'diagnosis' for a service; practitioners believing they do not have the knowledge and skills to work with a person with a dual diagnosis; staff attitudes that lead to silo thinking about service users, providing no flexibility to accommodate the person and acknowledge where they are on their dual diagnosis journey (Green, 2015: 89). In relation to S&F services, to perceive the service user as an individual who may require a number of different interventions at different times will support the view that diagnosing someone as 'dual diagnosis' is not that helpful. Using terms to represent an individual that encompass contemporary principles on mental health and substance use that are integral to recovery should ensure practitioners embrace the significance of therapeutic engagement that is flexible, sustainable and based on optimism and hope (Drake et al, 1993).

Summary of key learning points

- The term dual diagnosis should be considered more critically by the practitioner who should work with the presenting individual, irrespective of whether they present to mental health services with substance use problems or substance misuse services with mental health problems.
- Therapeutic interventions influenced by MI (Miller and Rollnick, 2012) can enable the S&F practitioner to support the service user in addressing their substance use.
- A drug and alcohol assessment should be viewed as integral to the mental health and forensic assessments because a holistic assessment can provide information to help make sense of the association between drug and/or alcohol use, mental state; criminal activity and the associated risks.
- Training of practitioners can significantly improve attitudes towards those who use drugs and/or alcohol.
- Service users need to be included in decisions about education requirements and where appropriate be co-producers of training. See the following useful resource from the New Economics Foundation on co-production in mental health commissioned by Mind https://neweconomics.org/uploads/files/ca0975b7cd88125c3e_ywm6bp3l1.pdf accessed 6/3/19

References

Bandura, A. (1977) 'Self-efficacy: towards a unifying theory of behavioural change', *Psychological Review*, 84: 191–215.

Barnes, M. and Bowl, R. (2001) *Taking over the asylum: empowerment and mental health.* Basingstoke: Palgrave.

Bartholomew, R. (2015) 'New psychoactive substances (legal highs)' in A. Pycroft (ed), *Key concepts in substance misuse.* London: Sage, pp 47–53.

Bonsack, C., Manetti, S.G., Favrod, J., Montagrin, Y., Besson, J., Bovet P. and Conus P. (2011) 'Motivational intervention to reduce cannabis use in young people with psychosis: a randomised controlled trial', *Psychotherapy and Psychosomatics*, 80: 287–297.

Centre for Suicide Prevention (2010) *National confidential inquiry into suicide and homicide by people with mental illness.* Annual Report, Manchester: University of Manchester.

Clark, T. and Sandbrook, J. (eds) (2013) *Standards for interventions to address problematic drug and alcohol use in medium security.* Royal College of Psychiatrists College, Centre for Quality Improvement.

Cromar-Hayes, M. and Chandley, M. (2014) 'Recovery in a high secure hospital in England', *Mental Health Practice*, 18(8): 32–37.

Department of Health (DOH) (2002) *Mental health policy implementation guide: dual diagnosis good practice guide.* London: HMSO.

DOH (2007) *Best practice guidance specification for adult medium-secure services.* London: Department of Health.

DOH (2009) *The Bradley Report: Lord Bradley's review of people with mental health problems or learning disabilities in the criminal justice system. Executive summary.* London: Department of Health.

Derry, A. and Batson, A. (2008) 'Getting out and staying out: does substance use treatment have an effect on outcome of mentally disordered offenders after discharge from medium secure units?', *British Journal of Forensic Practice*, 10(2): 13–17.

Drake, R., Bartel, S., Teague, G., Noordsy, D. and Clarke, R. (1993) 'Treatment of substance abuse in severely mentally ill patients', *The Journal of Nervous and Mental Disease*, 18(10): 606–611.

Durand, M.A., Lelliott, P. and Coyle, N. (2006) 'Availability of treatment for substance misuse in medium secure psychiatric care in England: a national survey', *Journal of Forensic Psychiatry & Psychology*, 17: 611–625.

Green, A. (2015) 'Dual diagnosis and the context of exclusion' in A. Pycroft (ed), *Key concepts in substance misuse.* London: Sage.

Green, A. and Joy, A. (2013) 'Providing a motivational interviewing (MI) informed intervention in conjunction with a cannabis drug urine screening for PICU service users: a feasibility project', *Advances in Dual Diagnosis*, 6(3): 121–131.

Guest, C. and Holland, M. (2011) 'Co-existing mental health and substance use and alcohol difficulties – why do we persist with the term "dual diagnosis" within mental health services?', *Advances in Dual Diagnosis*, 4(4): 162–169.

Handmaker, N., Packard, M. and Conforti, K. (2002) 'Motivational interviewing in the treatment of dual disorders', in W. Miller and S. Rollnick (eds), *Motivational interviewing: preparing people for change*, second edition. New York: Guilford Press.

Hipolito, M., Carpenter-Song, E. and Whitley, R. (2011) 'Meanings of recovery from the perspective of people with dual diagnosis', *Journal of Dual Diagnosis*, 7(3): 141–149.

Maden, A., Scott, F., Burnett, R., Lewis, G.H. and Skapinakis, P. (2004) 'Offending in psychiatric patients after discharge from medium secure units: prospective national cohort study', *BMJ*, 328: 1534.

Mezey, G., Kavuma, M. and Turton, P. (2010) 'Perceptions, experiences and meanings of recovery in forensic psychiatric patients', *The Journal of Forensic Psychiatry and Psychology*, 21(5): 683–696.

Miles, H., Dutheil, L., Welsby, I. and Haider, D. (2007) '"Just say no": a preliminary evaluation of a three-stage model of integrated treatment for substance use problems in conditions of medium security', *The Journal of Forensic Psychiatry and Psychology*, 18: 141–159.

Miller, W.R. and Rollnick, S. (2012) *Motivational interviewing. Helping people change*. Third edition. London: Guilford Press.

Moore, J. (2013) 'Dual diagnosis: training needs and attitudes of nursing staff', *Mental Health Practice*, 16(6): 27–31.

National Survivors Users Network (2011) *Unlocking Service user involvement practice in forensic settings*. London: USPAN.

Naylor, C., Parsonage, M., McDaid, D., Knapp, M., Fossey, M. and Galea, A. (2012) *Long term conditions and mental health: the cost of co-morbidities*. London: The King's Fund and Centre for Mental Health.

NICE (2011) *Alcohol Use Disorders: Clinical Guideline 115*. London: NICE.

Oddie, S. and Davies, J. (2009) 'A multi-method evaluation of a substance misuse program in a medium secure forensic mental health unit', *Journal of Addictions Nursing*, 20: 132–141.

Prochaska, J.O. and DiClemente, C.C. (1982) 'Transtheoretical therapy: Towards a more integrative model of change', *Psychotherapy: Theory, Research and Practice*, 10(3): 276–288.

Pycroft, A. and Green, A. (2015) 'Challenging the cultural determinants of dual diagnosis in the criminal justice system,' in J. Winstone (ed), *Perspectives on mentally disordered offending: key issues for justice and health responses*. Palgrave Macmillan, pp 147–166.

Pycroft, A., Wallis, A., Bigg, J. and Webster, G. (2015) 'Engagement, participation and change: an evaluation of the experiences of service users of the Unified Adolescent Team', *British Journal of Social Work*, 45(2): 422–439.

Rees, V.C., Copeland, J. and Smith, W. (1998) *A brief cognitive-behavioural intervention for cannabis dependence: therapists' treatment manual*. Sydney: National Drug and Alcohol Research Centre, University of New South Wales, https://ndarc.med.unsw.edu.au/sites/default/files/ndarc/resources/TR.064.pdf

Regier, D.A., Farmer, M.E., Rae, D.S., Locke, B.Z., Keith, S.J. and Judd, L.L. (1990) 'Comorbidity of mental disorders with alcohol and other drug abuse: results from the Epidemiologic Catchment Area (ECA) Study', *JAMA*, 264: 2511–2518.

Rössler, W. (2006) 'Psychiatric rehabilitation today: an overview', *World Psychiatry*, 5(3): 151–157.

Royal College of Psychiatrists Centre for Quality Improvement (2006) *Standards for medium secure units*. London: CCQI.

Sampl, S.K. (2001) *Motivational enhancement therapy and cognitive behavioral therapy for adolescent cannabis users*. Rockville, MD: Center for Substance Abuse Treatment, Substance Abuse and Mental Health Services Administration.

Scott, F., Whyte, S., Burnett, R., Hawley, C. and Maden, A. (2004) 'A national survey of substance misuse and treatment outcome in psychiatric patients in medium security', *Journal of Forensic Psychiatry & Psychology*, 15: 595–605.

Shaw, J., Baker, D. and Hunt, I. (2004) 'Suicide by prisoners: a national clinical survey', *British Journal of Psychiatry*, 184(3): 263–267.

Steinberg, K.R. (2005) *Brief Counseling for Marijuana Dependence: A Manual for Treating Adults*. Rockville, MD: Centre for Substance Abuse Treatment, Substance Abuse and Mental Health Services Administration.

Swain, E., Boulter, S. and Piek, N. (2010) 'Overcoming the challenges of evaluating dual diagnosis interventions in medium secure units', *British Journal of Forensic Practice*, 12(1): 33–37.

Webb, D. (2010) 'Consumer perspectives', in P. Phillips, O. McKeown and T. Sandford (eds), *Dual diagnosis: practice in context*. London: Wiley-Blackwell: pp 27–36.

Weldon, S. and Ritchie, G. (2010) 'Treatment of dual diagnosis in mentally disordered offenders: application of evidence from the mainstream', *Advances in Dual Diagnosis*, 3: 18–23.

Whyte, S. and Harrison, C. (2004) 'Substance misuse services in secure psychiatric units', *Medicine, Science and the Law*, 44: 71–74.

Further reading

Derry, A. (2008) 'The clinical response to substance use problems in forensic mental health services', *The British Journal of Forensic Practice*, 10(3): 20–23.

Durant, M.A., Lelliott, P. and Coyle, N. (2006) 'Availability of treatment for substance misuse in medium secure psychiatric care in England: a national survey', *The Journal of Forensic Psychiatry and Psychology*, 17: 611–625.

Edwards, R., Guy, R., Bartholomew, M. and Buckland, R. (2011) 'Reflecting on the delivery of a structured alcohol and drug group in a medium-secure forensic unit', *Advances in Dual Diagnosis*, 4(4): 180–189.

Moore, J. (2013) 'Dual diagnosis: training needs and attitudes of nursing staff', *Mental Health Practice*, 16(6): 27–31.

Wood, N., Patel, K., Skinner, J. and Thomson, K. (2009) 'Setting up a dual diagnosis service within a forensic inpatient setting: reflections one year on', *Advances in Dual Diagnosis*, 2(3): 20–24.

Ziedonis, D.M., Smelson, D., Rosenthal, R.N., Batki, S.L., Green, A.I. and Henry, R.J. (2005) 'Improving the care of individuals with schizophrenia and substance use disorders: consensus recommendations', *Journal of Psychiatric Practice*, 11: 3.

15

Offenders with mental health needs in the criminal justice system: the multi-agency challenge to provide solution-focused responses

Jane Winstone

Aims of the chapter
- To argue that providing services to offenders with mental health problems is a matter that requires multi-agency collaboration throughout.
- To explore 'good life' interventions as a framework.
- To identify the population under scrutiny.
- To highlight the problems posed for sentencing and service provision.
- To discuss solution focused responses.

Introduction

Since the Reed Report (1992) there have been repeated calls from professionals and academics for the provision for offenders with mental health needs to have access to multi-agency support and adequate funding, including pathways which can meet the identified social, health and emotional needs. The latest and most influential of these is the Bradley Report (2009), commissioned by the then Secretary of State, which made 82 recommendations, all of which were adopted by the government of the day. Its aim was to reduce offending by this vulnerable group of people and to improve their quality of life.

A long history of good intentions has seen its fair share of difficulties in bringing these to reality and sustaining the longevity of best practice strategies (Winstone and Pakes, 2010). Thus, despite initiatives aimed at fulfilling the Bradley Report recommendations – such as NHS England's five year forward view (King's Fund, 2015) – Durcan et al (2014) argued that the actual evidence of sustained improvement is limited. For example, as recently as 2017, the London Assembly Health Committee, reporting on offender mental health, stated that probation services were struggling to meet the needs of this group. They called for funding to support early and holistic intervention to address the challenges, particularly in relation to multiple, complex needs. They proposed the following: improving joint working and data sharing; enhancing strategies to support individuals away from the criminal justice pathway, widely known as liaison and diversion; supporting ex-offenders into housing and employment, interventions known to improve mental health and reduce the risk of offending (MIND, 2017, 2018); and to challenge the stigmatisation that impacts on all aspects of quality of life and wellbeing (Thornicroft, 2006; Pilgrim, 2014). These problems are not new and neither are the proposed strategies. They have been the subject of decades of research which has informed evidence-based theoretical paradigms.

Research in probation and rehabilitation has been influenced in the past decade by desistence scholarship (McNeill and Weaver, 2010; Canton, 2016). This has given credence to the evidence that 'social capital' – networks of social and emotional support embracing strong links with relationships, housing, employment and education – supports desistance from offending and reoffending. Those who recall the 'What Works' paradigm, influential evidence-based scholarship in the 1980s and 1990s (McGuire, 2016), will be familiar with these as a Risk, Needs, Responsivity (RNR) model (Andrews and Bonta, 2010). This was a concept of multiple criminogenic needs as dynamic risk factors that can be positively impacted on to reduce the risk of recidivism. Whereas What Works initiatives arose from a largely individualist perspective of responsibility for life choices, social capital has a focus on addressing the lives that offenders lead and associated multiple and complex needs, within a holistic framework that seeks to ameliorate the constraints on choices and promote strategies to motivate individuals towards coming to live 'good lives' (Ward and Brown, 2004; Ward and Maruna, 2007). The claim is that this will support offenders to establish constructive lifestyles as the quality of life transcends the need to resort to offending behaviour (Canton, 2016). Therefore, although What Works and the good lives model both target similar multiple and complex needs which are contributory factors to offending behaviour, they come from different theoretical perspectives and therefore offer different solutions.

Chu et al (2014) claim that the good lives model is complementary to the RNR model by offering a strengths-based theory of rehabilitation. Central to the good lives model is the notion that offenders, like all human beings, have goal directed behaviours that seek to maximise a sense of fulfilment and happiness. Ward and Gannon (2006) state that this includes access to primary human goods such as connection to wider social groups, expressing individuality through pro-social activities, autonomy and self-directedness, hobbies, freedom from stress and turmoil, knowledge and feeling informed, pleasure and positive relationship networks as well as having a purpose and meaning in life. Working on this assumption, the practitioner, in a three-phase approach, focuses on supporting the offender to explore their identity and their personal strengths alongside strategies to set positive personal goals and how to realise these. Being supported to achieve secure housing, access to medical support, education, training, embeddedness in the community and connectedness in positive relationships is seen as the framework within which the individual can grow and where recidivism is left behind as a style of living and of thinking that only inhibits the realisation of personal goals.

I am a firm advocate of the 'good lives' initiatives. But can this be addressed by the statutory services alone? In relation to offenders with mental health needs, we need to be realistic about the hurdles faced by people who experience the double stigmatisation and social exclusionary impacts of not only having a mental illness but also the labelling impacts of being an offender (Thornicroft, 2006; Pilgrim, 2014). Furthermore, we need to understand the scope of the problem and just how many individuals are affected and what they require in terms of health, social care and rehabilitative provision in order to fulfil the intentions of 'good life' interventions.

Reflection

What are the social exclusionary factors that people with mental health problems face, and how is this exacerbated by the criminal justice system?

The challenges for service provision

The issues outlined below are some of the most pressing, but do not represent the totality of the problems that services experience, which is beyond the scope of this short article to address. The National Audit Office (2017) concluded that NHS England, NOMS and Public Health England do not have reliable, current data that enable them to understand the prevalence, at a national level, of mental ill health among the offender population. So we need to turn to other sources of evidence to understand the scope of the problem facing the statutory and community services.

Turning first to the police. One in four people experience a mental health problem in any given year in the UK and many will come into contact with the police, either as victims of crime, witnesses, offenders or when detained under s.136 of the Mental Health Act (MHA, 2007). Estimates put the proportion of total police time spent dealing with those mental health issues at between 20% and 40% (HM Government, 2017). As first responders, police are spending at much as 40% of their time dealing with incidents triggered by some kind of mental health issue, against a backdrop of severe cuts in social and health services (House of Commons, 2015). Overall the number of incidents recorded in police logs as being related to mental health rose by a third between 2011 and 2014, including those experiencing florid symptoms of mental illness (House of Commons, 2015).

With evidence mounting as to the unsuitability of police cells being used as a place of safety for those detained under s.136 (MHA, 2007), the Crisis Care Concordat (2014) committed the government to a 50% reduction in the use of police cells. The House of Commons (2015) also reported that in 2008 the rate of detention of black and minority people under s.136 was almost twice that of white people and that even in 2015 children were still being detained in police custody in most police force areas.

The average length of time for those in police stations assessed by an Approved Mental Health Practitioner or s.12 approved doctor is 9.5 hours (HMIC et al, 2015). Compared to this, people brought by the police to a hospital A&E place of safety have to wait on average between six and eight hours before they receive a mental health assessment. In both settings the most common reason for delay is the availability of an appropriate professional.

Prison

It is widely accepted that up to 90% of prisoners have mental health needs (Prison Reform Trust, 2017). These include severe and enduring mental health disorders and also as many as 49% of women and 23% of male prisoners have been assessed as suffering from anxiety and depression compared to 16% of the general UK population (12% of men and 19% of women; National Audit Office, 2017). Prisons in the UK hold approximately 85,000 people (Brooker, 2014) and therefore it can be concluded that the numbers of people in prison in need of both mental health care and rehabilitation is significant. However, the primary function of prison is not that of health care. This led Bradley (2009) to observe that punishing individuals for their behaviours did not equate to providing them with second rate health care compared to mainstream services; and mainstream services are, as is well documented, severely underfunded and under-resourced. In addition, due to resource issues, to arrange a transfer between prison and a secure health facility continues to far exceed the recommended 14 days. This means that floridly mentally unwell individuals will be held in an environment wholly unsuited to ameliorate or treat their needs (Sharpe et al, 2016).

Probation and community rehabilitation centres (CRCs)

Brooker (2013) argues that there has been a paucity of research into the prevalence of mental illness among offenders on probation. The Lincoln Prevalence Study (Brooker, 2013) reported that a random sample of offenders across just one probation trust demonstrated that 39% of offenders had a current mental illness. The most prevalent category was anxiety disorders, estimated to affect 27% of the population. Prevalence rates for psychosis and dual diagnosis were also highly elevated in comparison to the general population (Brooker, 2013, 2014). More recently, supporting evidence for the findings of this study is provided by the Prison Reform Trust (2017), which reports that two fifths of those on community sentences have mental health needs.

What can we conclude from this about the scope of the problem? In March 2013 there were 222,000 people serving a probation order in 35 probation trusts. At that time, probation received three times less money that the prison sector, but worked to rehabilitate three times more offenders (Brooker, 2014). However, with the restructuring of the English probation service, approximately 70% of the probation population assessed as 'low risk' are managed by CRCs, often with payment linked to reductions in reoffending. CRCs in turn rely on the charity and voluntary sector to support provision for complex needs. This does not lessen the concerns. Mental illness, and the complexities it poses in supporting individuals across a range of health and social issues, is as prominent in the 'lower risk' group as in the 5–7% deemed to be high risk who continue to be supervised by the Probation Service. However, as evidenced in a recent study (Clinks, 2017a), expertise and resources to provide for the multiple complex needs of these offender groups does not simply vanish because there is a shifting of responsibilities and organisational roles.

Voluntary and community sector

A Clinks (2017a) study on the state of the voluntary and community sector in supporting the rehabilitation of offenders reports that 52% of organisations receive referrals from a CRC and 50% from the National Probation Service. In addition, 61% of organisations support people with mental health needs, 60% are those with problematic substance misuse issues (often linked to dual diagnosis) and 45% support people who are homeless. This study led to a headline in the *Guardian* (Dick, 2017) that claimed 'The UK's criminal justice system would fall apart without charities' and to observe that their funding status is precarious. It can therefore be concluded that the longevity of the services they provide is equally uncertain.

Identification of mental health needs in the criminal justice system

The unmet mental health needs of those passing through the criminal justice system is widely acknowledged and attributed to a range of factors. These include:

- Professionals working in the statutory setting have not received extensive training in the identification of mental health needs, yet will be responsible for identifying the need to start a screening process, for example, the police.
- Training to use screening tools needs to be improved.
- Screening tools in themselves do not accurately identify the presence of mental health needs.

- Where significant mental health problems are identified, a full assessment by a qualified mental health practitioner needs to be undertaken. The availability of the latter is limited; see for example the aforementioned length of time seriously ill individuals must wait for a full assessment in a police or health setting.

If a mental health need is not identified, then it cannot be met. To improve the process, the collaboration between criminal justice professionals and health professionals is paramount and this includes the role of the court in supporting these needs through appropriate sentencing provision.

Once the individual gets to court, it is often mentioned that offenders need mental health help but courts frequently require mental health input from mental health professionals in order to secure certain disposals, such as those under the Mental Health Act 2007 or the imposition of a community order with a Mental Health Treatment Requirement (MHTR). The relationship between criminal justice agencies and health agencies or mental health professionals is therefore multi-faceted (Winstone and Pakes, 2010).

A simple example will demonstrate the intrinsic difficulty of these relationships. Consider an offender sentenced to a community order with a MHTR that requires him/her to attend regular sessions with a local Community Mental Health Team. The offender must have agreed to that sentence, and must realise that failing to attend can constitute a breach of that Order. A breach can lead to imprisonment. When a client indeed fails to turn up for a health appointment, should the community psychiatric nurse tell the relevant probation officer knowing that that information could be used to place the client behind bars? Would health professionals become jailers by default, knowing full well that prison is more likely to exacerbate than ameliorate mental health issues? It is such blurring of roles and professional objectives that highlight the difficulty between mental health and criminal justice bodies.

Multiple complex needs and the multi-agency challenge

Once mental health and associated complex needs are identified (see Noyce, and also Green and Pycroft, this volume), the 'good life' research suggests that there would be individual and social benefits from addressing them. These adverse factors, associated with offending and social exclusion (NHS, 1999; SEU, 2004; Thornicroft, 2006; Pilgrim, 2014; Winstone, 2016; MIND, 2017) pose a significant multi-agency challenge as provision is not confined to the remit of the statutory and health sector. The most well documented are:

- **Unemployment:** People who are unemployed are twice as likely to suffer depression as people in work. The SEU report (2004) found that, in the UK, only 20% of those with severe mental health problems were employed. Even for people with more common types of mental illness such as depression, only half of these are competitively employed (Thornicroft, 2006: 50). Those with mental health problems who also offend face a particularly uphill struggle to find employment and despite the provisions of the Equality Act (2010), this profile has not been significantly impacted on (Hamilton et al, 2015). The explanation for this is largely attributed to the stigma attached to both mental illness and offending.

- **Poverty:** People living in poverty are three times more likely to have mental health problems. Poverty and unemployment tend to go hand in hand (SEU, 2004; MIND, 2017, 2018). As evidenced above by research, the challenges to find secure employment for those with mental disorder is significant. Poverty leads to debt management issues, which in turn lead to unstable housing and overall impoverishment of quality of life opportunities.

- **Homelessness:** Between a quarter and half of people who use night shelters or are sleeping rough may have a serious mental disorder (MIND, 2017, 2018). Poverty and unemployment also contribute to unstable housing and homelessness, which in itself exacerbates the rates of mental health and associated offending behaviours (Pilgrim, 2014).

- **Substance misuse and mental disorder:** Guest and Holland (2011: 163) argue that people with a dual diagnosis of mental disorder and substance misuse receive unpredictable care and treatment because the 'intricate and often complex relationship' between the different problems that the individual is experiencing does not always make sense to those working in mental health services. Pycroft and Green (2016: 148) further argue that 'the person with dual diagnosis may require different responses from health, social and criminal justice services' depending on their level of need and motivation. The problem being that neither clinical nor actuarial assessment can reliably identify which aspect should be treated first and as provisions are commissioned through different services and funding streams across the statutory and community sector, the pathway to provision remains unclear, for organisations and for service users alike. This contributes to problematic multi-agency working (Stone, 2003).

- **Friendship and relationship networks:** Thornicroft (2006) demonstrates the ways in which friendship and relationship networks, so important to leading a 'good life', often break down where mental disorder is present. The reasons are various and include social embarrassment, fears around unpredictable behaviours, emotional and health needs of the individual which test relationships, plus the unemployment, insecure housing and poverty which are so often linked to mental disorder.

- **Issues which impact specifically on women** (see Noyce this volume): In England and Wales the number of women sent to prison almost doubled between 1995 and 2010 and a total of 8,447 women were sent to prison in 2016, accounting for 10% of all prison receptions. Of these 25% had no previous convictions; 46% of women in prison report having suffered domestic violence, 53% report having experienced emotional, physical or sexual abuse during childhood and 31% have spent time in local authority care as a child (Women in Prison, 2018). Most women have neither a home nor a job to go to on release (Prison Reform Trust, 2017). These women therefore represent some of the most vulnerable in the prison population. Although the same numbers of men and women experience mental health problems, there are issues which specifically impact on women and there are differences, compared to men, in the drivers to offending behaviours. More women than men undertake primary care roles for their children and wider family networks. They are over-represented in low income, low status jobs, often part-time, and are more likely to live in poverty than men. Poverty, working mainly in the home on housework and concerns about personal safety can make women particularly isolated. All of which can have an impact of mental health and wellbeing. Physical and sexual abuse of girls and women is also recognised as having a long-term impact on women's mental health, especially if no support has been received around past abuses. This in turn means that the rates of depression, self-harm, anxiety, eating disorders and post-traumatic stress disorder are higher for women than men (Mental Health Foundation, 2018). Therefore, there are a range of dynamic risk factors for women which are predictors for both mental health and offending, which could be ameliorated to promote 'good life' outcomes, many of which fall outside of the criminal justice remit to respond to.

- **Black, Asian and minority ethnic (BAME) communities who have mental health needs:** In 2007 NACRO reported that:

  Research studies and data monitoring have consistently shown that of all the black and minority ethnic (BME) groups in Britain, those from black communities, in particular, are disproportionately represented in both the criminal justice and the mental health systems. This anomaly is compounded by the fact that both systems seriously disadvantage black people once within their remit.

Unfortunately, this situation has not changed in the past seven years, prompting Theresa May to state in 2016 'If you're black, you're treated more harshly by the criminal justice system than if you're white' (May, 2016). This claim is based on successive reviews into the criminal justice system, including the Young Review (2014), the Taylor Review (2016) and the Lammy Review (2016) of the treatment of, and outcomes for, BAME individuals in the criminal justice system.

These reviews have consistently demonstrated that this situation is aggravated by the high arrest rate for young black males, that individuals from the BAME community are more likely to be sent to prison from the Crown Court, that for every 100 white women given custodial sentences for drug offences, 227 black women are sentenced to custody for the same offence, and that BAME individuals are more likely to have severe mental health problems, be admitted to secure mental health facilities and experience poorer treatment outcomes than their white counterparts. The specific mental health issues include that BAME individuals disproportionately experience the impact of migration, including trauma in the country of origin, complications in navigating the migration process and hostile responses in the host country, material and socioeconomic disadvantage, including reduced access to employment and housing, exacerbated by the experience of racism and/or exclusion (Clinks, 2017b). All of which pose a significant challenge to the criminal justice process in relation to training and education to address unintentional bias in professional practice, and highlight the need for culturally appropriate support and multi-agency intervention to target social inclusionary strategies to reduce the social impacts of discrimination and stigma.

While the causal nature and complexity of the pathway that links social and health disadvantage with mental disorder remain unclear, one factor can be relied on: the dynamic risk factors could be positively addressed. Stone (2003) argues that multi-agency work is the most successful in doing so but, due to many factors, including lack of clarity in roles and responsibilities, funding streams, competing professional philosophies, information sharing, training, and so on, these arrangements too often become unsustainable over the medium and long term, not from a lack of professional goodwill, but from strategic and operational hurdles that are *not* insuperable.

Towards solution focused responses

Given the issues outlined above, a comprehensive multi-agency strategy for dealing with offenders with mental health difficulties throughout the criminal justice system is essential. This would enhance effectiveness, given that sentencing options that ignore mental health difficulties are more likely to be ineffective; promote expedience, in that unrecognised mental health difficulties may prove to be an obstacle at the sentencing stage causing delays; improve the quality of justice so that mental health problems are addressed to secure a just disposal; and reduce reoffending and risk of self-harm (Winstone and Pakes, 2010). The enhanced wellbeing resulting from this would be conducive for engagement with intervention designed to promote behaviour change – the 'good life'.

However, there is not a one-stop-shop for solutions, so I outline here a range of evidence-based strategies that have been or are being developed.

First responders

To address the issues identified by the police for first responders, nine street triage pilots have introduced mental health nurses to accompany officers to incidents of those in a mental health crisis. In addition to more mental health nurses being located at police stations, it is reported that this has helped to develop multi-agency relationships and to break down barriers between participating agencies (House of Commons, 2015). This demonstrates the importance of multi-agency working which exposes the providers to the advantages of shared philosophies and expertise.

Use of police cells

While there remains a paucity of data, it can be reported that the use of police cells as a place of safety has halved since 2011/12, but the situation continues to be far from satisfactory in terms of multi-agency clarity around roles, responsibilities, staffing, and appropriate provision of care settings.

To address this, in November 2017, Part IV of the Policing and Crime Act 2017 (PaCA) was introduced. This brought amendments to Part X of the MHA (1983), which had remained largely untouched by the MHA (2017) revisions, certainly in terms of the responsibilities of the police in relation to mental disorder and the legal framework which supports their professional roles and multi-agency collaboration. However, a note of caution should be sounded, in that the additional pressures on the decision-making process for the police have raised concerns as to the viability of the new arrangements.[1]

Liaison and diversion

Rogers and Ormston (2016) have reported in detail on a liaison and diversion provision in Sussex which was part of the NHS England pilot in response to the Bradley Report (2009) recommendations. With a potentially wide remit, the success of this scheme was founded on being able to establish the key strategic objectives: to develop processes to assess individuals arriving in the police custody suites for multiple vulnerabilities, including mental health and substance misuse; opportunities to divert the assessed individuals away from the criminal justice process and into relevant support services; and credible options to provide sentencers with alternatives to a sentence of imprisonment. To secure an overall vision they engaged with key stakeholders on a regular basis, proven project management tools were utilised, robust governance arrangements were secured by the early 'buy in' of senior leaders from their main delivery partners, including police, probation and health. Partnership decisions were informed by the collection and analysis of relevant data. On such a firm footing, the arrangements endured through the start-up and implementation phases before being successfully passed to the Sussex Criminal Justice Board and local Reducing Offending Boards, where they remain to this day (Rogers and Ormston, 2016: 239–240). A truly remarkable achievement given that the history of liaison and diversion schemes is littered with examples of short-term success and long-term unsustainability. It is also a demonstration of how successful solution focused responses can be when expertise is pooled from a range of professionals and agencies.

Mental health clinical nurse specialists in court

De Lacy (2016), who is a practising clinical nurse specialist in court, states that the value of this role is as a facilitator of both court and health process, as the defendant who is mentally unwell will straddle both systems. It enhances inter-agency liaison and problem solving focused on attaining a fair trial process and works for all stakeholders (court administration, judges, Crown and defence, probation, police, court cells, and so on), because the brokering of knowledge into the system empowers all parties to more effectively play their respective roles.

Women-centred approaches

Petrillo (2016) has conducted a study which explores the experiences of women in detention in relation to mental health. She argues for a trauma-informed approach and gender-responsive programme designs which address the complex needs of these women. This study identifies the paucity of current responses and more fruitful pathways to pursue. This approach is lent support by the government white paper on Prison Safety and Reform (November 2016). This recognises the evidence that specific approaches to women's issues are the most effective in supporting women into constructive lifestyles and wellbeing, and a commitment was made to introduce early and targeted interventions to reduce the numbers of women being sent to custody. The Prison Reform Trust (2017) also argues that most of the solutions to women's offending lie in improved access to community based support services, including women's centres. These enable women to address underlying problems which may lead to offending but that the criminal justice system cannot solve (Prison Reform Trust, 2017).

Training to improve collaborative practice

Hean et al (2016), with a background in inter-professional practice, respond to the Bradley (2009) call to improve multi-agency relationships by joint training between agencies, particularly in relation to mental health provision. They note that despite the issue being repeatedly raised regarding joint training, there is little that suggests what content or format this training should take. There are examples, but these tend to be piecemeal and usually consist of local initiatives to respond to identified cross-agency needs. While making the case for collaborative practice, they argue for a systems approach to training between health and justice professionals. They explore at a micro level how this would be conducted (Hean et al, 2016: 252–253) and demonstrate how collaborative competencies could be enhanced in a detailed model based on evidence drawn from other collaborative training settings. This is a good example of how looking more widely to identify expertise to inform multi-agency training in offender mental health provision could serve well the need to develop national, evidenced based, programmes for professionals working in the health and justice sector.

BAME communities

There is very little in the way of progress regarding criminal justice responses to the issues facing the BAME community and mental health concerns. The House of Lords (2017) reported that progress and best practice in this area have tended to come when the community and the voluntary sector have been involved and cited examples from initiatives in Brent, Lambeth and Birmingham of BME community-led voluntary organisations working with GPs and hospitals to deliver services. However, they also pointed out that these organisations are the first to get cut at a time of pressure on local authority and health budgets, while stating that 'they are, in fact, the last organisations we should be cutting out of the picture, because they are a depository of good practice and understanding and a gateway into the service for the community' (House of Lords, 2017).

Unemployment

Individual Placement Support (IPS) and vocational rehabilitation are current initiatives which seek to address these issues for both the individual and potential employers. However, while the research findings are in the right direction, further investment in research and development of the initiatives is needed (Kinoshita et al, 2013).

Homelessness

In 2016 the Mental Health Foundation published a policy paper which acknowledged the difficulties in housing provision per se and for this group in particular. However, they were able to arrive at realistic solutions to address this, which included recommendations to invest in co-production, that is, the adoption of joint planning with residents, representative groups and other expert advisors in the design and development of buildings and services. However, improving community awareness to address exclusionary practices and improve access to housing stock cannot, alone, address all the problems. So, for example, the report also recommended targeted investment in staff training to support skill development to undertake intensive work with individuals. While this policy is still aspirational, it lays down clear markers for cooperation with housing stock providers, the community and multi-agency collaboration, which, for offenders with mental health needs, includes the statutory services, in order to begin to ameliorate the types of problems identified by the London Assembly Health Committee (2017).

Conclusion

There is consistent evidence from academic scholarship and a plethora of reports that addressing the social and health needs of offenders, particularly offenders with mental health needs, would lead to a reduction in offending behaviours, as per the 'good lives' model. A few of the very many examples of solution focused initiatives and best practice have been given in this chapter to support my claim that there are solutions out there. However, there is a major caveat – *if* there were sufficient resources available.

The mental health trusts saw their budgets fall by more than 8% in real terms over the course of the coalition government (2010–2015). It is calculated that this amounts to a reduction of almost £600m, while at the same time referrals to the service rose by nearly 20% (McNicoll, 2015). The chronic underfunding is proving hard to reverse. In 2017, following funding cuts in five regions, there was a call to the government, from charities, to address the growing mental health crisis and to fulfil the promises that had been made regarding funding and resources. The health sector has fared no better (King's Fund, 2018) and the Ministry of Justice, whose budget covers prison, probation and the legal system, confirmed that official figures show it will have taken a real terms cumulative budget decrease of 40% since 2010/11 (Emmerson and Pope, 2017). It is in this resource climate that solutions have to be found and Bradley (2009) set out the social and economic costs of failing to do so.

While this may seem a pessimistic note on which to leave this chapter, the plight of those with mental health needs seems, in the past 12 months, to have struck a chord in the social conscience of those with political and public responsibilities to set the tone of how the debate and commissioning initiatives should be taken forward. And it is optimistic that the 'good life' interventions point the way.

Summary of key learning points

- Mental health issues affect all sectors of the population, however, contributory factors associated with social exclusion, such as poverty, can trigger as well as exacerbate existing mental health needs and are also linked to offending behavior

- Multi-agency collaboration can be problematic but, when it works, it is the most effective solution to addressing the multiple complex needs of those with mental health issues who offend

- 'Good Life' interventions offer a constructive framework for intervention and supporting offenders with mental health needs

- A long history of underfunding has contributed to a lack of provision for those with mental health needs in the secure and community sector

- BAME individuals are disproportionately represented in both the criminal justice and mental health systems and further disadvantaged by a continued lack of specific provision for their needs

- Solution-focused responses have been discussed for the past three decades and current debates continue to support strategies of liaison and diversion but have become more nuanced in response to research evidence arising from social exclusion, gender and BAME studies

Note

[1] See mentalhealthcop.wordpress.com

References

Andrews, D.A. and Bonta, J. (2010) *The psychology of criminal conduct*. Fifth edition. Cincinnati, OH: Anderson Publishing.

Bradley, Lord (2009) *Lord Bradley's review of people with mental health problems or learning disabilities in the criminal justice system*, https://webarchive.nationalarchives. gov.uk/20130123195930/http://www.dh.gov.uk/en/Publicationsandstatistics/ Publications/PublicationsPolicyAndGuidance/DH_098694

Brooker, C. (2013) 'An investigation into the prevalence of mental health disorders in an English probation population: an overview', *Eurovista: Probation and Community Justice*, 2(3): 154–160.

Brooker, C. (2014) 'Probation and mental health: who cares?', *British Journal of General Practice*, 64(621): 170–171.

Canton, R. (2016) 'Troublesome offenders, undeserving patients? The precarious rights of the mentally disordered offender', in J. Winstone (ed), *Mental health, crime and criminal justice: responses and reforms*. London: Palgrave Macmillan, pp 22–47.

Chu, C.M., Ward, T. and Willis, G. (2014) 'Practicing the good lives model', in I. Durnescu and F. McNeill (eds), *Understanding penal practice*. London: Routledge, pp 206–222.

Clinks (2017a) *The state of the sector: Key trends for voluntary sector organisations working with offenders and their families*, www.clinks.org/sites/default/files/2018-10/ clinks_state-of-the-sector-2015_final-web.pdf

Clinks (2017b) *Race, mental health and criminal justice: moving forward*, www.clinks. org/publication/race-mental-health-and-criminal-justice-moving-forward

Crisis Care Concordant (2014) *Mental Health Crisis Care Concordat: Improving outcomes for people experiencing mental health crisis*, www.crisiscareconcordat.org. uk/wp-content/uploads/2014/04/36353_Mental_Health_Crisis_accessible.pdf

De Lacy, C. (2016) 'The role of the mental health clinical nurse specialist in the Crown Court setting: towards a best practice model', in J. Winstone (ed), *Mental health, crime and criminal justice: responses and reforms*. London: Palgrave Macmillan, pp 167–183.

Dick, N. (2017) 'The UK's criminal justice system would fall apart without charities', *Guardian*, 12 July, www.theguardian.com/voluntary-sector-network/2017/jul/12/criminal-justice-charities-prison-probation

Durcan, G., Saunders, A., Gadsby, B. and Hazard, A. (2014) *The Bradley Report five years on. An independent review of progress to date and priorities for further development*. London: Centre for Mental Health.

Emmerson, C. and Pope, T. (2017) *Autumn 2017 Budget: options for easing the squeeze*, Institute for Fiscal Studies, 30 October, www.ifs.org.uk/publications/10010

Guest, C. and Holland, M. (2011) 'Co-existing mental health and substance use and alcohol difficulties – why do we persist with the term "dual diagnosis" within mental health services?', *Advances in Dual Diagnosis*, 4(4): 162–172.

Hamilton, I.S., Schneider, J., Kane, E. and Jordan, M. (2015) 'Employment of ex-prisoners with mental health problems, a realistic evaluation protocol', *BMC Psychiatry*, 15: 185, https://doi.org/10.1186/s12888-015-0553-3

Hean, S., Walsh, E. and Hammick, M. (2016) 'Training to improve collaborative practice: a key component of strategy to reduce mental ill health in the offender population', in J. Winstone (ed), *Mental health, crime and criminal justice: responses and reforms*. London: Palgrave Macmillan, pp 242–265.

HM Government (2017) *Government response to the Independent Review of Deaths and Serious Incidents in Police Custody*, October, www.gov.uk/government/uploads/system/uploads/attachment_data/file/660452/Government_Response_to_Angiolini_Review.pdf

HM Inspectorate of Constabulary (HMIC), HM Inspectorate of Prisons, the Care Quality Commission and Healthcare Inspectorate Wales (2013) *A criminal use of police cells? The use of police custody as a place of safety for people with mental health needs*, 20 June, www.justiceinspectorates.gov.uk/hmiprisons/inspections/a-criminal-use-of-police-cells-the-use-of-police-custody-as-a-place-of-safety-for-people-with-mental-health-needs/

House of Commons (2015) *Policing and mental health: eleventh report of session 2014–15*. HC 202.

House of Lords (2017) 'Mental health services: Black and minority ethnic communities', 28 November, Volume 787, hansard.parliament.uk/Lords/2017-11-28/debates/B4D24C68-A7DD-4A6B-A556-A3730A7F0417/MentalHealthServicesBlackAndMinorityEthnicCommunities

King's Fund (2015) 'The NHS five year forward view', www.kingsfund.org.uk/projects/nhs-five-year-forward-view

King's Fund (2018) 'Mental health funding gap widens further', 16 January, www.kingsfund.org.uk/press/press-releases/mental-health-funding-gap-widens-further

Kinoshita, Y., Furukawa, T.A., Kinoshita, K., Honyashiki, M., Omori, I.M., Marshall, M., Bond, G.R., Huxley, P., Amano, N. and Kingdon, D. (2013) 'Supported employment for adults with severe mental illness', Cochrane Database of Systematic Reviews, Issue 9, Art. No.: CD008297, https://doi.org//10.1002/14651858.CD008297.pub2

Lammy, D. (2016) *The Lammy Review: An independent review into the treatment of, and outcomes for, Black, Asian and Minority Ethnic individuals in the Criminal Justice System*, www.gov.uk/government/uploads/system/uploads/attachment_data/file/643001/lammy-review-final-report.pdf

London Assembly Health Committee (2017) 'Offender mental health', 14 September, www.london.gov.uk/about-us/london-assembly/london-assembly-publications/offender-mental-health

May, T. (2016) *Statement from the new Prime Minister Theresa May*, 13 July, www. gov.uk/government/speeches/statement-from-the-new-prime-minister-theresa-may

McGuire, J. (2016) 'Interventions and outcomes: accumulating evidence', in J. Winstone (ed) *Mental Health, Crime and Criminal Justice: responses and reforms*, London: Palgrave Macmillan, pp 48–66.

McNeill, F. and Weaver, B. (2010) *Changing Lives? Desistance research and Offender Management*. Scottish Centre for Crime and Justice Research Report No. 3/2010, www.sccjr.ac.uk/publications/changing-lives-desistance-research-and-offender-management/

McNicoll, A. (2015) 'Mental health trust funding down 8% from 2010 despite coalition's drive for parity of esteem', Community Care, 20 March, www. communitycare.co.uk/2015/03/20/mental-health-trust-funding-8-since-2010-despite-coalitions-drive-parity-esteem/

Mental Health Foundation (2018) 'Women and mental health', mentalhealth. org.uk/a-to-z/w/women-and-mental-health

MIND (2017) 'Mental health problems – an introduction: what causes them?', www.mind.org.uk/information-support/types-of-mental-health-problems/mental-health-problems-introduction/causes/#.WmR_Ba5l-M8

MIND (2018) 'Housing and mental health', www.mind.org.uk/information-support/guides-to-support-and-services/housing/#.WmHdQa5l-M8

NACRO (2007) *Black communities, mental health and the criminal justice system*, Mental health and crime briefing 2007, www.ohrn.nhs.uk/resource/policy/Nacroblackcommunities.pdf

National Audit Office (2017) *Mental health in prisons*, HC 42 Session 2017–2019, www.nao.org.uk/wp-content/uploads/2017/06/Mental-health-in-prisons.pdf

NHS (1999) *National service framework for mental health*, www.gov.uk/government/publications/quality-standards-for-mental-health-services

Petrillo, M. (2016) '"It made my mind unwell": trauma-informed approaches to the mental health needs of women in the criminal justice system', in J. Winstone (ed), *Mental health, crime and criminal justice: responses and reforms*. London: Palgrave Macmillan, pp 131–146.

Pilgrim, D. (2014) *Key concepts in mental health*. London: Sage.

Prison Reform Trust (2017) *Why focus on reducing women's imprisonment?* Prison Reform Trust briefing, www.prisonreformtrust.org.uk/Portals/0/Documents/Women/whywomen.pdf

Pycroft, A. and Green, A. (2016) 'Challenging the cultural determinants of dual diagnosis in the criminal justice system' in J. Winstone (ed), *Mental health, crime and criminal justice: responses and reforms*. London: Palgrave Macmillan, pp 147–156.

Reed, J. (1992) *Review of health and social services for mentally disordered offenders and those requiring similar services*. Department of Health/Home Office. London: HMSO.

Rogers, L. and Ormston, G. (2016) 'Successful strategies for working with mentally disordered offenders within a complex multi-agency environment', in J. Winstone (ed), *Mental health, crime and criminal justice: responses and reforms.* London: Palgrave Macmillan, pp 218–241.

Sharpe, R., Vollm, B., Akhtar, A., Puri, R. and Bickle, A. (2016) 'Transfers from prison to hospital under Sections 47 and 48 of the Mental Health Act between 2011 and 2014', *Journal or Forensic Psychiatry and Psychology*, 27(4): 459–475.

Social Exclusion Unit (SEU) (2004) *Mental health and social exclusion.* London: Office of the Deputy Prime Minister.

Stone, N. (2003) *A companion guide to mentally disordered offenders.* Second edition. Crayford: Shaw & Sons.

Taylor, C. (2016) *Review of the Youth Justice System in England and Wales.* Ministry of Justice, www.gov.uk/government/uploads/system/uploads/attachment_data/file/577103/youth-justice-review-final-report.pdf

The Young Review (2014) *The Young Review: Improving outcomes for young black and/or Muslim men in the Criminal Justice System*, final report, www.youngreview.org.uk/sites/default/files/clinks_young-review_report_dec2014.pdf

Thornicroft, G. (2006) *Shunned: discrimination against people with mental illness.* Oxford: Oxford University Press.

Ward, T. and Brown, M. (2004) 'The good lives model and conceptual issues in offender rehabilitation', *Psychology, Crime & Law*, 10(3): 243–257.

Ward, T. and Gannon, T.A. (2006) 'Rehabilitation, etiology, and self-regulation: The comprehensive good lives model of treatment for sexual offenders', *Aggression and Violent Behavior*, 11(1): 77–94, https://doi.org/10.1016/j.avb.2005.06.001

Ward, T. and Maruna, S. (2007) *Rehabilitation.* London: Routledge.

Winstone, J. (ed) (2016) *Mental health, crime and criminal justice: responses and reforms.* London: Palgrave Macmillan.

Winstone, J. and Pakes, F. (2010) 'Offenders with mental health problems in the criminal justice system: the multi-agency challenge' in A. Pycroft and D. Gough (eds), *Multi-agency working in criminal justice: control and care in contemporary correctional practice.* Bristol: Policy Press, pp 169–178.

Women in Prison (2018) 'Key facts', www.womeninprison.org.uk/research/key-facts.php

Further reading

NHS (2013) 'Mortality rate three times as high among mental health service users than in general population', 19 February, content.digital.nhs.uk/article/2543/Mortality-rate-three-times-as-high-among-mental-health-service-users-than-in-general-population

Rees, S. (2009) *Mental ill health in the adult single homeless population: a review of the literature.* Public Health Resource Unit, www.crisis.org.uk/media/20611/crisis_mental_ill_health_2009.pdf

16

Enforcement and rehabilitation: challenges to partnership working with substance using offenders

Marie-Edith Tiquet

Aims of the chapter
- To explore the link between substance misuse and crime.
- To provide an evaluation of consent in coerced treatment.
- To recognise the role and impact of organisational agendas on information sharing and partnership working.
- To understand the difference of success between crime control and public health approaches.

Introduction

Over the past 20 years, the British government has been taking a harsher approach to addressing acquisitive crime such as theft, robbery and burglary while maintaining the rhetoric of rehabilitation for substance misusing offenders. The perception was, and is, that substance misuse was one of the main causes of crime, and which had greatly impacted on communities across England and Wales and therefore needed to be controlled. The failure to address the 'drug problem' and its perceived links with crime had led to the introduction of coercive measures, with drug and alcohol treatment becoming sentencing options for the courts. This has reinforced an abstinence-based agenda (Home Office, 2008), with the desire to eradicate both substance misuse and crime which are perceived to be interlinked. Despite the lack of research evidence to support such measures (Strang and Gossop, 2005) and some jurisdictions moving towards decriminalisation, the UK maintained a war on drugs by moving towards legal enforcement to stamp out substance misuse. Multi-agency working became a requirement in the management of drug using offenders following the introduction of the 1995

255

National Drug Strategy (Home Office, 1995) which initiated the formalisation of partnership working between the police, drug services and other health and welfare agencies. Drug Action Teams (DAT) were established to commission services to respond to drug problems in local areas. The New Labour government held public health issues high on its agenda (Home Office, 1998), as well as social exclusion and crime. Under this approach the problem of drugs, particularly for inner city areas, was perceived as a key part of this nexus of problems and requiring of multi-agency responses. In addressing these issues, partnership working became a key requirement in the management of substance using offenders and expanded to include a variety of voluntary sector organisations, as well as statutory provision from probation, courts and prisons to manage public protection and assist in the rehabilitation of offenders (Skinner, 2010).

This chapter will explore the complex relationship between substance use and crime and identify the importance of social needs and partnership working in addressing both. By addressing the role of consent in England and Wales, it will increase our understanding of substance using offenders' motivation and the importance of partnership working in coerced treatment. Information sharing plays a key role in the success of partnership working in the management of substance using offenders. This chapter will also explore the challenges agencies' agendas plays in our understanding and management of risk. How outcomes are measured and defined greatly vary from public protection and public health agencies. With substance misuse funding streams from criminal justice sources reducing, how an approach to crime control for substance using offenders will consequently impact upon the success of partnership working will be explained.

Are substance use and crime related to each other?

Early drug strategies are criticised for their misplaced assumption that drugs and crime have a deep connection and that enabling access to drug treatment would eradicate a high number of crimes committed (Reuter and Stevens, 2008). This link was the basis for changes that occurred in the UK drug policy during the 1990s and has been one of the most researched areas of drug policy worldwide (Parker et al, 1988; McGregor, 2000; Bennett and Holloway, 2009; Seddon, 2006). The most widely cited explanation on the link between drugs and crime is Goldstein's tripartite conceptual framework (1985) which divided this into psychopharmacological, economic-compulsive and systemic elements. With elements of overlap between these, he felt that they could assist in our understanding of the link between substance use and crime. He described how psychopharmacological crime may occur as a result of specific substance use, such as alcohol or stimulant use, when an individual may become excitable, irrational, and exhibit violent behaviour. Economic-compulsive crime referred to instances where individuals engage in economically oriented crime to fund their substance use, and systemic crimes occur when it is intrinsic to the involvement with substance: following interaction within the system of drug distribution and use, disputes over territory, drug dealer retaliation, and punishment for failure to pay debts. Goldstein (1985) argued that drug-related offending results from drugs' ability to alter functions of the brain through decreasing inhibitions and cognitive functioning and their compulsion to fund their addictions through crime. Furthermore, he felt that drug users, traffickers and dealers abide by their own rules which fall outside society's. Drug users commit crime; however, this relationship is more complex than Goldstein perceived. His framework provided a theory on the relationship between drugs and crime, enabling a basic understanding of drug users' relationship with crime, and reasons as to why an individual may commit crime. The model has since been widely criticised as under-developed, specifically due to its lack of consideration of the causal relationship between different crimes and drugs, and whether drug use is a result of offending behaviour or if offending behaviour is the onset of substance misuse (Bennett and Holloway, 2009; Stevens, 2011a). The lack of consideration around the interconnections between the three parts of the model has also been condemned (Parker and Auerhahn, 1998). Furthermore, Stevens (2011b) identified various methodological failings within research. He highlights the lack of justification and definition around the precise link between drug use and crimes committed, whereby if drug use was present in any individual's criminal or personal records, it was deemed a contributing factor. As Hough (1996) noted while addressing the relationship between drug use and property crime, not all dependent drug users offend with the sole purpose of gaining funds for their drugs; this could also be for food, housing and other necessities. Failing to address the cause of the crime prior to it being committed has been the downfall of much research carried out to date. As Reuter and Stevens (2008) notably argued, findings based on the National Treatment Outcome Research Study (NTORS, which investigates outcomes for drug misusers treated in community and residential services and suggest that reductions in offending are as a result of drug treatment) could be linked to other consequences considering similar reductions perceived in untreated groups due to lack of comparison groups. Furthermore, Stevens (2011b) highlights that the use of arrestees within research are not a true representation of the offending or drug using population due to social inequalities. He notes that problematic drug use is higher in deprived areas with its harmful effects on society being more concentrated in those areas (Stevens, 2011b: 32). Thus, addressing underlying problems such as unemployment and poverty would be of assistance in tackling crime reduction and substance misuse, as adopting a crime reduction and treatment approach alone would not address these.

Whereas the government had not taken into consideration health and income inequalities and underlying personal and social disadvantages, it has become recognised that substance misuse treatment needs to consider these factors to effectively support individuals in moving away from problematic drug use. Individuals who offend and use substances have various interlinked needs such as unemployment, lack of stable accommodation and education and training opportunities, which requires a holistic approach to tackle the complexity of substance related offending (Hough et al, 2003).

With the lead National Treatment Agency for Substance Misuse subsumed into Public Health England in 2013, resources were deployed away from substance misuse and crime control towards a wider public health agenda. Ostensibly with the aim of protecting and improving health, and addressing inequalities as an integrated approach, the public health approach was broadly welcomed (especially with regard to alcohol). Because of this reorganisation substance misuse services have become expected to deliver additional interventions, putting further emphasis on the development of partnership working and multi-agency approaches to increase health outcomes. Although the 2010 drug strategy (Home Office, 2010) was criticised for its lack of detail and guidance on how this should be implemented, its approach enabled areas of the UK to identify where and how to use resources depending on the need of the area or region. It has successfully identified that one size does not necessarily fit all and that in order for resources to be most efficiently used, it is best left to local commissioning teams to identify what is best.

Key point

Research demonstrates that there is a connection between drug use and crime. However, the causal link between the two is extremely complex and with the provision of treatment not guaranteeing either a reduction in reoffending rates or ongoing drug use.

With the increasing recognition that substance misuse and offending are often embedded in social needs, the government's expansion of agencies involved in the management of drug using offenders would theoretically assist in addressing substance related crime. As Skinner identifies, however (2010), probation agencies are much concerned with risk management, public protection and ensuring elements of punishment are filtered through community sentences. On the other hand, drug and alcohol services are increasingly more concerned with public health and rehabilitation since funding streams and Key Performance Indicators are increasingly linked to public health rather than crime reduction sources and outcomes. Partnership working would therefore be challenging due to the agencies' differing agendas in their collaboration. Targets for probation would be linked to reductions in reoffending and completion of an order without being breached, whereas community drug and alcohol services' targets would relate to successful completions of treatment, improvements in health and abstinence of Class A drugs. With the recent cuts of Mayor's Office for Policing And Crime (MOPAC) funding, this will have further impact on community drug and alcohol services' ability to continue to make provision for partnership working with criminal justice agencies. Exploring the requirements placed on drug or alcohol using offenders to engage in substance related treatment as part of community orders will further assist in our understanding of how partnership working can effectively manage them from a crime reduction and rehabilitation perspective.

Consent, motivation and assessment

To address substance misuse and to comply with UN Conventions, the Misuse of Drugs Act (1971) established the principles of punishment and deterrence predicated on the concept of relative harm (the classificatory system of Class A, B and C drugs, with the latter the least harmful and in ascending order of harm). The legislation does allow for the setting up of treatment centres continuing the so-called 'British system' (Berridge, 2005) of drug control started in the 1920s (substitute prescribing). Imprisonment having had limited success in steering drug using offenders away from drugs and crime (Stevenson, 2011), Drug Treatment Testing Orders (DTTOs) were introduced through the Crime and Disorder Act in 1998. These new guidelines differed from previous orders as they enabled the courts to monitor individuals and their progress through reviews and mandatory drug testing. The launch of DTTOs established an expansion of structured drug treatment services to assist in the rehabilitation of drug using offenders and the reduction of drug-related crime. Although DTTOs were successful in reducing recidivism among individuals who had completed their orders, one of the main challenges DTTOs encountered were their ability to retain individuals in treatment. Hough and his colleagues (2003) identified difficulties to establish programmes and waiting times as contributing factors to their failings.

While successive governments' drug policies have come and gone, the 1971 legislation has remained intact with the only changes being new substances banned under the legislation and cannabis temporarily reclassified from Class B to Class C and then back again. The use of deterrence and punishment with respect to interventions for substance misuse has brought much controversy with respect to both the ethics and effectiveness of coerced treatment and its uses within the criminal justice system and the ways in which those principles of justice interface with wider networks of health and welfare organisations. These issues come to the fore in the establishment of treatment orders under the Criminal Justice Act (2003).

The Criminal Justice Act (2003) gave the police more powers to 'stop and search' and the ability to issue conditional cautions. As a result, major changes were made to sentencing practice, specifically relating to serious offences. Community orders were reviewed and new processes for dealing with crime were introduced. Continuing its move away from harm reduction in line with the United Nations Office on Drugs and Crime (UNODC)'s strategy on crime and punishment (Arlacchi, 1998), the aim was for sentencing to become tailored to the individual to maximise outcomes. All community sentences were replaced by one community order with a variety of requirements being added to it such as drug and alcohol treatment, unpaid work, curfews, mental health among others

(Sentencing Guidelines Council, 2016). Drug Rehabilitation Requirements (DRR) consequently replaced DTTO, which enabled treatment programmes to be more tailored to individual needs rather than a one size fits all approach. These new sentencing guidelines also saw the introduction of Alcohol Treatment Requirements (ATR), specifically introduced to tackle alcohol related violence, which had become increasingly prominent on the public agenda (NOMS, 2014).

In England and Wales, treatment is quasi-compulsory, which means that some form of consent is sought from individuals prior to their engagement in treatment, compared to other countries such as the United States where individuals are not given a choice. Seddon (2007) criticised this approach as he felt that consent given could be distorted. Among others, he makes some broad assumption that some individuals may perceive custody as a less attractive option. Stevens, Berto et al (2005), however, found that imprisonment can at times be seen as appealing to drug using offenders as it can provide entrenched, chaotic and homeless users with opportunities such as shelter and regular access to food, and the ability to address any physical health concerns they may have experienced or developed as a result of their substance use. Over the past ten years, treatment programmes within prisons in England and Wales have considerably developed. Whereby the majority of prisons used to detox individuals through methadone substitute prescribing, in recent years, many prisons across England and Wales have increased their treatment options to include maintenance as well as detoxification of both methadone and buprenorphine. Combined with more effective group and other one-to-one psychosocial interventions, prisons have become key in increasing the health of substance using offenders, delivering harm reduction interventions and initiating recovery. The assumptions that those coerced into treatment are unwilling candidates has therefore been extensively challenged (Farabee et al, 2002; Hiller et al, 2002). While Hough (1996: 36) argued that substance misuse treatment in British drug policy is 'an offer they can't refuse', therefore shifting the cost-benefit ratio in favour of treatment under the sentencing guidelines in the UK, the length of a DRR or Alcohol Treatment Requirement (as well as a previous DTTO) could potentially be longer than a custodial sentence, which could deter individuals from accepting treatment. For example, an individual may receive 28 days imprisonment for a shoplifting offence, whereas, were they to be sentenced to a DRR or ATR, the length of the order would be between six and 18 months. Custody may therefore be more attractive to those who have no interest in drug treatment and/or are not motivated to engage in it.

A key requirement of treatment orders under the Criminal Justice Act 2003 is that individuals must comply with drug and alcohol treatment where this is made part of their community order. The relation to 'the offender expresses his willingness to comply with the requirement' appears in various sections of the Act which highlights the importance of consent. Clear guidelines are also provided in the event of treatment plans or requirements being amended whereby the individual's consent must be sought prior to any changes being made. In addition to this, should an individual no longer wish to comply with treatment requirements and withdraw consent to engage, reference is made to orders being revoked and individuals being resentenced.

Key point

Subsection (1)(a) of section 209 of the Criminal Justice Act 2003 states that an individual:

> must submit to treatment by or under the direction of a specified person having the necessary qualifications or experience with a view to the reduction or elimination of the offender's dependency on or propensity to misuse drugs.

The assessment of a substance using offender is a complex process which requires a number of elements to be taken into consideration. Information sharing between probation and treatment services is crucial to enable an effective assessment of motivation and development of an effective treatment plan which would maximise the individual's ability to engage and remain in treatment as part of their orders. Previous convictions provide information relating to risk which is needed when engaging an individual in a treatment programme to explore the potential risk to other individuals but also to identify the extent of an individual's offending history. Sharing of DRR/ATR assessment and pre-sentence reports are also important as it will enable both agencies to identify and develop a full understanding of the individual's presenting needs to better compile treatment plans. This will also enable agencies to identify discrepancies in individuals' reported circumstances and provide the opportunity to potentially challenge reported motivation.

Substance misuse workers are trained to address and assess motivation with individuals during assessment and treatment, through the use of motivational interviewing, which has been a leading choice in the treatment of drug using offenders, providing a 'client-centred, directive method for enhancing intrinsic motivation to change by exploring and resolving ambivalence' (Miller and Rollnick, 2002: 25). This has been found to enable individuals to understand offenders' motivating factors to engage in treatment and will assist in increasing their motivation through treatment. This means that, if individuals are not ready to address their substance misuse but agree to treatment, the worker would not find them suitable for treatment unless there is a perception that change can occur. This will require effective communication between substance misuse services and probation to ensure the management of offenders. Alternative interventions such as Restrictions on Bail are available to assess and build motivation of substance using offenders. It is important for probation and treatment providers to work collaboratively in building treatment packages (and community orders) to reduce recidivism and address substance use.

However, as Stevens and his colleagues found, professionals do report difficulties in identifying whether individuals are 'ready for treatment or just trying to get out of prison' (2006: 11). Partnership working between probation and treatment services is key in further exploring an individual's motivation as it provides the opportunity to share information as previously mentioned but also discuss potential risk in the present context. Offenders are not necessarily motivated to address their substance misuse but Stevens and his colleagues (2005) identified that, despite lack of readiness for change or motivation, treatment can be an opportunity that individuals appreciate which can lead to positive behaviour change and recovery.

Multi-agency collaboration and the management of drug using offenders

The recognition of the need for substance using offenders to be managed through a multi-agency approach has played a vital role in the development of service provision for rehabilitation. However, increasing the capacity for addressing substance misuse also means increasing the number of agencies involved in an offenders' treatment plan. Although indispensable in terms of providing support for offenders and increasing recovery capital by exploring social, human, physical and cultural elements of an individual's life (Best and Laudet, 2010) to maximise reintegration into society away from substances and crime, partnership working becomes more complex in the management of drug using offenders. As identified thus far, agencies' agendas will play a very important role in our understanding of the effectiveness of partnership working. As Rees (2010) highlighted, the role of probation officer in the management of offenders has changed extensively over the years and has become increasingly concerned with risk management and public protection over rehabilitation and ensuring elements of punishment remain through the use of community orders. It is instead the responsibility of voluntary sector agencies to assist with rehabilitation and instilling change. However, as Skinner (2010) points out, probation officers are qualified in effectively addressing offending behaviour whereas third sector professionals are not, which inevitably entails difficulties from a crime control perspective. As previously identified, substance use and crime are not always interlinked and although drug and alcohol treatment will address substance use and its related social needs, it will not address offending behaviour if this is not linked to substance use, or not to the extent that a probation officer may do due to lack of training and knowledge in that area. This means that an individual may move away from substance use but if this is not linked to their offending behaviour, they may continue to commit crime. As Hough (1996) found, drug users, and consequently offenders, commit crime for a variety of reasons, which may be very different to the reasons for their substance use. Despite a holistic approach to substance use and the government's recommendation to increase individuals' recovery capital through treatment (Home Office, 2010), this may not fully explore and support a move away from offending behaviour. There would therefore be a need for probation officers to work closely with voluntary sector agencies to encourage the exploration of offending behaviour through treatment (whether substance use or mental health). This would require comprehensive partnership working through joint care planning and effective communication.

The challenges that criminal justice agencies and the voluntary sector face in relation to effective communication can be compared to those agencies face to safeguard children. There have been a number of high profile serious case reviews in the media in recent years relating to the lack of communication between agencies to safeguard children (Watson, 2010). Agencies involved often have a very different focus and aims. However, safeguarding children is everyone's responsibility, and this always supersedes the organisational focus and aims, and becomes a requirement. When it comes to public protection and the safeguarding of communities from crime, it is not always an expectation or requirement from organisations, nor is it common practice to bear this in mind, who work with individuals (offenders or not) unless there is a potential risk of serious harm to an individual. If someone is at a high risk of physical harm due to someone's substance use or mental health, for example, agencies will indeed act in accordance with confidentiality policies to ensure public safety. However, the extent of the risk they present to others is not easily measurable. Mental health services have the opportunity to section individuals who pose a risk to society but this is providing they have capacity. If someone does have capacity, information is shared with criminal agencies who are responsible for evaluating, addressing and managing this risk. In this instance, as with safeguarding children, it is imperative for information to be shared effectively. This will consequently be included in agencies' risk management plans for individuals through their treatment and addressed accordingly. However, the risk of committing other low-level crimes such as shoplifting and burglaries, despite constituting threats to communities and the public from a crime control perspective, would not be deemed a priority in terms of safeguarding for non-criminal justice agencies. This may contribute to the challenges of partnership working between the voluntary sector and criminal agencies as the primary focus and aim of organisations will supersede this 'lesser risk' to society.

Partnership working between probation and substance misuse services has always been positive in relation to information sharing. Although this can be better described as an effective exchange of information rather than a collaborative approach. Following the introduction of substance misuse services to crime control, a number of procedures were put in place to enable effective information sharing between agencies. To date, agencies have been successful in developing effective 'transactions' of information in the management of substance using offenders. However, how this information is subsequently used is worth exploring in relation to the effectiveness of partnership working. The type of information shared and how this is shared is an important element to explore. Watson (2010) identified in depth some of the challenges of partnership working to safeguarding children and drew on learning from serious case reviews which identified how agencies successfully shared information but how the lack of context lead to failings. These failings can be expanded to the management of substance using offenders from a public protection and risk management perspective. For example, substance misuse services are required to feedback daily on the attendance of offenders to groups and appointments. Should an individual fail to attend, information is seldom shared or provided regarding the potential risks failure to attend may present; whether in relation to their health, their social circumstances or their offending behaviour. Effective partnership working and information sharing would necessitate information to be shared in relation to risk, whether from a public protection or health perspective. This will inevitably lead to effective risk management which is a crucial element of both agencies, regardless of whether this is relating to managing risk to the public or risk to the individual as both will essentially be linked. A joint approach is sometimes adopted when offenders consistently fail to engage with parts of their requirements, and three-way meetings between the substance misuse worker, offender manager and offender are often used to explore ways of promoting engagement and prevent breach proceedings. However, offending behaviour and how this may impact or be linked to substance use or other social areas are seldom discussed during these meetings. From a public health perspective, this would be identified as good practice as it promotes the engagement of the individual and reduces the possibility of breach proceedings which would inevitably impact on treatment and the health of the individual. However, from a crime control perspective, this would have few benefits as it is not aimed at reducing or addressing reoffending as, as mentioned previously, substance use is not always if regularly, linked to offending behaviour.

Measuring success and its impact on partnership working

Alongside effective communication, it is essential to explore measures of success within an organisation which will inevitably impact on our understanding of the effectiveness of partnership working. Thus far, we have identified that the focus of probation is to reduce risk and public protection. In relation to DRRs and ATRs, performance is measured through the successful completion of an order and effective engagement of the offender with the required interventions. Guidelines relating to the delivery of ATR and DRR are very clear that the expectation is that offenders attend all appointments as directed, which usually entails structured treatment programme and supervision from probation officers. Furthermore, should an offender miss more than two appointments without a valid reason – if they were unwell and able to provide a doctor's certificate would be a justifiable reason – they should be breached and the case brought back to court where the offender may be required to continue with their order, with the possibility of increased requirements, or the order revoked and the individual sentenced to imprisonment. From experience, however, breach proceedings are not consistently initiated by offender managers. The reason for this varies widely. The ability to breach and having the necessary proof that the offender was informed and aware of the missed appointments can sometimes be a challenge. In addition, high caseloads and the amount of paperwork required to complete a breach can also impact on consistency. Relationships between the offender, offender manager and other social care workers may also impact on breach proceedings being initiated. If an individual previously engaged well but had recent difficulties that workers had been supporting them with, they may be allowed additional time to adjust to potential changes or to address issues. On the other hand, if an individual is known to not engage with services and presents a high risk to the public, such as someone with a history of violent offences when under the influence of substances, this may lead to quicker breach proceedings.

The next expectation, in relation to ATRs and DRRs, is for offenders to successfully comply and complete their orders. Although there is acknowledgement that if an offender commits another crime during their order, they will be brought back to court and the expectation would be that they be sentenced for the new offence and for their breach of their order. Depending on the nature of the new crime, there is the possibility for the offender to be sentenced to a new community order with increased requirements as compensation for the new offence. However, in relation to the individual's substance use, there are no expectations. Despite drug testing being used, there is no penalty associated with positive drug tests, nor is there any expectations for offenders to reach abstinence through their orders. Although there is an expectation that they will address and effectively reduce their substance use, providing the offender complied with the requirements of their order, there are no consequences for not addressing substance use. From a drug and alcohol service perspective, it is essential for an individual to fully engage with treatment programmes and make changes to behaviour for it to be effective. However, with the introduction of coercive measures, services have had to adapt and develop programmes to meet the needs of more resistant and resilient drug and alcohol users in order to support them through their recovery. It is rare for an offender to comply with the requirements of drug and alcohol treatment for the duration of an order if they have no motivation to address their substance use or make changes, so when an individual consistently engages for several weeks, it would be expected that there is an element of motivation regarding their substance use. However, recent drug strategies have been increasingly focused towards recovery and drug and alcohol services are measured against the number of individuals who successfully complete 'drug/alcohol free' or as 'occasional users' (Public Health England, 2017). This has put increasing pressure on treatment services to deploy resources towards programmes and individuals which will increase and support effective completion of treatment according to National Drug Monitoring System (NDTMS) definitions, which is rarely an offending cohort of individuals. An evaluation of the DTTO pilot scheme by Hough and his colleagues (2003) found that reconviction rates stood at 53% for those who had completed their orders compared to 91% for those who had breached their orders. Furthermore, 30% successfully completed their orders (Hough et al, 2003). Of these 30%, it is not known how many had reached abstinence or moved away from problematic substance use. The successful completion of an

ATR or DRR where the individual is still using substances would not be seen as a success for treatment services whereas it would for probation from a crime control perspective. These nuances in agencies' goals will also inevitably impact on partnership work and agencies' ability to fully work together and identify common ground as focus, goals and requirements vary across the board.

Conclusion

Heath (2010) identified the various definitions utilised by the government and public health agencies to describe partnership working, which provided insight into some of the challenges that agencies can face in developing effective approaches to offender care in criminal justice settings. This chapter has further identified the competing and incompatible agendas of the voluntary sector and criminal agencies. This consequently makes the evaluation of partnership working more challenging depending on the perspective one adopts.

In order to maximise outcomes for all involved, it would be beneficial for agencies to place additional emphasis on the type of information shared and the settings in which these are shared. Rees (2010), Skinner (2010) and Watson (2010) identified increased benefits of sharing premises in the management of offenders which encourages effective information sharing, communication and the development of shared goals. Communication is key to the rehabilitation of offenders and it is imperative that criminal justice agencies share their knowledge of offending behaviour and rehabilitation with the voluntary sector to reduce recidivism and increase effective reintegration of offenders into society. Criminal justice agencies are often seen as law enforcement agencies. However, probation staff are much more than that and the sharing of their knowledge and skills in the management of offenders is key to effective partnership working which will contribute to the success of all agendas.

Drug Intervention Programme (DIP) has been discontinued as a nationally managed and mandated programme, with the future of interventions becoming a matter for local discretion. An evaluation report due to be published in March 2018 has yet to be released, but 'offender need and demand in London may have changed since DIP Programmes were first introduced in 2003 and there is little evidence that they continue to be effective' (MOPAC, 2018). This will have a considerable impact on substance misuse services as the focus will continue to shift away from criminal justice initiatives, crime prevention and public protection, meaning that partnership working for substance using offenders will no longer be seen as a priority, if it ever was, potentially increasing risk to communities from a crime control perspective. Former budgets are no longer protected and are divided between Police and Crime Commissioners and Directors of Public Health. Funding will be absorbed into Crime Prevention Funds where each area will be able to apply for funding. Concerns have been raised relating to competing priorities and assessment of need carried out by criminal justice agencies who may have a different perspective on the effectiveness of treatment services and criminal justice interventions. As identified, success is measured differently when evaluated from a crime control or public health perspective. Services could reduce presence in criminal justice settings such as police stations, courts, prisons and probation, depending on viewed priorities and budget streams. As such, it is encouraged that clear definitions and expectations in relation to partnership working are provided with a common agreement and shared goal to support the rehabilitation of offenders from a crime control and public health perspective.

Summary of key learning points

- Addressing the cause of crime is paramount in understanding the relationship between substance use and crime as the two are not necessarily inter-related
- Substance misuse, health, social and financial needs are interlinked. To enable effective treatment, a holistic approach is necessary
- The sharing of information and communication between substance misuse agencies and probation is essential to formulate effective treatment plans which will support both rehabilitation and crime reduction agendas
- Context is key in partnership working and sharing of information to ensure effective assessment and management of risk
- Definition and understanding of success and agendas are key to enable effective partnership working

---

References

Arlacchi, P. (1998) 'Towards a drug-free world by 2008 – we can do it...', *UN Chronicle*, 35(2): 4–6.

Bennett, T. and Holloway, K. (2009) 'The causal connection between drug misuse and crime', *British Journal of Criminology*, 49(3): 513–531.

Berridge, V. (2005) 'The "British system" and its history', in J. Strang and M. Gossop (eds), *Heroin addiction and the British system: Volume 2 Treatment and policy responses*. Abingdon: Routledge.

Best, D. and Laudet, A. (2010) *The potential of recovery capital*. London: RSA.

Farabee, D., Shen H. and Sanchez, S. (2002) 'Perceived coercion and treatment need among mentally ill parolees', *Criminal Justice and Behavior*, 29(1): 76–86.

Goldstein, P. (1985) 'The drugs-violence nexus: a tripartite framework', *Journal of Drug Issues*, 15: 495–506.

Heath, B. (2010) 'The partnership approach to drug misuse', in Pycroft, A. and Gough, D. (eds) *Multi-agency working in criminal justice: Control and care in contemporary correctional practice*, Bristol: Policy Press, pp 185-200.

Hiller, M.L., Knight, K., Leukefeld, C. and Simpson, D.D. (2002) 'Motivation as a predictor of therapeutic engagement in mandated residential substance abuse treatment', *Criminal Justice and Behavior*, 29(1): 56–75.

Home Office (1995) *Tackling drugs together: a strategy for England 1995–1998.* London: HMSO.

Home Office (1998) *Tackling drugs to build a better Britain.* London: Home Office.

Home Office (2008) *Drugs: protecting families and communities.* London: Home Office.

Home Office (2010) *Reducing demand, restricting supply, building recovery: supporting people to live a drug free life.* London: Home Office.

Hough, M. (1996) *Drug misuse and the criminal justice system: a review of the literature.* London: Home Office.

Hough, M., Clancy, A., McSweeney, T. and Turnbull, P.J. (2003) *The impact of drug treatment and testing orders on offending: two-year reconviction results.* London: Home Office.

McGregor, S. (2000) 'Editorial: The drugs-crime nexus', *Drugs: Education, Prevention and Policy*, 7(4): 311–316.

MOPAC (2018) MPS Drug Testing & Drug Intervention Programmes Review, www.london.gov.uk/what-we-do/mayors-office-policing-and-crime-mopac/governance-and-decision-making/mopac-decisions-493

NOMS (2014) *Drug Recovery wings set up, delivery and lessons learned: Process study of first tranche DRW pilot sites.* London: Ministry of Justice Retrieved from www.gov.uk/government/uploads/system/uploads/attachment_data/file/286040/Drug-recovery-wings-process-study.pdf

Parker, R.N. and Auerhahn, K. (1998) 'Alcohol, drugs and violence', *Annual Review of Sociology*, 24: 291–311.

Parker, H., Bakx, K. and Newcombe, R. (1988) *Living with heroin: the impact of a drugs 'epidemic' on an English community.* Milton Keynes: Open University Press.

Public Health England (2017) 'Technical definitions for alcohol and drugs for healthier lives', https://healthierlives.phe.org.uk/documents/Alcohol_And_Drugs_Healthier_Lives_Technical_Definitions.pdf

Rees, A. (2010) 'Dual diagnosis: issues and implications for criminal justice partnerships', in Pycroft, A. and Gough, D. (eds) *Multi-agency working in criminal justice: Control and care in contemporary correctional practice*, Bristol: Policy Press, p 201.

Reuter, P. and Stevens, A. (2008) 'Assessing UK drug policy from a crime control perspective', *Criminology and Criminal Justice*, 8(4): 461–482.

Seddon, T. (2006) 'Drugs, crime and social exclusion: social context and social theory in British drug-crime research', *British Journal of Criminology*, 46(4): 680–703.

Seddon, T. (2007) 'Coerced drug treatment in the criminal justice system: conceptual, ethical and criminological issues', *Criminology and Criminal Justice*, 7(3): 269–286.

Sentencing Guidelines Council (2016) Imposition of community and custodial sentences.

Skinner, C. (2010) 'Clients or offenders? The case for clarity of purpose in multi-agency working', in Pycroft, A. and Gough, D. (eds) *Multi-agency working in criminal justice: Control and care in contemporary correctional practice*, Bristol: Policy Press, pp 35–50.

Stevens, A. (2011a) 'Recovery through contradiction?', *Criminal Justice Matters*, 84(1): 20–21.

Stevens, A. (2011b) *Drugs, crime and public health. The political economy of drug policy.* Abingdon: Routledge.

Stevens, A., McSweeney, T., van Ooyen, M. and Uchtenhagen, A. (2005) 'On coercion', *International Journal of Drug Policy*, 16(4): 207–209, DOI: 10.1016/j.drugpo.2005.04.004

Stevens, A., Berto, D., Heckmann, W., Kerschl, V., Oeuvrau, K., Van Ooyen, M., Steffan, E. and Uchtenhagen, A. (2005) 'Quasi-compulsory treatment of drug dependent offenders: an interventional literature review', *Substance Use and Misuse*, 40(3), 269–283. DOI: 10.1081/JA-200049159

Stevens, A., Berto, D., Frick, U., Hunt, N., Kerschl, V., McSweeney, T., Oeuvray, K.F., Puppo, I.G., Santa Maria, A.H., Schaaf, S.C., Trinkl, B.I., Uchtenhagen, A.C. and Werdenich, W. (2006) 'The relationship between legal status, perceived pressure and motivation in treatment for drug dependence: results from a European study of quasi-compulsory treatment', *European Addiction Research*, 12(4): 197–209.

Stevenson, B. (2011) 'Drug policy, criminal justice and mass imprisonment', working paper prepared for the first meeting of the Global Commission on drug policies, Geneva, 24–25 January, www.globalcommissionondrugs.org/wp-content/themes/gcdp_v1/pdf/Global_Com_Bryan_Stevenson.pdf

Strang, J. and Gossop, M. (2005) *Heroin addiction and the British system: Volume 1 Origins and evolution.* Abingdon: Routledge.

Watson, A. (2010) 'Sharing or shifting responsibility? The multi-agency approach to safeguarding children', in Pycroft, A. and Gough, D. (eds) *Multi-agency working in criminal justice: Control and care in contemporary correctional practice*, Bristol: Policy Press, p 123.

Further reading

Farabee, D., Prendergast, M. and Anglin, M. (1998) 'The effectiveness of coerced treatment for drug-abusing offenders', *Journal of Correctional Philosophy and Practice*, 62(1): 3–10.

Gregoire, T.K. and Burke, A.C. (2004) 'The relationship of legal coercion and readiness to change among adult with alcohol and other drug problems', *Journal of Substance Abuse Treatment*, 26: 35–41.

Hiller, M.L., Knight, K., Broome, K.M. and Simpson, D.D. (1998) 'Legal pressure and treatment retention in a national sample of long-term residential programs', *Criminal Justice Behaviour*, 25(4): 463–481.

Perkins, N., Smith, K., Hunter, D.J., Bambra, C. and Joyce, K. (2010) '"What counts is what works"? New Labour and partnerships in public health', *Policy & Politics*, 38(1): 101–117, DOI:10.1332/030557309X458425

Sellman, D. (2009) 'The 10 most important things to know about addiction', *Addiction*, 105: 6–13.

Stevens, A. (2007) 'When two dark figures collide: evidence and discourse on drug-related crime', *Critical Social Policy*, 27(1): 77–99.

Stevens, A., Radcliffe, P., Sanders, M. and Hunt, N. (2008) 'Early exit: estimating and explaining early exit from drug treatment', *Harm Reduction Journal*, 5: 13, DOI: 10.1186/1477-7517-5-13

Szasz, T. (1963) *Law, liberty and psychiatry: an inquiry into the social uses of mental health practices.* New York: Macmillan.

17

The decline of youth offending teams: towards a progressive and positive youth justice

Nicholas Pamment

Aims of the chapter

- To introduce multi-agency youth offending teams and consider their impact.
- To explore the major barriers to effective multi-agency working.
- To outline alternative and progressive approaches to address youth crime.

Multi-agency working within youth justice

In 1996 an Audit Commission (1996) report argued that an immense amount of money had been invested into the youth justice system (YJS) but the interventions remained inefficient and ineffective. The Labour government capitalised on this finding and suggested that under the Conservatives, the YJS was in disarray and they proposed a radical change (Labour Party, 1996). After entering office in 1997, the Labour Party embarked on what was a major reform (Home Office, 1997) and the Crime and Disorder Act (CDA) 1998 was introduced. The Act put in place the specific requirement that youth offending is addressed through a multi-agency response, something which was suggested almost ten years earlier by the Morgan Report (Home Office, 1991).

Youth offending teams (YOTs) were subsequently formed, replacing social workers within local authority social services. They have been described as teams not belonging to a single department but consisting of representatives from the police, probation, social services, health, education, drugs, alcohol misuse and housing officers (Souhami, 2007: 208). YOTs work in conjunction with other statutory, voluntary and corporate services engaged within crime reduction strategies and, as Souhami (2007: 209) has previously suggested, they therefore embody multi-agency and inter-agency working. Staff can be seconded to YOTs by the varying agencies or they can be employed directly within the team by local authorities and they work towards the principle aim of 'preventing offending by children and young persons' (CDA 1998, s.37). Sometimes called Youth Offending Service (YOS), they are centrally monitored and controlled by the Youth Justice Board (YJB) which was also set up as part of the CDA 1998 (See Pamment, 2016; Case et al, 2017; YJB, 2017).

The expansion of multi-agency working can be considered against wider developments in thinking with regard to crime and its management (Souhami, 2007; Newburn, 2007). A new 'corporatist' strategy for dealing with offenders appeared outside the traditional 'welfare' and 'justice' approaches at the end of the 1980s. This was primarily concerned with efficiently managing the offending population rather than offender rehabilitation. It has been strongly argued that multi-agency arrangements are merely utilised as a way of bureaucratically managing performance and monitoring cost efficiency (Bottoms, 1995; Pitts, 2001). Alongside the 'corporatist' strategy, evaluative research started to show that certain forms of criminal justice intervention could reduce recidivism and therefore there was a focus on 'what works' with offenders (for a brief overview, see Pamment, 2016: 22). It became accepted that offending should be combated at an early stage, as reflected in the principle aim of YOTs, through tough interventions as this was arguably more effective but also less expensive (Case et al, 2017). Furthermore, it was acknowledged that crime is inherently complex with young offenders having multiple needs and these cannot be met by a single agency (Souhami, 2007). The Home Office (1997) argued that offending by young people is linked to a number of problems and it is important to bring experience and skills from varying agencies together. This approach would increase overall efficiency and avoid any duplication of effort (Burnett and Appleton, 2004).

During the early introduction of YOTs, the Home Office (1999) issued guidance on the roles of the different officers from the varying agencies but research suggested that YOT personnel were carrying out the same tasks, despite differences in professional background, training and qualifications (see Ellis and Boden, 2005). This raised concern that YOT personnel were not developing a 'fusion' or 'unifying' model of joint working (Burnett and Appleton, 2004; Ellis and Boden, 2005). However, Burnett and Appleton (2004) in their study of one YOT area discovered that, regardless of parent agency, there was a unifying social work ethic between the YOT staff. Ellis and Boden (2005) conducted a later study within a different YOT and also concluded that 'a social work ethic is alive and well' (p 19), indicating cohesive working, as desired.

The YJB has acknowledged that YOTs are key to the success of the YJS, claiming that because they incorporate a number of representatives from a wide range of services, the needs of young offenders are addressed in a 'comprehensive manner' (see YJB, 2017). According to Souhami (2007: 208), multi-agency working has been most fully developed within the YJS and therefore one would expect that YOTs are successful in tackling the multiple needs of young offenders. Following the introduction of YOTs, the YJB stated that joined-up working was an 'unqualified success' (YJB News, December 2000, cited by Burnett and Appleton, 2004: 48). Not only was this statement rather premature but in making this claim, it has been argued that the YJB was highly selective of independent evaluations, ignoring research which contained less positive results. As Burnett and Appleton (2004: 48) pertinently state, 'the unabated self-congratulation of the YJB, endorsed by government ministers, has been hard to swallow' (for an analysis of research manipulation and distortion, see Ellis et al, 2009; Walters, 2005; Goldson, 2000; Muncie, 2002). In reality, academic commentators have been extremely critical of the Labour government's youth justice reforms, of which multi-agency work forms a major part.

Reflection

How does multi-agency working within youth justice differ from adult supervision?

A damning verdict

Research regarding multi-agency working tends to centre on the process of integration and the perceptions of professionals about the impact of the service (Burnett and Appleton, 2004; Blagg, 2000) and there exists only limited evidence on any outcomes (Brown and White, 2006). However, central to the argument here is Solomon and Garside's (2008) independent and comprehensive audit of the Labour government's youth justice reforms, from 1998–2008. The results were far from positive and the evaluation shows that YOTs missed targets in relation to key areas of offender need, including accommodation; education, training or employment; mental health and substance misuse. Perhaps most importantly, there was no significant or substantial reduction in reconviction rates and the principle aim of the YJS set out in the CDA 1998, to prevent offending by young people, was not achieved (Solomon and Garside, 2008: 11).

Solomon and Garside's (2008) audit is not in isolation and a number of other reports have drawn attention to the YOTs' inability to meet the needs of young people. For example, an HM Inspectorate of Probation report published in 2007 found that despite young people having physical health needs (15%), emotional or mental health needs (40%), schooling difficulties (62%) and learning difficulties (15%), they were not being met or adequately addressed by YOTs. Additionally, the statutory entitlement to 25 hours' education for school age children and young people was rarely achieved (HM Inspectorate of Probation, 2007). A further example of YOTs' inability to address individual needs is the Intensive Supervision and Surveillance Programme (ISSP).

ISSP case study

ISSP was introduced in England and Wales in 2001, with an initial investment of £45 million. Uncritically, it became hailed as 'the most robust and innovative community-based programme available for persistent and serious offenders' (Gray et al, 2005: 9). Offenders were subject to monitoring up to 24 hours/7 days a week, with at least one form of direct surveillance (tracking; electronic tagging; voice verification) or intelligence led policing (Gray et al, 2005: 28–29). Lasting a period of six months, offenders received five core intervention modules, including education/training; restorative justice; offending behaviour; interpersonal skills and family support (Gray et al, 2005). Importantly, the YJB set three objectives for the ISSP, one of which was to tackle young offenders' underlying problems effectively. Certainly, given the multi-agency make-up, coupled with increased contact time, this should have been achievable; however, this was not the case.

The YJB commissioned an evaluation of ISSP in two stages (see Moore et al, 2004; Gray et al, 2005) and researchers discovered many examples of homelessness, unmet mental health needs, ignored special educational needs and poor social work intervention. Furthermore, practitioners reported a number of difficulties in accessing education, accommodation, mental health and drug services (Gray et al, 2005: 32). Most importantly, however, there was a substantially high reconviction rate of 89% after 12 months, increasing to 91% after 24 months (Moore et al, 2004; Gray et al, 2005), hardly a ringing endorsement for intensive multi-agency working.

An independent study also examined the impact of the ISSP, reporting similar negative findings. It explored young offender and staff perceptions of the programme within two YOT areas and discovered that the ISSP was failing on a number of levels (see Ellis et al, 2009). In particular, young offenders were asked whether the intervention addressed individual needs and, using a Likert Scale data collection method (see Likert, 1932), 27 offenders responded with a negative mean score of 3.2 (7 being the best possible result). This negative score is best explained in the young offenders' own words:

> 'I was given a school bullying pack to do when I was not even at school; the interventions are all based on the same thing.'

> 'I have to do teen talk packs which are really childish and nothing to do with me.'

> 'I was made to play with plastic men and told to move them through an imaginative grand chamber of feelings. I was embarrassed coz I was nearly 18.'

Throughout the study, it was evident to the researchers that much of the programme content was designed for a younger age group and ineffective at addressing underlying problems. Driven primarily through political expediency and principles of robust enforcement, it is perhaps unsurprising the ISSP lacked programme integrity and positive results (Tonry, 1990; Ellis et al, 2009).

Barriers to effective multi-agency working

It would appear, given the evidence cited above, that multi-agency success within youth justice is marginal and we certainly have not seen massive improvements that would perhaps have been expected with a 'comprehensive' multi-agency response. This is hard to fathom considering the clear benefits of this form of working, which have been comprehensively discussed elsewhere (see Souhami, 2007). It has been argued that multi-agency working can lead to shared knowledge, easier access to other services, expertise and improved referral processes, all of which can contribute towards a 'seamless service' without communicational blocks or delays, bureaucratic divisions and defensive professional boundaries (Burnett and Appleton, 2004: 37). It certainly has 'commonsense appeal' (Burnett and Appleton, 2004), where the 'ideology of unity' (Crawford, 1994) is generally considered an 'unproblematically good thing' (Blagg et al, 1988). For the government, it has the advantage of being extremely good for public relations (Gilling, 1994) and as Burnett and Appleton (2004: 35) state, 'there can be few more worthy sounding ideals than that of collaboration'.

In reality, joint working can be extremely difficult to achieve in practice and interestingly, even before the introduction of the CDA 1998, incidents had highlighted difficulties faced with regard to multi-agency working. The National Society for the Prevention of Cruelty to Children (NSPCC) argued that since the 1970s repeated enquiries into child abuse cases have exposed serious failings (Cloke, 2007; see also Fox, this volume). For instance, the report into the death of Maria Colwell argued that there was a lack of communication and liaison (Department of Health and Social Security, 1974). Furthermore, a report into child abuse in Cleveland discovered a lack of understanding between agencies and it was stated that, 'it is unacceptable that the disagreements and failure of communication of adults should be allowed to obscure the needs of children' (Department of Health, 1988).

Culture

According to Liddle and Gelsthorpe (1994) the most significant barrier to multi-agency collaboration can be found in the informal responses and complexities within the workforce. The term 'culture' is regularly cited as having the most impact on the success of this type of working (see Souhami, 2007; Gilling, 1994). Ogbonna and Harris (1998: 35) have described the notion of organisational culture as an enigma but it can be described as an umbrella term incorporating a number of aspects primarily centred on the idea of identity. Sergiovanni and Corbally (1984: viii) provide a comprehensive definition, they state that culture is:

the system of values, symbols, and shared meanings of a group including the embodiment of these values, symbols, and meanings into material objects and ritualised practices ... the 'stuff' of culture includes customs and traditions, historical accounts be they mythical or actual, tacit understandings, habits, norms and expectations.

When discussing 'culture' as a barrier to effective multi-agency working, it is argued that conflicts in the cultures of different agencies may negatively affect working relationships, thus obstructing any form of collaboration (Souhami, 2007: 220). Sloper (2004: 572) argues that multi-agency working requires change at an individual and organisational level, this will inevitably challenge any existing culture and workers may fear such transformation, finding reasons for its failure (see Burnett and Appleton, 2004). It is not hard to find examples of cultural barriers within the YJS. For instance, Bailey and Williams (2000) discovered 'shotgun marriages' and 'turf wars' between different agencies in their study of early shadow YOTs. Holdaway et al (2001) discovered conflict over implementation of case working and obstructiveness regarding attempts to introduce evidence-based practice. Burnett and Appleton (2004) also encountered underlying cultural issues with regard to appropriate language use within their study of an Oxfordshire YOT. These cultural issues will inevitably appear 'on the ground' in the form of communicational breakdowns and ultimately, poor working relationships within YOTs. However, Crawford and Jones (1995) argue that conflicts in the workplace are always present and inevitable and Souhami (2007) suggests that these conflicts are 'integral' to multi-agency provision as it is the merging of diverse approaches to work. Indeed, it must be remembered that culture can have both a positive and negative impact. Nevertheless, it is perhaps all too easy to focus on culture as the main barrier to effective multi-agency working and this detracts from assessing whether our YJS is effective in the first place.

Reflection

How might the cultures of the varying agencies differ?

A negative, risk-based and interventionist system

Smith (2007) suggests that the public presentation of the Labour government's youth justice reform programme was seamless, comprehensive and based on the best evidence about effective interventions. However, within the past few decades there has been a major shift from a 'welfare' approach to dealing with young people to that of a punitive response, through increased criminalisation, punishment and exclusion (Muncie, 1999; Goldson, 2000; Pratt et al, 2005; Case et al, 2017).

For example, through structural separation, the YOT model introduced discrete services for 'offenders'. Additionally, the CDA 1998 introduced several risk-focused, net widening and early interventions, including Antisocial Behaviour Orders (ASBOs) and Curfew and Child Safety Orders (CCSOs), conflating 'immaturity, indiscretion and everyday incivility' (Byrne and Brooks, 2015: 4–5; Dugmore et al, 2006).

Such a 'tough on crime' approach has failed to address underlying social conditions and the causes of offending (Newburn, 2007). Solomon and Garside (2008: 65) highlight the years of disinvestment in social responses to youth crime, whereby substantial amounts of money have been transferred from policy areas critical to tackling the underlying causes of youth crime. Interestingly, a large proportion of funding for YOTs has stemmed from the budgets of social spending, health, education and social services. Solomon and Garside (2008: 64) question whether YOTs can actually address the complex economic and social factors causing youth offending. They suggest a more effective solution may be found outside of the YOT system in the delivery of coordinated services through *mainstream* local authority children's and young people's provision and more effective children's services that can effectively address the causes of offending. They state:

> After a number of years of expansion should youth justice be scaled back and social support-led prevention scaled up ... A decade on from the creation of the YJB and YOTs, and at a time of rising concerns about youth 'gangs' and violence involving guns and knives, the time has come to reappraise the role and purpose of the YJS and to consider what it can realistically achieve in addressing youth offending. (Solomon and Garside, 2008: 12)

Reflection

What changes would you make to improve youth justice policy and why?

Towards a progressive youth justice

With the coalition administration in 2010 and the Conservative government in 2015, there has been a substantial shift in the direction of youth justice. As others have highlighted, alongside a less directive YJB, the YJS is developing less stigmatising and more progressive ways of addressing youth criminality (Case et al, 2017: 254–255; Haines and Case, 2015). These have been characterised as future orientated, through the promotion of positive behaviours, rather than a focus on negative past actions. One way to challenge the exclusionary practice of the CDA 1998, discussed above, is through diversion from the formal YJS (Muncie, 1999; Case et al, 2017; Creaney and Smith, 2014).

Diversion

It is widely acknowledged that formal justice processing increases the chance of further criminality, extending young people's criminal careers (McAra and McVie, 2007; Petrosino et al, 2010; Carlsson and Sarnecki, 2016). Young people who enter the YJS can adopt and internalise a 'deviant' identity, developed through the justice system's response, subsequent 'label' and targeting (see Becker, 1963; McAra and McVie, 2007). Moreover, there is a contagion effect, whereby peer influence creates enhanced negative attitudes, increasing the risk of prolonged criminality (Centre for Justice Innovation, 2016; Hoge, 2016). Crucially, research indicates that system contact can have the most detrimental impact on lower-risk young people (Wilson and Hoge, 2013; see also Little and Sodha, 2012).

Diversion from the YJS has, therefore, been described as a major protective factor against serious and prolonged offending (House of Commons, 2013). Proponents of diversion argue that troublesome young people should be supported and diverted away from the damaging influence of YJS contact, minimising overexposure, harmful labelling and net widening (Cohen, 1985; Bloomberg, 1983). Interventions offered through diversion should remain positive, supportive and for the majority, minimal and informal (Case et al, 2017; Centre for Justice Innovation, 2016; Adler et al, 2016).

An example of diversionary practice (or 'interventionist diversion', see Kelly and Armitage, 2015) was the coalition government's introduction of a new pre-court system, through the Legal Aid Sentencing and Punishment of Offenders Act (LASPO) 2012 (Yates, 2012; Creaney and Smith, 2014; Haines and Case, 2015; Case et al, 2017). In response to a hierarchical and negative out-of-court disposal process introduced by the previous Labour government (Reprimands – Final Warnings – Court), LASPO introduced a discretionary and non-escalatory system of: No Further Action, Community Resolution, Youth Caution and Youth Conditional Caution (see MOJ and YJB, 2013: 6–7).

Alongside LASPO 2012, guidance for Police and YOTs, suggested that any assessments of young people should not simply focus on risk, but consider intervention appropriateness, young person engagement and motivation (MOJ and YJB, 2013). According to Yates (2012: 5), LASPO allows for 'dialogue around costly, net widening, criminalising, counterproductive, and damaging institutional practices' (see also Byrne and Brooks, 2015). Arguably driven by fiscal pressures, such legislation indicates a move away from damaging and costly criminalisation, towards the promotion of further innovative and child-friendly practices (Creaney and Smith, 2014; Case et al, 2017).

Positive youth justice

A further departure from the negative and risk-based era of the CDA 1998 (Muncie, 1999; Vaughan, 2000) is an alternative model of youth justice termed *Children First, Offenders Second* (CFOS) (Case and Haines, 2015). First developed within the rights-based and pro-child policy context in Wales (see Case and Haines, 2015: 161), CFOS emphasises diversion for all and advocates a wider set of progressive ideals for delivering a positive youth justice (for a full and comprehensive overview, see Haines and Case, 2015).

One of the central tenets of the CFOS model is to view young offenders as children first, rather than focus on any 'deviant' identify or label (McAra and McVie, 2007). Thus, any response should be child-friendly and child-appropriate. It gives primacy to the promotion of positive behaviours and future orientated outcomes, viewing children as active problem-solvers. In line with the UNCRC 1989, it also highlights the importance of young people's perspectives in any decision making, something which has been advocated elsewhere (Ellis, Pamment and Lewis, 2009; Holt and Pamment, 2011). Finally, CFOS urges practitioners to view themselves as working primarily *for* the children. Such principles can influence every decision making stage, creating a YJS viewed as fair, just and legitimate, encouraging greater engagement and desistance (Case and Haines, 2015).

The ideals of the CFOS approach have gained considerable academic and practitioner attention within England and Wales and an example of implementation can be found in Surrey, through two key child-centred reforms. First, the YOT model was abandoned in 2012, in favour of an informal and integrated response to youth criminality, within a wider Youth Support Service (YSS; Case et al, 2017: 256). According to Byrne and Brooks (2015), this change was motivated by the need to move beyond discrete and stigmatising services for 'offenders', towards a holistic and citizen-centred approach. Importantly, much of the help and guidance is provided through a designated Youth Support Officer, and the same opportunities are available to all young people, irrespective of entry route (offending, homelessness, mental health, unemployment, or 'child in need' status; Byrne and Brooks, 2015: 12).

Second, Surrey Police and the YSS have formed an integrated response to gatekeeping the formal YJS. Central to this was the introduction of the pre-court and diversionary Youth Restorative Intervention (YRI) in 2009. As the 'default disposal' available for young people under 18 who admit an offence, it seeks to prevent reoffending, reduce criminalisation, increase victim satisfaction, provide value for money and ultimately, improve the experience of the YJS for all (Byrne and Brooks, 2015: 6).

The YRI contains a number of restorative and progressive characteristics. For example, all needs are assessed before seeking the active involvement of both victim and offender (see Marshall, 1999; Gavrielides, 2008; Wilcox and Hoyle, 2004). Due to previous negative relationships or environmental experiences, it recognises that offenders also require restoration, encouraging access to services offered by the integrated YSS, outlined above. Finally, after direct or indirect mediation, offenders make amends, through letter of apology, direct or indirect reparation (see Pamment, 2016), attendance requirement or good behaviour contract. Most importantly, following completion of the YRI, there is no criminal conviction (for a comprehensive overview of the organisation and operation of the YRI, see Mackie et al, 2014).

Through the integration of services and diversion, it is perhaps unsurprising that the results of an independent evaluation into the YRI were highly positive (Mackie et al, 2014). Most notably, the reoffending rate of YRI participants was 27%, in contrast to 33% for the control group. Between October 2012 and September 2013, YJB data identified 189 first-time entrants per 100,000 young people, the lowest in England and Wales. Victims also reported positive, fair and just processes, alongside an overall satisfaction rate of 91% (see Reed, 2013). Finally, at £360 per case, the YRI represented good value for money, avoiding approximately £1,040 in current and future public sector costs (for a full analysis see Mackie et al, 2014).

Conclusion

Since their inception within the CDA 1998, multi-agency YOTs have shown a prolonged inability to address the needs of offenders. The most comprehensive assessment of youth justice reforms under the Labour government demonstrated that YOTs missed most YJB targets in relation to key areas of need (accommodation, education, training or employment, mental health and substance misuse), with no significant or substantial reduction in reconviction rates. With regard to multi-agency achievements, the highly negative conclusion is best delivered in Solomon and Garside's (2008: 11) own words:

> The overall picture is of a YJS that was designed with the best intentions of providing effective multi-agency provision but that in practice is struggling to meet the needs of a group of vulnerable children and young people who require carefully coordinated specialist support. YOTs do not appear to successfully meet the complex needs of children and young people.

This conclusion is not in isolation. Sloper (2004) found limited evidence surrounding the effectiveness of multi-agency working in producing results for children and their families. Blagg (2000) has also argued that despite the rhetoric, not everyone benefits from the process.

Is it unfair to argue that multi-agency working is the failure? Certainly, it is wrong to believe that crime can only be reduced through better coordination and cooperation, a belief that has been in existence for some time (Blagg, 2000). While it is acknowledged that multi-agency working can bring substantial rewards, through shared knowledge, easier access to services and speed efficiency (Souhami, 2007), it must be remembered that it is a process operating within the YJS, which must be evidence-led and able to address the underlying causes of youth crime. However, as this chapter has argued, much of our current provision is based on principles of criminalisation, punishment and exclusion, and it is failing to deliver positive outcomes for young people.

Recent progressive ideals (CFOS) and developments in diversion (LASPO and YRI) represent a partial and positive departure from this negative, risk-based and interventionist approach. The abandonment of the YOT model in Surrey and the appointment of proponent Ben Byrne to the YJB (MOJ and YJB, 2018) presents an exciting opportunity to further pursue non-stigmatising, child-centred and integrated support services for young people, across England and Wales. However, to end on a cautionary note, in the ever-changing and highly politicised arena of youth justice, the 'pendulum could swing again' (Byrne and Brooks, 2015: 17).

Review question

Can you list the ways in which CFOS and diversion are considered progressive forms of youth justice?

Summary of key learning points
- Arguably, YOTs are unable to meet the complex needs of vulnerable young people.
- Better coordination and cooperation cannot solely address the complexities of youth offending.
- Child-friendly ideals and developments in diversion represent a positive departure from the risk-based era of the CDA 1998.
- Non-stigmatising and integrated support services for young people should be developed, across England and Wales.

References
Adler, J., Edwards, S., Scally, M., Gill, D., Puniskis, M., Gekoski, A. and Horvath, M. (2016) *What works in managing young people who offend? A summary of the international evidence.* London: Ministry of Justice.

Audit Commission (1996) *Misspent youth: young people and crime.* London: Audit Commission.

Bailey, R. and Williams, B. (2000) *Inter-agency partnerships in youth justice: implementing the Crime and Disorder Act, 1998.* Sheffield: University of Sheffield, Joint Unit for Social Service Research.

Becker, H. (1963) *The outsiders*. New York: Free Press.

Blagg, H., Pearson, G., Sampson, A., Smith, D. and Stubbs, P. (1988) 'Inter-agency co-ordination: rhetoric and reality', in T. Hope and M. Shaw (eds), *Communities and crime reduction*. London: Home Office.

Blagg, H. (2000) 'Multi-agency work, marginal communities and crime prevention'. Paper presented at the conference 'Reducing Criminality: Partnerships and Best Practice', Perth 31 July/1 August. Available https://aic.gov.au/publications?search_api_views_fulltext=multi-agency%20work&sort=&order=&page=1

Bloomberg, T. (1983) 'Diversion's disparate results and unresolved questions: an integrative evaluation perspective', *Journal of Research in Crime and Delinquency*, 20: 24–38.

Bottoms, A. (1995) 'The politics of sentencing reform', in R. Morgan (ed), *The philosophy and politics of punishment and sentencing*. Oxford: Oxford University Press, pp 17–49.

Brown, K. and White, K. (2006) *Exploring the evidence base for integrated children's services*. Scottish Executive Education Department, www.scotland.gov.uk/Publications/2006/01/24120649/0

Burnett, R. and Appleton, C. (2004) 'Joined-up services to tackle youth crime', *British Journal of Criminology*, 44(1): 34–54.

Byrne, B. and Brooks, K. (2015) *Post-YOT youth justice*. London: Howard League for Penal Reform.

Case, S., Johnson, P., Manlow, D., Smith, R. and Williams, K. (eds) (2017) *Criminology*. Oxford: Oxford University Press.

Case, S. and Haines, K. (2015) 'Children first, offenders second: positive promotion: reframing the prevention debate', *Youth Justice Journal*, 15(3): 226–39.

Carlsson, C. and Sarnecki, J. (2016) *An introduction to life-course criminology*. London: Sage.

Centre for Justice Innovation (2016) *Valuing youth diversion: a toolkit for practitioners*, http://justiceinnovation.org/wp-content/uploads/2017/01/Valuing-Youth-Diversion-A-Toolkit.pdf

Cloke, C. (2007) *Safeguarding children: the importance of multi professional and multi-agency working*. London: NSPCC.

Cohen, S. (1985) *Visions of social control: crime, punishment and classification*. Cambridge: Polity Press.

Crawford, A. (1994) 'The partnership approach: corporatism at the local level?', *Social and Legal Studies*, 3: 497–519.

Crawford, A. and Jones, M. (1995) 'Inter-agency co-operation and community-based crime prevention: some reflections on the work of Pearson and colleagues', *British Journal of Criminology*, 35(1): 17–33.

Creaney, S. and Smith, R. (2014) 'Youth justice back at the crossroads', *Safer Communities*, 13(2): 83–87.

Department of Health (1988) *Report of the inquiry into child abuse in Cleveland*. London: HMSO.

Department of Health and Social Security (1974) *Report of the committee of inquiry into the care and supervision provided in relation to Maria Colwell*. London: HMSO.

Dugmore, P., Pickford, J. and Angus, S. (2006) *Transforming social work practice: youth justice and social work*. Exeter: Learning Matters.

Ellis, T. and Boden, I. (2005) 'Is there a unifying professional culture in youth offending teams? A research note', *British Society of Criminology Conference Proceedings*, 2004 (Volume 7).

Ellis, T., Pamment, N. and Lewis, C. (2009) 'Public protection in youth justice? The Intensive Supervision and Surveillance Programme (ISSP) from the inside', *International Journal of Police Science and Management*, 11(4): 393–413.

Gavrielides, T. (2008) 'Restorative justice: the perplexing concept. Conceptual fault lines and power battles within the restorative justice movement', *Criminology and Criminal Justice Journal*, 8(2): 165–183.

Gilling, D.J. (1994) 'Multi agency crime prevention: some barriers to collaboration', *Howard Journal*, 33: 246–57.

Goldson, B. (2000) 'Wither diversion: interventionism and the new youth justice', in B. Goldson (ed), *The new youth justice*. Lyme Regis: Russell House Publishing.

Gray, E., Roberts, C., Merrington, S., Waters, I., Fernandez, R., Hayward, G. and Rogers, R. (2005) *ISSP: the final report*. London: YJB.

Haines, K. and Case, S. (2015) *Positive youth justice: children first, offenders second*. Bristol: Policy Press.

HM Inspectorate of Probation (2007) *Joint inspection of youth offending teams annual report 2006–2007*. London: HM Inspectorate of Probation.

Hoge, R. (2016) 'Application of pre-charge diversion programs', *Criminology and Public Policy*, 15(3): 991–999.

Holdaway, S., Davidson, N., Dignan, J., Hammersley, R., Hine, J. and Marsh, P. (2001) *New strategies to address youth offending: the national evaluation of the pilot youth offending teams*. Research, Development and Statistics Directorate Paper No. 69. London: Home Office.

Holt, A. and Pamment, N. (2011) 'Overcoming the challenges of researching "young offenders": using assisted questionnaires – a research note', *International Journal of Social Research Methodology*, 14(2): 125–133.

Home Office (1991) *Safer communities: the local delivery of crime prevention through the partnership approach (Morgan Report)*. London: Home Office.

Home Office. (1997) *No more excuses: a new approach to tackling youth crime in England and Wales*. London: Home Office.

Home Office (1999) *Inter-departmental circular on establishing youth offending teams*. London: Home Office.

House of Commons Justice Committee (2013) *Youth justice: seventh report of session 2012–13*, https://publications.parliament.uk/pa/cm201213/cmselect/cmjust/339/339.pdf

Kelly, L. and Armitage, V. (2015) 'Diverse diversions: youth justice reform, localised practices, and a "new interventionist diversion"?', *Youth Justice*, 15: 117–133.

Labour Party (1996) *Tackling youth crime: reforming youth justice*. London: Labour Party.

Liddle, M. and Gelsthorpe, L. (1994) *Crime prevention and inter-agency co-operation*. Crime Prevention Unit Paper 53. London: Home Office.

Likert, R. (1932) 'A technique for the measurement of attitudes', *Archives of Psychology*, No.140.

Little, M. and Sodha, S. (2012) *Prevention and intervention in children's services*. Dartington: The Social Research Unit.

Mackie, A., Cattell, J., Reeder, N. and Webb, S. (2014) *Youth restorative intervention evaluation: final report*, London: GtD.

Marshall, T. (1999) *Restorative justice: an overview*. London: Home Office.

McAra, L. and McVie, S. (2007) 'Youth justice? The impact of system contact on patterns of desistance from offending', *European Journal of Criminology*, 4(3): 315–34.

Ministry of Justice (MOJ) and Youth Justice Board (YJB) (2013) *Youth out-of-court disposals guide for police and youth offending services*. London: MOJ.

MOJ and YJB (2018) 'Appointment of 10 members of the Youth Justice Board', 8 January, www.gov.uk/government/news/appointment-of-10-members-of-the-youth-justice-board

Moore, R., Gray, E., Roberts, C., Merrington, S., Waters, I., Fernandez, R., Hayward, G. and Rogers, R. (2004) *ISSP: The Initial Report, Summary*. London: YJB.

Muncie, J. (1999) 'Institutional intolerance: youth justice and the 1998 Crime and Disorder Act', *Critical Social Policy*, 19(2): 147–175.

Muncie, J. (2002) 'Policy transfers and "what works": some reflections on comparative youth justice', *Youth Justice*, 1(3): 27–35.

Newburn, T. (2007) *Criminology*. Cullompton: Willan.

Ogbonna, E. and Harris, L. (1998) 'Organizational culture: it's not what you think', *Journal of General Management*, 23(3): 35–49.

Petrosino, A., Turpin-Petrosino, C. and Guckenberg, S. (2010) *Formal system processing of juveniles: effects on delinquency*. Campbell Systematic Reviews.

Pamment, N. (2016) *Community reparation for young offenders: perceptions, policy and practice*. Basingstoke: Palgrave Macmillan.

Pitts, J. (2001) 'Korrectional karaoke: New Labour and the zombification of youth justice', *Youth Justice*, 1(2): 3–16.

Pratt, J., Brown, D., Brown, M., Hallsworth, S. and Morrison, W. (2005) *The new punitiveness: trends, theories, perspectives*. Cullompton: Willan.

Reed, R. (2013) *Youth restorative intervention victim satisfaction survey*. Surrey Police: Force Analysis Unit.

Sergiovanni, T. and Corbally, J. (eds) (1984) *Leadership and organizational culture*. Urbana, IL: University of Illinois Press

Sloper, P. (2004) 'Facilitators and barriers for co-ordinated multi-agency services', *Child Care, Health and Development*, 30(6): 571–580.

Smith, R. (2007) *Youth justice: ideas, policy and practice*. Second edition. Cullompton: Willan Publishing.

Solomon, E. and Garside, R. (2008) *Ten years of Labour's youth justice reforms: an independent audit*. London: Centre for Crime and Justice Studies.

Souhami, A. (2007) 'Multi-agency working: experiences in the youth justice system', in D. Green, E. Lancaster and S. Feasey (eds), *Addressing offending behaviour*. Cullompton: Willan.

Tonry, M. (1990) 'Stated and latent functions of ISP', *Crime and Delinquency*, 36: 174–191.

Vaughan, B. (2000) 'The government of youth: disorder and dependence?', *Social and Legal Studies*, 9(3): 347–366.

Walters, R. (2005) 'Boycott, resistance and the role of the deviant voice', *Criminal Justice Matters*, 62: 6–7.

Wilcox, A. and Hoyle, D. (2004) *The national evaluation of the Youth Justice Board's restorative justice projects*. London: YJB.

Wilson, H. and Hoge, R. (2013) 'The effect of youth diversion programs on recidivism: a meta-analytic review', *Criminal Justice and Behavior*, 40(5): 497–551.

Yates, J. (2012) 'What prospects youth justice? Children in trouble in the age of austerity', *Social Policy and Administration*, 46: 432–447.

YJB (2017) *Business plan 2017/18*, www.gov.uk/government/uploads/system/uploads/attachment_data/file/660018/yjb-business-plan-2017-18.pdf

Index

Note: Page numbers for figures appear in italics.